Please send me a copy of the

MOTHERWELL COLLEGE PROSPECTUS & COURSE DIRECTORY

Name

_____

_____

Address

_____

_____

_____

Post Code

_____

Tel

_____

Send coupon to:

MOTHERWELL COLLEGE DALZELL DRIVE MOTHERWELL ML1 2DD

COURSES IN SCOTLAND

To use the Provider Section, simply look up the code/number (**B1, C8, S78** etc) listed against the appropriate entry in the Classes & Courses Section. Where more than one reference is given, you can use the code to find the Provider most convenient to where you wish to attend.

You will find additional useful addresses on pages 219-220 as well as the Community Education Department addresses on pages 24-26, the TAP's on pages 29 and 194, and the Local Enterprise addresses on pages 30-32.

When you contact a Provider for further information,
you may wish to make mention of
PART-TIME CLASSES & COURSES in Scotland.

PART-TIME
Classes &
Courses
IN SCOTLAND
1995–96

For
TRAINING
CAREER DEVELOPMENT
and LEISURE

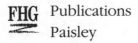 Publications
Paisley

In association with the Network of Scottish Tap Agencies

Acknowledgements

The Publishers are grateful to Scottish Enterprise, Highlands and Islands Enterprise, the Local Enterprise Companies and the Network of TAP Agencies for permission to use extracts from the national TAP database and in particular to Dennie Colley and Lewis Goram for their co-operation and assistance.

For help and advice we are also grateful to Matthew Johnson and Elizabeth Bryans of SCEC, Fiona McIntosh of SCOTVEC, Anne McLeod of SFEU, Jordanhill, Wylie Wright of Strathclyde Gateway, Jack Dyce of Strathclyde Community Education, to Helen McCrumb and most especially to Gordon McGuinness, both of Renfrewshire Enterprise.

Finally we thank the universities, colleges, other organisations and individuals who through their advertising entries have made publication possible and whose classes and courses we commend for widest support.

ISBN 1 85055 210 X
© FHG Publications and the Network of Scottish TAP Agencies 1995

Cover: W Tindle, Glasgow

Typeset by RD Composition Ltd., Glasgow.
Printed and bound by Bemrose, Derby

Distribution – Book Trade: WLM, Downing Road, West Meadows Industrial Estate, Derby, Derbyshire, DE21 6HA
(Tel: 01332 343332. Fax: 01332 340408/340464).
News Trade: United Magazine Distribution Ltd, 16–28 Tabernacle Street, London EC2A 4BN.
(Tel: 0171-638 4666. Fax: 0171-638 4665).

Published by FHG Publications Ltd.,
Abbey Mill Business Centre, Seedhill, Paisley PA1 1TJ   (0141-887 0428. Fax: 0141-889 7204).

Publisher's Introduction

Every year all over Scotland, thousands of students of all sorts are engaged in some kind of part-time education. It may be a short skills-training course or a year's intensive Certificate study. It may be a marathon effort for an Open University degree or it may simply be a term's pre-holiday 'brush-up' of conversational French.

Common as part-time learning may be, it could have even greater popularity if there was wider awareness of what is available, both near to home and perhaps also at a distance. Its provision, too, might be all the more effective and efficient if duplication could be more easily identified.

However, the aim of PART-TIME CLASSES & COURSES IN SCOTLAND 1995–96 is to help spread the good news of the endless possibilities of part-time learning opportunities to a general readership in a straightforward and inexpensive way. The foresight of those who set up the network of TAP Agencies has provided a resource which has now been selectively harvested and carefully re-presented to reach what we hope is an interested consumer market. In turn these consumers can taste some of the benefits of 'life-long learning' and thereby improve the quality of both life and work.

By its nature, part-time education is an elusive subject, often bursting into life with little notice and equally soon burning-out for lack of attention. We are aware that there is a wealth of local daytime, evening and weekend education which time and other practical considerations prevent us from including in this first edition of PART-TIME CLASSES AND COURSES. With the continuing co-operation of the many providers, future editions will hopefully extend their coverage and grow in authority.

USING THE GUIDE

Apart from the Introductions and Indexes, Parts One and Two are the core of the book. **Part One** contains the details of almost 7,000 separate classes and courses, carefully classified under the headings shown in the Contents and in the Subject Index. There is a small amount of duplication where it has been felt that a class/course should properly appear under more than one category or heading. The codes for each entry in Part One lead easily to the Providers listed in **Part Two**, where full contact details are given. By matching the entry in Part One with the provider in Part Two, we hope that you can identify and enroll at the most convenient location for the particular part-time class or course which fits your needs.

Contents

HEALTH & PERSONAL CARE 139

Dental, ophthalmic & audiology services **139**. Health (general) & health administration **139**. Medical technology & pharmacology **140**. Medicine, surgery, complementary medicine **140**. Nursing **140**. Personal care, hair, beauty **141**. Personal health care & fitness, first aid **143**. Physiotherapy, occupational & speech therapy **145**. Psychiatry, psychology **145**.

LANGUAGE, COMMUNICATION & SELF-HELP 146

Audio & visual media **146**. Basic skills, reading, writing, arithmetic, social **147**. Career change, job search, retirement **148**. Communication for and with disabled people **150**. Communication, writing, journalism, speaking, mass media **151**. English & UK 'ethnic' languages **152**. Foreign languages **155**. Language Studies **164**. Print & publishing **165**. Self-help, counselling, personal development **166**.

LAW, POLITICS & ECONOMICS 169

Economics **169**. Law **169**. Politics **171**.

MINERALS, MATERIALS & FABRICS 172

Chemical engineering & technology **172**. Furniture manufacture **172**. Materials engineering, metallurgy & technology **172**. Mining oil & minerals technology **172**. Paper & board **173**. Textiles fashion & furnishings **173**.

MUSIC & PERFORMING ARTS 174

Dance **174**. Music history & theory **174**. Music performance **174**. Music of specific cultures **175**. Music of specific kinds **175**. Theatre & dramatic arts **175**.

SCIENCES & MATHEMATICS 176

Astronomy **176**. Chemistry **176**. Earth sciences **177**. Mathematics, statistics **178**. Natural history, life sciences **180**. Physics **181**. Science & technology (general) **183**. Surveying & cartography **184**.

SPORTS, GAMES & RECREATION 185

Air sports **185**. Athletics, gymnastics, fitness training, combat sports **185**. Ball & related games **185**. Indoor, computer & card games **185**. Outdoor & animal sports **185**. Sports studies & combined sports **186**. Water sports **187**. Winter sports **187**.

TRANSPORT SERVICES & VEHICLE ENGINEERING 188

Aviation **188**. Driving & road safety **188**. Freight handling **188**. Marine & waterway transport **188**. Road transport: passenger, freight, inspection, legislation **190**. Transport (general) **190**. Vehicle maintenance & repair **191**. Vehicle manufacture, motor trade & sales **192**.

Part Two: Providers 195

Other Useful Addresses 219.

Abbreviations 221.

A-Z Subject Index 223.

Further Education in Scotland

Scotland has a history of providing quality education. The colleges of further education have a reputation for innovative and flexible delivery of vocational and general education and training.

Scotland's Colleges

There are 46 further education colleges located throughout Scotland. Each college is unique in serving its particular local community and specific sectors of industry, commerce and the professions. However, all colleges have aims, purposes and characteristics in common: they provide opportunities for people to learn and take qualifications throughout their lives and they support the Scottish economy through the development of a highly trained and qualified workforce.

Colleges Welcome Everyone

People of all ages and at all stages of their lives can benefit from college services. College students are a good mixture of people. Classes can be made up of young people progressing from school and men and women learning new skills. Regardless of age, qualification or experience the Scottish colleges of the 90s offer a comprehensive range of courses and services.

Further education colleges offer their students a supportive learning environment. Before starting a course and during the programme individuals have access to personal guidance and support. Prospective students are helped to choose the right course and mode of study and are provided with information on finance and child care. As a result, most people complete and succeed in their courses.

Thinking of Going to College?
Your Questions Answered

What are Further Education Colleges?

They are local colleges providing a very wide range of courses in general education and vocational training in a welcoming friendly environment. Colleges run full time, part-time and open learning courses. This means that you can continue adding to your qualification at your own time and pace, even when you are working.

How will going to College help you?

A college education means something. It can boost confidence, help with career

prospects and enhance self respect. Skills learned in further education colleges are directly related to the workplace thus improving your job opportunities.

Going to college also enables you to meet new people with similar interests and it can be good fun.

What courses can you do at College? Full-Time & Part-Time?

Colleges are committed to providing opportunities for lifelong learning. College courses are now designed to enable people to progress easily from one qualification to the next. The system is very flexible. Full-time study is not the only option, part-time courses, open learning, drop-in learning and short courses allow people to gain qualifications and skills when it is convenient for them and at their own pace. Previous work experience can be taken into account and accredited at the outset of programmes.

Colleges offer the widest range of options available. Courses are available for people with no or few qualifications up to degree level and are structured to help you progress easily from one qualification to the next.

Many of the qualifications awarded for college courses are Scottish Council For Vocational Education and Training (SCOTVEC) certificates. These are nationally

recognised by industry and other education providers. A wide range of National Certificate (NC) non advanced courses and all 1100 advanced SCOTVEC qualifications, Higher National Certificate (HNC) and Higher National Diploma (HND) courses are available in colleges throughout Scotland. Colleges also offer the new Scottish qualifications Scottish Vocation Qualifications (SVQs) and general SVQs (GSVQs) which have been designed by education and industry working together.

Most courses are built of individual units or modules. These units and modules are blocks of study on a particular subject which last for 40 hours. You will build up your qualification with a group of relevant units of modules.

What range of subjects can I study?

Courses cover the skills and knowledge required by key Scottish industries including, electronics, tourism, fish farming, banking, business studies, and catering. The list is too long to mention all areas of training here. Many colleges also offer a range of leisure classes. These are designed to help you find out more about subjects which interest you, and they can also help you to pursue new hobbies.

How will I be assessed?

Assessment is normally carried out throughout the course and is usually based on the students' ability to provide evidence that they understand and can put into practice the key elements of their course. Students with today's qualifications can demonstrate that they are competent.

New forms of assessment allow individuals to gain qualifications more readily. Accreditation of prior learning allows past experience to be recognised towards a qualification, and where individuals already have the necessary knowledge and skills, assessment can be proved independently of teaching programmes. Colleges can also provide assessment on demand services.

A feature of learning in colleges of the 90s is that students are encouraged and supported in taking responsibility for their personal and professional development.

What is College life like?

College life is very different from being at school. It is an adult environment and there will be a wide range of different age groups in your class. There is an interesting range of subjects to choose from and most courses include some sort of work experience. You will be expected to take a great deal of responsibility for your own learning as much of the classwork is project or skills development based. Whilst at college you will have access to guidance services which will help you plan your future.

How will you get funding for your course?

As a full-time student you may be eligible for a bursary or grant to cover course fees and help with living and travel expenses.

If you are considering applying for a National Certificate course (NC) you should contact your local Regional education department for a bursary. The number will be in the telephone directory.

If you are applying for a HND or HNC course you can get information on student grants and an applications form from, The Scottish Office Education Department's Awards Branch on (0131 244 5823).

How can you find out more?

Most colleges have trained guidance staff who will consider your previous qualifications, experience and interests, and help you choose a course which is suitable for you.

Some part-time students may be eligible for assistance, usually through the local Benefits Agency office. Leisure classes usually have a fee, though some students – unemployed, retired – may have concessions.

If you want general information you can write to SFEU, University of Strathclyde, Southbrae Drive, Glasgow G13 1PP and ask for '*FE for the 90's*' to be sent to you.

Grampian
Regional Council

Community Education Service

Community Based Adult Learning aims to offer a wide range of learning opportunities which are locally accessible to people throughout Grampian. The Community Education Service, in co-operation with colleges, universities, schools, training providers and voluntary organisations provides opportunities for

* **gaining knowledge and new skills**
* **preparing to return to further education and work**
* **being active in local decision-making**
* **working towards qualifications such as SCOTVEC modules, Standard Grades and Highers**
* **improving their basic communication skills or everyday maths.**

Programmes are developed locally through Management Committees made up of local people who respond to identified need.

For information about Community Based Adult Learning in your area – contact:

ABERDEEN
Cath Hamilton 01224 644431
Donna Stewart 01224 208626

BANFF / BUCHAN
Moira Watson 01888 544692

GORDON
Elizabeth Barrow 01467 620218

KINCARDINE / DEESIDE
Caroline Hay-Crawford
01569 762020

MORAY
Wendy Jamieson 01343 541144

or drop in to your local Community Education Centre

Get Qualified – with SCOTVEC!

If you're reading this, you already know how important it is to have the right qualifications. You are probably looking for training to help you do one or more of these things:

- Get a job.
- Change direction.
- Improve your career.
- Start work again after spending time away.
- Have the chance to go to college or university.
- Take up a new interest or hobby.

Whichever is most important to you, you need to choose a course with the right qualification at the end of it. To help you make your decision, the next few pages explain what kinds of vocational qualifications are available.

SCOTVEC

All these vocational qualifications are SCOTVEC qualifications. SCOTVEC, the Scottish Vocational Education Council, was set up by the Government in 1985, and given overall responsibility for vocational qualifications in Scotland. At SCOTVEC, we work closely with employers to make sure that our qualifications are relevant and up-to-date.

What are vocational qualifications?

There are vocational qualifications for just about every career you can imagine. Vocational qualifications prove to an employer that you are capable of doing a job and can do it well. Some are quite broad - giving you a range of job opportunities. For example:

- National Certificate technology.
- National Certificate design.
- National Certificate business administration.

Others cover particular skills and are ideal if you know exactly the kind of job you're interested in. For example.

- SVQ construction; painting and decorating.
- SVQ vehicle body fitting.
- SVQ catering and hospitality management: housekeeping.
- SVQ child care and education: pre-school provision.
- HNC computer graphic design and production.
- HNC horticulture.
- HND accounting.
- HND journalism.

- Certificate in quality assurance.
- Advanced Certificate in engineering practice: electrical and electronic.
- Diploma in management with marketing.
- Advanced Diploma in software engineering.

There are also vocational qualifications that are less to do with particular jobs and more to do with the skills and knowledge almost everyone needs. For example:

National Certificate Modules:
- Communication.
- Numeracy.
- Information technology.
- Problem solving.
- Interpersonal skills.

Finally, there are qualifications that help you to develop your hobbies, or take up a new interest. For example:

National Certificate Modules:
- Drawing skills: figure/life drawing.
- Jewellery design: basic enamelling.
- Ceramics and pottery: throwing techniques.
- Working with wood.
- Fabric crafts: embroidery.

Altogether, there are several thousand vocational qualifications available – so there's almost certainly one that's right for you.

Are they for you?

Vocational qualifications are available to people from age 16 upwards, in every walk of life. You can do them part-time, full-time, day-release or block-release. You can take them at college, school, work, training centres, at evening class, or by distance learning. Also, in some universities. Most importantly, you take them at a pace that suits you.

What do I get to show for it?

When you take a SCOTVEC qualification, you get a personal certificate called a Record of Education and Training. Each new qualification you get is *automatically* added to the certificate, and a new copy sent to you. For some qualifications, like SVQs or HNDs, you also get a separate certificate.

Step by step

All the qualifications listed below are based on a simple idea – you can build up to a qualification bit by bit. The building blocks of each qualification are called *units*. Each one takes around 40 hours of study.

There are three different kinds of unit:

- National Certificate Modules
- Higher National Units
- Workplace Assessed Units

You can take as many units as you like – or as few. Each one is recognised as a valuable achievement by employers and by admissions staff in colleges and universities. Each is listed separately on your Record of Education and Training. And if you choose the right units, you can get one of the more comprehensive vocational qualifications described below.

National Certificates

National Certificate Modules

There are over 3,000 National Certificate Modules covering a huge range of subjects. Modules can be taken on their own or put together into different combinations to make full National Certificate awards.

National Certificates (GSVQs)

GSVQ stands for *General Scottish Vocational Qualification.* GSVQs are a good option if you're not sure exactly what career you want. They are especially suitable if you are:

- a 16–19 year old in full-time education.
- an adult returning to work after a break.

They are broad qualifications which will help you learn a wide range of job skills – so you can choose from a number of careers, or go on to further and higher education. There are GSVQs at three levels, and at the higher levels you can get a merit grade.
GSVQs are made up of either 12 or 18 National Certificate Modules.

SKILLSTART

SKILLSTART 1 is made up of six National Certificate Modules. Aimed at slower learners, including those with mild to moderate learning difficulties, Skillstart 1 offers the chance to get a qualification that recognises their abilities.

SKILLSTART 2 is made up of nine National Certificate Modules. Most suitable for people who have no formal qualifications, Skillstart 2 helps to improve their chances of getting a job. It also offers a step up to further training or education.

HNC's and HND's

HNCs are *Higher National Certificates* and HNDs are *Higher National Diplomas.* You can take them at college and some universities, often part-time or by open learning.
   They are recognised by employers and by many professional and technical bodies too. They are accepted for admission to some degree courses, and can often get you straight into the second or third year of a degree programme.

HNCs and HNDs are all made up of 12 or 30 Higher National Units, and you can get each unit with a merit grading.

SVQs

SVQ stands for *Scottish Vocational Qualification.* SVQs are a special type of qualification, designed *by* employers *for* employers. They can be taken in the workplace or at training centres and sometimes at college.

There are SVQ's for nearly all occupations in Scotland, and they are equivalent to the National Vocational Qualifications available elsewhere in the UK.

Like all SCOTVEC qualifications, SVQs are made up of units, so they can be built up gradually. SVQs are available at five levels.

Professional Development Awards

If you have already got an HNC, an HND, or a degree, or have experience in a particular occupation, you may want to consider taking a Professional Development Award. There are four kinds:

- Certificate
- Advanced Certificate
- Diploma
- Advanced Diploma.

All Professional Development Awards are designed for people who want to develop their careers, and for those who want to make a career change.

Further Information

If you would like more information about any of these qualifications, please contact the *Publications Section, SCOTVEC, Hanover House, 24 Douglas Street, Glasgow G2 7NQ (Tel: 0141 242 2168).*

PUBLISHERS' NOTE

Because of local government re-organisation, details of providers for some courses, in particular for leisure pursuits, cannot be confirmed as we go to print. Libraries and other local sources should be consulted and the Community Education contacts on pages 24 to 26 may also be of assistance.

Strathclyde EDUCATION

Community Education Service

AYR DIVISION

Value for people

There's nothing to do in Ayrshire!

Except ... Dressmaking, French, Calligraphy, Keyboard Skills, Gardening, Cookery, Fly Tying, Photography, Spanish, First Aid, Yoga, Bridge, Microwave Cookery, Pottery, Creative Video, Woodwork, Keep Fit, German, Embroidery, Gaelic, Golf, Self-Defence, Public Speaking, Cake Decoration, Current Affairs, Oil Painting, Look After Yourself, Typewriting, Adult Basic Education, Shorthand, Word Processing, Open University Courses, Upholstery, Italian, Art and Crafts . . . . and much more . . . . *if you live in Ayrshire, why not contact your local Community Education Office (addresses below).*

Carrick Area:
42 Ladyland Road,
MAYBOLE KA19 7DH
Tel: 01655 882105;
Fax: 01655 882598

Kyle Area:
25 Wellington Square,
AYR KA7 1EZ
Tel: 01292 267278;
Fax: 01292 287788

Cumnock and Doon Valley Area:
228 Main Street,
AUCHINLECK KA18 2BE
Tel: 01290 420163;
Fax: 01290 425723

Kilmarnock Area:
Gateway Centre,
Foregate Square,
KILMARNOCK KA1 1LN
Tel: 01563 525628;
Fax: 01563 543921

Irvine and Garnock Valley Area:
47 Townhead,
IRVINE KA12 0BH
Tel: 01294 279233;
Fax: 01294 277832

Ardrossan Area:
12 Princes Street,
ARDROSSAN KA22 8BP
Tel: 01294 465401;
Fax: 01294 469720

The Scottish Community Education Council

Established in 1982, the Scottish Community Education Council is the national focal point for community education, promoting and supporting the informal education services provided by local authorities and voluntary organisations. Its main areas of activity are:

- Adult Education
- Community Work
- Youth Work and Schools
- International Services
- CeVe (Community Education Validation and Endorsement): setting training standards for community education

SCEC itself is not a direct provider of classes and courses, whether part-time or full-time. However it is closely involved in the work of Community Education Officers, providing information, advice and support, and plays an important role in supporting Adult Education in the community. Its publication 'SCAN' is designed to raise

awareness of community education, to publicise good practice and to carry community education news, projects and issues to professionals in the field, while the *'Young Scot'* magazine is a lively interactive medium for young consumers and school-leavers and the issues which affect them.

'Learning is a lifelong process' is the starting-point and the underlying philosophy of all community education work and it is the aim of the Scottish Community Education Council to enable this philosophy to be put into practice in a constructive and effective way.

Contact details for SCEC and for the main regional offices of Community Education as are follows:

Scottish Community
Education Council,
Roseberry House,
9 Haymarket Terrace,
EDINBURGH EH12 5EZ
Tel: 0131 313 2488
Fax: 0131 313 6800

Principal Community
Education Officer,
Regional Headquarters,
Education Department,
Borders Regional Council,
NEWTOWN ST.
BOSWELLS TD6 0SA
Tel: 01835 823301
Fax: 01835 822145

SCOTTISH

**COMMUNITY
EDUCATION
COUNCIL**

For further information on the
work of the Scottish Community
Education Council,
please contact the
Marketing and Public Affairs Unit,
Scottish Community Education
Council, Rosebery House,
9 Haymarket Terrace,
Edinburgh EH12 5EZ
Tel: 0131-313 2488
Fax: 0131-313 6800

The Council supports the providers of community education to help them meet the learning needs of people in communities by:

● Influencing public policy and awareness
● Promoting best practice
● Providing information, products and services

The Council is active in five main areas:

● Adult Education
● Community Work
● Youth Work
● International Services
● Setting training standards for community education (CeVe)

Principal Community
Education Officer,
Education Offices,
Dumfries & Galloway
Regional Council,
30 Edinburgh Road,
DUMFRIES
Tel: 01387 260406
Fax: 01387 60453

Community Education
Service Manager,
Central Regional Council,
Grendon,
9 Snowdon Place,
STIRLING FK8 2NH
Tel: 01786 442336
Fax: 01786 442340

Principal Officer,
Community Education
Services Office,
Fife Regional Council,
189 Nicol Street,
KIRKCALDY
Tel: 01592 4123241/2
Fax: 01592 412345

Community Education
Training Officer,
Community Education Service,
Grampian Regional Council,
Woodhill House,
Westburn Road,
ABERDEEN AB9 2LU
Tel: 01224 664695
Fax: 01224 664615

Community Education Officer,
Lothian Regional Council,
40 Torphichen Street,
EDINBURGH EH3 8JJ
Tel: 0131 479 2291

Principal Community
Education Officer,
Ayr Division (Strathclyde),
Wellington Square,
AYR KA7 1DR
Tel: 01292 612241
Fax: 01292 612261

Principal Community
Education Officer,
Glasgow Division (Strathclyde),
129 Bath Street,
GLASGOW G2 4SQ
Tel: 0141 227 6753
Fax: 0141 227 6864

Principal Community
Education Officer,
Renfrew Division
(Strathclyde),
Regional Buildings,
Cotton Street,
PAISLEY PA1 1LA
Tel: 0141 842 5631
Fax: 0141 842 5699

Principal Officer,
Cultural and Community
Education Services,
Western Isles Council,
Town Hall, South Beach Street,
STORNOWAY
ISLE OF LEWIS
Tel: 01851 703773
Fax: 01851 704209

Divisional Manager –
Community Work,
Shetland Islands Council,
Leisure & Recreation Department,
Dales Voe Base, Lerwick,
SHETLAND ZE1 0HD
Tel: 01595 6606
Fax: 01595 5224

Principal Community
Education Officer,
Community Education Office,
Highland Regional Council,
3 High Street,
DINGWALL IV15 9HL
Tel: 01349 864962
Fax: 01349 63781

Principal Community
Education Officer,
Education Offices,
Argyll & Bute Division (Strathclyde),
2 Tom-a-Mhoid Road,
DUNOON PA23 7HN
Tel: 01369 6918
Fax: 01369 3045

Principal Community
Education Officer,
Dunbarton Division (Strathclyde),
Regional Council Offices,
Garshake Road,
DUMBARTON G82 3PU
Tel: 01389 727349
Fax: 01389 27070

Principal Community
Education Officer,
Lanark Division (Strathclyde),
Regional Offices,
Almada Street,
HAMILTON ML2 0AE
Tel: 01698 454466
Fax: 01698 454467

Principal Community
Education Officer,
Community Education Department,
Tayside Regional Council,
15 Albert Square,
Meadowside,
DUNDEE DD1 1DJ
Tel: 01382 227129
Fax: 01382 227184

Assistant Director of Education,
Orkney Islands Council,
Education Department,
Kirkwall,
ORKNEY KW15 1NY
Tel: 01856 873535
Fax: 01856 876327

PUBLISHERS' NOTE

Whilst every care has been taken to ensure that the information contained in this book is accurate, the Publishers and the Network of TAP Agencies cannot accept responsibility for errors, omissions or changes which may have taken place after passing for press.

Tap Training Information Services

TAP (literally, Training Access Points) is a network of local education and training information services aimed at individuals and employers looking for education and training opportunities. The overall objectives of TAP are:

- To help improve the take-up of work-related education and training.
- To produce a comprehensive database of education and training opportunities.
- To provide ready access to this information via a range of delivery mechanisms (e.g. TAP points, mobile TAPs, databases leased to intermediaries and companies, telephone helplines, 'shop-front' advisory services, etc.).
- To help users make the best use of this information.

In Scotland, local TAP Agencies are funded by their respective Local Enterprise Companies (LECs). In addition, Scottish Enterprise National (SEN) and Highlands and Islands Enterprise (HIE) fund the Scottish TAP Network Agency whose role is to help co-ordinate the activities of the local TAP's and to compile the Scottish Training Database from the local TAP databases. The range of services available

locally can vary from area to area – depending on local needs and on LEC priorities. Core services, however, include database compilation and the maintenance of a wide range of computerised information points ('TAP points'). Each TAP database contains information on:-

a) Full time, part-time, day-release, open learning opportunities – from short ½ day courses to post-graduate degrees.
b) Entry requirements, costs, qualifications.
c) When and where courses are run.
d) Detailed course content information.
e) Courses available in a range of sectors – Further Education, Higher Education, Private Training Provision and Government funded training.

TAP has been highly successful across Scotland. In 1994 over 200,000 people used TAP – bringing the total in the last few years to over **1 million users**. A substantial proportion of users have gone on to find an education or training opportunity as a result of using TAP. Over **1,200** Scottish training providers are now represented on the database. There are now in excess of **300** information outlets across the whole of Scotland.

The network of TAP agencies across Scotland are delighted to be working with FHG on 'Classes and Courses'. Part-time provision accounts for approx. 50% of

the information on the Scottish TAP database. In association with FHG we have customised this information for inclusion in this exciting new Directory. Undoubtedly part-time provision is a growing market – as both employers and individuals increasingly seek flexible access to education and training courses.

For information on TAP services across Scotland contact:

SCOTTISH TAP NETWORK AGENCY
Room 1M1
1 Parliament Square
EDINBURGH
EH1 1RF
Tel: 0131 469 3464

LOTHIAN TAP AGENCY
8 St Mary's Street
EDINBURGH
EH1 1SU
Tel: 0131 557 5822

CAREERS CENTRAL LTD
TAP Training Information Service
Cape Unicentre
Kerse Road
STIRLING
FK7 7RW
Tel: 01786 446150

DUMFRIES & GALLOWAY TAP
AGENCY
The Penninghame Centre
Auchendoon Road
NEWTON STEWART
DG8 6HD
Tel: 01671 403530

FIFE TRAINING INFORMATION
SERVICES
9–10 Flemington Road
GLENROTHES
KY7 5OW
Tel: 01592 611231

HIGHLANDS & ISLANDS TAP
Inverness Business Centre
Seafield Road
INVERNESS
IV1 1SJ
Tel: 01463 710019

STRATHCLYDE TAP AGENCY
(inc. LANTRACS)
Network Scotland
57 Ruthven Lane
GLASGOW
G12 9JQ
Tel: 0141 357 1774

MORAY, BADENOCH &
STRATHSPEY TAP
Elgin Business Centre
Maisondieu Road
ELGIN
IV30 1RH
Tel: 01343 551858

TAP TRAINING INFORMATION
Scottish Borders Enterprise
Bridge Street,
GALASHIELS
TD1 1SW
Tel: 01896 758991

TAYSIDE TAP AGENCY
New Directions (Tayside) Ltd
88 Commercial Street
DUNDEE
DD1 2AP
Tel: 01382 206116

STEP*ahead*
381 Union Street
ABERDEEN
AB1 2BX
Tel: 01224 210300

The Enterprise Organisations

Scottish Enterprise National (SEN) and Highlands & Islands Enterprise (HIE) were set up in 1991 with Scottish Office funding to undertake a wide-ranging role in the economic development of Scotland. Among their priorities is Training and this is generally organised through the network of Local Enterprise Companies (LEC's) all over Scotland. The TAP Agencies are one example of the work of the network of LEC's which can be found regionally as follows:

HIGHLANDS & ISLANDS ENTERPRISE
Bridge House
20 Bridge Street
INVERNESS IV1 1QR
Tel: 01463 234171

ARGYLL and the ISLANDS ENTERPRISE
Stag Chambers,
Lorne Street,
LOCHGILPHEAD PA31 8LU
Tel: 01546 602281

ARGYLL and the ISLANDS
ENTERPRISE
Queen's Hall
DUNOON
PA23 7HJ
Tel: 01369 5511

ARGYLL and the ISLANDS
ENTERPRISE
(Cowal Initiative)
7A Alexandria Parade
DUNOON
PA23 8AB
Tel: 01369 2023

ARGYLL and the ISLANDS
ENTERPRISE
4 George Street
OBAN PA34 5RX
Tel: 01631 66368

ARGYLL and the ISLANDS
ENTERPRISE
Hazelbank Business Park
Milknowe
CAMPBELTOWN
PA28 6HA
Tel: 01586 553777

ARGYLL and the ISLANDS ENTERPRISE
25 Victoria Street
Rothesay
PA20 0JA
Tel: 01700 504830

**CAITHNESS AND SUTHERLAND
ENTERPRISE**
2 Princes Street
THURSO
Caithness
KW14 7BQ
Tel: 01847 66115

**INVERNESS AND NAIRN
ENTERPRISE**
Castle Wynd
INVERNESS
IV1 3DW
Tel: 01463 713504

LOCHABER LIMITED
5 Cameron Square
Fort William PH33 6AJ
Tel: 01397 702160

**MORAY, BADENOCH AND
STRATHSPEY ENTERPRISE**
(*jointly with Scottish Enterprise*)
Elgin Business Centre
ELGIN, Moray
IV30 1RH
Tel: 01343 550567

MORAY, BADENOCH AND
STRATHSPEY ENTERPRISE
67 High Street
FORRES, Moray
IV36 0AE
Tel: 01309 675520

MORAY, BADENOCH AND
STRATHSPEY ENTERPRISE
The Square
GRANTOWN-ON-SPEY
PH26 3HF
Tel: 01479 3288

ORKNEY ENTERPRISE
14 Queen Street
KIRKWALL KW15 1JE
Tel: 01856 874638

ROSS and CROMARTY ENTERPRISE
62 High Street
INVERGORDON
Ross and Cromarty IV18 9DH
Tel: 01349 853666

SHETLAND ENTERPRISE
Toll Clock Shopping Centre
20 North Road
LERWICK ZE1 0PE
Tel: 01595 3177

**SKYE AND LOCHALSH
ENTERPRISE**
Bridge Road
PORTREE
Isle of Sky IV51 9ER
Tel: 01478 2841

WESTERN ISLES ENTERPRISE
3 Harbour View
Cromwell Street Quay
STORNOWAY
Isle of Lewis PA87 2DEF
Tel: 01851 703625

WESTERN ISLES
ENTERPRISE
Balivanich
BENBECULA PA88 5LA
Tel: 01870 2438

SCOTTISH ENTERPRISE
120 Bothwell Street
GLASGOW G2 7JP
Tel: 0141 2482700

ENTERPRISE AYRSHIRE
17/19 Hill Street
KILMARNOCK
KA3 1HA
Tel: 01563 26623

**DUMFRIES AND GALLOWAY
ENTERPRISE COMPANY LTD**
Cairnsmore House
Bankend Road
DUMFRIES
DG1 4TA
Tel: 01387 54444

DUNBARTONSHIRE ENTERPRISE
2nd Floor, Spectrum House
Clydebank Business Park
Clydebank
GLASGOW G81 2DR
Tel: 0141 9512121

FIFE ENTERPRISE
Huntsman's House
33 Cadham Centre
GLENROTHES KY7 6RU
Tel: 01592 621000

FORTH VALLEY ENTERPRISE
Laurel House
Laurelhill Business Park
STIRLING FK7 9JQ
Tel: 01786 451919

GLASGOW DEVELOPMENT AGENCY
Atrium Court
50 Waterloo Street
GLASGOW G2 6HQ
Tel: 0141 2041111

GRAMPIAN ENTERPRISE LIMITED
27 Albyn Place
ABERDEEN AB1 1YL
Tel: 01224 211500

**LANARKSHIRE ENTERPRISE
COMPANY**
New Lanarkshire House
Willow Drive
Strathclyde Business Park
BELLSHILL ML4 3AD
Tel: 01698 754454

**LOTHIAN AND EDINBURGH
ENTERPRISE LIMITED**
Apex House
99 Haymarket Terrace
EDINBURGH EH12 5HD
Tel: 0131 313 4000

**RENFREWSHIRE ENTERPRISE
COMPANY**
25–29 Causeyside Street
PAISLEY PA1 1UL
Tel: 0141 848 0101

SCOTTISH BORDERS ENTERPRISE
Bridge Street
GALASHIELS TD1 1SW
Tel: 01896 58991

SCOTTISH ENTERPRISE TAYSIDE
45 North Lindsay Street
DUNDEE DD1 1HT
Tel: 01382 231000

Part-time Classes and Courses
IN SCOTLAND 1995–96

PART ONE

Classes and Courses

On the pages that follow, you will find details of approximately 7,000 part-time classes and courses available in 1995–96 in locations all over Scotland. The courses are listed in 17 main sections which are sub-divided into subject sections each with a number of individual sub-headings. There is a small amount of duplication where it has been felt appropriate to include a class/course under more than one category or heading. The Contents Pages (pages 8 to 9) and the headlines at the top of pages, will guide you through the various subjects and there is also an alphabetical Subject Index at the back of the book.

USING THE ENTRIES

The entry for each course contains three parts:

a) The name of the class/course. This will also normally be the name by which it is known by the provider and on the TAP database.
b) The 'outcome' – what qualification, award etc. you gain from the course, if any. In some cases, there is no formal outcome or simply a Certificate of Attendance. This Certificate can be important for Benefits or for an employer, if appropriate.
c) The 'Provider'. This is the college, university, company or other organisation who actually runs any particular course listed. Because most providers offer more than one course, we have used a simple coding system to identify providers. These codes lead you directly to the individual course provider whose contact details are listed by region in 'Part Two: Providers' on pages **195** to **218**.

ABBREVIATIONS

For reasons of space and to avoid repetition, commonly accepted abbreviations or shortened forms have been used in the entries for awards, professional bodies etc. Please refer to the 'Abbreviations' on pages **221** to **222** for an explanation of all abbreviations used.

Agriculture, Horticulture & Animal Care

AGRICULTURAL ENGINEERING

Agricultural & Horticultural Engineering - Accreditation of Prior Learning *SCOTVEC/NCMs & SVQs.*   **F4**

Agricultural And/Or Horticultural Engineering - NC *SCOTVEC/NC & College Certificate.*   **L64**

Agricultural Engineering - NC *SCOTVEC/NC will be awarded on successful completion of this course.*   **B2 T9**

Agricultural/Horticultural Engineering - NC *SCOTVEC/NC in Agricultural/Horticultural Engineering.*   **S87**

Crofting Short Courses *Participants will have gained skills in various aspects of crofting.*   **H31**

Food & Environment Protection Act Training: Crop Spraying *Foundation module (PAI) as tested by SAYFC.*   **L66**

Horticultural Engineering - NC *SCOTVEC/NC in Horticultural Engineering.*   **F3**

Horticultural Machinery Level III - SVQ *SCOTVEC/NC at the end of each year of study.*   **G17**

Horticultural Service Engineering - HNC *SCOTVEC/HNC in Horticultural Service Engineering.*   **F3**

Horticulture (Amenity & Commercial) - NC *SCOTVEC/NC in Horticulture. Possible progression to HNC in Horticulture.*   **C10**

Introductory Welding *An introduction to welding of ferrous & non ferrous metals using gas, arc & MIG welding equipment.*   **B2 B6**

MIG Welding *The SCOTVEC Module 64748.*   **B2 B6**

Part-Time Engineering/Agricultural Course for the Unemployed *A certificate for modules passed.*   **T9**

Pesticide & Sprayer Courses (FEPA) for Agriculture & Horticulture *Trainees will be issued with a certificate of attendance.*   **L64**

Practical Welding Skills *Skills in welding.*   **H31**

Small Engine Powered Machine Operation - NCM (SCOTVEC) *SCOTVEC/NCM in Small Engine Powered Machine Operation.*   **L64**

Tractor & Fork-Lift Truck Operation & Maintenance *SCOTVEC/NC. Fork-Lift Truck Operators Certificate.*   **F3**

Tractor Driving for Farmers Wives *College Certificate of Attendance.*   **B5**

Use of Hand Tools in Horticulture - NCM (SCOTVEC) *SCOTVEC/NCM.*   **L64**

Welding *Students will learn some basic skills of farm welding.*   **H30**

Welding - NCM (SCOTVEC) *SCOTVEC/NCM in Welding.*   **L64**

AGRICULTURAL & HORTICULTURAL MANAGEMENT & MAINTENANCE

Agriculture - Accreditation of Prior Learning *SCOTVEC Diploma in Agriculture.*   **F4**

Agriculture - NC *SCOTVEC/NC in Agriculture.*   **S79**

Animal Technology - HNC *SCOTVEC/HNC in Animal Technology. Qualification for Associate Membership of the Institute of Animal Technology.*   **L68**

Basic Marketing *Certificate of Attendance is awarded.*   **B6**

Concrete Practice & Paving - NCM (SCOTVEC) *SCOTVEC/NCM in Concrete Practice & Paving.*   **L64**

Countryside Woodwork & Access Facilities - NCM (SCOTVEC) *SCOTVEC/NCM in Countryside Woodwork & Access Facilities.*   **L64**

Customised Short Courses in Science & Technology   **L68**

Dry-Stone Dyking *Practical skills & knowledge will be gained by successful students.*   **S15**

Drystone Dykes - NCM (SCOTVEC) *SCOTVEC/NCM in Drystone Dyking.*   **L64**

Farm Accounts *Students will have an understanding of the skills needed to develop an accurate Accounting System.*   **H30**

Farm Business Management *SCOTVEC certificate will be awarded on successful completion.*   **B2**

Farm Business Management - NC *SCOTVEC/NC in Farm Business Management.*   **B2**

Farm Management - Accreditation of Prior Learning *SCOTVEC/NCMs & SVQs.*   **F4**

Fence Construction - NCM (SCOTVEC) *SCOTVEC/NCM in Fence Construction.*   **L64**

Game Fishing Course - Part 1 *Certificate of Attendance.*   **B5**

Game Fishing Course - Part 2 *Certificate of Attendance.*   **B5**

Golf Course Management - HNC *SCOTVEC/HNC in Golf Course Management.*   **F3**

Horticulture - HNC *SCOTVEC/HNC in Horticulture. Possible progression to HND level course.*   **C10**

How the Countryside Works: Land Use *No formal Certificate.*   **T23**

Integrated Rural Land Use - Accreditation of Prior Learning *SCOTVEC/NC. Skills associated with rangers, wardens & countryside technicians.*   **F4**

Integrated Rural Land Use - NC *SCOTVEC/NC. Skills associated with rangers, wardens & countryside technicians.*   **F3**

Introduction to Estate Maintenance - NCM (SCOTVEC) *SCOTVEC/NCM in Estate Maintenance.*   **L64**

Land Based Studies - NC *SCOTVEC/NC.*   **H49**

Livestock Record Keeping *SAC Certificate.*   **S122**

Pesticides Short Courses *Skills in the safe use of pesticides.*   **H31**

Quality Control for the Dairy Industry *SAC Certificate.*   **S122**

Rural Secretarial Studies - Accreditation of Prior Learning *SCOTVEC/NC for Rural Secretarial Studies.*   **F4**

Rural Skills Courses *Short courses in a variety of subjects relating to rural skills.*   **H27**

Safe Lifting Techniques *SAC Certificate.*   **S122**

Statutory Training On Abrasive Wheels *Certificate.*   **S122**

Use of Borders Produce *Certificate of Attendance.*   **B6**

AGRICULTURE & HORTICULTURAL STUDIES (GENERAL)

Agricultural Awarences for Statutory Authorities *SAC Certificate.*   **S122**

Agricultural Updating for River Board Personnel *SAC Certificate.*   **S122**

Agriculture (Part-Time) *Primarily for those starting a career in Agriculture. Modules are those required for SVQ level 2.*   **T1**

Agriculture - NC *SCOTVEC/NC will be awarded on successful completion.*   **B2**

Agriculture - NC (SCOTVEC) *SCOTVEC/NC in Agriculture.*   **L64**

Agriculture - SVQ Level I *A SVQ Level I Preliminary Certificate (SE0101001) in Agriculture.*   **B2**

Agriculture/Horticulture *No formal outcome.*   **S122**

Agriculture: General Crop & Livestock Production - SVQ Level II *A SVQ Level II Preliminary Certificate (SF0101008).*   **B2**

Basis: Crop Diseases & Control *Contributes to Basis Certificate.*   **S122**

Basis: Safety Legislation *Contributes to Basis Certificate.*   **S122**

Basis: Sales of Treated Seeds *Contributes to Basis Certificate.*   **S122**

Broiler Breeding *SAC Certificate.*   **S122**

Broiler Production *SAC Certificate.*   **S122**

Commercial Horticulture: General Practice - SVQ Level II *SVQ Level II (SF0102001).*   **B2**

Commercial Horticulture: Nursery Stock Production - SVQ Level II *SVQ Level II (SF0102005).*   **B2**

Computers On the Farm *SAC Certificate.*   **S122**

COSHH Regulations *Certification required by legislation.*   **S122**

Employment Training (Horticulture) *Practical experience in Horticulture.*   **C22**

Environment Management for Poultry Producers *SAC Certificate.*   **S122**

Environmentally Responsible Farming *SAC Certificate.*   **S122**

Farm Diversification *SAC Certificate.*   **S122**

Farm Pollution for Risk Assessors *SAC Certificate.*   **S122**

FEPA; Pa9 Fogging, Misting & Smokes *Contributes to FEPA Certificate of competence which is requirement of N/SVQ.*   **S122**

Free Range Egg Production *SAC Certificate.*   **S122**

Garden Centre Personnel *The names of plants and dividing plants into suitable groups.*   **M8**

General Agriculture - NC *SCOTVEC/NC. SVQ at Craftsman Level 2/3.*   **F3 T9**

General Horticulture Practice - Yt/Svq II *SCOTVEC SVQ, SVQ Level II Certificate.*   **S79**

Hatching Egg Management *SAC Certificate.*   **S122**

Hill & Upland Farming - NC *SCOTVEC/NC in Hill & Upland Farming.*   **T9**

Horticulture *SCOTVEC Certificate will be awarded on successful completion of the modules.*   **B11**

Horticulture (Amenity & Commercial) - NC *SCOTVEC/NC in Horticulture.*   **C10**

Horticulture (Part-Time) *Students will gain a knowledge of Horticulture relevant to their needs.* **T1**

Horticulture - Accreditation of Prior Learning *SCOTVEC/NCM & SVQ.* **F4**

Horticulture - Commercial or Amenity - NC *SCOTVEC/NC.* **S79**

Horticulture - HNC *SCOTVEC/HNC in Horticulture.* **C10 S15**

Horticulture - NC *SCOTVEC/NC will be awarded on successful completion.* **B2 S15 T9**

Horticulture - SVQ Level I *SVQ Preliminary Certificate Level I (SE0102002).* **B2**

Horticulture - SVQ Level I, Level II & Level III *SCOTVEC SVQs, Level I, Level II & Level III.* **L64**

Horticulture Short Courses *A variety of courses is available.* **H31**

Implications of Agricultural Change for Rural Land Use *SAC Certificate.* **S122**

Introductory Agriculture - Accreditation of Prior Learning *SCOTVEC/NC.* **F4**

Landbased Industries Practical Training Courses - NCMs *SCOTVEC/NCM.* **L64**

New Approaches to Better Sheep Breeding *SAC Certificate.* **S122**

Pest & Predator Control - Part 1 *First part of a three part syllabus for SCOTVEC Module 78431.* **B5**

Pest & Predator Control - Part 2 *Second part of a three part syllabus for SCOTVEC Module 78431.* **B5**

Pest & Predator Control - Part 3 *Third part of a three part syllabus for SCOTVEC Module 78431.* **B5**

Rodent Control And/Or Rabbit Control *SAC Certificate.* **S122**

Royal Horticulture Society Master of Horticulture *The Royal Horticulture Society's Master of Horticulture certificate.* **S81**

Safety Management - Basic *SAC Certificate.* **S122**

Welfare of Poultry Stock *SAC Certificate.* **S122**

AGRICULTURAL SCIENCES

Agricultural Science - HND *SCOTVEC/HND in Agricultural Science.* **S92**

Agriculture - NC *SCOTVEC/NC in Agriculture.* **S79**

FEPA Application by Hand Held Sprayers Course for Workers who Apply Pesticides . **D1**

FEPA Foundation Course for Forestry Workers who Apply Pesticides *A Foundation Course for existing operators.* **D1**

Laboratory Techniques *SAC Certificate.* **S122**

Northern Studies Courses *These courses are run on a wide variety of subjects for general interest & education.* **H50**

Pesticide & Sprayer Courses (FEPA) for Agriculture & Horticulture *Certificate of attendance.* **L64**

Pesticides *Participants will learn the regulations on the use of pesticides. Course members will receive Certificate of Attendance.*

Pesticides *Certificate of Attendance & Certificate of Competence.* **B2**

Pesticides Short Courses *Skills in the safe use of pesticides.* **H31**

Laboratory Science Technology Course - NC *SCOTVEC/NC in Laboratory Science Technology.* **L68**

ANIMAL HUSBANDRY, GAME-KEEPING, FISH-FARMING

Agriculture - NC *SCOTVEC/NC in Agriculture.* **S79**

Animal Medicines Training Regulatory Authority *Certification of nominated person.* **S122**

Aquaculture - Short Courses *SCOTVEC/NC(s) will be available in some subjects. Others will be College certificated.* **H37**

Bee Keeping *SCOTVEC/NC in Bee Keeping.* **S92**

BHS Progressive Rider Tests, 1 - 6 *BHS Award.* **F20**

BHS Stages 1,2 & 3 *BHS Stages 1,2 & 3.* **F20**

Calf Rearing *No formal outcome although a College Certificate of Attendance will be given.* **B5**

Commercial Egg Production *SAC Certificate.* **S122**

Crofting Short Courses *Participants will have gained skills in various aspects of crofting.* **H31**

Data Processing & Computing *Participants will have learned basic computing skills.* **H14**

Diseases of Sheep *There is no formal outcome although a College Certificate of Attendance will be given.* **B5**

Feeding Management of Sheep *There is no formal outcome although a College Certificate of Attendance will be given.* **B5**

Finance *Non-certificated course to help those involved in financial operations.* **H14**

First Aid *Participants will have gained skills in First Aid.* **H14**

Fish Farming Courses for Industry *Short courses in a variety of subjects relating to fishing/fisheries.* **H27**

Fish Farming Short Courses *Participants will have gained skills in various aspects of fish farming.* **H31**

Fish Industry Safety Courses *To increase safety awareness of those in the Industry.* **H14**

Fish Industry Short Courses *Short courses in a variety of subjects relating to fishing/fisheries are available.* **H14**

Fish Processing - Short Courses *Courses can lead to SCOTVEC, SVQ Qualifications.* **H37**

Food Hygiene Courses - REHIS *Courses are run at all levels of hygiene skills.* **H14**

Fork-Lift Truck *Participants will have improved their skills in operating a Fork-Lift truck.* **H14**

Game Bird Rearing Part 1 *First of three parts of the syllabus for the SCOTVEC module 88429.* **B5**

Game Bird Rearing Part 2 *Second of three parts of the syllabus for the SCOTVEC module 88429.* **B5**

Game Bird Rearing Part 3 *Third of three parts of the syllabus for the SCOTVEC module 88429.* **B5**

Game Bird Releasing Part 1 *First of four parts of the syllabus for the SCOTVEC Module 78432.* **B5**

Game Bird Releasing Part 2 *Second of four parts of the syllabus for the SCOTVEC Module 78432.* **B5**

Game Bird Releasing Part 3 *Third of four parts of the syllabus for the SCOTVEC Module 78432.* **B5**

Game Bird Releasing Part 4 *Fourth of four parts of the syllabus for the SCOTVEC Module 78432.* **B5**

Gamekeeping & Wildlife Conservation - Accreditation of Prior Learning *SCOTVEC/NCMs & SVQs.* **F4**

Gamekeeping & Wildlife Conservation - NC *NC in Gamekeeping & Wildlife Conservation.* **F3**

Gamekeeping & Wildlife Management - Accreditation of Prior Learning *SCOTVEC/NC in Gamekeeping & Wildlife Management.* **F4**

Gamekeeping & Wildlife Management - Diploma *SCOTVEC/NC in Gamekeeping & Wildlife Management.* **F3**

Gamekeeping & Wildlife Management - HNC *SCOTVEC/HNC.* **B2**

Gamekeeping - NC *SCOTVEC/NC.* **B2 F3**

Gamekeeping - SVQ Level II *A SVQ Level II (SF0103101) in Gamekeeping.* **B2**

Gamekeeping Short Courses *The courses cover a variety of topics relating to gamekeeping.* **H31**

General Agriculture - NC *SCOTVEC/NC. Participants can achieve modules necessary for SVQ at Craftsman Level 2/3.* **F3**

General Crop and Livestock Production - YT/SVQ Level II *SCOTVEC SVQ, SVQ Level II Certificate.* **S79**

Horse & Stable Management *BHS Stages 1 & 2.* **L91**

Horse Care & Management *BHS S/NVQ Level 1/2/3.* **G29**

Horse Management - Certificate *Certificate in Horse Management.* **G17**

Horse Management - HNC *SCOTVEC/HNC. Designed to prepare students for British Horse Society Stage III.* **B2**

Horse Management - NC *SCOTVEC/NC. British Horse Society Stages 1 & 2.* **B2**

Horse Owners Certificate (British Horse Society) Level 1 & 2 *HOC Level 1 & 2.* **F20**

Horsemanship Courses *Participants will learn how to handle and care for horses & ponies.* **T1**

Housing Sheep *There is no formal outcome although a College Certificate of Attendance will be given.* **B5**

Interviewing Techniques *Non-certificated course to help those involved in interviewing staff.* **H14**

Introductory Agriculture - Accreditation of Prior Learning *SCOTVEC/NC.* **F4**

Introductory Business Analysis Planning & Control for Fish Farmers *SAC Certificate.* **S122**

Lambing *Participants will be able to develop skills in caring for ewes at lambing time.* **F3**

Lambing Courses *There is no formal outcome although a College Certificate of Attendance will be given.* **B5**

Management At Lambing *SAC Certificate.* **S122**

Management Skills *Participants will have improved their management skills.* **H14**

Motivation & Communication *Non-certificated course improving managerial skills involved in the fishing trade.* **H14**

NVQ Horse Care - Levels 1,2 & 3 *NVQ in horse care.* **F20**

Part IV Air Diving: First Aid (HSE Regulation 7(1)(b)) *R.G.I.T. Part IV Air Diving: First Aid Certificate.* **H37**

Performance Appraisal *No formal certificate.* **H14**

Pest & Predator Control - Part 1 *First part of a three part syllabus for SCOTVEC Module 78431.* **B5**

Pest & Predator Control - Part 2 *Second part of a three part syllabus for SCOTVEC Module 78431.*
B5

Pest & Predator Control - Part 3 *Third part of a three part syllabus for SCOTVEC Module 78431.*
B5

Sea Fishing *SCOTVEC Level 2.* **G33**

Shearing *There is no formal outcome although a College Certificate of Attendance will be given.*
B5

Sheep Dog Handling *Participants will have gained skills in sheep dog handling.* **H31**

Sheep Shearing *SCOTVEC Module in Sheep Shearing. British Wool Marketing Board Bronze Seal.* **F3 T1**

Small Animal Care - NC *NC in Small Animal Care up to SVQ (SVQ) Level 2.* **F3**

Suckler Cow Management *SAC Certificate.*
S122

Supervision Skills *Short courses to help those involved in supervision or instruction.* **H14**

Training for Countryside Rangers *SAC Certificate & HNC Validation.* **S122**

CROP PRODUCTION

Environmental Studies *Practical skills & knowledge will be gained by successful students.*
S15

FEPA; Pa2 Ground Crop Sprayer *Contributes to FEPA Certificate of competence which is requirement of N/SVQ.* **S122**

FEPA; Pa6 Safe Hand Held Applicators *Contributes to FEPA Certificate of Competence which is requirement of N/SVQ.* **S122**

FEPA; Pa1 Safe Use of Pesticides *Contributes to FEPA Certificate of competence which is requirement of N/SVQ.* **S122**

Garden Centre Personnel *Delegates will be familiar with the names of plants and able to divide them into groups.* **M8**

Garden Centres & Nursery Practice - NC *SCOTVEC/NC in Garden Centres & Nursery Practice.* **S81**

General Agriculture - NC *SCOTVEC/NC. Participants can achieve modules necessary for SVQ at Craftsman Level 2/3.* **F3**

General Crop and Livestock Production - YT/SVQ Level II *SCOTVEC SVQ, SVQ Level II Certificate.*
S79

Introductory Agriculture - Accreditation of Prior Learning *SCOTVEC/NC.* **F4**

Mushrooms & Toadstools *Development of knowledge of mushrooms & toadstools.* **C41**

Tree & Shrub Planting - NCM (SCOTVEC) *SCOTVEC/NCM in Tree & Shrub Planting.* **L64**

FORESTRY

Amenity Tree Management - NC *SCOTVEC/NC in Amenity Tree Management.* **S81**

Arboriculture - NC *SCOTVEC/NC in Arboriculture.* **S79**

Arboriculture - SCOTVEC/NC *Certificate in Arboriculture; Forestry Training Council Certificate; Health & Safety First Aid Certificate.* **G17**

Basic Chainsaw *Basic skills required for the safe operation of chainsaws.* **H53**

Chain Saws (Including Tree Surgery) *CITB Certificate.* **G26**

Chainsaw Advanced/Tree Harvesting *This course leads to SCOTVEC Module.* **G17**

Chainsaw an Introduction - NCM (Scotvec) *SCOTVEC/NCM in Chainsaw Skills. National Proficiency Test Council Certificate.* **L64**

Chainsaw Operation *A Certificate of Attendance & Certificate of Competence.* **B2**

Chainsaw Operations for Those Proficient to NPTC/SSTS Level *National Proficiency Test Council and Scottish Skills Testing Service Certificates.* **D1**

Chainsaw Short Courses *Skills in the safe operation of chain saws.* **H31**

Forestry Short Courses *A variety of courses is available.* **H31**

Fork-Lift Driving *Skills needed to drive a Fork-Lift truck.* **H31**

Tree & Shrub Planting - NCM (SCOTVEC) *SCOTVEC/NCM in Tree & Shrub Planting.* **L64**

Tree Surgery *Skills gained in Tree Surgery.*
S79

GARDENING, FLORISTRY, SPORTSGROUNDS, AMENITY HORTICULTURE

Amenity Horticulture - HNC *SCOTVEC/HNC in Amenity Horticulture.* **F3**

Amenity Horticulture - NC *SCOTVEC. An Elmwood certificate will also be awarded.* **F3**

Amenity Horticulture - NC *SCOTVEC/NCMs in Amenity Horticulture.* **S81**

Amenity Horticulture - SVQ Level II-III   *SCOTVEC SVQ SVQ Level II & III in Amenity Horticulture.*   **C10**

Amenity Horticulture/Landscaping, Green Keeping/Sports Ground Maintenance   *SCOTVEC SVQ Certificate Level 2.*   **S131**

Amenity Tree Management - NC   *SCOTVEC/NC in Amenity Tree Management.*   **S81**

Basis: Crop Pests in Amenity Horticulture   *Contributes to Basis Certificate.*   **S122**

Basis: Soils & Nutrition   *Contributes to Basis Certificate.*   **S122**

Basis: Weed Control   *Contributes to Basis Certificate.*   **S122**

Building for Gardeners   *Landscape gardening skills.*   **L5**

Container Gardening; Design, Propagation & Husbandry   *SAC Certificate.*   **S122**

Floral Art   *No formal certificate.*   **H53**

Floristry   *SVQ Level 2 Certificate.*   **S131**

Floristry (Level 1) - SCOTVEC/NC   *Record of Educating Training (RET) & SCOTVEC Certificate in Floristry (Level I).*   **G17**

Floristry (Level I) - SCOTVEC National Preliminary Certificate   *SCOTVEC National Preliminary Certificate in Floristry (Level I).*   **G2**

Floristry (Level II) - SVQ   *SVQ: Floristry Level II.*   **G2**

Floristry - City & Guilds Stage III   *A City & Guilds stage 3 certificate in Floristry.*   **S81**

Floristry - HNC   *SCOTVEC/HNC.*   **L5**

Floristry - NC   *SCOTVEC/NC . This course also leads to a SVQ.*   **B2**

Floristry - NC SVQ Levels I-II   *SCOTVEC/NC in Floristry.*   **S81**

Floristry - SCOTVEC   *SCOTVEC .*   **B2**

Floristry - SVQ Level 1   *SVQ Level 1 in Floristry.*   **L5**

Floristry - SVQ Level 2   *SVQ Level 2 in Floristry.*   **L5**

Floristry - SVQ Level I   *SCOTVEC SVQ Level I in Floristry.*   **S15**

Floristry - SVQ Level II   *SCOTVEC SVQ Level II in Floristry.*   **S15**

Gardening Science - the Follow Up   *Individuals will gain an understanding of how plants work.*   **T13**

General Trowel Skills: for Gardeners NCM (SCOTVEC)   *SCOTVEC/NCM.*   **L64**

Golf Course Management - HNC   *SCOTVEC/HNC in Golf Course Management.*   **L64 S81**

Greenkeeping & Groundsmanship - NC   *SCOTVEC/NC in Green- keeping & Groundsmanship.*   **S81**

Greenkeeping & Groundsmanship - NC (SCOTVEC)   *SCOTVEC/NC in Greenkeeping & Groundsmanship. College Certificate.*   **L64**

Greenkeeping - NC   *SCOTVEC/NC. Basic skills in Golf Greenkeeping.*   **F3**

Greenkeeping Supervision - NC   *SCOTVEC/NC in Greenkeeping Supervision.*   **F3**

Hard Landscaping   *Practical skills & knowledge.*   **S15 S87**

Horticulture - Commercial or Amenity - NC   *SCOTVEC/NC in Horticulture - Commercial & Amenity.*   **S79**

Horticulture - HNC   *SCOTVEC/HNC in Horticulture.*   **S15**

Horticulture - NC   *SCOTVEC/NC. Practical skills in Horticulture.*   **S15**

Landscape Construction an Introduction - NCM (Scotvec)   *SCOTVEC/NCM in Landscape Construction.*   **L64**

Landscape Practice - NC   *SCOTVEC/NC in Landscape Practice.*   **S81**

Parks & Recreational Supervisory Management - NEBSM   *National Examining Board in Supervisory Management (NEBSM) Certificate.*   **S94**

Practical Horticulture & Gardening Skills   *Knowledge of domestic gardening skills.*   **H31**

Sportsground & Greenkeeping - Accreditation of Prior Learning   *SCOTVEC/NCMs & SVQs.*   **F4**

Use of Hand Tools in Horticulture - NCM (SCOTVEC)   *SCOTVEC/NCM in Use of Hand Tools in Horticulture.*   **L64**

VETERINARY SERVICES & PET CARE

Small Animal Care - NC   *NC in Small Animal Care up to SVQ Level 2.*   **F3**

Small Animal Care   *City & Guilds NVQ Level 1/2.*   **G29 S131**

Sheep Dog Handling   *Participants will have gained skills in Sheep Dog Handling.*   **H31**

Veterinary Nursing   *NVQ Level 3.*   **S131**

Architecture and Construction

ARCHITECTURE

Advanced Architectural Design - PgD   *A PgD in Advanced Architectural Design.*   **S105**

Architectural Technology (Built Environment) - HNC   *A HNC in Architectural Technology (Built Environment).*   **S68**

Architectural Technology - BSc / BSc (Honours)   *BSc Degree / Hons Degree in Architectural Technology.*   **L60**

Architectural Technology - HNC   *SCOTVEC/HNC in Architectural Technology.*
B6 C22 D5 H53 L5 T12

Architectural Technology/Building/ Quantity Surveying   *HNC in Architectural Technology.*   **G15**

Architecture - HNC   *Scottish HNC in Architecture.*   **F5**

Building Technician - NC   *SCOTVEC/NC.*   **B6**

Built Environment - HNC   *SCOTVEC/HNC in the Built Environment.*   **S15**

Built Heritage Conservation - Pgd/Msc   *PgD/MSc in Built Heritage Conservation.*   **G15**

Computer Aided Landscape Technology - HNC   *SCOTVEC/HNC in Computer Aided Landscape Technology.*   **F3**

Computer Aided Landscape Technology - HND   *SCOTVEC/HND in Computer Aided Landscape Technology.*   **F3**

Integrated Building Design - MSc   *An MSc in Urban Design.*   **S105**

Integrated Building Design - PgD   *A PgD in Urban Design.*   **S105**

Landscape Architecture - MLA   *Master of Landscape Architecture Degree.*   **L77**

Urban Design - MSc   *An MSc in Urban Design.*   **S105**

Urban Design - MSc/Postgraduate Diploma   *An MSc or PgD in Urban Design.*   **S109**

Urban Design - PgD   *A PgD in Urban Design.*   **S105**

Various Courses Available   *Outcome depends on level and subject matter of individual courses.B1 Advanced Architectural Design - MArch   S105   A MArch in Advanced Architectural Design.*   **T21**

BUILDING & CONSTRUCTION OPERATIONS

Advanced Craft - Brickwork - City & Guilds 588   *City & Guilds 588 certificate.*   **T9**

Advanced Craft - Painting & Decorating City & Guilds 594   *C & G Advanced painting & decorating certificate.*   **S2 T9**

Advanced Craft Certificate in Plumbing - NC   *SCOTVEC/NC.*   **F13**

Advanced Craft Painting & Decorating   *City & Guilds of London Institute Advanced Craft Painting & Decorating 594 Certificate.*   **S2**

Advanced Plastering Skills   *Increased plastering skills.*   **L5**

Advanced Stone Carving   *Increased stonemasonry skills.*   **L5**

Bricklaying - SVQ Level III   *SVQ Level III in Bricklaying.*   **B6**

Brickwork   *An Advanced Craft Level Certificate in Brickwork.*   **C22 S87**

Brickwork - Advanced Certificate   *SCOTVEC AC in Brickwork.*   **F13 S6**

Brickwork - Advanced Craft Certificate   *SCOTVEC AC in Brickwork.*   **S91**

Brickwork - C & G 588   *NVQ, NVQ City & Guilds Advanced Craft 588 Certificate in Brickwork.*   **S88**

Brickwork - NC   *SCOTVEC/NC - equivalent to the Craft City & Guilds Certificate.*   **F13 S88**

Brickwork - SCOTVEC AC   *SCOTVEC AC in Brickwork.*   **B6**

Brickwork - SCOTVEC/NC   *SCOTVEC/NC in Brickwork.*   **G2**

Brickwork - SVQ Level III   *SCOTVEC SVQ SVQ Level III in Brickwork.*   **C22 S6**

Brickwork Advanced Craft - C & G   *City & Guilds Advanced Craft Certificate.*   **L81**

Brickwork: Advanced Competition   *Acquisition of advanced bricklaying techniques. Competition practice.*   **L5**

Building & Civil Engineering - HNC   *Can lead to SCOTVEC/HND.*   **H31**

Building - HNC   *SCOTVEC/HNC in Building.*   **S6 S81**

Building - NC   *NC Programme in Building.*   **F5 F13 L81**

Building Craft - NC   *SCOTVEC/NC in Building Craft.*   **S81**

Building Crafts - YT/SVQ Level III   *SVQ Level III Certificate.*   **S73**

Building for Gardeners   *Basic skills required by landscape gardeners.*   **L5**

Building Programme - NC   *SCOTVEC/NC in Building Construction.*   **S88**

Building Services (ACIBASE Membership) - Post-HNC Course   *Can lead to registration with the Institute of Building Services Engineers.*   **L5**

Building Services (Heating & Ventilating) - Continuing Education Certificate   *CEC Building Services (H&V) leading to Associate Membership CIBSE.*   **S88**

Building Services (Heating & Ventilating) - HNC   *SCOTVEC/HNC in Heating & Ventilating.*   **S88**

Building Services (Heating & Ventilating) - NC   *SCOTVEC/NC in Heating & Ventilating.*   **S88**

Building Services Engineering - MSc/ Diploma   *MSc Degree/Diploma in Building Services Engineering.*   **L6**

Building Services Engineering Management - MSc/Diploma   *MSc Degree/Diploma in Building Services Engineering Management.*   **L6**

Building Technicians - NC   *SCOTVEC/NC in Building Technology.*   **S6**

CGLI 600 Series Supplementary Studies   *City & Guilds Certificate (CE).*   **T1**

Concrete Work   *No formal certificate.*   **S15**

Construction - NC   *SCOTVEC/NC in Construction. Possible progression to SVQ Level III in Building Trades.*   **C10**

Construction - YT/SVQ Levels I-II   *SCOTVEC SVQ, SVQ Levels I-II Certificate.*   **S79**

Construction Skills   *Skills gained in construction skills.*   **S81**

Construction Studies/Building/Civil Engineering - NC   *SCOTVEC/NC.*   **H53**

Construction Trades Craft Courses - SVQ   *SVQ in Construction Trades.*   **S75**

CORGI Gas Safety Registration   *CORGI Gas Safety Registration.*   **L5**

Damp Proof Plastering   *College Certificate.*   **L5**

Decorative Floorlaying - SVQ Levels II-III   *SCOTVEC SVQ, SVQ Levels II-III Certificate in Decorative Floorlaying.*   **S68**

Domestic Gas Safety (ACOP)   *SCOTVEC & the British Plumbing Employers Council offer certification.*   **H53**

Domestic Gas Safety (ACOP) Course   *Industry registration.*   **C22**

Electrical Installation - NC   *SCOTVEC/NC. NVQ Level III after achieving measurement test.*   **M7**

Engineering & Building Services - Customised Courses   *Various courses available.*   **L71**

Evening Courses in Decorating, Glazing & Signwork   *SCOTVEC/NCMs or increased skills.*   **L5**

Feature Slating   *Acquisition of techniques in feature slating.*   **L5**

Fence Erection   *SVQ Level 2.*   **S136**

Gas Distribution & Gas Service Engineering - NC   *SCOTVEC/NC in Gas Distribution & Gas Service Engineering.*   **S68**

Gas Installation (ACOP)   *Practical skills & knowledge in Gas Installation.*   **S15**

Gas Installation Inspection - Domestic   *Knowledge gained in Gas Installation Inspection.*   **S68**

Gas Installation Studies - C & G 598   *City & Guilds 598 Advanced Craft Certificate.*   **F13**

Gas Safety (Installation & Use)   *Knowledge gained in Gas Installation inspection & use.*   **S68**

Gas Service Engineering - NC   *SCOTVEC/NC.*   **F13**

Gas Service Engineers - SVQ   *SCOTVEC SVQ.*   **S68**

General Appreciation of Interior Finishes - NC   *SCOTVEC/NC.*   **C23**

General Appreciation of Interior Finishes - NCM   *SCOTVEC/NCM.*   **L81**

General Appreciation of Roofing - NCM   *SCOTVEC/NCM.*   **L81**

General Appreciation of Trowel Applied Finishes - NCM   *SCOTVEC/NCM.*   **L81**

General Appreciation of Underground Drainage - NCM   *SCOTVEC/NCM.*   **L81**

General Building Cutting & Fixing Building Materials -National Certificate   *SCOTVEC/NCM.*   **L81**

General Building Operations - SVQ Level I-II   *SCOTVEC SVQ, SVQ Level I-II in General Building Operations.*   **C10**

Glazing - SVQ Levels II-III   *SCOTVEC SVQ, SVQ Levels II-III Certificate in Glazing.*   **S68**

Hard Landscaping   *SCOTVEC Modules.*   **S87**

Heating & Ventilating Craft Fitters - NC   *SCOTVEC/NC in Heating & Ventilating for Craft Fitters.*   **S88**

Heating Installation   *Skills in heating installation.*   **S15**

Institute of Clerk of Works Course (Mature Entrants)   *To prepare practising Clerks of Works for the ICW Mature Entrants Examination.*   **S68**

Introduction to Decorative Skills - NCM   *SCOTVEC/NCM.*   **L81**

Introduction to Stonecutting   *Introduction to stonecutting techniques.*   **L5**

Introductory Trowel Skills - Walling - NCM   *SCOTVEC/NCM.*   **L81**

Introductory Trowel Skills - Walling NC   *SCOTVEC/NC.*   **C23**

Modern Decorative Renderings *Improved decoration skills.*   **L5**

Non-Advanced Vocational Courses for Adults *Skills in chosen subject.*   **S75**

Non-Domestic Gas Installations - Testing for Soundness & Purging Procedures *Knowledge gained in Gas Installation Testing.*   **S68**

Painting & Decorating *Advanced Craft Level Certificate in Painting & Decorating.*   **C22 S87**

Painting & Decorating (Part Time) - HN Advanced Units *For students who have achieved SVQ III.*   **T1**

Painting & Decorating - Advanced Certificate *SCOTVEC AC in Painting & Decorating.*   **S6**

Painting & Decorating - Customised Courses *Various.*   **L71**

Painting & Decorating - HNC *SCOTVEC/HNC in Painting & Decorating.*   **S75**

Painting & Decorating - NC *SCOTVEC/NC.*
L81 S2 S15 S88

Painting & Decorating - NVQ C & G *NVQ, NVQ City & Guilds Certificate in Painting & Decorating.*   **S75**

Painting & Decorating - SCOTVEC AC *SCOTVEC AC in Painting & Decorating.*   **B6**

Painting & Decorating - SCOTVEC/NC *SCOTVEC/NC leading to an SVQ Level III.*
G2 G17

Painting & Decorating - SVQ Level III *Scottish Vocational Certificate Level III in Painting & Decorating.*   **B6 C22 S6 T9**

Painting & Decorating - SVQ Levels I-III *SCOTVEC SVQ SVQ Level I-III in Painting & Decorating.*   **C10**

Painting & Decorating Advanced Craft - C & G *City & Guilds Advanced Craft Certificate.*   **L81**

Painting & Decoration - Advanced Certificate *SCOTVEC AC in Painting & Decorating.*   **F13**

Painting & Decoration - NC *SCOTVEC/NC equivalent to the Craft City & Guilds Certificate.*   **F13**

Plastering - Advanced Course *SCOTVEC Advanced Craft Certificate in Plastering.*   **S68**

Plastering - SVQ Level III *SVQ Level III in Plastering.*   **S6**

Plastering - SVQ Levels II & III *SCOTVEC SVQ, SVQ Levels II-III in Plastering.*   **S91**

Plastering - SVQ Levels II-III *SCOTVEC SVQ, SVQ Levels II-III Certificate in Plastering.*   **S68**

Plumbing - HNC *HNC in Plumbing.*   **S13 S15**

Plumbing - NC *SCOTVEC/NC in Plumbing.*
B6 F13 S15

Plumbing - SCOTVEC/NC *SCOTVEC/NC.* **G17**

Plumbing - SVQ Level I & II *SCOTVEC SVQ Levels I & II in Plumbing.*   **S12**

Plumbing - SVQ Level II *SVQ Level II (SF0304205) in Plumbing.*   **B6**

Plumbing - SVQ Level III *SCOTVEC SVQ SVQ Level III in Plumbing.*   **C22 S6 T9**

Plumbing - YT *Contact for details.*   **S73**

Plumbing Technician *SCOTVEC/NC.*   **S15**

Plumbing Technician - NC *SCOTVEC/NC in Plumbing for Building Technicians.*   **S12**

Plumbing Technician - NC *SCOTVEC/NC - Plumbing Technician Programme.*   **F13 S91**

Reinforced Concrete Detailing *College certificate.*   **L5**

Roof Slating & Tiling - Advanced Certificate *SCOTVEC AC in Roof Slating & Tiling.*   **F13**

Roof Slating & Tiling - NC *SCOTVEC/NC equivalent to the Craft City & Guilds Certificate.*
F13

Roof Slating & Tiling - SVQ Level III *SVQ Level III in Roof Slating & Tiling.*   **S6**

Short Courses in Decorating, Glazing & Signwork *SCOTVEC/NCMs or increased skills.*   **L5**

Stone Carving *Stone carving skills.*   **L5**

Stonemasonry - Advanced Certificate *SCOTVEC AC in Stonemasonry.*   **S68**

Stonemasonry - SVQ Levels II-III *SCOTVEC SVQ, SVQ Levels II-III Certificate in Stonemasonry.*   **S68**

Stonework *Practical skills & knowledge.* **S15**

Trowel Skills *College Certificate.*   **L81**

Trowel Trades (Brickwork) City & Guilds *Students will follow City & Guilds course to advanced craft levels.*   **T1**

Trowel Trades - Customised Courses *Various courses available.*   **L71**

Unvented Domestic Hot Water Storage Systems *Will enable the student to sit CITB Multi-Choice Examination.*   **T9**

Unvented Hot Water Systems *Knowledge of unvented hot water systems.*   **H53 S15**

Various Courses Available .   **S149**

Wall & Floor Tiling - SVQ Levels II-III *SCOTVEC SVQ, SVQ Levels II-III Certificate in Wall & Floor Tiling.*   **S68**

BUILDING CONSTRUCTION STUDIES GENERAL

Advanced Certificate in Construction Practice   *8 SCOTVEC units which contribute to the new HNC Award in Construction Practice.*   **C23**

Architectural Technology - HNC   *SCOTVEC/HNC in Architectural Technology.*   **B6 C22 D5 L5**

Building - CIOB Membership Part 2   *Prepares students for the professional examinations of the Chartered Institute of Building (CIOB) Part 2.*   **L59**

Building - HNC   *HNC in Building.*   **T12**

Building - NC   *SCOTVEC/NC in Building. Possible progression to HNC level course.*   **C10 F13**

Building - Stage I - NC   *SCOTVEC/NC in Building (Stage 1).*   **L5**

Building - Stage II - NC   *SCOTVEC/NC in Building (Stage II).*   **L5**

Building - Stage III - NC   *SCOTVEC/NC in Building (Stage III).*   **L5**

Building Construction - General   *SCOTVEC/SVQ III.*   **S9**

Building Control - BSc / BSc (Honours)   *BSc Degree / Hons Degree in Building Control.*   **L60**

Building Operatives - NC   *SCOTVEC/NC.*   **S15**

Building Services Engineering - BSc   *A BSc in Building Services Engineering.*   **S45**

Building Technician - NC   *SCOTVEC/NC.*   **B6**

Building Technology - Years 1 & 2 - NC   *SCOTVEC/NC in Building Technology.*   **C22**

Building, Architectural Studies & Quantity Surveying - NC   *SCOTVEC/NC in Building, Architectural Studies & Quantity Surveying.*   **S68**

Chartered Institute of Building Direct Membership   *To prepare candidates for membership of the Institute.*   **S8**

Chartered Institute of Building Part I (CIOB)   *Institute of Building Part 1 (CIOB).*   **S8**

Chartered Institute of Building Part II   *Institute of Building Part II.*   **S8**

Concrete Technology & Construction - NVQ C & G 629 Certificate   *NVQ, City & Guilds 629 Certificate.*   **S68**

Construction & Surveying - Scottish Wider Access   *Recognised group of SCOTVEC Modules & University subject.*   **G2**

Construction - NC   *SCOTVEC/NC. Possible progression to SVQ Level III in Building Trades.*   **C10**

Construction - Supplementary Studies - C & G 600   *City & Guilds 600 Certificate in Construction.*   **C23**

Construction Courses for Industry   *Various courses available.*   **H53**

Construction Craft Supplementary Studies - C & G   *City & Guilds Certificate.*   **S91**

Construction Crafts Supplementary Studies - C & G 600   *City & Guilds Certificate.*   **L5**

Construction Crafts Supplementary Studies - City & Guilds 600   *HNC in Building.*   **G2**

Construction Drawing: an Introduction   *SCOTVEC Module.*   **H54**

Construction Practice - Advanced Craft Certificate   *Advanced Craft Certificate in Construction Practice.*   **C22**

Construction Practices - HNC   *SCOTVEC/HNC in Construction Practices.*   **S9**

Construction Studies/Building/Civil Engineering - NC   *SCOTVEC/NC.*   **H53**

Construction Trades - SCOTVEC/NC   *SCOTVEC/NC.*   **G2**

Institute of Clerks of Works   *ICW Certificate for Clerks of Works.*   **D5**

Institute of Clerks of Works - Final Part I   *Certificate from the Institute of Clerks of Works - Part 1.*   **C23**

Introductory to Building Craft Science - NCM   *SCOTVEC/NCM.*   **L81**

Quantity Surveying - HNC   *Scottish HNC in Quantity Surveying.*   **F5 L5**

SVQ in General Building Operation   *Level II SVQ.*   **S136**

Technology - GSVQ Level I   *SCOTVEC SVQ GSVQ Level I in Technology.*   **C10**

Various Courses Available   *Outcome depends on level and subject matter of individual courses.*   **T21**

Vocational Preparation in Construction Crafts   *SCOTVEC/NC.*   **S9**

CIVIL ENGINEERING

Blast Design - Certificate   *Blast Design Certificate from the Quarry Products Training Council.*   **S6**

Building & Civil Engineering - HNC   *SCOTVEC/HNC.*   **H31**

Building Services Engineering - BSc   *A BSc in Building Services Engineering.*   **S45**

Civil Engineering - HNC   *HNC in Civil Engineering.*   **F5 H53 L45 S94 T12**

Civil Engineering - NC   *NC in Civil Engineering Progression is possible to the Higher Certificate in Civil Engineering.*   **F5 S94**

Civil Engineering - Years 1 & 2 - HNC   *SCOTVEC/HNC in Civil Engineering.*   **C22**

Civil Engineering - Years 1 & 2 - NC
SCOTVEC/NC in Civil Engineering. **C22**

Civil Engineering Technician - SCOTVEC/NC
SCOTVEC. **G17**

Civil/Structural Engineering - NC *SCOTVEC/NC in Civil/ Structural Engineering.* **S94**

Civil/Structural Engineering - Stage I NC
SCOTVEC/NC in Civil/ Structural Engineering (Stage I). **L5**

Civil/Structural Engineering - Stage II NC
SCOTVEC/NC in Civil/ Structural Engineering. **L5**

Civil/Structural Engineering - Stage III NC
(SCOTVEC) SCOTVEC/NC in Civil/ Structural Engineering. **L5**

Construction Courses for Industry *Various courses available.* **H53**

Construction Studies/Building/Civil Engineering - NC *SCOTVEC/NC.* **H53**

Energy & Environmental Systems - MSc *A MSc in Energy & Environmental Systems.* **S46**

Energy & Environmental Systems - PgC *A PgC in Energy & Environmental Systems.* **S46**

Energy & Environmental Systems - PgD *A PgD in Energy & Environmental Systems.* **S46**

Engineering Council Civil Engineering
Registration with the Institution of Civil Engineers. **S94**

Engineering Design of Buildings MSc/PgD
MSc/Postgraduate Diploma in Engineering Design of Buildings. **S101**

Renewal of CITB Plant Operators Certificates
Various courses available. **H31**

Roadworks - Advanced Craft Course *City & Guilds of London Institute (No 623) Advanced Craft Certificate in Roadworks.* **S68**

Roadworks - Craft Course *City & Guilds of London Institute (No 614) Craft Certificate in Roadworks.* **S68**

Transportation Engineering - MSc/ Postgraduate Degree *MSc Degree in Transportation Engineering.* **L59**

Urban Property Appraisal - MSc/PgD
MSc/Postgraduate Diploma in Urban Property Appraisal. **S101**

CONSTRUCTION & PROPERTY MANAGEMENT

Access to Higher National Construction/ Building Courses *SCOTVEC/NCM.* **T9**

Building - Institute of Building Control Part II *This course prepares students for the Institute of Building Control's Part II examinations.* **L43**

Building Control (Built Environment) - HNC *HNC in Building Control.* **S68**

Building Control - Advanced Diploma *An advanced diploma in building control.* **S68**

Building Defects & Their Implications *Attendance Certificate.* **L10**

Building Management - Advanced Diploma *An advanced diploma in building management.* **S68**

Building Site Supervision *SCOTVEC & CITB, SVQs, SVQ Level 111 (SG0301301) in Building Site Supervision.* **H53**

Building Supervision (Built Environment) - HNC *HNC in Building Supervision (Built Environment).* **S68**

Certificate/Diploma in Site Management
Certificate/Diploma. CIOB Membership. **S146**

CIOB Site Management - Certificate *Certificate in Site Management Studies.* **L5**

CIOB Site Management - Diploma *Diploma in Site Management Studies.* **L5**

Construction - SCOTVEC/NC *SCOTVEC.* **G17**

Construction - Supplementary Studies - C & G 600 *A City & Guilds 600 Certificate in Construction.* **C23**

Construction Courses for Industry *Various courses available.* **H53**

Construction Craft Supplementary Studies - C & G 600 *City & Guilds 600 Craft Supervision Studies Certificate.* **F13**

Construction Law - LLM *LLM in Construction Law.* **S105**

Construction Law - PgD *PgD in Construction law.* **S105**

Construction Management (Building Maintenance) - MSc/Diploma *MSc Degree/Diploma in Construction Management (Building Maintenance).* **L6**

Construction Management (Built Environment - HNC *HNC in Construction Management (Built Environment).* **S68**

Construction Management (Contracting & Management) MSc/Diploma *MSc Degree/Diploma in Construction Management (Production Management).* **L6**

Construction Management (Corporate Strategy) - MSc/Diploma　*MSc Degree/Diploma in Construction Management (Corporate Strategy).*　**L6**

Construction Management (Project Management)- MSc/Diploma　*MSc Degree/Diploma in Construction Management (Project Management).*　**L6**

Construction Management - HNC *SCOTVEC/HNC which may provide entry requirements for Degree level work.*　**H53 L5 S5**

Construction Management - MSc　*MSc in Construction Management.*　**S50**

Construction Management - PgC　*PgC in Construction Management.*　**S50**

Construction Management - PgD　*PgD in Construction Management.*　**S50**

Construction Management - Years 1 & 2 HNC *SCOTVEC/HNC in Construction Management.*　**C22**

Construction Practice - Advanced Craft Certificate *Advanced Craft Certificate in Construction Practice.*　**C22**

Construction Practice - HNC　*SCOTVEC/HNC in Construction Practice.*　**C10 S68**

Construction Practice - HND　*HND in Construction Practice.*　**S68**

Construction Practice - SCOTVEC AC *SCOTVEC AC in Construction Practice.*　**C10**

Construction Practices - HNC　*SCOTVEC/HNC in Construction Practices.*　**S9**

Estate Management - BSc / BSc (Honours)　*BSc Degree / Hons Degree in Estate Management.*　**L60**

Facilities Management - MSc　*MSc in Facilities Managements.*　**S105**

Facilities Management - PgD　*PgD in Facilities Management.*　**S105**

General Site Safety　*Skills in identifying safe site procedures and potential site hazards.*　**M8**

Health & Safety (Site Management)　*CITB Certificate.*　**G26**

Institute of Clerks of Works　*Institute of Clerks of Works Certificate for Clerks of Works.*　**D5 T9**

Land Economics - Diploma　*Diploma in Land Economics.*　**S101**

One Day Site Safety Awareness Course *Certificate.*　**G26**

Planning, Supervisory Skills, Site Practice, General Courses　*Various Certificates awarded.*　**S146**

Project Management in Construction　*Attendance Certificate.*　**L10**

Urban Property Appraisal - MSc/PgD *MSc/Postgraduate Diploma in Urban Property Appraisal.*　**S101**

CONSTRUCTION SITE PRACTICE

180 Degree Back Hoe Loaders　*CITB Certificate.*　**G26**

360 deg. Cranes (Wheeled or Crawled)　*CITB Certificate.*　**G26**

Advanced Certificate in Construction Practice　*8 SCOTVEC units contributing to the new HNC Award in Construction Practice.*　**C23**

Banksman/Slinger's Course　*CITB Certificate.*　**G26**

Construction Plant Maintenance - NC *SCOTVEC/NC in Construction Plant Maintenance.*　**S88**

Construction Plant Maintenance - NVQ C & G 393 Part II-III　*NVQ, NVQ City & Guilds 393 Parts II-III in Construction Plant Maintenance.*　**S88**

Construction Plant Maintenance - NVQ C & G 620 Part III　*NVQ, NVQ City & Guilds 620 Parts III in Construction Plant Maintenance.*　**S88**

Construction Practice - HNC　*SCOTVEC/HNC in Construction Practice.*　**C10**

Construction Practice - SCOTVEC AC *SCOTVEC AC in Construction Practice.*　**C10**

Construction Site Safety *Skills in Health & Safety considerations on site.* **C10**

Construction/Contractors Plant - Mechanics Programme *This programme leads to a skilled mechanic status.* **S87**

Dump Trucks (35 cwt) *CITB Certificate.* **G26**

Dump Trucks (Articulated or Fixed) *CITB Certificate.* **G26**

Dump Trucks (Under 10 Tonnes): Basic Operator *CITB Certificate.* **H53**

Elevated Work Platforms *CITB Certificate.* **G26**

General Building Operations - SVQ Level I-II *SCOTVEC, SVQ Level I-II in General Building Operations.* **C10**

Health, Safety & Hygiene *No formal certificate.* **H42**

Hoists *CITB Certificate.* **G26**

Institute of Clerks of Works *Institute of Clerks of Works Certificate for Clerks of Works.* **D5**

Loading Shovel (Wheeled or Crawled) *CITB Certificate.* **G26**

Lorry Loaders *CITB Certificate.* **G26**

Overhead/Gantry Cranes *CITB Certificate.* **G26**

Renewal of CITB Plant Operators Certificates *Various courses available.* **H31**

Rigger/Slinger Course *CITB Certificate.* **G26**

Scaffold Inspection *College Certificate.* **L5**

Scaffolding Appreciation *No formal Certificate.* **C10**

Site Management Safety Training Course (CITB) *Construction Site Managers Safety Certificate.* **L5**

Slinger/Banksman *Training in the safe use, storage of lifting tackle & the correct way of signalling cranes etc.* **H53**

Soil/Landfill Compact *CITB Certificate.* **G26**

Surveying & Levelling *College Certificate.* **T9**

Tower Cranes *CITB Certificate.* **G26**

Trowel Trades - Customised Courses *Various Courses available.* **L71**

Work Safety (SCOTVEC) *SCOTVEC/NCM.* **L5**

Workshop Practice *SCOTVEC Module.* **H54**

PLANNING, ESTIMATING, SURVEYING

Advanced Land Surveying (SCOTVEC) *SCOTVEC/NCM. Chartered Institute of Building Certificate in Site Surveying & Levelling.* **L5**

Building - NC *SCOTVEC/NC in Building.* **C10**

Building Defects & Their Implications *Attendance Certificate.* **L10**

Building Operatives - NC *SCOTVEC/NC.* **S15**

Building Surveying - BSc / BSc (Honours) *BSc Degree / Hons Degree in Building Surveying.* **L60**

Building, Architectural Studies & Quantity Surveying - NC *SCOTVEC/NC.* **S68**

Clerk of Works *Institute of Clerks of Works Certificate.* **S15**

Construction Surveying (Built Environment) - HNC *HNC in Construction Surveying (Built Environment).* **S68**

Construction Surveying - Advanced Diploma *An advanced diploma in construction surveying.* **S68**

Estimating *Certificate course.* **S146**

General Surveying - HNC *SCOTVEC/HNC in General Surveying.* **S68**

General Surveying Foundation *A Certificate in General Surveying Foundation.* **S68**

Housing Studies - Diploma *Diploma in Housing Studies.* **L11**

Introduction to Land Surveying Techniques *SCOTVEC/NCM. Chartered Institute of Building Certificate.* **L5**

Land Economics - Diploma *Diploma in Land Economics.* **S101**

Managing Urban Environments - HNC *SCOTVEC/HNC in Urban Environmental Management.* **C22 C23**

Planning - HNC *SCOTVEC/HNC in Planning.* **S68**

Planning - NC *SCOTVEC/NC in Planning.* **S68**

Quantity Surveying - BSc (Honours) *A BSc (Honours) in Quantity Surveying.* **S49**

Quantity Surveying - BSc / BSc (Honours) *BSc Degree / Hons Degree in Quantity Surveying.* **L42**

Quantity Surveying - HNC *SCOTVEC/HNC in Quantity Surveying.* **L5**

Site Surveying *Exemption from the appropriate associate examinations of the Chartered Institute of Building.* **L59**

Town & Country Planning - Diploma *PgD in Town & Country Planning.* **L11**

Urban & Regional Planning - MSc *An MSc in Urban & Regional Planning.* **S105**

Urban & Regional Planning - PgD *A PgD in Urban & Regional Planning.* **S105**

Urban Development - MSc *An MSc in Urban Development.* **S105**

Urban Development- PgD *A PgD in Urban Development.* **S105**

STRUCTURAL ENGINEERING

Civil/Structural Engineering - NC   *SCOTVEC/NC in Civil/ Structural Engineering.*   **S94**

Civil/Structural Engineering - Stage I NC *SCOTVEC/NC in Civil/ Structural Engineering.*
L5

Civil/Structural Engineering - Stage II NC *SCOTVEC/NC in Civil/ Structural Engineering.*
L5

Civil/Structural Engineering - Stage III NC *SCOTVEC/NC in Civil/ Structural Engineering.*
L5

Construction Practice - HNC   *SCOTVEC/HNC in Construction Practice.*   **C10**

Construction Practice - SCOTVEC AC *SCOTVEC AC in Construction Practice.*   **C10**

Engineering Design of Buildings MSc/PgD *MSc/Postgraduate Diploma in Engineering Design of Buildings.*   **S101**

Finite Element Analysis   *Knowledge gained in elementary & advanced Finite Element Analysis.*
S8

Introductory to Building Craft Science - NCM *SCOTVEC/NCM.*   **L81**

Structural Engineering : MSc/Diploma   *MSc Degree/Diploma in Structural Engineering.*   **L6**

Structural Engineering Computational Technology - MSc/Diploma   *MSc Degree/Diploma.*   **L6**

Structural Steelwork Detailing   *College certificate.*
L5

WOOD & WOODWORKING

Advanced Craft - Carpentry & Joinery City & Guilds 585   *City & Guilds Advanced Certificate.*
T9

Advanced Craft Carpentry & Joinery   *City & Guilds of London Institute Advanced Craft Carpentry & Joinery 585 Certificate.*   **S2**

Advanced Craft Certificate in Carpentry & Joinery - C & G 585   *A City & Guilds Certificate in Advanced Craft Carpentry & Joinery.*   **S91**

Basic Woodworking Skills   *Skills required for simple repairs & construction of wooden items.*
H53

Building Crafts - YT/SVQ Level III   *SVQ, SVQ Level III Certificate.*   **S73**

Building Programme - NC   *SCOTVEC/NC in Building Construction.*   **S88**

Cabinet Making - SVQ Levels II-III   *SCOTVEC SVQ, SVQ Levels II-III Certificate in Cabinet Making.*   **S68**

Carpentry & Joinery   *Advanced Craft Level Certificate in Carpentry & Joinery.*   **C22**

Carpentry & Joinery - Advanced Certificate *SCOTVEC AC in Carpentry & Joinery.*
F13 H30 S6 S68

Carpentry & Joinery - C & G 585/2 Advanced Craft *City & Guilds 585/2.*   **H31**

Carpentry & Joinery - City & Guilds   *City & Guilds Advanced Craft Certificate in Carpentry & Joinery.*
S81

Carpentry & Joinery - HNC   *Successful students will be awarded SCOTVEC/HNC in Carpentry & Joinery.*   **S75**

Carpentry & Joinery - NC   *SCOTVEC/NC equivalent to the Craft City & Guilds Certificate.*
F13 S2 S88

Carpentry & Joinery - NVQ C & G   *NVQ, NVQ City & Guilds Certificate.*   **S75**

Carpentry & Joinery - Part-Time City & Guilds *Students will follow City & Guilds course to advanced craft levels.*   **T1**

Carpentry & Joinery - SCOTVEC AC   *SCOTVEC AC in Carpentry & Joinery.*   **B6 C10**

Carpentry & Joinery - SVQ Level I-III   *SCOTVEC, SVQ Level I-III in Carpentry & Joinery.*   **C10**

Carpentry & Joinery - SVQ Level II   *SCOTVEC, SVQ Level II in Carpentry & Joinery.*   **C23**

Carpentry & Joinery - SVQ Level III   *SVQ Level III in Carpentry & Joinery.*   **B6 C22 S6 S13**

Carpentry & Joinery - SVQ Levels II-III *SCOTVEC, SVQ Levels II-III Certificate in Carpentry & Joinery.*   **S68**

Carpentry & Joinery I - NC Stage I   *SCOTVEC/NC stage I in Carpentry & Joinery.*   **S81**

Carpentry & Joinery II - NC Stage II *SCOTVEC/NC Stage II in Carpentry & Joinery.*
S81

Carpentry & Joinery Advanced Craft Certificate - CGLI-585   *A CGLI-585 Carpentry & Joinery Advanced Craft Certificate.*   **G2**

Carpentry & Joinery Course - Advanced Certificate *SCOTVEC AC in Carpentry & Joinery.*   **S9**

Carpentry & Joinery Craft Programme - NC *SCOTVEC/NC.*   **F5**

Carpentry & Joinery- CITB Programme *SCOTVEC/NC leading to an SVQ Level III.*   **G2**

Construction Trades Craft Courses - SVQ   *SVQ in Construction Trades.*   **S75**

Craft & Design - SCE H Grade
C4 C5 C20 C25 C26 C27 C28 C29 C30 C33 C34 C36 C45

ESF Heritage Woodwork   *Skills gained in woodwork.*   **S81**

Introduction to Basic Woodworking   *Introductory knowledge of woodwork.*   **L68**

Joinery   *NVQ Level 3.*   **G39**

Joinery   *SCOTVEC Modules.*   **S87**

Machine Woodworking - Advanced Certificate
SCOTVEC AC in Machine Woodworking.   **S68**

Machine Woodworking - SVQ Levels II-III
*SCOTVEC, SVQ Levels II-III Certificate in Machine
Woodworking.*   **S68**

Machine Woodworking Stage 4 - City & Guilds of
London Institute   *City & Guilds of London Institute.*
                                              G17

Machine Woodworking/Lathe & Drillwork - NC
SCOTVEC/NC.   **G17**

Shopfitting - SVQ Levels II-III   *SCOTVEC SVQ
Levels II-III Certificate in Shopfitting.*   **S68**

Timber Trade Woodmachining Course -
Skillseekers/SVQ Level II   *SVQ Level II
Certificate.*   **S99**

Wood Finishing - SVQ Levels II-III   *SCOTVEC
SVQ, SVQ Levels II-III Certificate in Wood
Finishing.*   **S68**

Wood Machining - Years 1, 2 & 3 - NC
SCOTVEC/NC in Wood Machining.   **C22**

Woodwork   *No formal outcome.*   **B6**

Woodworking - SCOTVEC Module   *Participants
will gain SCOTVEC Module in Woodworking.*
                                              H49

Woodworking Machinery Regulations   *College
certificate.*   **T9**

Woodworking Machines Regulations 1974   *No
formal outcome.*   **M8**

Working with Wood   *SCOTVEC Module.*   **H54**

Working with Wood - Module (Household
Accessories)   *SCOTVEC Module in Woodwork.*
                                              M6

Working with Wood - NC   *SCOTVEC/NC &
College Certificate.*   **L81**

Working with Wood - NCM   *SCOTVEC/NCM.*
                                              L81

Arts, Crafts & Hobbies

ARTS, CRAFTS & HOBBIES

Classes for Physically Disabled Adults
Development of skills & creative ability.   **S81**

Pathways   *SCOTVEC/NCM.*   **L68**

CRAFTS (GENERAL) COLLECTING & ANTIQUES

Craft & Design - SCE H Grade   *Scottish
Certificate of Higher Education in Craft & Design.*
B10 D8

DECORATIVE ARTS & CRAFTS

Decorative Arts & Crafts - Leisure Course   *No
formal outcome.*   **S9**

Fine Art Courses   *Various short courses are on
offer.*   **H9**

Floral Art   *No formal outcome.*   **B3**

Floral Art - City & Guilds Part 1   *A City & Guilds
part I certificate in Floral Art.*   **S81**

Floral Art - City & Guilds Parts I & II   *A City &
Guilds parts I & II certificate in Floral Art.*   **S81**

Floristry - SCOTVEC   *SCOTVEC Certificate.*   **B2**

Flower Arrangement: Parts 1 & 2 - City & Guilds
*City & Guilds Certificate in Creative Studies -
Flower Arrangement (784).*   **L5**

Flower Arranging   *Experience in flower arranging.*
C16

Textile Workshops   *Knowledge & expertise in
textile techniques.*   **H22**

DESIGN (NON-INDUSTRIAL)

Advanced Diploma in Spatial Design   *Advanced
Diploma in Spatial Design.*   **L5**

Art   *SCOTVEC Certificate.*   **B11**

Art & Design   *Students can gain various
SCOTVEC modules.*   **S79**

Art & Design - CSYS   *Certificate of Sixth Year
Studies in Art & Design.*   **D7**

Art & Design - Foundation   *Portfolio for entry into
specialist art courses in higher education.*   **B3**

Art & Design - GCE A Level & SCE H Grade   *GCE
A Level in Art & Design SCE H Grade in Art &
Design.*   **L68**

Art & Design - General   *SCOTVEC
Modules/Higher Grade Art Portfolio of practical
work.*   **B3**

Art & Design - H Grade   *SCE H Grade.*   **S88**

Art & Design - NCMs   *SCOTVEC/NC. A variety of
modules is available.*   **H53**

Art & Design - Post Higher Portfolio   *Post Higher
Portfolio Year in Art & Design.*   **D7**

Art & Design - SCE H Grade   *SCE at H Grade in
Art & Design (recently revised course).*   **D7 S2**

Art & Design - SCE H Grade (Revised)   *SCE H
Grade Art & Design.*   **L1**

Art & Design - SCE S Grade   *SCE at S Grade in
Art & Design.*   **D7**

Art & Design - SCE Standard / SCE H Grade /
NCMs   *SCE Standard or H grade or the
appropriate SCOTVEC modules.*   **H13**

Art & Design - SEB H Grade   *An SEB H Grade in
Art & Design.*   **B11**

Art & Design - SEB H Grade (Revised)   *A SEB H
Grade.*   **B1**

Art & Design - SEB S Grade   *An SEB S Grade in
Art & Design.*   **B11**

Art & Design - SEB Sixth Year Studies   *An SEB
Certificate of Sixth Year Studies in Art & Design.*
B11

Art & Design Portfolio Preparation - NC
*SCOTVEC/NC in Art & Design Portfolio
Preparation.*   **S19**

Art & Design SCE Higher Part-Time   *SCE in
Higher Art & Design.*   **L81**

Art - SEB H Grade   *SEB H Grade in Art.*   **B10**

Art Craft & Design - NC   *SCOTVEC/NC in Art
Craft & Design.*   **S81**

Art- SCE H Grade   *SCE H Grade Art.*   **L68**

Batik   *SCOTVEC/NCM 61730 in Fabric Crafts.*
D7

Computer Application - Design (SCOTVEC)
*SCOTVEC/NCM 61101 Computer Application
(Design).*   **L3**

Computer Graphic Design & Production -
SCOTVEC/HND   *HND in Computer Graphic
Design & Production.*   **G17**

Craft & Design (Revised) - SCE Higher *SCE Higher - Craft & Design (Revised).* **B11 F7**

Craft & Design - SCE H Grade *SEB Certificate in Craft & Design at H Grade.* **B10 D8 M3**

Craft & Design - SEB S Grade *An SEB S Grade in Craft & Design.* **B11**

Design & Typography for Print - HNC *SCOTVEC/HNC.* **L5**

Design - GSVQ Level III *General Scottish Vocational Certificate Level III in Design.* **B3**

Design - Introductory *Various SCOTVEC modules.* **S2**

Design for Advertising 1 - HN Unit *SCOTVEC Higher National Unit.* **L5**

Design for Marketing 1 - HN Unit *SCOTVEC Higher National Unit.* **L5**

Design for Print 1 - HN Unit *SCOTVEC Higher National Unit.* **L5**

Design for Printing - HND *SCOTVEC/HND in Design for Printing.* **S68**

Design Studies 1 - HN Unit *SCOTVEC Higher National Unit.* **L5**

Design Studies: Screen Printing 1 *SCOTVEC/NCM 71925 in Screen Printing.* **D7**

Desktop Publishing - HN Unit *SCOTVEC Higher National Unit.* **L5**

Display & Design - NC *SCOTVEC/NC in Display & Design.* **S87**

Display (Introduction) - 93102 - SCOTVEC/NC *SCOTVEC/NC.* **T23**

Display Technician - British Display Society Certificate *The British Display Society Technician Certificate.* **S14**

Distribution & Display - NC *SCOTVEC/NCMs in Distribution & Display.* **S11**

Electronic Publishing - HNC *SCOTVEC/HNC in Electronic Publishing.* **S68**

Graphic Communication - SCE H Grade **C4 C5 C20 C21 C25 C26 C27 C28 C29 C30 C33 C36 C45 C46 D8**

Graphic Design *A knowledge of graphic design techniques.* **C41**

Graphic Design & Illustration - HNC *SCOTVEC/HNC in Graphic Design & Illustration.* **C10**

Graphic Design & Illustration - HND *SCOTVEC/HND in Graphic Design & Illustration.* **C10**

Graphic Design & Spatial Design - SCOTVEC/HNC *HNC in Graphic Design & Spatial Design.* **G17**

Graphic Design - SCOTVEC/HND *HND in Graphic Design.* **G17**

Graphic Design 1 Package - NCMs *SCOTVEC/NCM.* **L5**

Graphic Design 2 Package - NCMs *SCOTVEC/NCM.* **L5**

Graphical Communication - SEB S Grade *SEB S Grade in Graphical Communication.* **B11**

Illustration & Media Design - HNC *SCOTVEC/HNC.* **L5**

Illustration - HN Unit *SCOTVEC Higher National Unit.* **L5**

Information Design - HN Unit *SCOTVEC Higher National Unit.* **L5**

Interior Decoration *The course provides an introduction to the skills & techniques of Interior Design.* **H53**

Interior Design - HNC *SCOTVEC/HNC.* **L5**

Interior Design with New Technology - NC *SCOTVEC/NC in Interior Design with New Technology.* **C22**

Interior Planning & Basic Design Principles - NC *SCOTVEC/NC.* **C23**

Jewellery Design - Module *SCOTVEC/NCM.* **F8**

Knitwear Design & Marketing *No formal outcome.* **B3**

Magazine Design 1 - HN Unit *SCOTVEC Higher National Unit.* **L5**

Marketing Design - HNC *SCOTVEC/HNC.* **L5**

Media Design 1 - HN Unit *SCOTVEC Higher National Unit.* **L5**

National Assoc.of Goldsmiths Preliminary & Diploma Courses in Retail Jewellery *A Diploma in Retail Jewellery.* **S14**

Photography 1 - HN Unit *SCOTVEC Higher National Unit.* **L5**

Photography/Art & Design - Part-Time NC *SCOTVEC certificate.* **L81**

Portfolio Preparation Class - NC *SCOTVEC/NC in Portfolio Preparation.* **S81**

Print Technology 1 - HN Unit *SCOTVEC Higher National Unit.* **L5**

Spatial Design - SCOTVEC/HND *HND in Spatial Design.* **G17**

Spatial Design 2 Package - NCMs *SCOTVEC/NCM.* **L5**

Spatial Design Package - NCMs *SCOTVEC/NCM.* **L5**

Stitched Textiles & Fashion Design - HNC *SCOTVEC/HNC.* **L5**

Typography 1 - HN Unit *SCOTVEC Higher National Unit.* **L5**

Workshops - Knitwear *There is no formal outcome to this course.* **B3**

FABRIC CRAFTS

Batik   *SCOTVEC/NCM 61730 in Fabric Crafts.*
D7

Batik - Wax Relief & Printed Textiles (Week)   *No formal outcome.*   **H55**

Batik - Wax Relief & Printed Textiles (Weekend)   *No formal outcome.*   **H55**

Beginners Dressmaking   *No formal outcome.*
B3

Creative Embroidery Part I - City & Guilds 782   *City & Guilds Certificate 782.*   **L5**

Creative Embroidery Part II - City & Guilds 782   *City & Guilds Certificate 782.*   **L5**

Design Courses   *Various short courses.*   **H9**

Domestic Machine Knitting   *Skills in machine knitting.*   **H31**

Domestic Machine Knitting (For Disabled People)   *An introductory knowledge of machine knitting.*
L28

Domestic Machine Knitting - CENTRA 789   *CENTRA 789 Certificate in Domestic Machine Knitting.*   **S13**

Domestic Machine Knitting - NC   *NC in Domestic Machine Knitting.*   **S13**

Dressmaking   *No formal outcome.*
B8 C16 H49

Dressmaking & Sewing Skills   *Skills in dressmaking and sewing techniques.*   **H31**

Embroidery   *Experience in embroidery.*   **C16**

Embroidery & Fabric Crafts   *SCOTVEC/NC. A variety of modules is available.*   **H53**

Embroidery (Part 1) - C & G 790   *C & G 790 in Embroidery.*   **M7**

Embroidery (Part 2) - C & G 782   *C & G 782 in Embroidery.*   **M7**

Embroidery - C & G 7900 (Part I)   *NVQ, City & Guilds 7900 Certificate in Embroidery (Part I).*
S13

Embroidery - C & G 7900 (Part II)   *NVQ, City & Guilds 7900 Certificate in Embroidery (Part II).*
S13

Furniture Restoration   *Skills in restoration techniques.*   **H31**

Home Machine Knitting - CENTRA Course I   *NWRAC Certificate 789/1.*   **S87**

Home Machine Knitting - CENTRA Course II   *NWRAC Certificate 789/2.*   **S87**

Knitting   *Participants will have gained skills in knitting.*   **H31**

Knitting Certificate   *North West Region Advisory Council Knitting certificate parts I & II.*   **S7**

Knitting for Profit   *College Certificate.*   **S88**

Knitwear Design & Marketing   *Participants will gain knowledge & ideas which could improve their business.*   **B3**

Lacemaking   *Students will learn the art of lacemaking.*   **T9**

Machine Knitting   *Development of skills used in machine knitting.*   **C15 G13**

Machine Knitting (SCOTVEC)   *SCOTVEC Modules.*   **L27**

Machine Knitting - NC   *SCOTVEC/NC or The North West Regional Advisory Council Certificate.*   **S88**

Machine Knitting - Part I (CENTRA)   *Part I Course Certificate.*   **L27**

Machine Knitting - Part II (CENTRA)   *Part II Course Certificate.*   **L27**

Marketing - Knitwear   *No formal outcome.*   **B3**

Modular Fabric   *Skills gained in garment construction.*   **S81**

Patchwork & Quilting - CGLI 7900   *CGLI 7900 certificate.*   **L27**

Patchwork for Beginners   *No formal outcome.*
B6

Preparing Working Designs - City & Guilds   *A City & Guilds certificate.*   **S81**

Textile Craft - SCOTVEC   *SCOTVEC module in Textile Craft.*   **B10**

Textile Workshops   *Knowledge & expertise in textile techniques.*   **H22**

Upholstery   *No formal outcome.*   **B3 B6**

Upholstery - SVQ Levels II-III   *SCOTVEC SVQ, SVQ Levels II-III Certificate in Upholstery.*   **S68**

Workshops - Knitwear   *No formal outcome.*   **B3**

FINE & GRAPHIC ARTS

Advanced Art Classes   *No formal outcome.*   **L92**

Advanced Relief Printing   *Techniques needed to make a relief print.*   **H19**

Airbrush Art   *Basic airbrush techniques.*   **L68**

Airbrushing   *SCOTVEC Certificate.*   **T9**

Analytical Drawing 1 - Module   *SCOTVEC Module 61720 - Analytical Drawing 1.*   **F14**

Art   *No formal outcome.*   **B8 B11**

Art & Design   *Various SCOTVEC modules available.*   **S79**

Art & Design (Revised) - SCE Higher   *SCE Higher - Art & Design (revised).*   **F7**

Art & Design - CSYS   *Certificate of Sixth Year Studies in Art & Design.*   **D7**

Art & Design - Foundation *Portfolio for entry into specialist art courses in higher education.* **B3**

Art & Design - GCE A Level & SCE H Grade *GCE A Level in Art & Design SCE H Grade in Art & Design.* **L68**

Art & Design - General *SCOTVEC Modules/Higher Grade Art Portfolio of practical work.* **B3**

Art & Design - H Grade *SCE H Grade.* **S88**

Art & Design - NCMs *SCOTVEC/NC(s) will be awarded to successful students. A variety of modules is available.* **H53**

Art & Design - Post Higher Portfolio *Post Higher Portfolio Year in Art & Design.* **D7**

Art & Design - SCE H Grade
 C1 C4 C5 C6 C7 C20 C21 C25 C26 C27 C28 C29 C30 C33 C34 C36 C45 C46 D7 S2

Art & Design - SCE H Grade (Revised) *SCE H Grade Art & Design.* **L1**

Art & Design - SCE H Grade or CSYS *SCE in Art & Design at H Grade or Certificate of Sixth Year Studies.* **D3**

Art & Design - SCE S Grade *Scottish Certificate or Education at S Grade in Art & Design.* **D7**

Art & Design - SCE Standard / SCE H Grade / NCMs *SCE Standard or H grade or the appropriate SCOTVEC modules.* **H13**

Art & Design - SEB H Grade *An SEB H Grade in Art & Design.* **B11**

Art & Design - SEB H Grade (Revised) *A SEB H Grade.* **B1**

Art & Design - SEB S Grade *An SEB S Grade in Art & Design.* **B11**

Art & Design - SEB Sixth Year Studies *An SEB Certificate of Sixth Year Studies in Art & Design.* **B11**

Art & Design Portfolio Preparation - NC *SCOTVEC/NC in Art & Design Portfolio Preparation.* **S19**

Art & Design SCE Higher Part-Time *SCE in Higher Art & Design.* **L81**

Art & the Environment *A knowledge of contemporary issues facing artists.* **C41**

Art - NC *SCOTVEC/NCM.* **L68**

Art - SCE H Grade *The SCE H Grade in Art.*
 B2 B3 F5 F8 L5 L15 M5 S13 S14 S16 S79 S87

Art - SCE H Grade (Revised) *The SCE H Grade Certificate in Art.* **B3**

Art - SCE O Grade *SCE O Grade Certificate in Art.* **S14**

Art - SCOTVEC Module *SCOTVEC Module Art.* **H49**

Art - SCOTVEC Modules *SCOTVEC Modules in Art.* **D8**

Art - SEB H Grade *An SEB H Grade in Art.* **B10**

Art -SCE H Grade *SCE H Grade certificate.* **S6**

Art Craft & Design - NC *SCOTVEC/NC in Art Craft & Design.* **S81**

Art for Pleasure *The course introduces participants to the use of a variety of painting media.* **H53**

Art School Folio Class *Lets students prepare a body of work to present in support of an application to study at Art School.* **S15**

Art,woodwork *No formal outcome.* **T18**

Art- SCE H Grade *SCE H Grade Art.* **L68**

Batik *SCOTVEC/NCM 61730 in Fabric Crafts.* **D7**

Batik - Wax Relief & Printed Textiles (Week) *No formal outcome.* **H55**

Calligraphy *Experience in calligraphy.* **C16**

Ceramics: Introduction to Sculpture (SCOTVEC) *SCOTVEC/NCM 8356821 Ceramics: Introduction to Sculpture.* **L3**

Colour, Composition & Sculpture 1880-1920 *A review of the Post-Impressionists work & changes in European art culture.* **C41**

Design - GSVQ Level III *General Scottish Vocational Certificate Level III in Design.* **B3 C10**

Design for Printing - HNC *SCOTVEC/HNC in Design for Printing.* **S68**

Design Studies: Screen Printing 1 *SCOTVEC/NCM 71925 in Screen Printing.* **D7**

Develop Your Painting Skills *No formal outcome.* **B2**

Drawing *No formal outcome.* **G24**

Drawing & Painting *Experience in drawing & painting.* **C16 C41**

Drawing & Painting Course *No formal outcome.* **F22**

Drawing / Painting *Skills required for successful drawing or painting.* **H19**

Drawing Skills - Figure/Life Drawing 1 - NC *SCOTVEC/NC.* **C23**

Drawing Skills - Module *SCOTVEC/NCM. Preparation for anyone planning to apply for full-time NC in Design Studies course.* **F8**

Drawing Skills: Analytical Drawing 1 *SCOTVEC/NCM in Drawing Skills: Analytical Drawing 1.* **L1**

Drawing Skills: Analytical Drawing 2 *SCOTVEC/NCM in Drawing Skills: Analytical Drawing 2.* **L1**

Exploring Aberdeen Art Gallery *Delegates will have had a look at Aberdeen Art Gallery, its collections & patrons.* **G21**

Figure Life Drawing - Module *SCOTVEC/NCM - Figure & Life Drawing.* **F12**

Figure Painting & Drawing (Week) *No formal outcome.* **H55**

Figure Painting & Drawing (Weekend) *No formal outcome.* **H55**

Figure/Life Drawing 3 - Module *SCOTVEC Module 61724 - Figure/life Drawing 3.* **F14**

Fine Art Courses *Various short courses available.* **H9**

Floral Art *No formal outcome.* **B3**

Folio Preparation *Preparation of folio of art & design work for entry to National courses.* **L5**

General Painting (Landscape) *No formal outcome.* **H53**

Graphic Communication - SCE H Grade *Scottish Examination Board Certificate in Graphic Communication at H Grade.* **D8**

Graphic Design & Illustration - HNC *SCOTVEC/HNC in Graphic Design & Illustration.* **C10**

Graphic Design & Illustration - HND *SCOTVEC/HND in Graphic Design & Illustration.* **C10**

Illustration & Media Design - HNC *SCOTVEC/HNC.* **L5**

Illustration - HN Unit *SCOTVEC Higher National Unit.* **L5**

Illustration 1 Package - NCMs *SCOTVEC/NCM.* **L5**

Illustration 2 Package - NCMs *SCOTVEC/NCM.* **L5**

Introduction to Sculpture Techniques (SCOTVEC) *SCOTVEC/NCM 8350023 Introduction to Sculpture Techniques.* **L3**

Introductory Signwriting - NC *SCOTVEC/NC.* **C23**

K506: Living Arts Support Group *Focusing on key themes & issues in the arts & their role in contemporary experience.* **H39**

Landscape & Studio Course - Mixed Media (Week) *No formal outcome.* **H55**

Landscape Drawing, Painting & Printing (Week) *No formal outcome.* **H55**

Landscape Painting Holidays *No formal outcome.* **F22**

Life Drawing *No formal outcome.* **G24**

Life Drawing & Painting *No formal outcome.* **L92**

Life Model Workshops *No formal outcome.* **L92**

Medical Illustration *SCOTVEC Certificate in Medical Illustration.* **S68**

Metal Sculpture (SCOTVEC) *SCOTVEC/NCM.* **L5**

Mixed Media Package - NCMs *SCOTVEC/NCM.* **L5**

Mixed Media Work (Evening Classes) *No formal outcome.* **H55**

Mixed Media: Saturday Workshops *No formal outcome.* **H55**

Modern Studies, Management & Information Studies, Art & Design - SCE H Grade *Participants will gain an SCE H Grade.* **M9**

New Starters *No formal outcome.* **L92**

Oil/Acrylic/Pastel Painting *No formal outcome.* **G24**

Painting *No formal outcome.* **B3**

Painting & Drawing *No formal outcome.* **B2 B6**

Painting Techniques: Oils 1 - Module *SCOTVEC Module 61820 - Painting Techniques: Oils 1.* **F14**

Painting Techniques: Opaque - NC *SCOTVEC/NC.* **C45**

Painting Techniques: Water Based (SCOTVEC) *SCOTVEC/NCM in Painting Techniques: Water Based.* **L1**

Photography/Art & Design - Part-Time NC *SCOTVEC certificate.* **L81**

Portfolio Preparation Class - NC *SCOTVEC/NC in Portfolio Preparation.* **S81**

Portfolio Week *No formal outcome.* **H55**

Portfolio Week (Introduction) *No formal outcome.* **H55**

Portrait & Life Painting *No formal outcome.* **H53**

Practice in Drawing & Painting with a Model *No formal outcome.* **H53**

Printing Techniques *Participants will have gained practical skills in Printmaking techniques.* **H19**

Public Art - HNC *SCOTVEC/HNC in Public Art.* **L5**

Saturday Workshops (Age 11-17) *No formal outcome.* **H55**

SCE O Grade Art *SCE O Grade.* **T1**

Schools Workshops *No formal outcome.* **H55**

Sign Writing *Practical skills & knowledge.* **S15**

Signwork - NC *SCOTVEC/NC.* **L5**

Signwork - SVQ Levels II-III *SCOTVEC SVQ,
SVQ Levels II-III Certificate in Signwork.* **S68**

Signwork Advanced Craft - C & G 593 *City &
Guilds 593 Craft Certificate.* **F13**

Signwork Advanced Craft- C & G 593 *City &
Guilds 593 Advanced Craft Certificate.* **F13**

Signwriting *Development of ability to draw, lay
out & paint signs leading to SCOTVEC/NC.*
F5 L68

Stone Carving *Acquisition of stone carving skills.*
L5

Technical & Graphical Communications -
Skillseekers/NVQ Level I *NVQ, Level I in
Technical & Graphical Communications.* **S18**

Technical Graphics - HNC *SCOTVEC/HNC in
Technical Graphics.* **S68**

Technical Graphics - HND *SCOTVEC/HND in
Design for Printing.* **S68**

Technical Graphics - NC *SCOTVEC/NC in
Technical Graphics.* **S68**

The Art of Spontaneity in Art *Knowledge of the art
of spontaneity.* **C41**

Two Dimensional Design: Experimental
Printmaking (SCOTVEC) *SCOTVEC/NCM 61705
Two Dimensional Design: Experimental
Printmaking.* **L3**

Water-Based Painting Package - NCMs
SCOTVEC/NCM. **L5**

Watercolour Painting *No formal outcome.* **G24**

Wild Flower Painting *No formal outcome.* **H53**

Wood Engraving *No formal outcome.* **H53**

GLASS, CERAMICS & STONE CRAFTS

Art & Design *Students can gain various
SCOTVEC modules.* **S79**

Ceramic & Enamelled Jewellery *Skills will be
developed in the design & making of ceramic &
enamelled jewellery.* **S87**

Ceramics *No formal outcome.* **B3 S87**

Ceramics & Pottery - Module *SCOTVEC/NCM.*
F8

Ceramics: Combined Thrown & Hand-Built Shapes
- Module *SCOTVEC Module 8356792.* **F14**

Ceramics: Decorated Tiles & Dishes - Module
*SCOTVEC Module 8356802 - Ceramics:
Decorated Tiles & Dishes.* **F14**

Design & Make: Stained Glass - NC
SCOTVEC/NC. **C23**

Design Courses *Various short courses available.*
H9

Gemmology - Diamond Diploma *Gemmological
Association of Great Britain Diamond Diploma.*
L5

Gemmology - Preliminary *Students will sit the
Preliminary Examination of the Gemmological
Association of Great Britain.* **L5**

Gemmology Diploma *Fellowship Diploma of the
Gemmological Association of Great Britain
(F.G.A.).* **L5**

Handmade Pottery Skills *Basic skills in Pottery.*
H31

Introduction to Stonecutting *Introduction of
stonecutting techniques.* **L5**

Pottery *No formal outcome.* **B2**

Stained Glass *Students will learn the art of
making stained glass.* **T9**

Stained Glass Workshop *Appreciation of Stained
Glass.* **C43**

Stone Carving *Acquisition of stone carving skills.*
L5

PUBLISHERS' NOTE

Because of local government re-organisation, details of providers for some courses, in particular for leisure pursuits, cannot be confirmed as we go to print. Libraries and other local sources should be consulted and the Community Education contacts on pages 24 to 26 may also be of assistance.

HOME MAINTENANCE CRAFTS, DIY

General Appreciation of Interior Finishes - NC
SCOTVEC/NC.   **C23**
General Appreciation of Interior Finishes - NCM
SCOTVEC/NCM.   **L81**
Introduction to Decorative Skills - NCM
SCOTVEC/NCM.   **L81**
Joinery/Woodwork   *YT Preparatory Course.*
                                                         T16
Painting & Decorating   *No formal outcome.*   **B6**

METAL CRAFTS, JEWELLERY

Ceramic & Enamelled Jewellery   *Design & making
of ceramic & enamelled jewellery.*   **S87**
Decorative Metalwork   *Knowledge of basic metal
working techniques.*   **L68**
Design Courses   *Various short courses available.*
                                              H9
Etching   *Skills achieved in various etching
techniques.*   **H19**

Jewellery & Enamelling   *Jewellery making &
enamelling.*   **T1**
Jewellery Design - Module   *SCOTVEC/NCM.*
                                               F8
Metal Ironwork (SCOTVEC)   *SCOTVEC/NCM.*
                                               L5
Metalwork   *Basic metalwork skills.*   **H31**

WOODWORK & BASKETRY CRAFTS

Craft & Design (Revised) - SEB H Grade   *An SEB
H Grade in Craft & Design.*   **B11**
Craft & Design - SCE H Grade   *SEB Certificate in
Craft & Design at H Grade.*   **D8**
Craft & Design - SEB S Grade   *An SEB S Grade
in Craft & Design.*   **B11**
Customised Short Courses in Science &
Technology   *College. Certificate.*   **L68**
Furniture Renovation   *No formal outcome.*   **B6**
Furniture Restoration   *Restoration techniques.*
                                              H31
Furniture Restoration Skills (Upholstery)   *The
development of re-upholstery skills.*   **F5**
Picture Framing   *No formal outcome.*   **B6**
Rural Skills Courses   *Various short courses
available.*   **H27**
Speciality Woodworking Skills   *Skills in woodwork.*
                                              H31
Stick Dressing   *No formal outcome.*   **B2**
Woodturning   *Introduction to the skills &
techniques of woodturning.*   **H53**
Woodwork   *No formal outcome.*   **B6**
Woodwork / Basketry - Leisure Course   *No formal
outcome.*   **S9**

Business & Management

BUSINESS ENTERPRISES, SMALL BUSINESSES, CONSULTANCY

'Intro Business' - Start-Up & Business Management Skills *New Start-Up & development of business skills.* **S124**

Accounting & Finance *To improve knowledge & working practices of Accounting and finance.* **T2**

Accounting Towards Profit *Issues involved in accounting procedures.* **H51**

Ace-Start *Skills necessary to operate a small business.* **C2**

Achieving Through Being Assertive *Improvement of communication skills.* **H40**

Achieving Through Better Business Planning *Improvement of managerial skills.* **H40**

Achieving Through Meetings *Improvement of management skills.* **H40**

Action Learning *Development of effective business skills.* **C32**

Advertising *An understanding of effective advertising techniques.* **H47**

Advertising & Promotion *How to get your message across to your customers.* **C2 C35 H3**

Assertiveness *Improvement of existing skills or acquisition of new skills.* **C35**

Basic Accounting *All aspects of a basic accounting system.* **T8**

Book-Keeping *First steps in Financial Record Keeping for the smaller business.* **C2 C35 H51**

Book-Keeping & VAT *Knowledge of Book-Keeping.* **H3**

Book-Keeping *Understanding of all aspects of book-keeping.* **T8**

Business / Management Skills Courses *Can lead to appropriate SCOTVEC Certificate.* **H46**

Business Development Counselling *Organised on a one-to-one basis.* **H1**

Business Enterprise Programme - Main Course *Knowledge advice & practical assistance to set up a business.* **T8**

Business Planning *Knowledge in creating a Business Plan.* **H3**

Business Planning Seminar   *Various topics of interest to the small business.*   **H43**

Business Skills Seminar   *Various courses available.*   **H43**

Business Skills Seminars   *Development of skills necessary to operate a small business.*   **C2 C35**

Business Start-Up Course   *Working practices of the small business.*   **T2**

Business Start-Up Course   *Aspects involved in setting up a business.*   **H1 H24 H43**

Business Start-Up Programme   *Elements of running a business, & a written business plan.*   **C35**

Business Start-Up Training   *Skills for successfully starting a new business.*   **H3**

Childcare Business Training   *SCOTVEC National Certificate.*   **S152**

Communicate for Profit   *Improving profitability & efficiency through communication.*   **C2**

Communication Skills   *Improvement of existing skills or acquisition of new skills.*   **C35**

Computers in Business   *Terminology, hardware, software & computer applications.*   **T8**

Credit Control   *Setting up & implementing a successful credit control system.*   **H3 H11**

Customer Care   *Achievement of long term customer satisfaction.*   **C2 C35 H3 H51**

Debt Recovery   *Improvement of existing skills or acquisition of new skills.*   **C35**

Direct Marketing   *Knowledge to produce an effective direct mail and/or telemarketing campaign.*   **C2**

Dynamic Marketing (Marketing with new technology)   *City & Guilds in Information Technology.*   **S152**

Effective Management   *How to plan, make decisions, lead & motivate.*   **C2 C35 H3 H11 H51**

Employing People   *How to plan, motivate & part with staff.*   **C2 C35**

Employing People   *The importance of recruiting & keeping a good team of people.*   **T8**

Enterprise Allowance Scheme - Business Start-Up   *Knowledge gained in starting-up in business.*   **S14**

Enterprise Evenings   *No formal outcome.*   **S147**

Essential Selling Skills   *Skills in selling.*   **H40**

Export Marketing   *How to market your business abroad.*   **C2**

Finance for Non-Financial Managers   *Improve managerial skills.*   **H40**

Finding a Market for Your Product   *Knowledge of how to gather & utilise information gained from market research.*   **H3**

General Management   *No formal outcome.*   **T2**

Hairdressing & Salon Organisation - HNC   *SCOTVEC/HNC in Hairdressing & Salon Organisation.*   **S10**

Improving Time & Self Management   *Skills in time & self management.*   **H40**

Interviewing & Negotiation Skills   *Improvement of existing skills or acquisition of new ones.*   **C35**

Management Education & Development - the Scottish Enterprise Foundation   *Development of small business management skills.*   **C44**

Managing Growth   *Managing the growth of a business in a systematic & planned manner.*   **T8**

Managing the Enterprise Culture   *No formal qualification.*   **S82**

Marketing   *Basic marketing skills.*   **H47 T2**

Marketing Your Business   *Market research skills & techniques.*   **C2 C35 H3 H51**

More Profit - Fast!   *Increase profits by correct pricing.*   **C2**

Negotiating Skills   *No formal outcome.*   **C2**

Newstart - Training for Work   *No formal outcome.*   **S89**

Office Administration - HNC   *SCOTVEC/HND in Office Administration.*   **S14**

Personal Selling Skills   *Greater confidence in face-to-face selling techniques.*   **C2 C35 H51**

Practical Marketing   *Market research questionnaire design & implementation.*   **C2 C35**

Presenting with Confidence   *The course aims to improve presentation skills.*   **H40**

Pricing for Profit   *Effectively setting prices. .*   **H3**

Sales Promotion Workshop   *Various forms of advertising media explained.*   **T8**

Selling Skills   *Practical seminar on basic sales techniques.*   **H3**

Selling Techniques   *Issues involved in selling.*   **H47**

Setting Up a Business Computer   *Basic knowledge of setting up a business computer system.*   **H3**

Small Business Consultancy - Marketing For Profit   *No formal outcome.*   **S142**

Small Business Development Programme   *No formal outcome.*   **S150**

Small Business Management   *No formal outcome.*   **S145**

Small Business Management - HNC   *SCOTVEC/HNC in Small Business Management.*   **S8**

Sources of Finance   *Determining financial needs & identify sources of borrowing & investing.*   **T8**

Spreadsheets   *No formal outcome.*   **H3**

Start Your Own Business   *Business Plan/ Business Start-up.*   **S147**

Structure of Business Organisations - HN Unit
SCOTVEC Higher National Unit.   **L5**

Successful Negotiating *Skills in negotiating.*
                                                    H40

Taxation *Personal and business taxation.*
                                    C2 H3 H51

Telephone Sales *Essential skills for effective tele-sales.*   **H3**

Time, Stress & Crisis Management *Dealing positively with stress & crisis.*   **C2 C35**

Understanding Finance *Run your business more profitably.*   **C2**

Understanding Finance I *Improvement of existing skills or acquisition of new skills.*   **C35**

Understanding Finance II *Improvement of existing skills or acquisition of new skills.* **C35**

Using a Business Computer *Knowledge of using a business computer system.*   **H3**

Various Courses Available *Company Certificate awarded.*   **S149**

Women into Business *Skills necessary to operate a small business/return to work.*   **C2**

BUSINESS & MANAGEMENT (GENERAL)

Access to Business Administration *Entry to HND Courses in:- Business Administration, Commerce, Public Administration.*   **S3**

Accounting - HNC *SCOTVEC/HNC in Accounting.*   **S87**

Administration(RSA) *NVQ Level 3.*   **G39**

Administration - SVQ Level 3 *SVQ Level 3 in Administration.*   **G17**

Administration Management - HNC *HNC in Administration Management.*   **F5**

Administrative Management - Diploma *Diploma in Administrative Management.*   **S5**

Agricultural & Farm Business Management *Contributes to RICS Chartered Surveyors APC.*
                                                  S122

Arts Management - HNC *SCOTVEC/HNC in Arts Management.*   **S19**

Automotive Management with Technology - HNC *SCOTVEC/HNC in Automotive Management with Technology.*   **S16**

Building Services Engineering Management - MSc/Diploma *MSc Degree/Diploma.* **L6**

Buildings & Fixed Equipment *Contributes to RICS Chartered Surveyors APC.* **S122**

Business & Management I - (P/T Degree Unit) *Units can be accumulated towards a degree.*
C42

Business & Management III - (P/T Degree Unit) *Units can be accumulated towards a degree.*
C42

Business / Management Courses for Industry *Various courses available.* **H31 H46**

Business / Management Skills Courses *Various courses available.* **H46**

Business Administration *SCOTVEC Module/Level 2. Vocational qualification.* **G35**

Business Administration & Travel & Tourism - HND *SCOTVEC/HND in Business Administration & Travel & Tourism.* **B6**

Business Administration (Administration) - SVQ Level II *SVQ level II in Business Administration.*
F5

Business Administration (Financial) - SVQ Level II *SVQ level II in Business Administration.* **F5**

Business Administration (Mature Entrants) - SVQ *SCOTVEC/NC.* **G17**

Business Administration (Secretarial) - SVQ Level II *SVQ level II in Business Administration.* **F5**

Business Administration (Travel & Tourism) - HNC *HNC in Business Administration (Travel & Tourism).* **F5**

Business Administration (Travel & Tourism) - HND *HND in Business Administration (Travel & Tourism).* **F5**

Business Administration - DBA (Doctor of Business Administration) *DBA in Business Administration.* **S96**

Business Administration - GSVQ Level I & II *GSVQ Level I & II.* **S79**

Business Administration - GSVQ Level II & III *SCOTVEC General Scottish Vocational Certificate, GSVQ Level II & III.* **S91**

Business Administration - GSVQ NC (Level II) *GSVQ: NC (Level II) Business Administration.*
G2

Business Administration - GSVQ NC (Level III) *GSVQ: NC (Level III) Business Administration.*
G2

Business Administration - HNC *SCOTVEC/HNC in Business Administration.*
C10 C23 D5 F5 F8 F13 H31 H49 H53 L5 L68 L81 M7 S3 S5 S8 S11 S14 S15 S16 S19 S71 S75 S79 S81 S87 S88 S91

Business Administration - HNC Individual Units *SCOTVEC/HNC in Business Administration.* **L81**

Business Administration - HND *SCOTVEC/HND in Business Administration.*
B6 C10 F5 F8 H49 S11 S15 S16 S87

Business Administration - Masters *Masters degree in Business Administration.* **S34**

Business Administration - MBA/Diploma *Diploma in Business Administration MBA.* **L6**

Business Administration - NC *SCOTVEC/NC in Business Administration.*
C10 C22 H49 L5 L68 S87 S91

Business Administration - NC (GSVQ II) *SCOTVEC/NC - GSVQ II.* **F8**

Business Administration - NC (GSVQ III) *SCOTVEC/NC - GSVQ III.* **F8**

Business Administration - NC/GSVQ Level III *SCOTVEC/NC/GSVQ Level III.* **H53**

Business Administration - Scottish Wider Access *Recognised group of SCOTVEC Modules & University subject.* **G2**

Business Administration - Skillseekers/ HNC *HNC Business Administration.* **S19**

Business Administration - Skillseekers/ NVQ Level III *NVQ Pitman Level III Certificate.*
S83 S84 S85 S86

Business Administration - SVQ *SCOTVEC/NC in Business Administration.* **S75**

Business Administration - SVQ Level I *SCOTVEC SVQ Level I in Business Administration.*
C22 S155

Business Administration - SVQ Level II *SCOTVEC SVQ SVQ Level II in Business Administration.* **C22 S155**

Business Administration - SVQ Level III *SCOTVEC SVQ SVQ Level III in Business Administration.* **C22 F5**

Business Administration - SVQ SCOTVEC Modular Course *SCOTVEC/NC.* **G17**

Business Administration - Years 1 & 2 - HNC *SCOTVEC/HNC in Business Administration.*
C22

Business Administration HNC *SCOTVEC/HNC.*
L16

Business Administration with Purchasing - HNC *SCOTVEC/HNC Business Administration with Purchasing.* **S14**

Business Administration with Retailing - HNC *SCOTVEC/HNC in Business Administration with Retailing.* **S13**

Business Administration with Travel & Tourism (Year 1) - HNC *HNC in Business Administration with Travel & Tourism.* **C22**

Business Administration with Travel & Tourism - HNC *HNC in Business Administration with Travel & Tourism.* **S13 S75 S91**

Business Administration/Accounting - NC
*SCOTVEC/NC in Business
Administration/Accounting.*   **S16**

Business Administration/Medical Reception -
YT/SVQ Level II   *SCOTVEC, SVQ Level II
Certificate.*   **S79**

Business Administration/Travel & Tourism - HND
SCOTVEC/HND.   **S15**

Business Computing - NC   *SCOTVEC GSVQ in
Technology at Level II.*   **H49**

Business Skill Seminar - Management Skills
Development of management skills.   **C24**

Business Skills Seminars   *Improvement of
existing/ acquisition of new skills.*   **C35**

Business Studies   *Specific skills are developed in
specialist areas according to the needs of
participants.*   **F8**

Business Studies (Accounting) - NC   *NC in
Business Studies (Accounting).*   **F8**

Business Studies (Travel & Tourism) - NC
*SCOTVEC/NC in Business Studies (Travel &
Tourism).*   **S14**

Business Studies - BA/BA (Honours)   *Bachelor of
Arts Degree/Honours Degree in Business Studies.*
     L50

Business Studies - HNC   *NC in a Business
Studies Programme.*   **S14**

Business Studies - NC   *SCOTVEC/NC in
Business Studies.*
     L81   S5   S11   S13   S15   S71   S76   S81

Business Studies - NC (3 Day Programme)
SCOTVEC/NC in Business Studies.   **S78**

Business Studies - NCMs   *SCOTVEC/NC in
Business Studies.*   **L81**

Business Studies - SCOTVEC Modules
SCOTVEC Modules in Business Studies.   **D8**

Business Studies Evening Classes (SCOTVEC)
SCOTVEC/NCM.   **L68**

Business Studies Programme - NC   *NC in a
Business Studies Programme.*   **S14**

Business Studies with Purchasing - HNC   *HNC in
Business Studies with Purchasing.*   **S14**

Business Studies: Marketing (P/T Degree Unit)
Units can be accumulated towards a degree.
     C42

Business/Secretarial Studies - NC   *SCOTVEC/NC
in Business/Secretarial Studies.*   **S76**

Cap Reform, Quotas & Business Changes for
Financial Advisors   *SAC Certificate.*   **S122**

Certificate in Administrative Management
*Certificate in Administrative Management (Institute
of Administrative Management).*   **L68**

Certificate in Public Sector Management
SCOTVEC Certificate.   **S38**

Chartered Secretaries & Administrators (ICSA)
*Professional Membership of Institute of Chartered
Secretaries & Administrators.*   **S94**

Computer Aided Electronics with Management
Studies - HND   *SCOTVEC/HND.*   **F8**

Computer Aided Manufacture with Management
Studies - HNC   *SCOTVEC/HNC.*   **F8**

Computer Aided Manufacture with Management
Studies - HND   *SCOTVEC/HND.*   **F8**

European Business Management - HNC
SCOTVEC/HNC.   **F5   S91**

European Business Management - HND
SCOTVEC/HND.   **F5**

European Business Studies - NC   *SCOTVEC/NC
in European Business Studies.*   **S91**

European Industrial Management - Diploma
FEPIMS   *FEPIMS Diploma in European Industrial
Management (DEIM).*   **F8**

European Information Systems - HNC
SCOTVEC/HNC.   **L5**

European Policy, Law & Management - PgD/MSc
PgD/MSc.   **G15**

European Studies with Marketing - HNC
*SCOTVEC/HNC in European Studies with
Marketing.*   **S91**

Eurospeak   *Skills in communicating more
effectively with foreign visitors and business
associates.*   **T9**

Executive MBA Programme   *MBA.*   **S82**

Finance, Economics & Taxation   *Contributes to
RICS Chartered Surveyors APC.*   **S122**

Golf Course Management - HNC
SCOTVEC/HNC in Golf Course Management.
     F3

HNC Management (For Engineers)   *HNC.*   **S127**

Industrial Management - Post Graduate Diploma
Post Graduate Diploma in Industrial Management.
     F5

Information & Office Management - HND
*SCOTVEC/HND in Information & Office
Management.*   **C10   S87**

Institute of Administrative Management -
Certificate / Diploma   *Institute of Administrative
Management - Certificate/Diploma.*   **S14**

Institute of Chartered Secretaries & Administrators
- Grad ICSA   *ICSA - Grad ICSA (Professional).*
     L59

Institute of Management Services - Certificate &
Diploma   *Institute of Management Services
Certificate & Diploma.*   **S94**

Institute of Motor Industry - Certificate of
Management   *Institute of Motor industry
Certificate of Management.*   **S88**

Internal Quality Auditing   *IQA IRCA Registration.*
     S135

Introduction to Management   *NEBSM Award.*
S110

Introduction to Office Management - NC
SCOTVEC/NC.   **C23**

ISO 9000   *Training to ISO 9000 Accreditation.*
S124

ISO 9000 Lead Assessor Course   *IQA IRCA
Registration.*   **S135**

Languages for the European Market   *European
language for business purposes.*   **L28**

Law with Administrative Studies - BA   *BA in Law
with Administrative Studies.*   **S37**

Law with Administrative Studies - Certificate
Certificate in Law with Administrative Studies.
S37

Law with Administrative Studies - Diploma
Diploma in Law with Administrative Studies.   **S37**

Logistics - MSc   *MSc in Logistics.*   **S48**

Logistics - PgD   *PgD in Logistics.*   **S48**

Maintenance Systems Engineering & Management
- MSc   *MSc in Maintenance Systems Engineering
& Management.*   **S51**

Maintenance Systems Engineering & Management
- PgC   *PgC in Maintenance Systems Engineering
& Management.*   **S51**

Maintenance Systems Engineering & Management
- PgD   *PgD in Marketing - HNC   S087
SCOTVEC/HNC in Marketing.*   **S51**

Marketing - HND   *SCOTVEC/HND in Marketing.*
S87

MBA - Stage 1   *CNAA MBA leading to Stage 2 of
the MBA or Diploma in Management Studies.*
L59

MBA - Stage 2 & 3   *CNAA MBA Degree .*   **L59**

MBA Diploma   *MBA Degree/ Diploma in Business
Administration.*   **L77**

Modern Studies, Management & Information
Studies, Art & Design - SCE H Grade   *SCE H
Grade.*   **M9**

National Examination Board for Supervisory
Management   *Development of Supervisory
Management skills.*   **C22**

Nautical Examination Board Supervisory
Management Course   *Introductory Award Level 1.*
G32

Office Administration - HNC   *HNC in Office
Administration.*   **F5 F8 H49 S11 S75**

Office Administration - NC (SVQ II)
SCOTVEC/NC in Office Administration (SVQ II).
F8

Office Administration - SVQ   *SVQ in Office
Administration.*   **G2**

Professional & Business Ethics - MSc   *MScs
Degree / PgD in Professional & Business Ethics.*
L65

Public Sector Management - Diploma   *SCOTVEC
Diploma in Public Sector Management.*   **S38**

Quality Assurance - HNC   *SCOTVEC/HNC in
Quality Assurance.*   **S94**

Science & Technology Studies - MSc/Diploma in
Social Sciences   *MSc/Diploma in Social Sciences.*
L77

Science with Management Studies - HNC
*SCOTVEC/HNC in Science with Management
Studies.*   **L5**

Short Courses & Consultancy   *Various courses
available.*   **D5**

The Institute of Chartered Secretaries &
Administrators - Grad ICSA   *ICSA - Grad ICSA
(Pre-Prof).*   **L59**

The Management of Care Services - Diploma   *A
Diploma in The Management of Care Services.*
S23

Tourism Management - MSc   *MSc in Tourism
Management.*   **S59**

Tourism Management - PgC   *A PgC in Tourism
Management.*   **S59**

Tourism Management - PgD   *A PgD in Tourism
Management.*   **S59**

Various Courses available   *Outcome depends on
level and subject matter of individual courses.*
T21

Wastes Management - HNC   *SCOTVEC/HNC in
Wastes Management.*   **S94**

FINANCE, INSURANCE, ESTATE AGENCY, VALUATION

Accounting & Accounting Technicians - NC
SCOTVEC/NC in Accounting.   **C22**

Accounting & Finance   *SCOTVEC Certificate.*
B1

Accounting & Finance - Certified Diploma
Certified Diploma in Accounting & Finance.   **F5**

Accounting & Finance - SCE H Grade   *A SCE at H
Grade in Accounting & Finance.*   **C45 L1 S14**

Accounting & Finance - SCE Higher   *SCE Higher -
Accounting & Finance.*   **F7**

Accounting & Finance - SEB H Grade   *A SEB H
Grade.*   **B1 B11**

Accounting - AAT/SVQ   *Association of Accounting
Technicians Certificate.*   **S94**

Accounting - AAT/SVQ Level II   *SCOTVEC SVQ,
SVQ Level II approved by Association of
Accounting Technicians.*   **S91**

Accounting - ACCA   *ACCA Certificate in
Accounting.*   **L53**

Accounting - Chartered Institute of Management Accountants *Chartered Institute of Management Accountants qualification.* **S75**

Accounting - CIMA *ACMA - Chartered Institute of Management Accountants.* **L55**

Accounting - Higher Certificate *Napier Higher Certificate in Accounting.* **L51**

Accounting - Higher Diploma *Napier Higher Diploma in Accounting.* **L51**

Accounting - HNC
B6 C10 C23 F5 F8 G2 H49 H53 M7 S5 S8 S14 S15 S16 S19 S30 S75 S87 S91 T9

Accounting - HND *SCOTVEC/HND in Accounting.* **C10 F5 F13 G2 H53 S8**

Accounting - NC *SCOTVEC/NC.*
C45 S14 S91

Accounting - SCE H Grade *SCE H Grade in Accounting.*
C4 C5 C6 C7 C20 C21 C25 C26 C27 C28 C29 C30 C33 C34 C36 C45 C46 D8 L5 S16 S79

Accounting - SCE H Grade (Day) *SCE H Grade in Accounting.* **L68**

Accounting - SCE H Grade (Evening Class) *SCE H Grade in Accounting.* **L68**

Accounting - SCE Higher *SCE Higher - Accounting.* **F7**

Accounting - SCE O Grade *SCE O grade in Accounting.* **S14**

Accounting - SCE Standard / SCE H Grade / NCMs *SCE Standard or H Grade or appropriate SCOTVEC modules.* **H13**

Accounting - SCOTVEC Module *Higher Accounting or SCOTVEC Accounting 1, Costing 1.* **M3**

Accounting - SCOTVEC Modules *SCOTVEC/NCMs in Accounting.* **L68**

Accounting - SEB H Grade *An SEB H Grade in Accounting.* **B10**

Accounting - SVQ Levels II-IV *SVQ Levels II-IV Certificate in Accounting.* **S75**

Accounting 1 (SCOTVEC) *SCOTVEC/NCM in Accounting 1.* **L1 L2 L5**

Accounting 1 - 92253 - SCOTVEC/NC *SCOTVEC/NCM.* **G6**

Accounting 1 - NC *SCOTVEC/NC.* **C23**

Accounting 2 (SCOTVEC) *SCOTVEC/NCM in Accounting 2.* **L1 L5**

Accounting 2 - NC *SCOTVEC/NC.* **C23**

Accounting HNC *HNC Accounting.* **L16 L17**

Accounting NC *SCOTVEC/NC.* **L16**

Accounting Programme - NC *NC in an Accounting Programme.* **S14**

Accounting Technician - Association of Accounting Technician Membership *AAT Membership.* **D5**

Accounting Technician Studies - HNC *SCOTVEC/HNC in Accounting Technician Studies.* **S14**

Accounting Towards Profit *Issues involved in accounting procedures.* **H51 T8**

Accounting Year 1 & 2 - HNC *SCOTVEC/HNC in Accounting.* **C22**

Accounts - SCE H Grade *H Grade in Accounts.* **M4 S13**

Accounts - SCE Higher *SCE Higher Certificate in Accounts.* **H49**

Accounts - SCE O Grade *O Grade in Accounts.* **M4**

Accounts, Book-Keeping & Payroll - Short Contract Courses *Various courses available.* **L81**

Associateship of the Chartered Institute of Bankers in Scotland *The Associateship of CIBS.* **S8 S24**

Association of Accounting Technicians - SVQ Level III *SVQ Level III.* **S14**

Association of Accounting Technicians 3 (AAT3) *Membership of the Association of Accounting Technicians.* **T9**

Association of Accounting Technicians Examination *Associateship of the Association of Accounting Technicians.* **L68 S14**

Banking - Chartered Institute of Bankers Stage 2 - Associateship *Stage 2 Examination of CIBS.* **L57**

Banking - Chartered Institute of Bankers Stage 3 Members *Stage 3 Examination of CIBS.* **L57**

Basic Accounting *Aspects of a basic accounting system.* **T8**

Basic Accounts *No formal outcome.* **B3 B6**

Basic Financial Recording *SCOTVEC Certificate.* **B2 B4**

Book-Keeping *Financial Record Keeping for the smaller business.* **C2 C35 H51 T8**

Book-Keeping & Accounting for Adult Returners - SCOTVEC/NC *SCOTVEC/NC.* **G17**

Book-Keeping & Accounts - SCE H Grade *SCE H Grade in Book-keeping & accounts.* **M5**

Book-Keeping & VAT *Knowledge of Book-Keeping.* **H3**

Book-Keeping *Aspects of book-keeping.* **T8**

Budgetary Control *No formal outcome.* **B6**

Business & Management Development - Customised Programmes *Various courses available.* **L71**

Business / Management Courses for Industry *Various courses available.* **H31 H46**

Business Administration - GSVQ Level I & II *A GSVQ Level I & II.* **S79**

Business Administration - HNC Individual Units *SCOTVEC/HNC in Business Administration.* **L81**

Business Administration/Accounting - NC
*SCOTVEC/NC in Business
Administration/Accounting.* **S16**

Business Skill Seminar - Accounting Towards
Profit *Development of skills in accounting.* **C24**

Business Skill Seminar - Book-Keeping
Development of skills in Book-Keeping. **C24**

Business Skill Seminar - Understanding Finance
Development of skills in understanding finance.
C24

Business Skill Seminar - More Profit Fast *Skills in
profit making & customer loyalty.* **C24**

Business Skills Seminars *Skills necessary to
operate a small business.* **C2**

Business Studies - NC *SCOTVEC/NC in
Business Studies.* **S11**

Business Studies - NCMs *SCOTVEC/NC in
Business Studies.* **L81**

Business Studies - SCOTVEC Modules
SCOTVEC Modules in Business Studies. **D8**

Business Studies Banking Programme - NC
*SCOTVEC/NC in Business Studies (Banking
Programme).* **L68**

Business Studies Evening Classes (SCOTVEC)
SCOTVEC/NCM. **L68**

Business Studies Section Short Course Provision
College Certificate. **L19**

Certificate of Insurance Practice - Chartered
Insurance Institute *Certificate of Insurance
Practice - CII award.* **L68**

Certificate of Insurance Practice - Revision for
Exams (Short Courses) *Preparation for CIP
exams.* **L68**

Certificate of Professional Development in
Residential Estate Agency *Prof. Dev. in
Residential Estate Agency Certificate.* **S109**

Chartered Association of Certified Accountants
Chartered Association of Certified Accountants.
F5

Chartered Association of Certified Accountants -
Level III *Chartered Association of Certified
Accountants.* **S29**

Chartered Association of Certified Accountants
Professional Stage Module E *ACCA Professional
Stage - Module E.* **S8**

Chartered Association of Certified Accountants
Professional Stage Module F *ACCA Professional
Stage - Module F.* **S8**

Chartered Institute of Bankers in Scotland -
Associateship *Associateship of the Chartered
Institute of Bankers in Scotland.* **S14**

Chartered Institute of Management Accountants
Chartered Institute of Management Accountants.
F5

Chartered Institute of Management Accountants
(CIMA) Stages II, III & IV *CIMA Stages II, III & IV.*
S8

Chartered Institute of Management Accountants -
Stage II *Chartered Institute of Management
Accountants Stage II.* **S29**

Chartered Institute of Management Accountants -
Stage III *Chartered Institute of Management
Accountants Stage III.* **S29**

Chartered Institute of Management Accountants -
Stage IV *Chartered Institute of Management
Accountants Part IV.* **S29**

Chartered Institute of Public Finance &
Accountancy - Foundation Course *CIPFA
Foundation course.* **S31**

Chartered Institute of Public Finance &
Accountancy - Part I *Chartered Institute of Public
Finance & Accountancy Part I.* **S31**

Chartered Institute of Public Finance &
Accountancy - Part II *Chartered Institute of Public
Finance & Accountancy Part II.* **S31**

Chartered Institute of Public Finance &
Accountancy - Part III *Chartered Institute of
Public Finance & Accountancy Part III.* **S31**

Chartered Insurance Institute - NC
SCOTVEC/NC in a programme of modules. **S14**

Chartered Insurance Institute Associateship
Chartered Insurance Institute Associateship.
S24

Corporation Tax & VAT - HNU *SCOTVEC Higher
National Unit 6400149 Corporation Tax & VAT.*
F5

Cost Control *No formal outcome.* **B6**

Costing 1 - NC *SCOTVEC/NC.* **C23**

Credit Control *Knowledge of how to set up &
implement a successful credit control system.*
H3 H11

Debt Recovery *Improvement of existing skills or
acquisition of new skills.* **C35 S82**

Debt Recovery & Cash Control *No formal
outcome.* **D2**

Farm Accounts *Skills needed to develop an
accurate Accounting System.* **H30**

Finance *Non-certificated course.* **H14**

Finance for Non-Financial Managers *Improve
managerial skills.* **H40**

Finance for the Non-Financial Manager
*Knowledge to analyse & understand the financial
data.* **G16 S57 S87**

Financial Control *Ability to maintain a much
tighter financial control over business.* **T8**

Financial Control Systems for the Vehicle Industry
SCOTVEC/HNC. **H53**

Financial Management & Accounting - Customised
Training Programmes *Financial management &
accounting skills.* **L4**

Financial Management for Line Managers Supervisors & Admin/Tech Staff (M5) *Skills in cost effectiveness.* **S94**

Financial Record Keeping *Skills gained in financial record keeping.* **S81**

Financial Record Keeping - 82250 *SCOTVEC/NCM in Financial Record Keeping 82250.* **D6**

Financial Record Keeping - NC *SCOTVEC/NC in Financial Record Keeping.* **S19**

Financial Record Keeping - Skillseekers/ SVQ Levels I-III *SVQ Financial Record Keeping Levels I- III.* **S19**

Financial Record Keeping I - SCOTVEC/NC *SCOTVEC/NC Financial Record Keeping I.* **C23 F3 F8 L3 L5 L31 T23**

Financial Record Keeping II & III *Skills gained in financial record keeping.* **S81**

Financial Record Keeping II *SCOTVEC/NCM - Financial Record Keeping II.* **F8 L5 T23**

Financial Record Keeping III *SCOTVEC/NCM.* **F8 L5 T23**

Financial Services - HNC *SCOTVEC/HNC in Financial Services.* **S8**

Hospitality Operations - HNC *SCOTVEC/HNC in Hospitality Operations.* **C10**

ICM Professional Qualification Course *Professional Membership of ICM.* **G17 L5 S14**

Income Tax - HNU *SCOTVEC Higher National Unit 6400139 Income Tax.* **F5**

Institute of Credit Management *Skills in Credit Management.* **S14**

Institute of Credit Management - Final Stage *Institute of Credit Management (Final Stage).* **L5**

Institute of Rating & Valuation - Years I & II *Rating & valuation principles.* **C22**

Insurance Studies - Associateship Diploma of the Chartered Insurance Inst *Associateship Dip CII.* **L58**

Interpretation of Financial Data - HN Unit *SCOTVEC/HN Unit.* **L5**

Introduction to Finance for Managers *No formal outcome.* **G38**

Introduction to VAT *Knowledge of VAT accounting techniques at an introductory level.* **H30**

Job Costing - Sage *A Certificate of Competence.* **B6**

Management (Part Time) HNC *HNC in Management.* **L81**

Management - HNC *SCOTVEC/HNC in Management.* **S75**

Managing Budgets (For NHS Managers) *Understanding financial procedures.* **S57**

Managing Resources in Organisations *Middle management responsibility.* **T13**

Medical - Financial Management of Practices *Financial management of Medical Practices.* **D5**

Membership of the Chartered Institute of Bankers in Scotland *Membership of the Chartered Institute of Bankers.* **S24**

Office Administration & Technology - NC *SCOTVEC/NC in Office Administration & Technology.* **L81**

Office Administration - HNC *SCOTVEC/HNC in Office Administration.* **S11**

Office Administration - HNC Individual Units *SCOTVEC/HNC in Office Administration. .* **L81**

PAYE *No formal outcome.* **B6 H30**

Payments Handling - 92255 - SCOTVEC/NC *SCOTVEC/NC.* **T23**

Payroll - Sage Popular Payroll *Certificate of Competence.* **B6**

Payroll - Sage Sterling Payroll *Certificate of Competence.* **B6**

Payroll Preparation *College Certificate.* **L18**

Payroll Procedures - NC *SCOTVEC/NC.* **C23**

Preparing Final Accounts *SCOTVEC/NCM.* **L1**

Preparing Financial Forecasts - HN Unit *SCOTVEC Higher National Unit.* **L5**

Producing Business Accounts - HN Unit *SCOTVEC Higher National Unit.* **F8**

Quality - Cost of Quality *Quality - Ability to cost Quality procedures.* **D5**

Reception Skills *Skills, knowledge & attitude appropriate to reception duties..* **H42**

Record Keeping *Skills & knowledge appropriate to keeping office records.* **H42**

Recording of Financial Transactions *SCOTVEC/NCM in Recording of Financial Transactions.* **L1**

Reducing Quality Costs *Skills in assessing Quality costs.* **S102**

Resource Management *No formal outcome.* **B6**

Sage Popular Accountant *Skills using the Sage computer package.* **B6**

Sage Popular Accountant Plus *Certificate of Competence.* **B6**

Sage Popular Book-Keeping *Skills using the Sage computer package.* **B6**

Sage Popular Financial Controller *Certificate of Competence.* **B6**

Sage Sterling Accountant *Skills using the Sage computer package.* **B6**

Sage Sterling Accountant Plus *Certificate of Competence.* **B6**

Sage Sterling Book-Keeping *Skills using the Sage computer package.* **B6**

Sage Sterling Financial Controller   *Certificate of Competence.*   **B6**

Social Service Management - MSc/ PgD Certificate   *MSc/Diploma certificate in Social Service Management.*   **L33**

Sources of Finance   *Determine needs & identify sources of borrowing & investing.*   **T8**

Supervisory Management Skills   *Skills & attitudes appropriate to the first line supervisor or junior manager.*   **H42**

Taxation   *Personal & business taxation.*
C2 H3 H51 T8

The Pensions Management Institute Course   *Knowledge gained in the field of pensions management.*   **S14**

Understanding Finance   *Using financial information to run a business more profitably.*
C2 T8

Understanding Finance II   *Improvement of existing skills or acquisition of new skills.*   **C35**

Various Courses Available   *Company Certificate awarded.*   **S149**

VAT Appreciation   *Training in the methods used to apply VAT to accounts.*   **H30**

Women into Business   *Development of skills necessary to operate a small business/return to work.*   **C2**

HUMAN RESOURCES: DEVELOPMENT, MANAGEMENT

Action Centred Leadership (M8)   *Skills used in identifying key tasks & objectives within an organisation.*   **S94**

Bakery Supervisory Management SCOTVEC/HNC.   **H53**

Better Delegation   *No formal outcome.*   **G34**

Business & Management Development - Customised Programmes   *Various.*   **L71**

Business Administration - HNC Individual Units SCOTVEC/HNC in Business Administration.   **L81**

Career Management   *No formal outcome.*   **G34**

Certificate in Personnel Practice   *Certificate in Personnel Practice.*   **C22 T9**

Certificate in Personnel Practice (IPM)   *Institute of Personnel Management Certificate in Personnel Practice.*   **L67**

Certificate in Supervisory Management (NEBSM)   *NEBSM Certificate in Supervisory Management.*
L67 L82

Certificate in Supervisory Management NEBSM Part-Time   *NEBSM Certificate.*   **L82**

Certificate in Supervisory Studies (NEBSM)   *Certificate in Supervisory Studies (NEBSM).*   **L18**

Designing an Induction Training Programme   *No formal outcome.*   **M8**

Diploma in Supervisory Management (NEBSM)   *Diploma in Supervisory Management from NEBSM.*   **L5**

Diploma in Training Management   *The Institute of Training & Developments Diploma in Training Management.*   **L82**

Disciplinary Interviews & Grievance Handling   *No formal outcome.*   **B6**

Discipline & Grievance Handling   *Certificate of Attendance.*   **B6**

Effective Appraisal Interviewing   *No formal outcome.*   **G34**

Effective Leadership   *No formal outcome.*   **G34**

Effective Meetings   *No formal outcome.*   **G34**

Effective People Management   *No formal outcome.*   **G34**

Effective Presentations   *No formal outcome.*
G34

Effective Report Writing   *No formal outcome.*
G34

Effective Requirement Interviews   *No formal outcome.*   **G34**

Effective Time Management   *No formal outcome.*
G34

Employing People   *How to plan, motivate & part with staff.*   **C2**

Employing People (P.E.P.)   *Skills in recruiting & keeping a good team of people.*   **T8**

Employment Law & Practice - PgD/MSc   *PgD/MSc in Employment Law & Practice.*   **G15**

Employment Law - Short Course   *Knowledge of Employment Law.*   **L81**

Equality & Discrimination - MSc   *MSc in Equality & Discrimination.*   **S107**

Essay Writing for Professional Exams   *No formal outcome.*   **G34**

Greenkeeping Supervision - NC   *SCOTVEC/NC in Greenkeeping Supervision.*   **F3**

Hospitality Operations - HNC   *SCOTVEC/HNC in Hospitality Operations.*   **C10**

Human Resources Management - Customised Training Programmes   *Improved performance in people management skills.*   **L4**

Human Resources Management - HND SCOTVEC/HND in Human Resources Management.   **S14**

Human Resources Management - MSc   *MSc in Human Resources Management.*   **C38**

Institute of Employment Consultants - Certificate in Recruitment Practice   *Institute of Employment Consultants - Certificate.*   **S14**

Institute of Personnel Management   *Institute of Personnel Management.*   **F5**

Institute of Personnel Management Certificate in Personnel Practice P/Time   *Course certificate.*
L82

Interpersonal Skills for Managers   *Supervisory skills & techniques.*   **S87**

Interview Techniques   *No formal outcome.*
S142

Introduction to Community Education   *Prepares participants for work in the community.*   **C22**

Introduction to Supervisory Management (NEBSM)   *NEBSM Certificate.*   **L18**

Introduction to Supervisory Skills   *College Certificate.*   **L18**

Introductory Certificate in Supervisory Management (NEBSM)   *Introductory Certificate.*
L5

Investment in Excellence   *Certificate of completion.*   **C49**

Issues in Supervision & Management - HN Unit   *HN Unit.*   **F8**

Job Applications & Interviews   *No formal outcome.*
G16

Law in Employment (SCOTVEC)   *SCOTVEC/NCM.*   **L5**

Management & Supervisory Skills - Practical   *Improvement of management effectiveness.*
G22

Management - HNC   *HNC in management.*   **F8**

Management of Training   *Knowledge of HRD techniques.*   **G16**

Management Support Services & Skills   *SCOTVEC Certificate.*   **S78**

Managing People for Results   *No formal outcome.*
B6

Managing Projects Successfully   *No formal outcome.*   **G38**

Managing Resources in Organisations   *Knowledge of middle management responsibility.*
T13

Manpower Planning   *Development, management & motivation skills.*   **S57**

Manufacturing & Service Industries Supervisory Management - NEBSM   *NEBSM Certificate.*
S94

National Examination Board for Supervisory Management   *Development of Supervisory Management skills.*   **C22**

Negotiation Skills   *No formal outcome.*   **S142**

Operations Management - Diploma   *Diploma in Operations Management.*   **S87**

Organisation & Methods (M2)   *Knowledge of method study.*   **S94**

Organising Work   *No formal outcome.*   **B6**

Parks & Recreational Supervisory Management - NEBSM   *NEBSM Certificate.*   **S94**

PAYE   *There is no formal outcome to this course.*
B6

People & Work - SCOTVEC/NC   *SCOTVEC Certificate.*   **G17**

Performance Appraisal   *Skills needed to appraise performance.*   **H14**

Personnel Management (IPM)   *Graduateship of the Institute of Personnel Management.*   **L59**

Personnel Management - MSc   *MSc in Personnel Management.*   **S35 S105**

Personnel Management - PgD   *PgD in Personnel Management.*   **S35 S105**

Personnel Practice - Certificate   *Certificate in Personnel Practice of the Institute of Personnel Management (IPM).*   **F8**

Personnel Practice - IPM Certificate   *Institute of Personnel Management approved certificate.*   **D5**

Practical Supervision (M6)   *Skills required to be a supervisor.*   **S94**

Professional Development Award in Supervisory Care Management   *For care workers involved in staff supervision.*   **C22**

Promoting Equal Opportunities - SCOTVEC/NC   *SCOTVEC/NC.*   **T23**

Quality - Total Quality Management   *Implications & procedures involved in Total Quality Management.*   **D5**

Rating (Assessment) Clinic (M3)   *No formal outcome.*   **S94**

Social Service Management - MSc/ PgD Certificate   *MSc/Diploma certificate in Social Service Management.*   **L33**

Supervision of Care Service Management - Advanced Certificate   *AC in Supervision of Care Service Management.*   **S75**

Supervision of Social Care Staff - HN Unit   *HN Unit.*   **C23**

Supervision Skills   *Various short courses available.*   **H14**

Supervisory Management (Intro) - NEBSM   *National Examining Board in Supervisory Management (NEBSM) Certificate.*   **S94**

Supervisory Management (NEBSM)   *National Exam Board for Supervisory Management (NEBSM) Certificate.*   **F13**

Supervisory Management - Certificate   *NEBSM Certificate.*   **S14**

Supervisory Management - Certificate NEBSM   *Supervisory skills.*   **F8**

Supervisory Management - Introductory NEBSM   *L067 NEBSM Introductory Course Certificate.*
F8

Supervisory Management - ISM Certificate *ISM Certificate in Supervisory Management Studies.*
B6

Supervisory Management - National Examination Board *National Examination Board for Supervisory Management Certificate.* **S11**

Supervisory Management - National Examining Board (NEBSM) *NEBSM Certificate.* **S75**

Supervisory Management - NEBSM Certificate *National Examination Board Supervisory Management Certificate.* **S16**

Supervisory Management - NEBSM *NEBSM Certificate.* **D5 H49 S5 S15 S79**

Supervisory Management - NEBSM Diploma *Diploma from the National Examinations Board for Supervisory Management.* **S15**

Supervisory Management - NEBSM Introductory Certificate *Introductory Certificate in Supervisory Management.* **G2 H35**

Supervisory Management for the Motor Industry *Certificate of the Licentiateship of the City & Guilds of London.* **T9**

Supervisory Management Level III - SVQ *Nationally recognised qualification.* **G2**

Supervisory Management Skills *Skills & attitudes appropriate to the first line supervisor or junior manager.* **H42**

Supervisory Skills *Identify & develop supervisory skills at work.* **G16**

Supervisory Skills - Instructional Techniques *Skills in instructional techniques.* **H35**

Team Building *No formal outcome.* **G34**

The Certificate Course in Supervisory Management (NEBSM) *Certificate in Supervisory Management.* **L5**

The Role of the Supervisor *No formal outcome.* **M8**

The Work Environment - SCOTVEC/NC *No formal outcome.* **T23**

Training & Development - Diploma *Diploma of the Institute of Training & Development.* **S94**

Training & Development NVQ Levels III & IV *NVQ Level III & IV.* **C49**

Waste Management - NEBSM *National Examining Board in Supervisory Management Certificate.* **S94**

INFORMATION & LIBRARY MANAGEMENT

Business & Management I - (P/T Degree Unit) *Accumulation of units leading to a Degree.* **C42**

Business Information Management - HNC *SCOTVEC/HNC in Business Information Management.* **C22**

Business Information Systems - HNC *SCOTVEC/HNC in Business Information Systems.* **S15**

Business Information Systems - HND *SCOTVEC/HND in Business Information Systems.* **S8**

Classification, Cataloguing & Indexing (SCOTVEC) *SCOTVEC/NCM 7130011.* **L5**

Cultural Services Management - MSc/ PgD *MSc/Diploma/Certificate in Cultural Services Management.* **L33**

European Information Systems - HNC *SCOTVEC/HNC.* **L5**

Information & Library Management - NC *SCOTVEC/NC.* **S9**

Information & Library Management - HNC *SCOTVEC/HNC.* **S9**

Information & Library Studies - MSc *An MSc in Information & Library Studies.* **S105**

Information & Library Studies - PgD *A PgD in Information & Library Studies.* **S105**

Information & Office Management - HND *SCOTVEC/HND in Information & Office Management.* **C10 F5 F8 H49 H53**

Information & Office Management - SCOTVEC/HND *SCOTVEC/HND in Information & Office Management.* **G17**

Information Management - MA/PgD *Master of Arts Degree / PgD in Information Management.* **L65**

Information Management Systems - MSc *MSc in Information Management Systems.* **S28**

Information Management Systems - PgD *PgD in Information Management Systems.* **S28**

Information Studies - NC *SCOTVEC/NC.* **C23**

Information Systems - MSc / PgD *MSc Degree / PgD in Information Systems.* **L62**

Information Technology *SCOTVEC Module/Level 2. Vocational qualification.* **G35**

Introduction to Database Management Systems - HN Unit *SCOTVEC Higher National Unit.* **F8**

Librarianship & Information Science - HNC *SCOTVEC/HNC.* **L5**

Library & Information Science - NC *SCOTVEC/NC in Library & Information Science.* **L5 S14**

Library & Information Science - SCOTVEC/NC *SCOTVEC/NC certificate.* **G17**

Library & Information Units in Modern Society (SCOTVEC) *SCOTVEC/NCM 7130021.* **L5**

Library & Information Work Routines: Design & Equipment *SCOTVEC/NCM 7130031.* **L5**

Library & Information Work Routines: Services (SCOTVEC) *SCOTVEC/NCM 7130041.* **L5**

Library & Information Work Routines: Stock (SCOTVEC) *SCOTVEC/NCM 7130051.* **L5**

Local Investigations 2 (SCOTVEC) *SCOTVEC/NCM 81213.* **L5**

Management & Information Studies - SCE H Grade *SCE H Grade.* **B3 C20 C21 C25 C28 C29 C33 C34 C36 L5**

Management & Information Studies - SCE Higher *SCE Higher - Management & Information Studies.* **F7**

Management & Information Studies - SEB H Grade *SEB H Grade.* **B11**

Management (Part Time) HNC *HNC in Management.* **L81**

Management Information Systems *No formal outcome.* **B6**

Office Administration - HNC *SCOTVEC/HNC in Office Administration.* **C10 C23 S15**

Office Administration - Years I & II - HNC *SCOTVEC/HNC in Office Administration.* **C22**

Project in Library & Information Work (SCOTVEC) *SCOTVEC/NCM 7130061.* **L5**

Software Quality Engineering - MSc *MSc in Software Quality Engineering.* **S28**

Software Quality Engineering - PgD *PgD in Software Quality Engineering.* **S28**

Sources of Information: Bibliographic (SCOTVEC) *SCOTVEC/NCM 7130071.* **L5**

Sources of Information: Quick Reference (SCOTVEC) *SCOTVEC/NCM 7130081.* **L5**

User Services in Library & Information Units (SCOTVEC) *SCOTVEC/NCM 7130091.* **L5**

Working in Libraries *SCOTVEC/NCM. User services in libraries & information units.* **M7**

MANAGEMENT SKILLS, SYSTEMS & TECHNIQUES

'Working With' Masterclass Series *No formal outcome.* **L97 S148**

Accounting for Profit *Understanding of business accounts.* **S110**

Achieving Through Being Assertive *Communication skills.* **H40**

Achieving Through Better Business Planning *Managerial skills.* **H40**

Achieving Through Meetings *Improving management skills.* **H40**

Action Learning *Development of effective business skills.* **C32**

Action Skills for Managers *Various skills & techniques used in many areas of management.* **S57**

Advanced Business Presentation Skills *No formal outcome.* **C51**

Advanced Interviewing Skills *Certificate of Attendance.* **B6**

Advanced Supervisory Skills (Sep 11-12 Falkirk) *No formal outcome.* **G38**

An Introduction to Counselling *No formal outcome.* **S57**

Assertiveness *Improvement of existing skills or acquisition of new skills.* **C35 S6 S57**

Assertiveness in the Workplace *Improvement of new skills & acquisition of new ones.* **M8**

Assertiveness Skills *Communicate effectively & efficiently with others.* **G16 S142**

Assertiveness Training *Increased self-confidence & improved inter-personal skills.* **D5 G17**

Assertiveness Training for Women - Beginners *No formal outcome.* **T13**

Automotive Management with Technology - HNC *SCOTVEC/HNC in Automotive Management with Technology.* **S16 S19**

Bar Management *Practical skills & knowledge.* **S15**

Basic Interviewing Skills   *Certificate of
Attendance.*   **B6**

Basic Management Studies   *Certificate of
Attendance.*   **B6**

BPICS - Diploma in Production & Inventory
Management   *BPICS Diploma.*   **F8**

BS 5750   *Improving efficiency within the work
place.*   **S87**

BS 5750 Quality Systems Management   *Napier
University Certificate.*   **L48**

Burnout: Stress in People-Centred Work   *Effects
& strategies to help manage burnout.*   **G16**

Business & Management Development -
Customised Programmes   *Various courses
available.*   **L71**

Business / Management Courses for Industry
Various courses available.   **H31 H46**

Business / Management Skills Courses   *Various
courses available.*   **H46**

Business Administration - HNC   *SCOTVEC/HNC
in Business Administration.*   **S87**

Business Administration - HNC Individual Units
SCOTVEC/HNC in Business Administration.   **L81**

Business Administration - HND   *SCOTVEC/HND
in Business Administration.*   **L5 S87**

Business Administration - Masters   *Masters
degree in Business Administration.*   **S34**

Business Administration - TFW - RSA VQ Level II
Development of skills in Business Administration.
                                                            C8

Business Communication & Report Writing
Accurate & persuasive business communication.
                                                            G16

Business English - Advanced   *Improved
comprehension & fluency in English in a variety of
business contexts.*   **L13**

Business English - Intermediate   *Improved
comprehension & fluency in English in a variety of
business contexts.*   **L13**

Business Management - Customised Training
Programmes   *Skills in an area of business
management.*   **L4**

Business Skill Seminar - Management Skills
Development of management skills.   **C24**

Business Studies Section Short Course Provision
College Certificate.   **L19 L27**

Certificate in Management   *Institute of
Management Certificate.*   **S138**

Certificate in Supervisory Management   *NEBSM
Certificate or S/NVQ Level III.*   **S138**

Committee Skills   *Understanding the roles of the
chairperson, secretary & members of the
committee.*   **H42**

Committee Skills (SCOTVEC)   *SCOTVEC/NCM.*
                                                            L5

Communicate for Profit   *Improvement in the
profitability & overall efficiency in a small business.*
                                                            C2

Communication & Personal Skills - Assertiveness
Training   *Improved communication & personal
skills - assertiveness.*   **D5**

Communication & Personal Skills - Interviewing
Skills   *Improved communication & personal skills -
interviewing techniques.*   **D5**

Communication & Personal Skills - Motivational
Interviewing   *Improved communication & personal
skills - motivational interviewing.*   **D5**

Communication & Personal Skills - Negotiation
Skills   *Improved communication & personal skills -
negotiation techniques.*   **D5**

Communication & Personal Skills - Presentation
Skills   *Improved communication & personal skills -
presentation skills.*   **D5**

Communication & Personal Skills - Stress
Management   *Improved communication &
personal skills - stress management.*   **D5**

Communication & Personal Skills - Time
Management   *Improved communication &
personal skills - time management.*   **D5**

Communication 4 - Part-Time NC   *SCOTVEC
module.*   **L81**

Communication for Business - HNC
SCOTVEC/HNC in Communication for Business.
                                                            L5

Communication for Business - SCOTVEC/HNC
HNC in Business Communication.   **G17 L68**

Communication Skills   *Improvement of existing
skills or acquisition of new skills.*   **C35**

Communication Skills - Customised Courses
Various courses available.   **L71**

Communications for Business   *Basic
communications skills.*   **S14**

Computers/Administration   *YT Preparatory
Course.*   **T16**

Confidence Building   *Skills gained in confidence
building.*   **S6**

Counselling Skills   *Helping staff to solve their own
problems.*   **G16**

Creative Problem Solving   *No formal outcome.*
                                                            B6

Creative Problem Solving & Decision Making
Certificate of Attendance.   **B6**

Customer Care   *Skills in dealing with the general
public & customer relations.*   **H42**

Customer Care - (M12)   *Skills gained in customer
care.*   **S94**

Customer Relations & Care   *Certificate of
Attendance.*   **B6**

Decision Making Techniques   *Skills in decision
making.*   **S87**

Developing Leadership Skills   *Developing leadership skills vital to effective performance.*
G16

Diploma in Management   *Institute of Management Diploma.*   **S138**

Diploma in Training Management   *Institute of Training & Development Diploma in Training Management.*   **L82**

Discipline & Grievance Handling   *Certificate of Attendance.*   **B6**

Effective Management   *Skills to increase efficiency & profitability.*
C2   C35   H3   H11   H51   T8

Effective Meetings   *Skills needed to get more out of meetings.*   **H30   L27   T13**

Effective Report Writing   *Developing concise written communication skills.*   **M8**

Effective Report Writing for Managers   *Developing concise written communication skills for those in management.*   **M8**

Effective Supervision (Sep 13-15 Falkirk : Oct 25-27 Aberdeen)   *No formal outcome.*   **G38**

Energy Management   *No formal outcome.*   **S87**

Environmental Management Systems BS 7750   *Napier University certificate.*   **L48**

European Business Management - HNC   *SCOTVEC/HNC in European Business Management.*   **F5**

European Business Management - HND   *SCOTVEC/HND in European Business Management.*   **F5**

Facilities Layout & Materials Handling Systems   *No formal outcome.*   **S87**

Finance for the Non-Financial Manager   *Skills in understanding finance.*   **S87**

Fish Farming Courses for Industry   *Various courses available.*   **H27**

General Education Section Short Course Provision   *College Certificate.*   **L27**

Goals & Goal Setting   *Deriving the maximum benefit for the organisation.*   **S57**

Health & Safety Management   *No formal outcome.*   **S87**

Health & Stress (S4)   *Strategies to avoid heart disease.*   **S94**

Housing Management   *Practical skills in housing management.*   **S15**

Improving Communications   *Improving communications skills.*   **S57**

Improving Time & Self Management   *Skills in time & self management.*   **H40**

Information & Office Management - HND   *SCOTVEC/HND in Information & Office Management.*   **S87**

Innovation & Entrepreneurship   *No formal outcome.*   **S82**

Intermediate Management Skills   *No formal outcome.*   **B6**

Interpersonal Skills   *No formal outcome.*   **G16**

Interpersonal Skills for Managers   *Improving interpersonal skills within the workplace.*   **S87**

Interview Skills   *Improved interview skills.*   **S6**

Interviewer Skills - Part-Time NC   *SCOTVEC module.*   **L81**

Interviewing & Negotiation Skills   *Improvement of existing skills or acquisition of new skills.*   **C35**

Interviewing Skills   *No formal outcome.*   **B6   D5**

Interviewing Skills for Interviewers & Interviewees   *Skills for interviewing, and being interviewed.*   **L6**

Interviewing Techniques   *Non-certificated course.*
H14

Introduction to Project Management   *Napier University certificate.*   **L48**

Introduction to Transactional Analysis   *Development of effective communication skills.*
C41

Introductory Business Presentation Skills   *No formal outcome.*   **G51**

Issues in Supervision & Management - HN Unit   *HNU.*   **F8**

Job Applications & Interviews   *No formal outcome.*
G16

Leadership & Motivation At Work - NC   *SCOTVEC/NC.*   **C23**

Leadership & Motivation At Work - SCOTVEC/NC   *SCOTVEC/NC.*   **G17**

Learn to Manage Effectively   *No formal outcome.*
S142

Listening & Counselling Skills Weekend   *Development of listening & counselling skills in a variety of contexts.*   **L6**

Making Meetings Effective   *Communication skills in meetings.*   **M8**

Making Successful Presentations   *Preparing & delivering a Presentation.*   **M8**

Management & Information Studies - SCE H Grade   *SCE H Grade.*
B3   C20   C21   C25   C28   C29   C33   C34   C36   D8   L5

Management & Office Studies - SCE H Grade or CSYS   *SCE in Management & Office Studies at H Grade or CSYS.*   **D3**

Management (Part Time) HNC   *HNC in Management.*   **L81**

Management - Diploma   *Successful candidates will gain SCOTVEC Advanced Diploma in Management.*   **M7   S8   S14   S87**

Management - HNC   *Successful candidates will gain SCOTVEC/HNC in Management.*
M7 S3 S5 S14 S16 S19 S75 S87

Management - SVQ   *SCOTVEC & the Management Charter Initiative (MCI) Levels III & IV Certificate.*   **C23**

Management - Year 1 - HNC   *SCOTVEC/HNC in Management..*   **C22**

Management Education & Development - the Management Development Unit   *Practical experience in management development.*   **C44**

Management Effectiveness   *No formal outcome.*   **S87**

Management Information Systems   *No formal outcome.*   **B6**

Management Science/Mathematics & Its Applications - BSc Hons [UCAS G1N1]   *BSc Hons course.*   **C37**

Management Skills   *Improved management skills.*   **S6**

Management Skills - Customised Training Programmes   *Improved performance in various management skills as required.*   **L4**

Management Techniques   *Improved management techniques.*   **S6**

Management with Marketing - Diploma   *Diploma in Management with Marketing.*   **S14**

Managing Change Projects   *No formal qualification.*   **S82**

Managing for the First Time   *Basic managerial skills.*   **L6**

Managing Growth   *Managing the growth of business in a systematic & planned manner.*   **T8**

Managing Meetings   *No formal outcome.*   **S87**

Managing People for Results   *Certificate of Attendance.*   **B6**

Managing the Marketing Plan   *No formal outcome.*   **S87**

Managing the Pressure   *Training on coping with pressure in the workplace.*   **S87**

Marketing   *Certificate of Attendance.*   **B6**

Marketing for Managers   *No formal outcome.*   **S87**

Materials Management - MSc/PgD   *MSc/Postgraduate Diploma in Marketing.*   **S101**

Media Presentation Skills   *Improved communication & presentation skills.*   **C22**

Meeting Customer Needs - HN Units   *2 credits towards a HNC in Management Studies.*   **C23**

Minuting of Meetings   *Knowledge of how to successfully record proceedings during a meeting.*   **H30**

Motivation & Communication   *Non-certificated course.*   **H14**

Motivational Leadership (Oct 9-11 Falkirk)   *No formal outcome.*   **G38**

National Examination Board for Supervisory Management   *Development of Supervisory Management skills.*   **C22**

NEBSM Management   *National Examining Body for Supervisory Management (NEBSM).*   **S87**

NEBSM Management Certificate   *Certificate in Supervisory Management.*   **C47**

NEBSM Management Introductory Award   *Introductory Award in Supervisory Management.*   **C47**

Negotiation Skills   *Basic skills of Negotiation & Conflict Management & possible SCOTVEC Certification.*   **C2 D5 G16 S6**

Office Technology & Administration - NC   *SCOTVEC/NCM in Office Technology & Administration.*   **L68**

Operational Research - MSc   *MSc in Operational Research.*   **S105**

Operations & Industrial Management - IIM Certificate   *Certificate from the Institute of Industrial Managers.*   **S15**

Operations & Industrial Management - IIM Diploma   *PgD from the Institute of Industrial Managers.*   **S15**

Operations & Industrial Management - IIM Post Graduate Diploma *PgD in operations & industrial management.*   **S15**

Operations Management - Diploma *Diploma in Operations Management.*   **S87**

Oral Presentation (SCOTVEC) *SCOTVEC/NCM in Oral Presentation.*   **L5**

Oral Presentation Skills *Improved oral presentation skills.*   **C22**

Organisation & Methods (M2) *Knowledge of method study.*   **S94**

Organising Work *No formal outcome.*   **B6**

Practical Recruitment, Interviewing & Selection Skills (M9) *Interviewing & selection Skills.*   **S94**

Practical Talking Skills (SCOTVEC) *SCOTVEC/NCM in Practical Talking Skills.*   **L5**

Practical Telephone Skills (SCOTVEC) *SCOTVEC/NCM in Practical Telephone Skills.*   **L5**

Practical Writing Skills (SCOTVEC) *SCOTVEC/NCM in Practical Writing Skills.*   **L5**

Presentation Skills *No formal outcome.*   **B6 G16 L6 S57**

Presentation Skills - Team *Increased confidence in a range of presentation situations.*   **G22**

Presentation Skills Course *Certificate of Attendance.*   **B6**

Presenting with Confidence *Improvement of Presentation skills.*   **H40**

Problem Solving & Creativity *Problem solving & how it can be improved.*   **G16**

Production & Inventory Management - BPICS Diploma *British Production & Inventory Control Society Diploma.*   **S15**

Project Management - Pertmaster (P10) *All aspects of project control & management.*   **S94**

Project Management Techniques - I *Training in project management.*   **M8**

Project Management Techniques - II *Improving project management techniques.*   **M8**

Project Management Techniques - III *Entering, monitoring & reporting projects.*   **M8**

Public Relations *No formal outcome.*   **S87**

Public Sector Management - Certificate *Certificate in Public Service Management.*   **S8**

Public Sector Management - Diploma *Diploma in Public Service Management.*   **S8**

Purchasing & Supply Management - (Professional Stage) *Chartered Institute of Purchasing & Supply - Certificate.*   **F8**

Purchasing & Supply Management - an Introduction *Chartered Institute of Purchasing & Supply - Introduction.*   **F8**

Quality - BS5750 Awareness Course *Quality - BS5750 awareness.*   **D5**

Quality - Cost of Quality *Quality - ability to cost Quality procedures.*   **D5**

Quality - Internal Auditing of Quality Systems - DTI *Quality - Department of Trade & Industry Certificate.*   **D5**

Quality - Total Quality Management *Understanding of the implications & procedures involved in Total Quality Management.*   **D5**

Reception Skills *Skills, knowledge & attitude appropriate to members of staff working in the reception.*   **H42**

Reception/Telephone Techniques *Non-certificated course.*   **S14**

Recruitment & Selection *No formal outcome.*   **S87**

Report Writing *No formal outcome.*   **B6 L27**

Report Writing for Managers *Improved report writing skills & increased organisational efficiency.*   **D5**

S/NVQ in Management *S/NVQ in Management at levels 3,4 & 5.*   **S138**

SCOTVEC/MCI First Level Management *SVQ Level 4 or units towards.*   **C47**

SCOTVEC/MCI Supervisory Management *SVQ Level 3 or units towards.*   **C47**

Secretarial Section Short Course Provision *College Certificate.*   **L27**

Selection Interviewing *Skills for interviewing within the context of a systematic selection procedure.*   **G16**

Selection Interviewing Skills *Certificate of Attendance.*   **B6**

Self Appraisal Workshop *College Certificate.*   **L18**

Self Presentation & Public Speaking *No formal outcome..*   **G16**

Selling in the Oil Industry (Sep 11-13 Aberdeen) *No formal outcome.*   **G38**

Service Sector Management - BA *BA in Service Sector Management.*   **S58**

Service Sector Management - BA (Hons) *BA (Hons) in Service Sector Management.*   **S58**

Setting Goals *Skills needed to set goals properly for the benefit of organisations.*   **L6**

Setting Goals & Objectives *No formal outcome.*   **B6**

Short Courses & Consultancy *Various courses available.*   **D5**

Strategic Planning *No formal outcome.*   **B6**

Stress & Stress Management   *Managing stress in the workplace.*   **G16**

Stress Management   *Improved personal effectiveness & well being.*   **D5 G17 S6 S57**

Successful Business Presentations (Oct 1 1 - 13 Glasgow)   *No formal outcome.*   **G38**

Successful Negotiating   *Improving skills in negotiating.*   **H40**

Supervisory Management   *NEBSM Certificate.*   **S144**

Supervisory Management - Certificate NEBSM   *Developing & improving supervisory skills.*   **F8**

Supervisory Management - NEBSM   *National Examining Board for Supervisory Management Certificate.*   **D5**

Supervisory Management Course   *Certificate of Attendance.*   **B6**

Supervisory Management Skills   *Knowledge, skills & attitudes appropriate to the first line supervisor or junior manager.*   **H42**

Systematic Selection & Selection Interviewing Skills   *Skills required for effective selection interviewing.*   **G16**

Task Oriented Performance Strategies (TOPS)   *Skills in implementing a clearly defined company strategy.*   **L6**

Team Building   *No formal outcome.*   **B6 S87**

Team Building Seminar   *Certificate of Attendance.*   **B6**

Team Work   *No formal outcome.*   **B6**

Teambuilding   *Possible SCOTVEC certification.*   **D5**

Teams & Team-Building   *Understanding of the nature of teams & how to develop effective teamwork.*   **G16**

Telephone Skills   *Training in telephone techniques & skills.*   **H30**

The Assertive Woman At Work   *Development of assertiveness skills.*   **C41**

The Managing Context - HN Unit   *2 Credits towards a HNC in Management Studies.*   **C23**

The Practice of Counselling   *Preparing, conducting and evaluating a counselling interview..*   **G16**

Time & Self Management   *No formal outcome.*   **B6**

Time Management   *Certificate of Attendance.*   **B6 G16 L18 M8 S6 S57 S87**

Time Management for Managers   *Increased personal efficiency & organizational effectiveness.*   **D5**

Time, Stress & Crisis Management   *Coping with time, & dealing positively with stress & crisis.*   **C2 C35 T8**

Using Assertiveness   *Skills and methods of assertiveness.*   **L6**

Various Courses Available   *Company Certificate awarded.*   **S149**

Verbal Communication   *English language skills in a working environment.*   **H42**

Women into Management   *No formal outcome.*   **S142 S147**

Working with People & Teams - HN Unit   *SCOTVEC Higher National Unit.*   **L5**

Workplace Education - Personal Development   *SCOTVEC certificate. Skills relevant to each individual.*   **C16**

Written Communication   *English language skills useful in a working environment.*   **H42**

MARKETING, SALES, ADVERTISING, PUBLISHING, DISTRIBUTION

Advanced Sales Skills (Dec 7 - 8 Edinburgh)   *No formal outcome.*   **G38**

Advertising   *Effective advertising techniques.*   **H47**

Advertising & Promotion   *How to get your message across to your customers.*   **C2 C35 H3 T8**

Advertising & Promotions   *No formal outcome.*   **S142**

Advertising & Public Relations Skills   *Development of successful advertising & public relation techniques.*   **C22**

Advertising - 63112 - SCOTVEC/NC   *SCOTVEC/NCM.*   **T23**

Advertising - Diploma   *Diploma in Advertising.*   **S14**

Advertising Copywriting - HNC   *SCOTVEC/HNC in Advertising Copywriting.*   **S75**

Advertising, Marketing & Public Relations - SCOTVEC/HNC   *SCOTVEC/HNC in Advertising, Marketing & Public Relations.*   **G17**

Applied Consumer Studies - SCOTVEC/HNC   *SCOTVEC/HNC.*   **G17**

Association of Supervisors in Purchasing & Supply Cert. in Purchasing & Stores   *1st & 2nd Certificates in Purchasing & Stores.*   **S14**

Basic Marketing   *Certificate of Attendance.*   **B6**

Basic Retail Skills - 93124 - SCOTVEC/NC
SCOTVEC/NC.   **T23**

Building Profits From Marketing (6 Days)
Introduction to the principles of marketing.   **S132**

Business Administration - HNC Individual Units
SCOTVEC/HNC in Business Administration.   **L81**

Business Administration with Retailing - HNC
*SCOTVEC/HNC in Business Administration with
Retailing.*   **S13**

Business Skill Seminar - Direct Marketing
Development of skills in Marketing.   **C24**

Business Skill Seminar - Personal Selling Skills
Development of skills in Selling.   **C24**

Business Skill Seminar Customer Care
Development of skills in customer care.   **C24**

Business Skill Seminar More Profit Fast
*Development of skills in profit making & customer
loyalty.*   **C24**

Business Skill Seminar Practical Marketing
Development of skills in marketing.   **C24**

Business Skills Seminars   *Development of skills
necessary to operate a small business.*   **C2**

Business Studies - NC   *SCOTVEC/NC in
Business Studies.*   **S11**

Business Studies Section Short Course Provision
College Certificate.   **L19**

Business Studies with Purchasing - HNC   *HNC in
Business Studies with Purchasing.*   **S14**

Business Studies: Marketing (P/T Degree Unit)
Accumulation of units leading towards a degree.
C42

Certificate in Retailing - SCOTVEC Level I VQ
Certificate in Retailing at Level I.   **C9**

Certificate in Retailing - SCOTVEC Level II VQ
Certificate in Retailing at Level II.   **C9**

Certificate in Retailing - YT - SCOTVEC Level III
VQ   *Certificate in Retailing at Level III.*   **C9**

Certificate in Warehousing - YT C & G Level I VQ
Certificate in Warehousing at Level I.   **C9**

Certificate in Warehousing - YT C & G Level II VQ
Certificate in Warehousing at Level II.   **C9**

Certificate of Marketing - CIM   *Chartered Institute
of Marketing's Certificate of Marketing.*   **L68**

Certificate of the Chartered Institute of Marketing
Certificate of the Chartered Institute Of Marketing.
L27

Chartered Institute of Marketing (CIM)
Professional Qualification. Certificate in Marketing.
G17

Chartered Institute of Marketing Certificate
*Chartered Institute of Marketing's 'Certificate in
Marketing'.*   **F8**

Chartered Institute of Marketing Diploma
Chartered Institute of Marketing Diploma.   **F5**

Chartered Institute of Purchase & Supply:
Foundation Stage   *Chartered Institute of
Purchase & Supply Certificate.*   **L5 S14**

Chartered Institute of Purchasing & Supply -
Professional Stage   *CIPS Professional Stage
Certificate.*   **S14**

Communication Studies (CAM Certificate)
*Communication, Advertising & Marketing
Foundation Certificate.*   **L68**

Communication, Advertising & Marketing
Education Foundation - Certificate   *CAM
Certificate.*   **S14**

Communication, Advertising & Marketing
Education Foundation - Diploma   *Diploma in
Communication, Advertising & Marketing.*   **S14**

Computer Aided Estimating & Tendering for
Building Works   *College Certificate.*   **L5**

Customer Care   *Achieving customer satisfaction.*
**C2 C35 D5 D6 H3 H30 H42 H51 M8 S6 S57
S87 T8**

Customer Care - Reception Skills   *Skills in serving
the customer at reception.*   **D5**

Customer Care - Telephone Skills   *Representing
the organisation & serving the customer when
using the telephone.*   **D5**

Customer Contact - 93125 - SCOTVEC/NC
SCOTVEC/NC.   **T23**

Customer Relations   *Knowledge of customer
relations.*   **L18**

Customer Relations & Care   *Certificate of
Attendance.*   **B6**

Customer Skills Course   *SCOTVEC/NC.*   **S78**

Design for Marketing 1 - HN Unit   *SCOTVEC
Higher National Unit.*   **L5**

Developing & Using an Effective Marketing
Database   *Enhanced sales support skills.*   **S139**

Diploma in Distribution Studies   *Diploma in
Distribution Studies.*   **S87**

Diploma in Management & Diploma in
Management with Marketing   *Diploma courses.*
S14

Diploma in Marketing - CIM   *Chartered Institute of
Marketing Diploma in Marketing.*   **L68**

Direct Marketing   *Knowledge to produce an
effective direct mail and/or telemarketing
campaign.*   **C2 T8**

Distribution & Display - NC   *SCOTVEC/NCMs in
Distribution & Display.*   **S11**

Distribution - Part-Time NC   *SCOTVEC/NC
(Distribution studies).*   **L81**

Distribution Studies - HNC   *HNC in Distribution
Studies.*   **S14**

Distribution Supervisory Management - HNC
SCOTVEC/HNC.   **L5**

Distributive Administration - NC   *SCOTVEC/NC in
Distributive Administration.*   **S14**

Effective Advertising & Sales Promotion *Advertising, public relations & sales promotion on a promotional campaign.* **S57**

Essential Selling Skills *Skills in selling.* **H40**

European Studies with Marketing - HNC *SCOTVEC/HNC in European Studies with Marketing.* **S91**

Eurospeak *Communicate more effectively with foreign visitors & business associates.* **T9**

Export Marketing *Skills in marketing your business abroad.* **C2 T8**

Exporting with Marketing *SCOTVEC/HNC in Exporting with Marketing.* **S8**

Face to Face Selling (1 Day) *No formal outcome.* **S132**

Fashion Marketing *Leading to HNC in Knitwear Design & Production.* **B3**

Field Sales Management Part 2 (Advanced) *No formal outcome.* **G38**

Financial Aspects of Marketing *Chartered Institute of Marketing's Certificate in Marketing.* **F8**

Finding New Products *Skills in identifying and developing new markets.* **T8**

Floristry - SCOTVEC *SCOTVEC Certificate.* **B2**

Institute of Export - Professional Examinations *Institute of Export - Professional Examinations.* **S14**

Institute of Purchasing & Supply Professional Examinations *Membership of the Institute of Purchasing & Supply.* **S14**

Introduction to Distribution - NC *NC in an Introduction to Distribution Programme.* **S14**

Introduction to Marketing (SCOTVEC) *SCOTVEC/NCM.* **L5**

Knitwear Design & Marketing *No formal outcome.* **B3**

Management Education & Development - the Institute for Retail Studies *Practical experience in retailing.* **C44**

Management Studies (Distribution Specialism) - HNC *SCOTVEC/HNC in Management Studies.* **L36**

Management with Marketing - Diploma *Diploma in Management with Marketing.* **S14**

Managing the Marketing Plan *No formal outcome.* **S87**

Market Research *SCOTVEC/NCM.* **C49**

Market Research Society - Diploma *Diploma in Market Research.* **S14**

Marketing *Certificate of Attendance.* **B6 S110**

Marketing & Promotion - NC *SCOTVEC/NC in Marketing & Promotion.* **S87**

Marketing - Advanced Certificate (Effective Management for Marketing) *Management skills in a marketing context.* **G17**

Marketing - Advanced Certificate (Management Information) *Skills in setting up and controlling budgets & marketing systems.* **G17**

Marketing - Advanced Certificate (Promotional Practice) *Promotional practices & industry.* **G17**

Marketing - Chartered Institute of Marketing Diploma *Chartered Institute of Marketing - Diploma in Marketing.* **L59 S14**

Marketing - Customised Training Programmes *Improved performance in marketing skills.* **L4**

Marketing - Diploma *Diploma in Marketing.* **G15**

Marketing - HNC *SCOTVEC/HNC in Marketing.* **F8 S5 S14 S87**

Marketing - HND *SCOTVEC/HND in Marketing.* **S14 S87**

Marketing - Knitwear *No formal outcome.* **B3**

Marketing - MSc/PgD *MSc/Postgraduate Diploma in Marketing.* **S101**

Marketing - NC *SCOTVEC/NC in Marketing.* **S14**

Marketing 1 - HN Unit *SCOTVEC Higher National Unit.* **L5**

Marketing Design - HNC *SCOTVEC/HNC.* **L5**

Marketing for Managers *Principles of marketing in private & public sectors.* **S57 S87**

Marketing for Non-Marketing Personnel (M7) *Understanding the potential of marketing techniques.* **S94**

Marketing Overhaul *Skills in developing a Marketing Plan.* **T8**

Marketing Skills & Service Quality *No formal outcome.* **B6**

Marketing Techniques *Improved marketing techniques.* **S6**

Marketing Your Business *Accrual of market research skills & techniques.* **C2 C35 T8**

Media Presentation Skills *Improved communication & presentation skills.* **C22**

More Profit - Fast! *Enables companies to increase their profits by correct pricing.* **C2**

More Profit...Fast! *Skills in setting prices & negotiating prices with customers.* **T8**

National Assoc.of Goldsmiths Preliminary & Diploma Courses in Retail Jewellery *A Diploma in Retail Jewellery.* **S14**

Operational Salesmanship - Certificate *Institute of Sales & Marketing Management - Certificate in Operational Salesmanship.* **S14**

Personal Selling Skills *Greater confidence in face-to-face selling techniques.* **C2 C35 H51 T8**

Practical Marketing   *Experience in market research questionnaire design & implementation.*
                                           C2 C35 T8

Practical Marketing for SME's   *No formal outcome.*   **S145**

Preparing & Marketing Plan   *Practical benefit.*
                                                 S139

Pricing for Profit   *Setting prices and setting them effectively.*   **H3**

Print Sales & Marketing - HNC   *SCOTVEC/HNC in Print Sales & Marketing.*   **S68**

Printing (Administration) - NC   *SCOTVEC/NC in Printing (Administration).*   **S68**

Production & Inventory Management - BPICS Diploma   *British Production & Inventory Control Society Diploma.*   **S15**

Public Relations - Be Your Own P.R. Person   *No formal outcome.*   **S142**

Public Relations Skills (SCOTVEC)   *SCOTVEC/NCM in Public Relations Skills.*   **L5**

Purchasing & Supply Management   *Graduate/Corporate Membership of the Institute of Purchasing & Supply.*   **L59**

Purchasing & Supply Management - (Professional Stage)   *CIPS (Professional Stage).*   **F8**

Purchasing & Supply Management - an Introduction   *CIPS - Introduction to Purchasing & Supply Management.*   **F8**

Purchasing & Supply Management - Certificate   *Certificate in Purchasing & Supply Management.*
                                                  S5

Purchasing, Distribution & Stock Control - Short Contract Courses   *Various courses available.*
                                                 L81

Reception Skills   *Skills, knowledge & attitude appropriate to members of staff working in the reception role.*   **H42**

Retail - SVQ Level II   *SVQ level II in Retail.*   **F5**

Retail Business - HNC   *SCOTVEC/HNC in Retail Business.*   **S8**

Retail Display Design - SCOTVEC National Certificate   *SCOTVEC/NC.*   **G17**

Retail Distribution - HNC   *SCOTVEC/HNC in Retail Distribution.*   **F5**

Retail Distribution - NC   *SCOTVEC/NC.*   **T1**

Retail Marketing - HNC   *SCOTVEC/HNC in Retail Marketing.*   **S14**

Retail Merchandising (Introduction) - 93099 - SCOTVEC/NC   *SCOTVEC/NC.*   **G6**

Retail Training - C & G VQ Level I & II   *Development of skills in retail.*   **C8**

Retailing - NC   *NC in a Retailing Programme.*
                                                 S14

Retailing - YT/SVQ Level II   *Successful candidates will gain a SVQ Level II (SF0703201) in Retailing.*   **L84**

Sales & Marketing - Short Contract Courses   *Various courses available.*   **L81**

Sales Development Course   *No formal outcome.*
                                                 S132

Sales Promotion Workshop   *Skills in choosing & making the best use of various forms of advertising media.*   **T8**

Sales Training Course (Dec 4 - 6 Glasgow).   *No formal outcome.*   **G38**

Selling by Telephone (1 Day)   *No formal outcome.*
                                                 S132

Selling Skills   *Understanding the sales process & using basic sales techniques.*   **H3**

Selling Skills (Introduction) - 93126 - SCOTVEC/NC   *SCOTVEC/NC.*   **T23**

Selling Techniques   *Awareness of issues involved in selling.*   **H47**

Selling Workshop   *Skills in all aspects of selling.*
                                                  T8

Service Sector Management - BA   *BA in Service Sector Management.*   **S58**

Service Sector Management - BA (Hons)   *BA (Hons) in Service Sector Management.*   **S58**

Stock Control - SCOTVEC/NC   *SCOTVEC/NC.*
                                                 T23

Storage & Warehousing   *SCOTVEC Modules in Storage & Warehousing.*   **S87**

Supervisory Management Skills   *Knowledge, skills & attitudes appropriate to the first line supervisor or junior manager.*   **H42**

Telephone Sales   *Essential skills for effective tele-sales.*   **H3**

Telesales   *Knowledge of selling skills, communication skills & telephone technique.*
                                                 L27

The Chartered Institute of Marketing Diploma   *Diploma in Marketing (Dip M).*   **L54**

The Fundamentals of Marketing   *Understand marketing.*   **S139**

The Fundamentals of Selling   *Improved performance.*   **S139**

Tourism - NC   *SCOTVEC/NC in Tourism.*   **C10**

Trading Standards - Diploma   *Diploma in Trading Standards.*   **S63**

Warehousing & Transportation - 63106 - SCOTVEC/NC   *SCOTVEC/NC.*   **T23**

Warehousing & Wholesaling YT/SVQ Level II   *SVQ Level II.*   **L84**

Wholesaling, Warehousing & Stores   *NVQ Level 2.*   **G39**

Wholesaling - NC   *NC in a Wholesaling Programme.*   **S14**

Women into Business   *Skills necessary to operate a small business/return to work.*   **C2**

OFFICE AND SECRETARIAL SKILLS

'Two Fingers' to Touch Typing Conversion Course 4.51/Typing Crash Course   *Skills in touch typing.*
H41

Access to Higher Education - SCOTVEC Computing (SCE O/S Equivalent)   *SCOTVEC.*
D5

Administration - SVQ Level 3   *6 credits towards HNC in Office Administration.*   **F13**

Adult Secretarial Courses   *Ability to use a wordprocessor for inputting, storing, revising & retrieving documents.*   **F5**

Advanced Displaywrite 4   *College Certificate.*
L27

Advanced Microsoft Word   *College Certificate.*
L27

Advanced Wordstar 6   *College Certificate.*   **L27**

Ami - Part 1   *Certificate of Competence.*   **B6**

Ami - Part 2   *Certificate of Competence.*   **B6**

Ami Pro - Part 1   *Certificate of Competence.*   **B6**

Ami Pro - Part 2   *Certificate of Competence.*   **B6**

Ami Pro for Windows - Introduction   *ITec certificate.*   **H17**

An Introduction to Displaywrite 4   *College Certificate.*   **L27**

An Introduction to Microsoft Word   *College Certificate.*   **L27**

An Introduction to Word Processing   *Knowledge of basic computer concepts & word processing.*
L27

An Introduction to Wordstar 6   *College Certificate.*
L27

Audio Typewriting - Module   *SCOTVEC/NCM - Audio Typewriting.*   **F3**

Audio Typing - TFW   *Development of skills in audio typing.*   **C8**

Beginners Shorthand   *Skills gained in shorthand.*
S81

Beginners Shorthand - NC   *SCOTVEC/NC.*   **C23**

Business & Office Technology - Diploma - NVQ Level II (C&G) - Training for Work   *C & G Diploma.*
L32

Business / Computing Short Courses *SCOTVEC/NC.*   **H30**

Business Administration   *SVQ Level 2 or units towards.*   **C47**

Business Administration (Finance) - SVQ Level II *SVQ Level II.*   **S98**

Business Administration (Secretarial) - SVQ Level II   *SVQ Level II.*   **S98**

Business Administration - HNC   *SCOTVEC/HNC.*
S3 S79

Business Administration - Skillseekers/ NVQ Levels I-II   *NVQ Pitman Levels I-II Certificate.*
S83 S84 S85 S86

Business Administration - SVQ Level I   *SCOTVEC SVQ Level I in Business Administration.*   **C22**

Business Administration - SVQ Level II *SCOTVEC SVQ Level II in Business Administration.*   **C22**

Business Administration - SVQ Level III *SCOTVEC SVQ Level III in Business Administration.*   **C22**

Business Administration - SVQ   *SVQ in Business Administration with Financial, Administrative or Secretarial options.*   **L68**

Business Administration - TFW - RSA VQ Level II *Skills in Business Administration.*   **C8**

Business Administration - YT RSA or LCCI Level II *RSA or LCCI Level II Certificate in Business Administration.*   **C9**

Business Administration - YT RSA or LCCI Level III   *RSA or LCCI Level III Certificate in Business Administration.*   **C9**

Business Administration 1   *City & Guilds VQ.*
H54

Business Administration/Medical Reception - YT/SVQ Level II   *SCOTVEC, SVQ Level II Certificate.*   **S79**

Business Computing - NC (GSVQ II) *SCOTVEC/NC - GSVQ II.*   **F8**

Business French - European Social Fund   *Skills necessary to communicate in the French business environment.*   **H18**

Business Information Systems - HNC *SCOTVEC/HNC in Business Information Systems.*
S15

Business Letter Writing   *Skills needed to write succesful business letters.*   **H30**

Business Studies - SCOTVEC Modules *SCOTVEC Modules in Business Studies.*   **D8**

Business Studies Section Short Course Provision *College Certificate.*   **L27**

Business Technology Skills for Women   *No formal outcome.*   **S123**

Business Writing 1   *Basic skills & experience in writing business documents.*   **S14**

Business Writing 2   *Skills & experience in writing business documents.*   **S14**

Business, Secretarial & Computing Studies - Skillseekers/SVQ Levels I-III *SCOTVEC modules Levels I-III.* **S98**

Business/Secretarial Studies - NC *SCOTVEC/NC in Business/Secretarial Studies.* **S76**

Communication & Personal Skills - Letter Writing *Improved communication & personal skills - letter writing.* **D5**

Computer / Technology Courses for Industry *Various courses available.* **H31 H46 H53**

Computer Application Package (Word Processing) - 91100 - SCOTVEC Nat Cert *SCOTVEC/NC.* **T23**

Computer Application Package (Wordprocessing) - Module *SCOTVEC/NCM - Computer Application Package.* **F8 L5 L30**

Computer Applications - Word Processing NC *SCOTVEC/NC.* **C23**

Computer Applications - Word Processing NC (Scotvec) *SCOTVEC/NC.* **L5**

Computer Applications : Word Processing Word Perfect (SCOTVEC) *SCOTVEC/NCM.* **L27**

Computer Applications: Wordprocessing - Wordperfect 5.1 (SCOTVEC) *SCOTVEC/NCM 91100.* **L5**

Computer Literacy & Information Technology - RSA Level 1 *RSA Foundation level qualification.* **H26**

Computer Programming - NC *SCOTVEC/NC - GSVQ III Progression is possible to the HNC/D.* **F8**

Computer Training *Training is available in various computer functions.* **H16**

Computing *Specific skills are developed in specialist areas according to the needs of participants.* **F8**

Computing & Word Processing *Experience in computing & word processing.* **C16**

Computing - NC *SCOTVEC/NC. Progression is possible to the HNC/D in Computing.* **F8 S15**

Computing - NC (GSVQ Information Technology) *SCOTVEC/NC & a VQ in Computing.* **B6**

Computing Courses *Participants will have gained skills in basic computer applications.* **H28**

Computing Section Short Course Provision *College Certificate.* **L27**

Customer Care - Reception Skills *Customer Care - Understanding of how to best serve the customer at reception.* **D5**

Customer Care - Telephone Skills *How to best represent the organisation & serve the customer when using the telephone.* **D5**

Displaywrite Assistant *College Certificate.* **L27**

Document Processing - HN Unit *1 credit towards a HNC in Computing.* **C23 F8 L5**

Effective Business Letter Writing *Skills in writing better Business Letters.* **M8**

Efficiency in the Office/Secretarial Development *Effective organisation in the office.* **M8**

Financial Record Keeping - 82250 *SCOTVEC/NCM in Financial Record Keeping.* **D6**

Flexible Updating & Retraining Provision in Secretarial Skills N C *SCOTVEC/NC.* **L27 L28**

French - Telephone Receptionists *A Certificate of Attendance.* **B6**

German - Telephone Receptionists *A Certificate of Attendance.* **B6**

Graphic Communication - SCE H Grade *Scottish Examination Board Certificate in Graphic Communication at H Grade.* **D8**

Individual Training for Wordperfect *Participants will gain a knowledge of the computer package of their choice.* **H41**

Information & Office Management - SCOTVEC/HND *SCOTVEC/HND.* **C10 F5 F8 G17 H49 H53**

Information Technology - GSVQ *GSVQ Certificate in Information Technology.* **S71**

Information Technology - Office Applications - NC *SCOTVEC/NC.* **C23**

Information Technology Courses *SCOTVEC or RSA Certificates.* **H46 H48**

Information Technology: Office Applications (SCOTVEC) *SCOTVEC/NCM in Information Technology: Office Applications.* **L1 L3 L83**

Intensive Secretarial Skills Course for Graduates/Adult Returners. *SCOTVEC/NCM.* **L68**

Intensive Secretarial Skills for Graduates/Adult Returners *3 SCOTVEC modules & a College certificate.* **L68**

Introduction to Computer Application Package (Database) - 81098 *SCOTVEC/NCM.* **D5**

Introduction to Computer Application Package (Spreadsheet) - 91099 *SCOTVEC/NCM.* **D5**

Introduction to Computer Application Packages (SCOTVEC) *SCOTVEC/NCM.* **L3**

Introduction to Computer Application Packages - 81095 *SCOTVEC/NCM.* **D5**

Introduction to Computers *SCOTVEC Module in Computers.* **M1**

Introduction to Keyboarding - TFW *Development of skills in keyboarding.* **C8**

Introduction to Office Management - NC *SCOTVEC/NC.* **C23**

Introduction to Windows/Word Processing *No formal outcome.* **B2**

Introduction to Word Processing *No formal outcome.* **B6 C12 G7 H3 S81**

Introduction to Word Processing (SCOTVEC) *SCOTVEC/NCM Introduction to Word Processing.* **L1 L3 L5 L31 L83**

Introduction to Word Processing - (Wordperfect 5.1) - NCM *SCOTVEC/NC.* **H53**

Introduction to Word Processing *Non-certificated course though an ITec certificate is available.* **H17**

Introduction to Word Processing - Module *SCOTVEC Module - Introduction to Word Processing.* **F1 F2 F9 F10**

Introduction to Word Processing - NC *SCOTVEC/NC.* **C23 C45**

Introduction to Word Processing - NCM (6180090) *SCOTVEC/NCM.* **H29**

Introduction to Word Processing Skills *Knowledge of Word Processing using Wordperfect 5.1.* **H31**

Introduction to Word Processing Using Word Perfect *SCOTVEC/NC.* **L27**

Introduction to Wordprocessing *College Certificate if required.* **L68**

Introductory to Wordprocessing *Students will gain skills & knowledge in Word Processing.* **S70**

Italian - Telephone Receptionists *A Certificate of Attendance.* **B6**

Keyboard Skills - Module *SCOTVEC module in Keyboarding.* **D3**

Keyboard Skills Using a Computer *SCOTVEC Module Using a Keyboard.* **T9**

Keyboarding *No formal outcome.* **B8**

Keyboarding Skills / Text Processing - NCM *SCOTVEC/NC.* **H53**

Keyboarding/Simple Word Processing *Basic skills in word processing.* **T10**

Keyboarding/Text Processing - Intermediate *SCOTVEC Module.* **F3**

Keyboarding/Text Processing - Introductory *SCOTVEC Module.* **F3**

Learn to Keyboard for the Unemployed *Certificate of Attendance.* **H17**

Learn Windows Software *Certificate of Attendance.* **H17**

Legal Secretarial Studies - NC *SCOTVEC/NC in Legal Secretarial Studies.* **S71**

Legal Secretaries - NC *Successful students will be awarded with SCOTVEC/NC.* **S75**

Letter Writing for Managers *Possible SCOTVEC Certification.* **D5**

Management & Office Studies - SCE H Grade or CSYS *SCE at H Grade or Certificate of Sixth Year Studies.* **D3**

Medical Secretarial - NC *SCOTVEC/NC in Medical Secretarial.* **S87**

Medical Terminology (SCOTVEC) *SCOTVEC/NCM in Medical Terminology (Double Module).* **L68**

Microsoft Word - Advanced *ITec certification is given on completion of course.* **H17**

Microsoft Word - Introduction *ITec certification is given on completion of course.* **H17**

Microsoft Word for Windows 2.0 *Skills useful in a Windows environment.* **M8**

Multimate IV *Skills gained in the use of Multimate IV.* **S6**

Office & Information Studies - SEB S Grade *An SEB S Grade in Office & Information Studies.* **B11**

Office Administration *SCOTVEC Higher National Unit 6400150 credit value 3.* **D5**

Office Administration & Technology - NC *SCOTVEC/NC in Office Administration & Technology studies.* **L81**

Office Administration & Technology - NCMs *SCOTVEC/NC in Office Administration & Technology.* **L81**

Office Administration (Day Release) - HNC *A HNC in Office Administration.* **T9**

Office Administration (Medical) - HNC *SCOTVEC/HNC.* **H53**

Office Administration - HNC *SCOTVEC/HNC.* **B6 C10 C23 F5 F13 H49 H53 L5 L81 M7 S3 S5 S8 S13 S14 S15 S16 S71 S75 S79 S81 S87 S91**

Office Administration - HNC Individual Units *SCOTVEC/HNC in Office Administration.* **L81**

Office Administration - NC *SCOTVEC/NC in Office Administration.* **B2 B3 B6 S79 S87 S91**

Office Administration - SVQ *SVQ in Office Administration.* **G2 S75**

Office Administration - Years 1 & 2 - HNC *SCOTVEC/HNC in Office Administration.* **C22**

Office Administration HNC *SCOTVEC/HNC.* **L27**

Office Administration with Medical Options - HNC *SCOTVEC/HNC in Office Administration with Medical Options.* **S91**

Office Information Processing - NC *SCOTVEC/NC in Office Information Processing.* **S10**

Office Management *SCOTVEC Higher National Unit 6400170 credit value 2.* **D5**

Office Skills *Up to 6 SCOTVEC Modules.* **S144**

Office Skills & Administration - Evening Classes *SCOTVEC/NCMs, HNUs, RSA Certificate & Certificate of Institute of Administrative Management.* **L68**

Office Skills - NC *SCOTVEC/NC in Office Skills.* **S78 S87 S88**

Office Skills - Skillseekers/SVQ Levels I-V *SCOTVEC modules.* **S20**

Office Studies - HNC *HNC In Office Studies.* **T1**

Office Studies - HND *HND In Office Studies.* **T1**

Office Studies - NC *SCOTVEC/NC in Office Studies.* **C10 T1**

Office Systems *Skills & knowledge required to plan, design & implement efficient & effective office systems.* **H42**

Office Technology & Administration - NC *SCOTVEC/NCMs in Office Technology & Administration.* **L68 S16**

Office Technology & Administration NC *SCOTVEC/NC.* **L27 S16**

Office Technology & Administration Workshops *Individual SCOTVEC modules or Higher National Units.* **T9**

Office Technology - NC *SCOTVEC/NC in Office Technology.* **S14**

Office/Secretarial/Administration/ Information - NCMs / HN Units *SCOTVEC/NC or Higher National Units.* **H53**

Pitmans Shorthand Course in Speed Development - NC *SCOTVEC/NC.* **T1**

Producing Business Documents - HN Units *2 credits towards a HNC in Office Technology.* **C23**

Producing Complex Business Documents - HN Unit *1 credit towards a HNC in Office Technology.* **C23**

Producing Text (Word Processing) *Successful candidates will receive SCOTVEC Module 6180011.* **M1**

Producing Text - Module *Participants will gain the SCOTVEC/NCM: Textprocessing 3.* **F12**

Reception & Telephone Techniques *College Certificate.* **L27**

Reception - NC *SCOTVEC/NC.* **C23**

Reception Skills *Skills in reception duties.* **H30 H42**

Reception/Telephone Techniques *Non-certificated course.* **S14**

Receptionist *Certificate of Attendance.* **B6**

Record Keeping *Skills & knowledge appropriate to keeping office records.* **H42**

RSA Shorthand - Teeline *RSA Certificate will be awarded.* **B6**

RSA Typewriting Skills 1 *RSA Certificate.* **L5**

RSA Typewriting Skills 2 *RSA Certificate.* **L5**

RSA Typewriting Skills 3 *RSA Certificate.* **L5**

RSA Word Processing *RSA Certificate will be awarded.* **B3**

Rural Secretarial Studies - Accreditation of Prior Learning *SCOTVEC/NC for Rural Secretarial Studies.* **F4**

SEC Studies with Word Processing - SCE *SCE Higher - SEC Studies with Word Processing.* **F7**

Secretarial & Computing Studies - NC *SCOTVEC/NC listing the modules studied & learning outcomes achieved.* **S98**

Secretarial - Training for Work *SCOTVEC/NCM.* **S98**

Secretarial Section Short Course Provision *College Certificate.* **L27**

Secretarial Skill Subjects *SCOTVEC or RSA certificate of completion.* **M7**

Secretarial Skills - NC *SCOTVEC/NC in Secretarial Skills.* **L28 S5**

Secretarial Studies & Information Technology - NC *SCOTVEC/NC in Secretarial Studies & Information Technology.* **F13**

Secretarial Studies (Legal) - NC *SCOTVEC/NC in Secretarial Studies (Legal).* **G17 S91**

Secretarial Studies (Medical) - NC *SCOTVEC/NC in Secretarial Studies (Medical).* **S91**

Secretarial Studies - NC *SCOTVEC/NC in Secretarial Studies.* **S10**

Secretarial Studies - NC *SCOTVEC/NC in Secretarial Studies.* **S71 S78 S81 S91 S98**

Secretarial Studies - NC (3 Day Programme) *SCOTVEC/NC in Secretarial Studies (3 Day Programme).* **S78**

Secretarial Studies - SCE H Grade *SCE H Grade in Secretarial Studies.*
**C1 C4 C5 C6 C7 C20 C21 C25 C26 C27
C28 C29 C30 C34 C36 C46 D8 L1**

Secretarial Studies - SCE H Grade (Word Processing Option) *SCE at H Grade in Secretarial Studies.* **D7**

Secretarial Studies - SCE H Grade or CSYS *SCE at H Grade or Certificate of Sixth Year Studies.* **D3**

Secretarial Studies - SEB H Grade *SEB H Grade in Secretarial Studies.* **B10**

Secretarial Studies for Beginners *SCOTVEC.* **B1**

Secretarial/Administration/Computing - NCM / HN Units *SCOTVEC/NC or Higher National Units.* **H53**

Secretarial/Clerical - NC *SCOTVEC/NC in Secretarial/Clerical.* **C22**

Secretary/Linguist - SCOTVEC/NC *SCOTVEC/NC.*   **G17**

Shorthand   *NCM. Practical skills are gained in Shorthand.*   **F8 G30 T1**

Shorthand - 6180201   *SCOTVEC/NCM in Shorthand Transcription.*   **D6**

Shorthand - Beginners   *Basic knowledge of shorthand skills.*   **H53**

Shorthand - Intermediate   *SCOTVEC modules at various speeds.*   **F3**

Shorthand - Introductory   *Progression is likely to more advanced speeds.*   **F3**

Shorthand - Pitman - TFW   *Development of skills in shorthand.*   **C8**

Shorthand - RSA Workshop   *Relevant certificate on successful completion of the course.*   **T9**

Shorthand - Speed Development   *HNU. Practical skills are gained in Shorthand & Speed Development.*   **F8**

Shorthand 2 (SCOTVEC)   *SCOTVEC/NCM.*   **L5**

Shorthand 3 - 70Wpm   *SCOTVEC/NC.*   **L5**

Shorthand 4 - 80 Wpm (SCOTVEC) *SCOTVEC/NCM.*   **L5**

Shorthand 5 - 90 Wpm   *SCOTVEC/NCM.*   **L5**

Shorthand 6 - 100 Wpm (SCOTVEC) *SCOTVEC/NCM.*   **L5**

Shorthand for Beginners/Refresher (Pitmans)   *No formal outcome.*   **B2**

Shorthand I (SCOTVEC)   *SCOTVEC/NCM.*   **L5**

Shorthand Transcription - NC   *SCOTVEC/NC.*   **C23**

Shorthand Transcription 1 (50 Wpm) - Module *SCOTVEC/NCM (x3) - 6180201.*   **F8 F12 L1**

Shorthand Transcription 2 (60 Wpm) - Module *SCOTVEC/NCM (x3) - 6180211.*   **F8 F12**

Shorthand Transcription 3 (70 Wpm) - Module *SCOTVEC/NCM - 6180221.*   **F8 F12**

Shorthand Transcription 4 (80 Wpm) - Module *SCOTVEC/NCM - 6180231.*   **F8 F12**

Shorthand Transcription 4 (80 Wpm) Legal - Module   *SCOTVEC/NCM: 6180251.*   **F12**

Shorthand Transcription 4 (80 Wpm) Medical - Module   *SCOTVEC/NCM: 6180241.*   **F12**

Shorthand Transcription 5 (90 Wpm) - Module *SCOTVEC/NCM - 6180261.*   **F8 F12**

Shorthand Transcription 5 (90 Wpm) Legal - Module   *SCOTVEC/NCM: 6180281.*   **F12**

Shorthand Transcription 5 (90 Wpm) Medical - Module   *SCOTVEC/NCM: 6180271.*   **F12**

Shorthand Transcription 6 (100 Wpm) - Module *SCOTVEC/NCM - 6180291.*   **F8**

Speed Shorthand   *Skills gained in speed shorthand.*   **S81**

Spreadsheets, Elementary & Intermediate *Diploma/Certificate credited towards NVQ .*   **G30**

Study Skills Course   *Preparation for employment or further education courses.*   **C17**

Taking & Processing Shorthand 1 (100 Wpm) - HN Unit   *SCOTVEC/HNU.*   **F8**

Taking & Processing Shorthand 2 (110 Wpm) - HN Unit   *SCOTVEC/HNU.*   **F8**

Taking & Processing Shorthand 3 (120 Wpm) - HN Unit   *SCOTVEC /HNU.*   **F8**

Taking & Processing Shorthand 4 (130 Wpm) - HN Unit   *SCOTVEC /HNU.*   **F8**

Taking & Processing Shorthand 5 (140 Wpm) - HN Unit   *SCOTVEC /HNU.*   **F8**

Teach Yourself /Wordperfect 6   *Knowledge of Wordperfect 6.*   **H41**

Teach Yourself /Understanding Word for Windows 6   *Knowledge of Word for Windows 6.*   **H41**

Teach Yourself/Understanding Wordperfect for Windows 6   *Knowledge of Wordperfect 6.*   **H41**

Telephone Skills in the Foreign Language (French or German)   *Appropriate phraseology for making telephone calls.*   **M8**

Text Processing   *Skills gained in text processing.* **S81**

Text Processing - Advanced   *SCOTVEC. Skills are gained in typewriting theory & practice.*   **F3**

Text Processing - Module   *SCOTVEC 1/2 Module - Text Processing.*   **F9 F10**

Text Processing 1   *SCOTVEC certificate.*   **B3**

Text Processing 1   *SCOTVEC/NCM in Text Processing 1.*   **L1 L3 L83**

Text Processing 1 - Module   *SCOTVEC (half module)-Text Processing I.*   **F1 F2 F11 F12**

Text Processing 1, 2 or 3 - 6180021 or 31 or 41 *SCOTVEC/NCM in Text Processing 1, 2 or 3.*   **D6**

Text Processing 2   *SCOTVEC/NCM in Text Processing 2.*   **B3 L1 L3 L5 L83**

Text Processing 2 - Half Module   *SCOTVEC (half module)-Text Processing 2.*   **F1 F2 F11 F12**

Text Processing 2 - NC   *SCOTVEC/NC.*   **C23**

Text Processing 3   *SCOTVEC/NCM in Text Processing 3..*   **B3 F12 L1 L5**

Text Processing 4   *SCOTVEC/NCM in Text Processing 4.*   **L1 L5**

Text Processing 5 (General, Legal or Medical) *SCOTVEC/NCM.*   **L5**

Text Processing 5   *SCOTVEC/NCM in Text Processing 5.*   **L1**

Text Processing I   *SCOTVEC/NCM.*   **L5**

Text/Word Processing   *RSA Certificate.*   **B6**

Textprocessing - Module   *SCOTVEC module in Textprocessing.*   **D3**

Timber Trade Clerical/Administration - Skillseekers/SVQ Level II *SVQ Level II Certificate.*   **S99**

Touch Typing, Word Processing & Shorthand *Pitman Certificate.*   **L89**

Training in Keyboard Skills *RSA Qualification.* **H6**

Tuition for People with a Disability *Advice on educational opportunities for people with a disability or health problem.*   **H32**

Typewriting *NCM. Practical skills are gained in typing.*   **F8**

Typewriting (Beginners) - NC *SCOTVEC/NC.* **T1**

Typewriting - Advanced *Improvement of typewritting skills.*   **T1**

Typewriting Skills - RSA 1 *Relevant certificate on successful completion of the course.*   **T9**

Typewriting Skills - TFW *Development of skills in keyboarding.*   **C8**

Typing - NCMs / RSA *RSA or SCOTVEC Certification.*   **H13**

Typing Crash Course *Basic typing skills.* **T23**

Typing, Stages 1,2 & 3 *Diploma/Certificate credited towards NVQ .*   **G30**

Understanding Ami Professional *Knowledge of Ami Pro.*   **H41**

Uniplex - Advanced *ITec certification.*   **H17**

Uniplex Wordprocessing - Introduction *ITec certification.*   **H17**

Updating Reception & Telephone Skills *College Certificate.*   **L27**

Using a Keyboard & Introduction to Word Processing *Understanding of Keyboarding & Word Processing.*   **G7**

Using a Keyboard (SCOTVEC) *SCOTVEC/NCM in Using a Keyboard.*   **L1 L5**

Using a Keyboard - Module *SCOTVEC (half module) Using a Keyboard.*   **F1 F9 F10 F11**

Using a Keyboard/Text Processing 1 - NC *SCOTVEC/NC.*   **C23**

Women into Technology *Practical skills & knowledge.*   **S15**

Women Returners Computing Course *Introduction to computers & their applications.* **H17**

Women Returners Course *RSA Computer Literacy & Information Technology I.* **H5 H12 H33**

Women Returning to Work - Office Skills *SCOTVEC/NCMs Introduction to Word Processing & Information Technology.*   **D6**

Word for Windows - Advanced *ITec certification.* **H17**

Word for Windows - Introduction *ITec certification.*   **H17 S94**

Word Perfect *Skills gained in word perfect.* **S81**

Word Perfect/Desk Top Publishing *Skills gained in Word Perfect/desk top publishing.*   **S81**

Word Processing *SCOTVEC module.* **B4 B8 C19 F5 T3 T7**

Word Processing & Text Processing - NCMs. *SCOTVEC/NCM.*   **L68**

Word Processing - Basic - TFW *Development of skills in word processing.*   **C8**

Word Processing - H Grade *H Grade in Word Processing.*   **B1**

Word Processing - Module *SCOTVEC module.* **F3 F5 M4**

Word Processing - NCM (91100) *SCOTVEC/NCM.*   **H29**

Word Processing - NCMs / RSA *RSA or SCOTVEC Certification. Various courses available.*   **H13**

Word Processing - RSA I - TFW *Development of skills in word processing.*   **C8**

Word Processing - RSA II - TFW *Development of skills in word processing.*   **C8 T9**

Word Processing - RSA III - TFW *Development of skills in word processing.*   **C8**

Word Processing - Samna One Word Plus *Certificate of Competence.*   **B6**

Word Processing - Samna Plus IV *Certificate of Competence.*   **B6**

Word Processing - Samna Plus IV Part 2 *Certificate of Competence.*   **B6**

Word Processing - Samna Word IV *Certificate of Competence.*   **B6**

Word Processing - Samna Word IV Part 2 *Certificate of Competence.*   **B6**

Word Processing - Samna Word IV Plus Part 2 *Certificate of Competence.*   **B6**

Word Processing - SCOTVEC *SCOTVEC module in Word Processing.*   **B10 G4 G18 H49**

Word Processing Beginners & Advanced Levels *Diploma Credited towards NVQ.*   **G30**

Word Processing Short Course *Wordperfect skills.*   **T1**

Word Processing Skills *SCOTVEC/NCM in Word Processing Skills.*   **F1 L1 L3 L5 L83 S81**

Word Processing Skills - NC *SCOTVEC/NC.* **C45**

Word Processing Skills - Wordperfect NC *SCOTVEC/NC.*   **L27**

Word Processing/Keyboarding for Beginners *SCOTVEC Module.*   **G4**

Word V.5   *Skills gained in the use of Word V.5.*
S6

Wordperfect 5.1   *Skills gained in the use of Wordperfect 5.1.*
S6

Wordperfect 5.1 - Advanced   *ITec certification.*
H17

Wordperfect 5.1 - Advanced Training Course
Advanced skills on Wordperfect.
M8

Wordperfect 5.1 - Introduction   *ITec certificate.*
H17

Wordperfect 5.1 - Introduction (C8)   *Students will gain the basic skills of Wordperfect.*
S94

Wordperfect 5.1 - Introductory Training Course
Intoductory skills for Wordperfect.
M8

Wordperfect 5.1 - Macro Programming Workshop
ITec certification.
H17

Wordperfect for Windows   *Training in the use of this software package.*
H30 M8

Wordperfect for Windows - Advanced   *ITec certification.*
H17

Wordperfect for Windows - Introduction   *ITec certification.*
H17

Wordperfect for Windows - Macro Programming
ITec certification.
H17

Wordprocessing   *No formal outcome.*
B6

Wordprocessing - Intermediate Wordperfect Workshop   *Relevant certificate on successful completion of the course.*
T9

Wordprocessing - Introduction to Wordperfect Workshop   *Relevant certificate on successful completion of the course.*
T9

Wordprocessing - Module   *SCOTVEC module in Wordprocessing.*
D3

Wordprocessing - RSA I   *Relevant certificate on successful completion of the course.*
T9

Wordprocessing - Wordperfect   *SCOTVEC/NCM.*
D5

Wordprocessing - Wordstar 6   *SCOTVEC/NCM.*
D5

Wordprocessing - Wordstar Professional
SCOTVEC/NCM.
D5

Wordprocessing Skills   *Skills & knowledge in Word Processing.*
S70

Wordstar - Advanced   *ITec certification.*
H17

Wordstar - Introduction   *ITec certification.*
H17

Wordstar 5.5   *Skills gained in the use of Wordstar 5.5.*
S6

Wordstar 6 - Introduction (C7)   *Basic skills of Wordstar.*
S94

Working in an Office   *SCOTVEC Module.*
H54

Working in Reception   *SCOTVEC Module.*
H54

Workplace Education - Computer Applications
Appropriate SCOTVEC qualification.
C16

PUBLISHERS' NOTE

Whilst every care has been taken to ensure that the information contained in this book is accurate, the Publishers and the Network of TAP Agencies cannot accept responsibility for errors, omissions or changes which may have taken place after passing for press.

PUBLIC ADMINISTRATION

Administration - SVQ Level 3 *6 credits towards HNC in Office Administration.*   **F13**

Arts Management - HNC *SCOTVEC/HNC.*   **L5**

Business Administration - HNC *SCOTVEC/HNC in Business Administration.*   **L81**

Chartered Institute of Public Finance & Accountancy - Foundation Course *CIPFA Foundation course.*   **S31**

Chartered Institute of Public Finance & Accountancy - P1 *Chartered Institute of Public Finance & Accountancy P1 stage.*   **S31**

Chartered Institute of Public Finance & Accountancy - P2 *Chartered Institute of Public Finance & Accountancy P2 stage.*   **S31**

Chartered Institute of Public Finance & Accountancy - P3 *Chartered Institute of Public Finance & Accountancy P3 stage.*   **S31**

Cultural Services Management - MSc/ PgD *MSc/Diploma/Certificate in Cultural Services Management.*   **L33**

Diploma in Public Sector Management *Diploma in Public Sector Management.*   **L5**

Housing - HNC *SCOTVEC/HNC in Housing.*
                                     L5 S68

Housing - NC *SCOTVEC/NC in Housing.*   **S68**

Housing Administration - NC *NC in a Housing Administration Programme.*   **S14 S15 S87**

Housing Administration - Years 1 & 2 - NC *SCOTVEC/NC in Housing Administration.*   **C22**

Housing Administration 1 (SCOTVEC) *SCOTVEC/NCM.*   **L5**

Housing Administration 2 (SCOTVEC) *SCOTVEC/NCM.*   **L5**

Housing Administration Studies - NC *SCOTVEC/NC.*   **L5**

Housing Law (SCOTVEC) *SCOTVEC/NCM.* **L5**

Housing Management *Skills in housing management.*   **S15**

Housing Studies - Diploma *Diploma or Master's Degree in Housing Administration.*   **C40 L11**

Office Administration - HNC *SCOTVEC/HNC in Office Administration.*   **F13**

Public Administration - HNC *SCOTVEC/HNC.*
   D5 H31 H53 L5 M7 S2 S8 S14 S15 S S75 S91

Public Administration - NC *SCOTVEC/NC.*
                            L5 S11 S75 S91

Public Administration - SCOTVEC/HNC *SCOTVEC/HNC in Public Administration.*   **G17**

Public Administration - Years 1 & 2 - NC *SCOTVEC/NC in Public Administration.*   **C22**

Public Adminstration - HNC *HNC in Public Administration.*   **S5**

Public Management - MSc *PgD in Public Management.*   **S105**

Social & Public Policy - MSc / Diploma *MSc Degree / Diploma in Social & Public Policy.* **L77**

Computers, Electrical & Electronic Engineering

COMPUTER PROGRAMMING SYSTEMS SOFTWARE ENGINEERING

Advanced C Programming Workshop   *Napier University certificate.*   **L48**

Advanced C++   *Advanced skills in C programming.*   **G16**

Advanced Computer Programming - C, Pascal, Basic   *Advanced techniques in computer programming.*   **L27**

Analysis & Design of Object Orientated Software   **S151**

Business Information Systems - HNC   *SCOTVEC/HNC in Business Information Systems.*   **S8**

C Programming   *SCOTVEC/NC.*   **D5**

C Programming Workshop   *Napier University certificate.*   **L48**

C++ Programming 1   *Increased knowledge of C++.*   **L5**

C++ Programming 2   *Increased knowledge of C++.*   **L5**

C++ Workshop Hands-On Object Oriented Programming   *Napier University certificate.*   **L48**

Cognitive & Computational Neuroscience   *Development of cognitive & computational neuroscience.*   **C44**

Computer / Information Technology Courses for Industry   *Various courses available.*   **H49**

Computer Application: Graphics (SCOTVEC)   *SCOTVEC/NCM.*   **L5**

Computer Applications (Database) - 81098   *SCOTVEC/NCM Computer Applications Package (Database).*   **D6**

Computer Applications (Spreadsheet) - 91099   *SCOTVEC/NCM.*   **D6**

Computer Data Processing - NC   *SCOTVEC/NC.*   **S16**

Computer Hardware (Introduction) - 71092 - SCOTVEC/NC   *SCOTVEC/NCM.*   **T23**

Computer Programming - Cobol NC   *SCOTVEC/NC.*   **C23**

Computer Programming - Pascal NC   *SCOTVEC/NC.*   **C23**

Computer Programming in Cobol or Pascal   *Skills in Computer Programming & problem-solving techniques.*   **F8**

Computer Programming Project (SCOTVEC)   *SCOTVEC/NCM.*   **L5**

Computer Science - MSc / Diploma   *MSc / Diploma in Computer Science.*   **L79**

Computer Software (Introduction) (PC Version) - 81093 - SCOTVEC Nat Cert   *SCOTVEC/NCM.*   **G6**

Computer Software - NC   *SCOTVEC/NC.*   **C23**

Computer Studies - HNC   *HNC in Computer Studies.*   **T1**

Computer Studies - NC   *SCOTVEC/NC in Computing.*   **C10 S10**

Computer Studies - SCE H Grade   *SCE H Grade in Computer Studies.*
C1 C4 C5 C6 C7 C20 C21 C25 C26 C27 C28 C29 C30 C33 C34 C36 C46

Computer Studies - SCE H Grade or CSYS or module   *SCE in Computer Studies, H Grade, CSYS or SCOTVEC Module.*   **D3**

Computer Studies - SEB H Grade   *SEB H Grade.*   **B1**

Computer Studies - SEB H Grade (Two Year)   *SEB H Grade.*   **B1**

Computer Systems Software (SCOTVEC)   *SCOTVEC/NCM.*   **L5**

Computer Systems Support - HNC   *SCOTVEC/HNC in Computer Systems Support.*   **S91**

Computers - Windows   *Skills in understanding of the software package.*   **H30**

Computing   *SCOTVEC Certificate.*   **B11**

Computing & Electronics - HNC   *SCOTVEC/HNC in Computing & Electronics.*   **S15**

Computing - Advanced Diploma   *Advanced Diploma in Computing. Management.*   **C22**

Computing - Beginners Group   *Introduction to basic computer programming.*   **C14**

Computing - HNC   *SCOTVEC/HNC.*
B6 C10 C23 D5 F8 F13 H29 H53 L5 M7 S2 S6 S11 S15 S75 S78 S79 S91 S94 T9

Computing - HNC (Day Release)   *SCOTVEC/HNC in Computing.*   **L68 L81**

Computing - HNC (Evening Class)   *SCOTVEC/HNC in Computing.*   **L68**

Computing - HNC/HND   *HNC/Diploma in Computing.*   **L59**

Computing - HND   *SCOTVEC/HND in Computing.*   **S15**

Computing - NC   *SCOTVEC/NC.*
F5 L81 S78 S79 S91

Computing - NC (Day Release or Evening Class) *SCOTVEC/NC in Computer Studies.* **L68**

Computing - NC (GSVQ Information Technology) *SCOTVEC/NC & a VQ in Computing.* **B6**

Computing - NCM *SCOTVEC/NC.* **H53**

Computing - SCE H Grade *SEB Computing at H Grade.* **D8 S13**

Computing - SCE Higher *SCE Higher in Computing.* **M3**

Computing - SCE S Grade / NCMs / RSA *Various courses available.* **H13**

Computing - SCOTVEC Modules *SCOTVEC Modules in computing.* **D8**

Computing - SEB H Grade *SEB H Grade in Computing.* **B10 B11**

Computing - SEB S Grade *SEB S Grade in Computing.* **B11**

Computing for Building Professionals - CIOB Associate Examinations Exemptions *Leads to Associate Examinations.* **L59**

Computing in Engineering I - NC *SCOTVEC/NC.* **C23**

Computing Science I - (P/T Degree Unit) *Units can be accumulated towards degree course.* **C42**

Computing Science III - (P/T Degree Unit) *Units can be accumulated towards degree course.* **C42**

Dbase 111 Plus - Programming *ITec certification.* **H17**

Dbase 1V - Programming *ITec certification.* **H17**

DOS - Introduction *Basic skills in DOS.* **M8**

Evening Classes in Computing *SCOTVEC/NCM.* **L68**

Graphic Communication - SCE H Grade *SCE H Grade in Graphic Communication.* **C4 C5 C20 C21 C25 C26 C27 C28 C29 C30 C33 C36 C45 C46**

Graphic Design & Illustration - HND *SCOTVEC/HND in Graphic Design & Illustration.* **C10**

Information Systems - MSc / PgD *MSc Degree / PgD in Information Systems.* **L62**

Information Technology (Software Engineering) - MSc /Postgraduate Diploma *CNAA MSc Degree / PgD in Information Technology.* **L37**

Information Technology (Systems Integration) - MSc /Postgraduate Diploma *MSc Degree or PgD.* **L37**

Information Technology - Customised Courses *Various.* **L71**

Information Technology - Knowledge Based Systems - MSc / Diploma *MSc Degree / Diploma in Information Technology.* **L74**

Introduction to C *Knowledge of the fundamental control & data structures.* **L5**

Introduction to C++ *Understanding of fundamental data types; function overloading; pointers; constructors; destructors.* **G16**

Introduction to Computer Programming - Basic Language *Basic computer programming.* **L27**

Introduction to Computer Programming - C Language (SCOTVEC) *SCOTVEC/NCM.* **L27**

Introduction to Computer Programming - Cobol Language *Basic computer programming.* **L27**

Introduction to Computer Programming - Comal - Module *SCOTVEC module.* **F11**

Introduction to Computer Programming - Pascal & Desktop Publishing 1 (SCOTVEC) *SCOTVEC/NCM.* **L83**

Introduction to Computer Programming - Pascal (SCOTVEC) *SCOTVEC/NCM in Introduction to Computer Programming - Pascal.* **L1 L3**

Introduction to Computer Programming - Pascal Language *Basic skills in computer programming.* **L27**

Introduction to Computer Programming Basic - 91111 - SCOTVEC National Cert *SCOTVEC/NCM.* **T23**

Introduction to Computers *No formal outcome.* **B6 T9**

Introduction to Computers - 81091 *SCOTVEC/NCM Introduction to Computers.* **D6**

Introduction to Computing *SCOTVEC/NCM.* **D5**

Introduction to Gem Applications *College Certificate.* **L27**

Introduction to MS DOS *SCOTVEC/NCM is possible.* **D5**

Introduction to MSDOS 5 & Windows *Napier University certificate.* **L48**

Introduction to MS-DOS *College certificate.* **T9**

Introduction to PCDOS/MSDOS/Windows *College Certificate.* **L68**

Introduction to Programming in Cobol (SCOTVEC) *SCOTVEC/NCM.* **L5**

Introduction to the PC & MS-DOS *College Certificate.* **L27**

Introduction to Windows *No formal outcome.* **B6 S87 T9**

Introduction to Windows/Word Processing *No formal outcome.* **B2**

Learn Windows Software - ESF *Certificate of attendance.* **H17**

Librarianship & Information Science *SCOTVEC/HNC in Librarianship & Information Science.* **S8**

Librarianship & Information Science - HNC *SCOTVEC/HNC in Business Information Systems.* **S8**

Metrics - an Aid to Controlling Software Projects *Napier University certificate.*   **L48**

Micro Computer Operating Systems   *College certificate of attendance.*   **B3**

Microcomputer Servicing & Support - HNC *SCOTVEC/HNC in Microcomputer Servicing & Support.*   **F8**

Microcomputer Servicing & Support - HND *SCOTVEC/HND in Microcomputer Servicing & Support.*   **F8**

Microcomputer Support - HNC   *SCOTVEC/HNC in Micro Computer Support.*   **C22**

Microcomputer Systems Support - HNC *SCOTVEC/HNC in Microcomputer Systems Support.*   **S75**

Microcomputers - Introduction   *ITec certification.*   **H17**

Microsoft Windows 3.1   *Basic understanding of the Windows environment.*   **M8**

MS DOS   *Certificate of Competence.*   **B6 S6**

MS DOS Level 2   *SCOTVEC/NCM.*   **D5**

MS-DOS - Advanced (C3)   *Knowledge of the MS-DOS operating system.*   **S94**

MS-DOS - Introduction   *ITec certification.*   **H17**

MS-DOS - Introduction (C2)   *Basics of MS-DOS operating system.*   **S94**

MS-DOS Operating System   *Knowledge & experience of the MsDos Operating System.*   **S87**

Multimedia Computing - Diploma   *Diploma Post Degree/HND in Multimedia Computing.*   **S75**

Netware System Administrator   *ITec certification.*   **H17**

Novell Appreciation - (C12)   *Basic concepts of Local Area Networks using Novell soft- ware.*   **S94**

Novell Netware - Introduction   *ITec certification.*   **H17**

Novell Networking - Introduction (C13) *Knowledge of Local Area Networks using Novell soft- ware.*   **S94**

Novell v3.x Workshop   *Napier University certificate.*   **L48**

Pascal Programming - NCM   *SCOTVEC/NCM in Pascal Programming.*   **L81**

PC Viruses - Understanding, Prevention & Cure *Napier University certificate.*   **L48**

Personal Computer Fault Finding Training *Understanding of the PC & its system.*   **H53**

Professor DOS   *Basic DOS commands.*   **T23**

Programming in Fortran   *Knowledge of the programming language Fortran 77.*   **S109**

Programming in Pascal 1 (SCOTVEC) *SCOTVEC/NCM.*   **L5**

Programming Languages - C++   *MEDC Course Certificate.*   **S151**

Programming Languages - Visual Basic   *MEDC Course Certificate.*   **S151**

Relational Database Methods & Programming - Skillseekers/NVQ Level III   *NVQ Level III.*   **S18**

RSA Core Text Processing   *RSA Certificate.*   **H54**

SAND - Structural Analysis & Design (P9)   *Basics of the SAND package.*   **S94**

Siemens Plc Programming   *Napier University certificate.*   **L48**

Software Development - HNC   *SCOTVEC/HNC in Software Development.*   **H29 S8**

Software Engineering - Advanced Diploma/ Post HND   *Advanced Diploma in Software Engineering.*   **S75**

Software Engineering - BEng / BEng (Honours) *BEng or BEng Hons Degree in Software Engineering.*   **L47**

Software Engineering - HNC   *SCOTVEC/HNC in Software Engineering.*   **L36**

Software Engineering - HND   *HND in Software Engineering.*   **L36**

Software Engineering for Established Engineers *SCOTVEC Certificate in Software Engineering.*   **L21**

Software Engineering Technology   *Development of software engineering skills.*   **C44**

Software Quality Engineering - MSc   *MSc in Software Quality Engineering.*   **S28**

Software Quality Engineering - PgD   *PgD in Software Quality Engineering.*   **S28**

Software Quality Management Systems   *Napier University certificate.*   **L48**

Software Technology - Msc/Postgraduate Diploma *MSc Degree / PgD in Software Technology.*   **L63**

SQL   *MEDC Course Certificate.*   **S151**

SSADM V4   *MEDC Certificate Course.*   **S151**

SSADM V4 Case Tools   *MEDC Course Certificate.*   **S151**

Structured Analysis & Design   *Napier University certificate.*   **L48**

Teach Yourself Lotus Freelance Plus   *Basic skills using Lotus Freelance Plus.*   **H41**

Teach Yourself/Understanding DOS 6   *Basic skills using DOS 6.*   **H41**

Uniplex - Introduction   *ITec certification.*   **H17**

Unix   *SCOTVEC/NCM.*   **D5**

UNIX   *MEDC Course Certificate.*   **S151**

Unix - Advanced   *ITec certification.*   **H17**

Unix - for System Administrators   *ITec certification.*   **H17**

Unix - Intermediate   *ITec certification.*   **H17**

Unix - Introduction *ITec certification.*   **H17**

Unix - Introduction (C14) *Knowledge of the UNIX file system & use the most common commands & utilities.*   **S94**

Unix - System Administration (C15) *Knowledge of the managing of a computer system running a variant of UNIX.*   **S94**

Utilising the Computer Resource - HN Unit *SCOTVEC/HNU.*   **F8**

Visual Basic *MEDC Course Certificate.*   **S151**

Windows *Skills gained in using windows.*   **S81**

Windows - Introduction *ITec certification.*   **H17**

Windows 3.1 - Introduction (C4) *Basic concepts of Windows 3.1.*   **S94**

CONTROL ENGINEERING

Application of Programmable Logic Controllers - HN Unit *SCOTVEC/HNU.*   **F8**

Applications of Programmable Logic Controllers (E1) *Basic Knowledge of Programmable Logic Controllers.*   **S94**

Electronic Engineering Practice - NC *ENTRA Parts 1 & 2; SCOTVEC named award in Electronic Engineering Practice.*   **H49**

Electronics & Programmable Logic Controller Technology *Delegates will have an understanding of Electronics & Programmable Logic Controller Technology.*   **G17**

Industrial Robots - Introduction (P1) *Knowledge & skills on a variety of Industrial Robots.*   **S94**

Introduction to Programmable Controllers *Applications of programmable controllers.*   **D5**

Machine Assembly Processes & Systems - NC *SCOTVEC/NC in Machine Assembly Processes & Systems.*   **S19**

Measurement & Control - SCOTVEC/NC *SCOTVEC/NC.*   **G17**

Mechanical Engineering - HNC *SCOTVEC/HNC in Mechanical Engineering (Manufacture or Plant).*   **S79**

Process Control - HNC *SCOTVEC/HNC in Process Control.*   **F8**

Programmable Logic Controllers *SCOTVEC Higher National Unit in PLCs.*   **H49 S87**

Programmable Logic Controllers (PLCs) *Various courses available.*   **H53**

Programming & Application of Programmable Logic Controllers *Skills gained in programming & application of programmable logic controllers.*   **S71**

Robotic Systems Engineering *Napier University certificate.*   **L48**

ELECTRICAL, COMPUTER & ELECTRONIC SERVICING

Audio Television Video & Service Engineering - HNC *SCOTVEC/HNC in Electrical Servicing Engineering.*   **S13**

Audio Visual Technology - HNC *SCOTVEC/HNC in Audio Visual Technology.*   **L68**

Elect & Electronic Engineering Section Short Course Provision *College Certificate.*   **L21**

Electrical, Computer & Electronic Servicing - HNC/NC *SCOTVEC/HNC/NC.*   **S9**

Electrical Skills Testing *Preparation for final electrical skills test.*   **T9**

Electronic Technology - NC *SCOTVEC/NC in Electronic Technology.*   **S16**

Electronics with Computer Maintenance - HNC *SCOTVEC/HNC in Computer Installation Support Engineering.*   **S13**

Electronics with Computer Maintenance - NC *SCOTVEC/NC in Electronic Engineering Practice.*   **S13**

Introduction to Electronics & TV Servicing - NC *SCOTVEC/NC in Electronic Engineering Practice.*   **S13**

Microcomputer Servicing & Interfacing *Necessary skills for Microcomputer Servicing.*   **S71**

Personal Computer Fault Finding Training *Basic skills in fault finding.*   **H53**

Various Courses Available *Company Certificate awarded.*   **S149**

ELECTRICAL ENGINEERING

16Th Edition IEE Wiring Regulations *Installation characteristics of Electrical Supply systems.*   **M8**

16Th Edition IEE Wiring Regulations Update *College Certificate of Completion.*   **L68**

16th Edition of the IEE Electricity At Work Regulations *Preparation for City & Guilds (2386) examinations.*   **S11**

16Th Edition of the IEE Regulations - C & G 238 *College Certificate.*   **F8**

16th Edition of the IEE Wiring Regulations *Preparation for the City & Guilds (2386) examinations.*   **S11**

16Th Edition Wiring Regulations - CITB, C & G 236-6-01 *City & Guilds.*   **D5**

AC Electrical Machines: Theory & Practice - HN Unit *SCOTVEC Higher National Unit - 2400149.*   **F8**

Advanced Certificate in Engineering Practice *Advanced Certificate in Engineering Practice Electrical & Electronic.* **C23**

Advanced Electrical Network Theory - HN Unit *SCOTVEC/HNU.* **F8**

Applying the 16th Edition - IEEIE Certified *IEEIE Certificate in Applying the 16th Edition Regulations.* **H53**

Basic Soldering & Diagnostic Techniques On Electronic Circuits *SCOTVEC/NC.* **T23**

Bridging Course in Electrical Engineering - NC *SCOTVEC/NCM.* **L68**

Broad Based Engineering Practice - National Certifcate GSVQ I *SCOTVEC/NC - Broad Based Engineering Practice (GSVQ I).* **F8**

Certificate in Electrical Installation Work - C & G 236 *City & Guilds 236 Electrical Science.* **F8**

Circuit Elements - Module *SCOTVEC/NCM.* **F8**

Circuits, Fields & Networks - HN Unit *SCOTVEC/HNU.* **F8**

Design, Verification & Testing of Electrical Installation - C & G 240 *A City & Guilds 240 Certificate in Electrical Installation.* **C22**

Drives & Power Engineering - MSc/ Diploma *MSc Degree/Diploma in Electrical Power Engineering.* **L6**

Earthing & Earth-Leakage Protection *Skills gained in modern installation protection techniques.* **S79**

Electrical *NVQ Level 3.* **G39**

Electrical & Electronic Craft Studies Part III - C & G 232 *A City & Guilds Certificate in Electrical & Electronic Craft Studies Part III.* **C22**

Electronic & Electrical Engineering Section Short Course Provision *College Certificate.* **L21**

Electrical & Electronic Engineering - HNC *HNC.* **F5 H49 L5 L28 S6 S19 S79 S87 S88**

Electrical & Electronic Engineering - NC *SCOTVEC/NC.* **L24 L26 L81 S6 S15 S19 S78 S79 S81**

Electrical & Electronic Engineering NCMs *Various courses available.* **H49**

Electrical & Electronic Engineering Technician - HN Units *SCOTVEC/HNU.* **H53**

Electrical & Electronic Engineering with Practice NC *SCOTVEC/NC in Electronic or Electrical Engineering with practice.* **L24**

Electrical & Electronic Engineering Yrs 2&3 - NC *SCOTVEC/NC.* **L81**

Electrical & Electronic Technician - NCMs *Various courses available.* **H53**

Electrical Craft Studies - C & G 236 *NVQ City & Guilds 236 Certificate.* **S15**

Electrical Engineering (Electrical Installation Bias)- NC *SCOTVEC/NC in Electrical Engineering.* **L68**

Electrical Engineering (Electrical Plant Bias) - NC *SCOTVEC/NC in Electrical Engineering.* **L68**

Electrical Engineering (Electronic Bias) 1St Year - NC *SCOTVEC/NC in Electrical Engineering with an Electronic Bias.* **S88**

Electrical Engineering (Plant Bias) 1St Year - NC *SCOTVEC/NC in Electrical Engineering with a Plant Bias.* **S88**

Electrical Engineering - HNC *SCOTVEC/HNC in Electrical Engineering.* **L68**

Electrical Engineering - NC *SCOTVEC/NC in Electrical Engineering.* **F8 F13**

Electrical Engineering with Electrical Plant *SCOTVEC/HNC in Electrical Engineering with Electrical Plant.* **C22**

Electrical Engineering: (Plant); (Measurement & Control) - National Cert *SCOTVEC/NC in Electrical Engineering.* **C22**

Electrical Essential Testing Module Number 4110180 *SCOTVEC/NCM.* **T9**

Electrical Fundamentals - 2160010 - SCOTVEC/NC *SCOTVEC/NC.* **T23**

Electrical Fundamentals - Module *SCOTVEC/NCM - 2160010.* **F8**

Electrical Fundamentals - NC *SCOTVEC/NC.* **C23**

Electrical Hand Skills *Participants will gain an initial understanding of Electrical Hand Skills.* **T1**

Electrical Installation - C & G 236 III C *City & Guilds 236 III Certificate ('C') in Electrical Installation.* **L68**

Electrical Installation - CGLI 236 C Course *City & Guilds 236 C Certificate.* **B6**

Electrical Installation - NC *SCOTVEC/NC.* **M7 S15 S75**

Electrical Installation - SVQ Level III *SCOTVEC SVQ Level III in Electrical Installation.* **C10**

Electrical Installation - Stage 2 - NC *SCOTVEC/NC in Electrical Installations.* **C22**

Electrical Installation 236/C St2 - City & Guilds of London Institute *City & Guilds of London Institute 236.* **G17**

Electrical Installation Advanced - C & G 236 Part III *City & Guilds 236 Part III.* **D5**

Electrical Installation Apprentice Training *Scottish Joint Industry Training approved qualification in Electrical Installation.* **D5**

Electrical Installation Part I *Part I Electrical Installation Training Board.* **S87**

Electrical Installation Part II *Part II of Electrical Installation.* **S87**

Electrical Installation Part III - NVQ C & G 236 C *Part III Electrical Installation C & G 236.* **S87**

Electrical Installation SJIB/ECA (SCOTVEC) *SCOTVEC/NCM.* **L68**

Electrical Installation Stage 1 - SCOTVEC/NC
SCOTVEC/NC.   **G17**

Electrical Installation Stage 2 - SCOTVEC/NC
SCOTVEC/NC.   **G17**

Electrical Installation Technicians - Part III - C & G
236   *City & Guilds 236 Certificate in Electrical
Installations (Part III).*   **C22**

Electrical Installation Techniques   *Practical
experience in electrical installation techniques.*
                                             L68

Electrical Installation Testing Methods   *College
certificate.*   **L68**

Electrical Installation Work - C & G 236 C Course
City & Guilds 236 C Certificate.
                              S6 S75 S91 T9

Electrical Installation Work - C & G 236 Course C
City & Guilds Certificate 236.   **S6**

Electrical Installation Work Stage 1 - NC
SCOTVEC/NC.   **S6**

Electrical Installation Work Stage II - NC
SCOTVEC/NC Stage II.   **S6**

Electrical Network Analysis - HN Unit   *SCOTVEC
Higher National Unit.*   **F8**

Electrical or Electronic Engineering - NC
*SCOTVEC/NC in Electrical or Electronic
Engineering.*   **S87**

Electrical Power Engineering - HNC
SCOTVEC/HNC Electrical Engineering.   **L23**

Electrical Power Engineering - MSc   *A MSc in
Electrical Power Engineering.*   **S105**

Electrical Power Engineering - PgD   *A PgD in
Electrical Engineering.*   **S105**

Electrical Principles - HN Unit   *SCOTVEC/HNU.*
                                             F8

Electrical/Electronic Engineering - HNC
SCOTVEC/HNC.   **L81 S15**

Electricity (Introducing) - 3171011 - SCOTVEC/NC
SCOTVEC/NC.   **T23**

Electricity At Work Act   *Awareness of the
Electricity at Work Act & how it applies in the work
place.*   **D5**

Electricity At Work Act & Small Appliance Testing
No formal outcome.   **H53**

Electricity At Work Regulations   *Increased
awareness of the requirements of the regulations.*
                                        L68 M8

Electricity At Work Regulations 1989 (E7)
Knowledge of the new Regulations.   **C10 S94**

Electricity Regulations   *City & Guilds 2380
Certificate.*   **T9**

Electromagnetism - Module   *SCOTVEC/NCM.*
                                             F8

Electronic & Electrical Engineering - BEng   *BEng
Degree.*   **L61**

Electronic & Electrical Engineering - BSc   *BSc
Degree in Electronic & Electrical Engineering.*
                                             L59

Electronic & Electrical Engineering - HNC
SCOTVEC/HNC.
  **C10 C23 D5 G17 L23 L59 S8 S11 S75 S91
S94**

Electronic & Electrical Engineering - HND UCAS
Code: 65Hh   *HND in Electronic & Electrical
Engineering.*   **G15**

Electronic & Electrical Engineering - NC
*SCOTVEC/NC in Electrical/Electronic
Engineering.*   **C10 H49 S75 S94**

Electronic & Electrical Engineering - SCOTVEC
National Awards   *SCOTVEC National Award in
Electrical Engineering; SCOTVEC National Award
in Electronic Engineering.*   **G2**

Electronic & Electrical Engineering Practice -
SCOTVEC National Awards   *SCOTVEC National
Award in Electrical Engineering; SCOTVEC
National Award in Electronic Engineering.*   **G2**

Electronic & Electrical Engineering with
Management - SCOTVEC/HND   *HND.*   **G17**

Electronic & Electrical Technology - NC   *Two
recognised NCs, in Electronic & Electrical
Engineering.*   **F8**

Electronic Project - 64315 - SCOTVEC/NC
SCOTVEC/NC.   **G6**

Electronic Systems & Servicing - NC
SCOTVEC/NC in Electronic Systems & Servicing.
                                             C10

Electronic/Mechanical Engineering - NC
*SCOTVEC/NC in Electronic Engineering &
SCOTVEC/NC in Mechanical Engineering.*   **H49**

Electronics & Electrical Engineering - HNC
SCOTVEC/HNC.   **F13**

Electronics - NC   *SCOTVEC/NC.*   **F13**

Electronics - SVQ Level II   *SCOTVEC SVQ SVQ
Level II in Electronics.*   **C10**

Electronics with Data Communication - HND
*SCOTVEC/HND in Electronics with Data
Communication.*   **S13**

Engineering - NC   *SCOTVEC/NC in Engineering.*
                                             B6

Engineering Council Part 2 Examination Course
*Chartered Engineer status without a traditional B
Eng or BSc course.*   **S94**

Engineering Council Part 2 Examination for
Electrical & Electronic Engineers   *Engineering
Council Part 2.*   **F5**

Engineering Practice: Electrical & Electronic -
Advanced Certificate (APL)   *Advanced Certificate
in Engineering Practice.*   **H31 L68**

Engineering Science - HN Unit   *SCOTVEC/HNU.*
                                             F8

Fibre Optic Systems for Electrical Engineers
North Glasgow College Certificate.   **S141**

Health, Safety & Hygiene   *No formal outcome.*
H42

IEE Electrical Wiring Regulations   *City & Guilds 238 Part 1 Certificate.*   **T1**

IEE Regulations - 16Th Edition   *Practical knowledge of the IEE regulations.*   **S15 S79**

IEE Regulations 16Th Edition - (E4)   *City & Guilds 238 Certificate.*   **S91 S94**

IEE Wiring Regulations   *Skills gained in IEE Wiring Regulations.*   **S6**

Introduction to Semi-Conductor Applications - SCOTVEC/NC   *SCOTVEC/NC.*   **T23**

Management of Electric Testing   *College certificate.*   **L68**

Mechatronic Engineering - HNC   *SCOTVEC/HNC Mechatronic Engineering.*   **F5**

Multiskill Engineering Technician Programme - NC   *SCOTVEC/NC in Multiskill Engineering.*   **F8**

Network Analysis - Module   *SCOTVEC/NCM.*
F8

Power Factor Improvement & Three-Phase Theory - Module   *SCOTVEC/NCM.*   **F8**

Single Phase AC - Module   *SCOTVEC/NCM.*
F8

Transformation & Rectification - Module   *SCOTVEC/NCM.*   **F8**

ELECTRONIC ENGINEERING, TELECOMMUNICATIONS

Advanced Certificate in Engineering Practice   *Advanced Certificate in Engineering Practice Electrical & Electronic.*   **C23**

Advanced Electronic Systems - MSc / PgD   *PgD / MSc Degree in Advanced Electronic Systems.*   **L59**

Amateur Radio Examination Course (City & Guilds)   *Radio Amateur Examination Certificate from City & Guilds.*   **L22**

Amplification - Module   *SCOTVEC/NCM.*   **F8**

Analogue Circuit Technology - HN Unit   *SCOTVEC/HNU.*   **F8**

Analogue Electronic Devices: Characteristics & Applications - HN Unit   *SCOTVEC/HNU.*   **F8**

Applied Physics with Microcomputing - BSc / BSc (Honours)   *BSc Degree / Hons Degree.*   **L41**

Audio/Video Production Technology - NC   *SCOTVEC/NC in Audio & Video Production Technology.*   **S16**

Auto Electrician/Electronics - NC   *SCOTVEC/NC - Auto Electrician/Electronics.*   **S87**

Autocad   *MEDC Course Certificate.*   **S151**

Broad Based Engineering Practice - National Certificate GSVQ I   *SCOTVEC/NC - Broad Based Engineering Practice (GSVQ I).*   **F8**

Combinational Logic & Digital Signal Conversion Using Integrated Circuits - HN Unit   *SCOTVEC/HNU.*   **F8**

Combinational Logic & Sequential Logic Circuit Design & Testing - HN Unit   *SCOTVEC/HNU.*
F8

Combinational Logic - Module   *SCOTVEC/NCM.*
F8

Communications, Control & Digital Signal Processing (CCDSP) - MSc   *MSc course.*   **S105**

Communications, Control & Digital Signal Processing (CCDSP) - PgD   *PgD course.*   **S105**

Computer Application Package (Database) - Module   *SCOTVEC/NCM.*   **F10**

Computer Application Package (Spreadsheet) - Module   *SCOTVEC/NCM.*   **F10**

Computer Data Processing - NC   *SCOTVEC/NC in Computer Data Processing.*   **S16**

Computer Integrated Manufacture - MSc   *MSc in Computer Integrated Manufacture.*   **S105**

Computer Integrated Manufacture - PgD   *PgD in Computer Integrated Manufacture.*   **S105**

Computer Studies - NC   *SCOTVEC/NC in Computer Studies.*   **S10**

Computers (Introduction) - 81091 - SCOTVEC/NC   *Basic knowledge of computer systems and various packages.*   **T23**

Computing & Electronics - HNC   *SCOTVEC/HNC in Computing & Electronics.*   **S15**

Computing - HNC   *SCOTVEC/HNC in Computing.*
S2 S8 S11 S13 S14

Computing - HND   *SCOTVEC/HND in Computing.*
S8

Computing - Module   *A vocational SCOTVEC module in computing.*   **D3**

Computing - NC   *SCOTVEC/NC in Computing.*
C22

Computing - SCOTVEC/HNC   *HNC in Computing.*
G17

Computing - SCOTVEC/HND   *HND in Computing.*
G17

Computing - SCOTVEC/NC   *SCOTVEC/NC.*
G17

Computing - SEB H Grade   *SEB H Grade in Computing.*   **B10**

Computing - Years 1 & 2 - HNC   *SCOTVEC/HNC in Computing.*   **C22**

Computing Programme - NC   *NC in Computing.*
S14

Computing with Confidence - SCOTVEC/NC   *SCOTVEC Certification.*   **G17**

Design & Make - Module   *SCOTVEC/NCM.*   **F8**

Desktop Publishing 1 - Module   *SCOTVEC/NCM..*
F10

Digital MSI Devices - Module   *SCOTVEC/NCM.*
F8

Digital Systems Engineering - MSc/ Diploma   *MSc Degree/Diploma in Digital Systems Engineering.*
L6

Electrical & Electronic Craft Studies Part III - C & G 232   *City & Guilds Certificate in Electrical & Electronic Craft Studies Part III.*   **C22**

Electrical & Electronic Engineering - HNC   *HNC course.*
F5 H49 L5 L28 S6 S19 S79 S87 S88

Electrical & Electronic Engineering - NC   *SCOTVEC/NC.*
C10 H49 L24 L26 L81 S6 S15 S19 S75 S78 S79 S81 S94

Electrical & Electronic Engineering NCMs   *Various courses available.*   **H49**

Electrical & Electronic Engineering Technician - HN Units   *SCOTVEC/HNU.*   **H53**

Electrical & Electronic Engineering with Practice NC   *SCOTVEC/NC in Electronic or Electrical Engineering with practice.*   **L24**

Electrical & Electronic Engineering Yrs 2&3 - NC   *SCOTVEC/NC.*   **L81**

Electrical & Electronic Technician - NCMs   *Various courses available.*   **H53**

Electrical Installation - NC   *SCOTVEC/NC in Electrical Installation.*   **S19**

Electrical or Electronic Engineering - NC   *SCOTVEC/NC in Electrical or Electronic Engineering.*   **S87**

Electrical/Electronic Engineering - HNC   *SCOTVEC/HNC in Electrical / Electronic Engineering.*   **L81 S15**

Electronic & Electrical Engineering - BEng   *BEng Degree.*   **L61**

Electronic & Electrical Engineering - BSc   *BSc Degree in Electronic & Electrical Engineering.*
L59

Electronic & Electrical Engineering - HNC   *SCOTVEC/HNC.*
C10 C23 D5 L59 S8 S11 S75 S91 S94

Electronic & Electrical Engineering - HND UCAS Code: 65Hh   *HND in Electronic & Electrical Engineering.*   **G15**

Electronic & Electrical Engineering - SCOTVEC National Awards   *SCOTVEC National Award in Electrical Engineering; SCOTVEC National Award in Electronic Engineering.*   **G2**

Electronic & Electrical Engineering - SCOTVEC/HNC   *SCOTVEC/HNC in Electronic & Electrical Engineering.*   **G17**

Electronic & Electrical Engineering HNC   *SCOTVEC/HNC.*   **L23**

Electronic & Electrical Engineering Practice - SCOTVEC National Awards   *SCOTVEC National Award in Electrical Engineering; SCOTVEC National Award in Electronic Engineering.*   **G2**

Electronic & Electrical Engineering with Management - SCOTVEC/HND   *HND course.*
G17

Electronic & Electrical Technology - NC   *Two recognised NCs, in Electronic & Electrical Engineering.*   **F8**

Electronic Components & Circuit Assembly Techniques - Module   *SCOTVEC/NCM.*   **F8**

Electronic Components & Circuit Assembly Techniques - NC   *SCOTVEC/NC.*   **C23**

Electronic Engineering - HNC   *SCOTVEC/HNC.*
B6 S13

Electronic Engineering - NC   *SCOTVEC/NC.*
B6 F8 H49 M7 S13 S91

Electronic Engineering - Part-Time NC   *SCOTVEC/NC in Electronic Engineering.*   **L81**

Electronic Engineering - SCOTVEC/NC   *SCOTVEC/NC.*   **L28**

Electronic Engineering Practice - NC   *ENTRA Parts 1 & 2 Engineering Training; SCOTVEC in Electronic Engineering Practice.*   **H49**

Electronic Maintenance - NC   *SCOTVEC/NC in Electronic Engineering.*   **S88**

Electronic Product Design & Manufacture - PgD   *PgD in Electronic Design & Manufacture.*   **S101**

Electronic Systems & Servicing - NC   *SCOTVEC/NC in Electronic Systems & Servicing.*
C10

Electronic Technicians - NC   *SCOTVEC/NC.*   **B6**

Electronic/Mechanical Engineering - NC   *SCOTVEC/NC in Electronic Engineering & SCOTVEC/NC in Mechanical Engineering.*   **H49**

Electronics   *No formal outcome.*   **B10 H31 M3**

Electronics & Electrical Engineering - HNC   *SCOTVEC/HNC.*   **F13**

Electronics - HNC   *SCOTVEC/HNC in Electronics.*   **M7**

Electronics - NC   *SCOTVEC/NC.*   **F13**

Electronics - SVQ Level II   *SCOTVEC SVQ Level II in Electronics.*   **C10**

Electronics for Electricians - Intro (E5)   *Skills in analogue & digital electronics.*   **S94**

Electronics Project (SCOTVEC)   *SCOTVEC/NCM in Electronics Project.*   **L1**

Electronics Project - Module   *SCOTVEC/NCM.*
F8

Electronics Technician - NC   *SCOTVEC/NC in Electronics - Technician.*   **S11**

Electronics with Computer Maintenance - HNC   *SCOTVEC/HNC in Computer Installation Support Engineering.*   **S13**

Electronics with Computer Maintenance - NC
SCOTVEC/NC in Electronic Engineering Practice.
S13

Electronics with Data Communication - HND
*SCOTVEC/HND in Electronics with Data
Communication.* **S13**

Electronics- NC *SCOTVEC/NC in Electronics.*
L68

Electronics/Electrical Plant - NC *SCOTVEC/NC
in Electronics (Electrical Plant).* **S2**

Engineering - NC *SCOTVEC/NC in Engineering.*
B6

Engineering Council Part 2 Examination for
Electrical & Electronic Engineers *Engineering
Council Part 2.* **F5**

Engineering Practice - Electrical & Electronic -
Advanced Certificate *Leads to an Advanced
Certificate.* **H31**

Engineering Practice: Electrical & Electronic -
Advanced Certificate (Apl) *Advanced Certificate
in Engineering Practice.* **L68**

Evening Classes in Electronics (SCOTVEC)
SCOTVEC/NCM. **L68**

Frequency Generation & Selection - Module
SCOTVEC/NCM. **F8**

Information Technology - NC *SCOTVEC/NC in
Information Technology.* **S6**

Internetworking *MEDC Course Certificate.*
S151

Introduction to Computer Application Packages -
Module *SCOTVEC/NCM.* **F10**

Introduction to Computer Hardware - Module
SCOTVEC/NCM. **F11**

Introduction to Computer Software - Module
SCOTVEC/NCM. **F10**

Introduction to Computers *No formal outcome.*
B6 G7

Introduction to Computers - Module
SCOTVEC/NCM. **F10 F12 G3**

Introduction to Electronic Systems & Electronic
Test Equipment - 1/2 Modules *SCOTVEC/NC.*
C23

Introduction to Electronics & TV Servicing - NC
SCOTVEC/NC in Electronic Engineering Practice.
S13

Introduction to Ms Dos 5 & Windows *Napier
University certificate.* **L48**

Introduction to New Technologies *SCOTVEC
Modules.* **L68**

Introduction to Semi-Conductor Applications - NC
SCOTVEC/NC. **C23**

Introduction to Semiconductor Applications -
Module *SCOTVEC/NCM.* **F8**

Logic Families & Digital System Analysis - Module
SCOTVEC/NCM. **F8**

Mechatronics - HNC *SCOTVEC/HNC in
Mechatronics.* **S94**

Mechatronic Engineering - HNC *SCOTVEC/HNC
Mechatronic Engineering.* **F5**

Mechatronics - HNC *SCOTVEC/HNC in
Mechatronics.*
C22 L26 S8 S13 S75 S87 S91

Micro Computer Operating Systems *College
Certificate.* **B3**

Microprocessor Applications *Knowledge gained
in Microprocessor Applications.* **S8**

Microprocessor Based Monitoring Systems -
Introduction (E3) *Skills in Microprocessor Based
Monitoring Systems.* **S94**

Multiskill Engineering Technician Programme - NC
SCOTVEC/NC in Multiskill Engineering. **F8**

Novell *MEDC Course Certificate.* **S151**

Optical Electronics - MSc *MSc in Optical
Electronics.* **S105**

Optical Electronics - PgD *PgD in Optical
Electronics.* **S105**

PC Interfacing - Introduction (E2) *Skills on many
aspects of Interfacing.* **S94**

Power Electronics - NC *SCOTVEC/NC.* **C23**

Power Electronics: Devices & Systems - HN Unit
SCOTVEC/HNU. **F8**

Practical Electronics *Participants will have skills
in practical electronics.* **H53**

Principles of Television Reception (1) *Experience
in TV servicing.* **L25**

Principles of Television Reception (2) *Experience
in TV servicing.* **L25**

Principles of Television Reception (3) *Experience
in TV servicing.* **L25**

Programmable Logic Controllers - NC
SCOTVEC/NC. **C23**

Radio Telephony VHF Only (RYA) *RYA
Certificate/Dept of Trade & Industry.* **L20**

Radiotelex *College Certificate.* **L22**

Restricted Radiotelephony Certificate Course *DTI
Certificate of Competence in Radiotelephony
Restricted.* **L22**

RYA Restricted Radiotelephony - Certificate *RYA
Restricted (VHF only) Radiotelephony certificate.*
S71

Satellite Dish Installation *CAI/City & Guilds
certificate of competence.* **S13**

Satellite TV Installation *Ability to install & adjust
domestic satellite TV installations.* **S71**

Satellite TV Servicing *Skills gained in satellite TV
servicing.* **S71**

Satellite TV Systems *City & Guilds of London
Institute (Part III) 224 Certificate.* **S71**

Sequential Logic - Module *SCOTVEC/NCM.* **F8**

Signal Processing   *MEDC Course Certificate.*
S151

Software Technology - Msc/Postgraduate Diploma
MSc Degree / PgD in Software Technology.   **L63**

Technological Studies - SCE H Grade   *SCE H
Grade in Technological Studies.*
**C1 C21 C25 C26 C27 C28 C29 C30 C33
C34 C36 C45**

Technology   *No formal outcome.*   **B10**

Telecommunication Radio Techniques & Circuits -
HN Unit   *SCOTVEC/HNU.*   **F8**

Testing & Inspection of Portable Electronic
Equipment (E8)   *Skills in testing of modern
Electronic equipment.*   **S94**

Vehicle Electrical System Diagnostics   *Knowledge
of Vehicle Electrical System Diagnostics.*   **S87**

VHF Radio Operations   *Department of Transport
Certificate.*   **H31**

INFORMATION
TECHNOLOGY & COMPUTER
APPLICATIONS

Access   *MEDC Course Certificate.*   **S151**

Access to Higher Education - SCOTVEC
Computing (SCE O/S Equivalent)   *Access to
Higher Education through SCOTVEC.*   **D5**

Access to Information Technology
*SCOTVEC/NCMs in Science, Technology &
Maths.*   **S11**

Access to Information Technology (Beginners
Course)   *Basic skills in using computers.*   **L5**

Accounting - HNC   *SCOTVEC/HNC in
Accounting.*   **S75**

Accounting - HND   *SCOTVEC/HND in
Accounting.*   **C10**

Accounting with Computers   *No formal outcome.*
T8

Advanced Autocad   *College Certificate.*   **L27**

Advanced Computer Aided Draughting - Autocad
College Certificate.   **L5**

Advanced Dataease   *College Certificate.*   **L27**

Advanced dbase IV   *College Certificate.*   **L27**

Advanced Lotus 1-2-3   *College Certificate.*   **L27**

Advanced Paradox   *College Certificate.*   **L27**

Advanced Reflex   *College Certificate.*   **L27**

Advanced Spreadsheet   *College Certificate.*
L27

Advanced Supercalc 5   *College Certificate.*   **L27**

Aldus Pagemaker   *Company Certificate awarded.*
S149

Amipro Advanced   *Advanced Knowledge of the
package.*   **G31**

Amipro Introductory   *Basic knowledge of Amipro.*
G31

An Introduction to Lotus 1-2-3   *College Certificate.*
L27

An Introduction to Microcomputers   *Basic
knowledge of microcomputers, their applications
and uses.*   **T13**

An Introduction to Spreadsheets   *College
Certificate.*   **L27**

An Introduction to Supercalc 5   *College
Certificate.*   **L27**

Apple-Mac Technology/Spreadsheets/Business
Packages   *Skills development to industry
standards .*   **S124**

Applications of PLCs - HN Unit   *1 credit towards a
HNC in Electronic & Electrical Engineering.*   **C23**

Applications Software for Engineers (P8)
Overview of software used in engineering.   **S94**

Applied Information Technology - NC   *Knowledge
of word processing, desktop publishing,
spreadsheets & databases.*   **C22**

Applied Technology - NC   *SCOTVEC/NC.*   **C23**

Auto Cad   *No formal outcome.*   **S87**

Autocad   *Skills gained in the use of Autocad.*   **S6**

Autocad (Computer Aided Draughting)   *Basic
knowledge of AUTOCAD (Computer Aided
Design).*   **L68**

Autocad (Computer Aided Draughting) - Drop-In
Service   *Knowledge of AUTOCAD, industry
standard CAD package.*   **L68**

Autocad - C & G 4351   *C & G 4351. Skills in
setting up & using Autocad.*   **B6**

Autocad - C & G 4354   *C & G 4354. Setting up &
using an Autocad system for a variety of specific
applications.*   **B6**

Autocad - City & Guilds 4351   *Relevant certificate.*
T9

Autocad for the Unemployed - ESF   *NVQ Level II
City & Guilds Certificate in CAD using Autocad
(Scheme 4351-01).*   **H17**

Basic Computing Courses   *Principles &
techniques of computer use.*   **H38**

Building - NC   *SCOTVEC/NC in Building.*   **C10**

Business & Office Technology - Diploma - NVQ
Level II (C&g) - Training for Work   *C & G Diploma.*
L32

Business / Computing Short Courses
SCOTVEC/NCs.   **H30**

Business Administration - DBA (Doctor of
Business Administration)   *DBA in Business
Administration.*   **S96**

Business Administration - HNC   *SCOTVEC/HNC
in Business Administration.*   **H49 S11 S71**

Business Administration - HND   *SCOTVEC/HND in Business Administration.*   **H49 S11**

Business Administration - NC/GSVQ Level 111   *SCOTVEC/NC/GSVQ Level 111.*   **H53**

Business Administration - Skillseekers/ NVQ Levels I-II   *NVQ Pitman Levels I-II Certificate.*   **S83 S84 S85 S86**

Business Computing - Foundation 1   *NCM. Understanding of basic computing concepts.*   **F8**

Business Computing - NC   *SCOTVEC GSVQ in Technology at Level II.*   **H49**

Business Computing - NC (GSVQ II)   *SCOTVEC/NC - GSVQ II.*   **F8**

Business Information Management - HNC   *SCOTVEC/HNC in Business Information Management.*   **C22**

Business Information Technology - HNC   *SCOTVEC/HNC in Business Information Technology.*   **L5**

Business Studies Section Short Course Provision   *College Certificate.*   **L19**

Business, Secretarial & Computing Studies - Skillseekers/SVQ Levels I-III   *SCOTVEC modules Levels I-III.*   **S98**

CAD (Computer Aided Drafting) (SCOTVEC)   *SCOTVEC/NCM.*   **L27**

CAD Drop-In   *Certification in Introduction to CAD and/or SCOTVEC CAD modules.*   **L5**

CAD Knitwear Principles/Practice   *No formal outcome.*   **B3**

CAD Systems Management - C & G   *City & Guilds Advanced CAD Systems Management Certificate.*   **H49**

CAD/CAM   *SCOTVEC/NCM.*   **D5**

CAD/CAM - Introduction (P7)   *Basic knowledge of CAD/CAM usage & application.*   **S94**

Certificate in CAD   *Certificate in Cad.*   **S87**

Chemistry with Information Technology & Instrumentation - BSc   *BSc course.*   **S55**

Chemistry with Information Technology & Instrumentation - BSc (Hons)   *BSc (Hons) course.*   **S55**

CNC & CAM - NC   *SCOTVEC/NC.*   **B6**

Community Based Adult Education   *Various courses available.*   **H7**

Computer & Information Technology Law - LLM   *MLL in Computer & Information Law.*   **S105**

Computer & Information Technology Law - PgD   *PgD in Computer & Information Technology Law.*   **S105**

Computer / Information Technology Courses for Industry   *Various courses available.*   **H49**

Computer / Technology Courses for Industry   *Various courses available.*   **H31 H46 H53**

Computer Aided Building Design - MSc   *MSc in Computer Aided Building Design.*   **S105**

Computer Aided Building Design - PgD   *PgD in Computer Aided Building Design.*   **S105**

Computer Aided Design   *Computer Aided Design experience.*   **F5**

Computer Aided Design & Draughting   *Knowledge gained in Computer Aided Design & Draughting.*   **S8**

Computer Aided Design & Manufacture   *HNC in Knitwear Design & Production.*   **B3 S8**

Computer Aided Design - C & G   *City & Guilds Certificate.*   **B6**

Computer Aided Design - HNC   *SCOTVEC/HNC.*   **S15**

Computer Aided Design - NC   *SCOTVEC/NC.*   **C45**

Computer Aided Design - Part-Time NC & College Cert.   *SCOTVEC Module Certificate for Introduction to CAD & CAD with a College certificate for Advanced CAD,.*   **L81**

Computer Aided Design Package - NCMs   *SCOTVEC/NCMs.*   **L5**

Computer Aided Draughting   *Computer Aided Draughting Certificate.*   **F5 H31 L5**

Computer Aided Draughting - Autocad Advanced Level Modules   *Authorised Training Centre registered with AutoDESK.*   **L48**

Computer Aided Draughting - Autocad Foundation Module   *Authorised Training Centre registered with AutoDESK.*   **L48**

Computer Aided Draughting - Intro (P3)   *Basic knowledge in Computer Aided Draughting.*   **S94**

Computer Aided Draughting - NC   *SCOTVEC/HNU.*   **S88 T1**

Computer Aided Draughting - NCM / C & G   *SCOTVEC module 226120 & City & Guilds Certificate 4351.*   **H49**

Computer Aided Draughting 1 - NCM   *SCOTVEC/NCM.*   **L81**

Computer Aided Draughting for Construction (AEC) - City & Guilds 4361   *City & Guilds Certificate.*   **T9**

Computer Aided Draughting in the Built Environment Using Autocad - NCM   *SCOTVEC Module in Computer Aided Draughting.*   **H53**

Computer Aided Drawing   *Skills gained in using the computer as a drawing tool.*   **S81**

Computer Aided Drawing & Manufacture   *SCOTVEC Modules in CAD & CAM.*   **G2**

Computer Aided Electronics with Management Studies - HND   *HND in Computer Aided Electronics with Management Studies.*   **F8**

Computer Aided Engineering   *Various courses available.*   **H53**

Computer Workshop - Module   *NCM. Skills will be gained in one of the major application packages in use in industry.*   **F8**

Computers for Small Businesses   *No formal outcome.*   **S150**

Computerised Accounts for Business Users   *Knowledge of computerised accounts.*   **L18**

Computers   *Knowledge of programming.*   **T10**

Computers & Their Uses   *No formal outcome.*   **H51**

Computers - SCOTVEC   *SCOTVEC module in Computers.*   **M5**

Computers for Businesses   *Basic use of computers in business.*   **T1**

Computers in Business   *Hardware, software & computer applications.*   **H51 T8**

Computers in Business   *Hardware, software & computer applications.*   **T8**

Computers in Engineering - Module   *SCOTVEC/NCM - Computers in Engineering.*   **F8**

Computers in Fabrication Engineering - Module   *SCOTVEC/NC.*   **F5**

Computing   *SCOTVEC Certificate.*   **B11 F8 T3 T6**

Computing & Word Processing   *Experience in computing & word processing.*   **C16**

Computing - Advanced Diploma   *Advanced Diploma in Computing Management.*   **C22**

Computing - Beginners Group   *Basic computer programming.*   **C14**

Computing - Database or Spreadsheet   *SCOTVEC Module in Computer Databases & Spreadsheets.*   **H49**

Computing - HNC   *SCOTVEC/HNC.*   **B6 C10 C23 D5 F8 F13 H29 S15 S16 S75 S78 S79**

Computing - HNC (Day Release)   *SCOTVEC/HNC.*   **L81**

Computing - HND   *SCOTVEC/HND in Computing.*   **S15**

Computing - NC   *NC.*   **F5 F8 L81 S15 S19 S78**

Computing - NC (GSVQ Information Technology)   *SCOTVEC/NC & a VQ in Computing.*   **B6**

Computing - NC/GSVQ Level II in Information Technology   *SCOTVEC/NC in Computing & GSVQ Level II in Information Technology.*   **S2**

Computing - NCM (Reflex Learning Unit)   *SCOTVEC/NCM in Computing.*   **S2 S4**

Computing - NCMs   *SCOTVEC/NC.*   **H53**

Computing - SCE H Grade   *SEB Certificate in Computing at H Grade.*   **D8 S79**

Computing - SCE Higher   *SCE Higher in Computing.*   **M3**

Computing - SCE S Grade/NCMs/RSA   *Various courses available.*   **H13**

Computing - SCOTVEC Modules   *Various courses available.*   **D8**

Computing - SEB H Grade   *SEB H Grade in Computing.*   **B10 B11**

Computing - SEB S Grade   *SEB S Grade in Computing.*   **B11**

Computing - Training for Work   *SCOTVEC/NCM.*   **S98**

Computing - Years 1 & 2 - HNC   *SCOTVEC/HNC in Computing..*   **C22**

Computing Courses   *Skills in basic computer applications.*   **H28 H31**

Computing for Building Professionals - CIOB Associate Examinations Exemptions   *Exemption from associate examinations of the Chartered Institute of Building.*   **L59**

Computing for Business & Commerce   *No formal outcome.*   **S71**

Computing for Medical Practices   *No formal outcome.*   **D5**

Computing for the Over 40's   *RSA (RSA) CLAIT I. Practical experience of Computing.*   **H17**

Computing for the Over 50's   *Practical experience of computing.*   **T13**

Computing in Engineering I - NC   *SCOTVEC/NC.*   **C23**

Computing Science I - (P/T Degree Unit)   *Units can be accumulated towards Degree.*   **C42**

Computing Section Short Course Provision   *College Certificate.*   **L27**

Computing Skills   *SCOTVEC Modules.*   **C48**

Computing Studies - NC   *SCOTVEC/NC.*   **S98**

Computing Studies - SCE Higher   *SCE Higher - Computing Studies.*   **F7**

Conceptual Design Tools Workshop   *Napier University certificate.*   **L48**

Controlling Use of Information Technology   *SVQ Level 3.*   **C47**

Corel Draw Graphics (User)   *Training to basic & intermediate levels.*   **S117**

Data Processing & Computing   *Basic computing skills.*   **H14**

Data Processing - Skillseekers/Nvq Level II   *NVQ Level II on Data Processing.*   **S18**

Database - NCM (81098)   *SCOTVEC/NCM.*   **H29**

Database - NCMs   *SCOTVEC/NCM.*   **L81**

Database - Various Courses Available   *Company Certificate awarded.*   **S149**

Database(access) - Introduction (C10)   *Basic knowledge of the database package - Access.*   **S94**

Databases - Dataease *SCOTVEC/NCM.*   **D5**

Databases - dbase *SCOTVEC/NCM.*   **D5**

Databases - Foxpro *SCOTVEC/NCM is possible.*
D5

Dataease *Certificate of Competence.*   **B6 G31**

Dataease 4.5 - Developing *ITec certification.*
H17

Dataease 4.5 - Introduction *ITec certification.*
H17 M8

Dataease Workshop *ITec certification.*   **H17**

Dbase *Basic skills using Dbase.*   **S57**

Dbase 3 & 4 *Skills gained in the use of DBase III & IV.*   **S6**

Dbase 3 Plus - Introduction *ITec certification.*
H17

Dbase 3 Plus - Programming *ITec certification.*
H17

Dbase 3 Plus - Workshop *ITec certification.*
H17

Dbase 4 - Introduction *ITec certification.*   **H17**

Dbase 4 - Programming *ITec certification.*   **H17**

Dbase 4 - Workshop *ITec certification.*   **H17**

Dbase 3+ - Advanced *Skilled use of Dbase3+.*
M8

Dbase 3+ - Introduction *Basic use of Dbase 3+.*
M8

Desktop Publishing *SCOTVEC.*   **B6**

Desktop Publishing & Information Processing - NC *SCOTVEC/NC in Desktop Publishing & Information Processing.*   **S16**

Desktop Publishing (User) *Training to basic level.*
S117

Desktop Publishing 1 - Module *SCOTVEC Module: 91128 - Desktop Publishing 1.*   **F10**

Desktop Publishing for Applemac *No formal outcome.*   **B3**

Document Engineering *MEDC Course Certificate.*
S151

Document Processing - HN Unit *1 credit towards a HNC in Computing.*   **C23**

Engineering & Building Services - Customised Courses *Various courses available.*   **L71**

Engineering - HNC *Can lead to SCOTVEC/HNC. Skills needed by higher technicians.*   **H31 S16**

Engineering - NC *SCOTVEC/NC in Engineering.*
S16

Engineering Practice - Manufacturing & Engineering Support - Advanced Cert *Advanced Certificate.*   **H31**

English, Arithmetic & Computers *Skilled level of Arithmetic & English.*   **T5**

Excel *A Certificate of Competence.*   **B6 S6**

Excel for Windows *MEDC Course Certificate.*
S151

Excel - Introduction (C6) *Knowledge of Excel.*
S94

Excel - Part 2 *Certificate of Competence.*   **B6**

Financial Record Keeping - 82250 *SCOTVEC/NCM in Financial Record Keeping.*
D6

Graphical Communication - SEB S Grade *SEB S Grade in Graphical Communication.*   **B11**

Graphics - Various Courses Available *Company Certificate.*   **S149**

Harvard Graphics for DOS *Knowledge of the Harvard Graphics.*   **G31**

Harvard Graphics for Windows *Knowledge of Harvard Graphics.*   **G31**

Hotel Reception - NC *SCOTVEC/NC in Hotel Reception.*   **S10**

How to Use Your PC *Knowledge of Personal Computers, how they work & how useful they can be.*   **H41**

IT & Computer Applications *Standard & H Grades.*   **L95**

Information & Office Management - HND *SCOTVEC/HND in Information & Office Management.*   **H49 H53**

Information Management Systems - MSc *MSc in Information Management Systems.*   **S28**

Information Management Systems - PgD *PgD in Information Management Systems.*   **S28**

Information Strategy - MSc *MSc in Information Strategy.*   **S105**

Information Technology & Computer Applications *SCOTVEC/NCM.*   **T14**

Information Technology (CLAIT Level 1) *RSA Certificate.*   **H54**

Information Technology (Computer Aided Engineering) CNAA MSc / PgD *CNAA MSc Degree / PgD in Information Technology.*   **L60**

Information Technology (Manufacturing Systems Engineering) - MSc / PgD *MSc Degree / PgD in Information Technology.*   **L60**

Information Technology - Customised Courses *Various.*   **L71**

Information Technology - Diploma Post Degree/HND *Diploma Post Degree/HND in information Technology.*   **S75**

Information Technology - GSVQ *GSVQ Certificate in Information Technology.*   **S71**

Information Technology - GSVQ Level II *GSVQ in Information Technology at Level 2.*
G17 M7 S10 S91

Information Technology - HNC *SCOTVEC/HNC in Information Technology.*   **H29 S75**

Information Technology - Office Applications -
Module *SCOTVEC/NCM.* **F15**

Information Technology 1 *SCOTVEC/NCM.*
H54

Information Technology 2 - Module
SCOTVEC/NCM. **F11**

Information Technology Applications - HN Unit
SCOTVEC/HNU. **F8 L5**

Information Technology Applications - HNC
*SCOTVEC/HNC in Information Technology
Applications.* **S11 S81**

Information Technology Computer Applications -
Module *SCOTVEC/NCM.* **F9**

Information Technology Courses *Various courses
available.* **H46 H48**

Information Technology for Business *No formal
outcome.* **G16**

Information Technology Office Applications -
Module *SCOTVEC Module - Information
Technology Office Applications.* **F1**

Information Technology Systems - HNC
*SCOTVEC/HNC in Information Technology
Systems.* **S14**

Information Technology: Office Applications
(SCOTVEC) *SCOTVEC/NCM in Information
Technology: Office Applications.* **L1 L83**

Information Technology: Office Applications -
Module *SCOTVEC/NCM.* **F8**

Interior Design with New Technology - NC
*SCOTVEC/NC in Interior Design with New
Technology.* **C22**

Internet-Surfing & Surfboards *MEDC Course
Certificate.* **S151**

Intro to Computer Aided Draughting *Chartered
Institute of Building Certificate, SCOTVEC/NC.*
L5

Intro to Computer Software *SCOTVEC/NC Units.*
S153

Intro to Hydraulics Circuit Computer Simulation
*Use of a computer simulation package for
hydraulic circuit drawings.* **F8**

Intro to Pneumatics Circuit Computer Simulation
*Use of a computer simulation package for
pneumatic circuit drawing.* **F8**

Introduction to Apple Macintosh *Introduction to
using the Apple Macintosh computer.* **C41**

Introduction to Application Packages - NC
SCOTVEC/NC. **C23**

Introduction to Autocad *SCOTVEC module in
Autocad.* **H53 S109**

Introduction to Autocad - Using Autosketch
SCOTVEC Module in Autocad using Autosketch.
H53

Introduction to CAD *College Certificate.* **L5**

Introduction to CAD - SCOTVEC Module
SCOTVEC certificate. **T9**

Introduction to CAD Using Autocad *College
Certificate.* **L27**

Introduction to Computer Aided Draughting
(SCOPTVEC) *SCOTVEC/NCM.* **L27**

Introduction to Computer Aided Draughting -
Module *SCOTVEC/NC half module Introduction
to Computer Aided Draughting.* **F8**

Introduction to Computer Aided Draughting - NC
SCOTVEC/NC. **C23 L81**

Introduction to Computer Application Package
(Database) (SCOTVEC) *SCOTVEC/NCM.* **L5**

Introduction to Computer Application Package
(Database) - 81098 *SCOTVEC/NCM
introduction to FOXPRO.* **D5**

Introduction to Computer Application Package
(Spreadsheet) - 91099 *SCOTVEC/NCM
introduction to SUPERCALC.* **D5**

Introduction to Computer Application Packages
(SCOTVEC) *SCOTVEC/NCM in Introduction to
Computer Application Packages.*
L1 L3 L31 L83

Introduction to Computer Application Packages -
Module *SCOTVEC Module - Introduction to
Application Packages.*
D5 F1 F8 F9 F10 F11 F15 T1

Introduction to Computer Applications *SCOTVEC
module.* **B4 B6 H49 L5**

Introduction to Computer Applications - NC
SCOTVEC/NC. **C45 L81**

Introduction to Computer Applications - NCM
SCOTVEC Certificate. **H53**

Introduction to Computer Skills *Introduction to
computers using software packages with practical
exercises.* **L27**

Introduction to Computer Software - Module
SCOTVEC/NCM. **F8 F10 F11 L1**

Introduction to Computers *SCOTVEC Certificate.*
**B2 B6 C12 D6 F1 F8 F9 F10 F11 F12 L
L2**

Introduction to Computers & Computing for
Housewives & Others (SCOTVEC)
SCOTVEC/NCM. **L27**

Introduction to Computers - NC *SCOTVEC/NC.*
C45

Introduction to Computers - NCM (81091)
SCOTVEC/NCM. **H29**

Introduction to Computers Application Packages
(SCOTVEC) *SCOTVEC/NCM.* **L2**

Introduction to Computing *No formal outcome.*
B6 D5 S81 S144

Introduction to Computing for the Young At Heart
Practical introduction to computers. **C41**

Introduction to Database *ITec certificate.* **H17**

Introduction to Database Management Systems -
HN Unit *SCOTVEC/HNU.* **F8**

Introduction to Databases   *College Certificate.*
L68

Introduction to Dataease   *College Certificate.*
L27

Introduction to Dbase 4   *College Certificate.*   **L27**

Introduction to Desktop Publishing   *No formal outcome.*   **B6**

Introduction to DOS   *Basic skills in DOS.*   **G31**

Introduction to Lotus 123   *College Certificate.*
T9

Introduction to Microsoft Works   *No formal outcome.*   **B6**

Introduction to New Technologies   *SCOTVEC Modules.*   **L68**

Introduction to Oracle - SQL   *Knowledge & experience of the Oracle - SQL software package.*
S87

Introduction to Paradox   *College Certificate.*
L27 S87

Introduction to PC's   *Basic PC skills.*   **G31**

Introduction to Project Management   *Napier University Certificate.*   **L48**

Introduction to Reflex   *College Certificate.*   **L27**

Introduction to Spreadsheet   *College Certificate.*
L68

Introduction to Spreadsheet - ESF   *ITec certificate.*   **H17**

Introduction to Spreadsheet Package (Quattro Pro)   *Knowledge & experience of the Quattro Pro software package.*   **S87**

Introduction to Spreadsheets   *No formal outcome.*
B6 L27

Introduction to the PC & MS-DOS   *College Certificate.*   **L27**

Introduction to the Personal Computer for the Unemployed - ESF   *ITec certificate.*   **H17**

Introduction to Windows/Word Processing   *No formal outcome.*   **B2**

Introduction to Word Processing   *Development of basic word processing skills.*   **C12**

Introduction to Word Processors Spreadsheets & Databases   *Practical experience of computer packages.*   **S109**

IT for Small Businesses   *RSA CLAIT Stage 1.*
S110

Job Costing - Sage   *Certificate of Competence.*
B6

Keyboarding   *SCOTVEC Module.*   **H54**

Lotus 1-2-3   *Construction & Manipulation of simple Spreadsheets.*   **G17 S6**

Lotus 1-2-3 - Advanced   *ITec certificate.*   **H17**

Lotus 1-2-3 - Advanced Training   *Extended knowledge of Lotus 1-2-3.*   **M8**

Lotus 1-2-3 - Forecasting & Analysis Techniques   *ITec certification.*   **H17**

Lotus 1-2-3 - Introduction   *Basic skills in Lotus 1-2-3.*   **M8**

Lotus 1-2-3 - Macro Programming   *ITec certification.*   **H17**

Lotus 1-2-3 Basic for Dos   *Basic knowledge of Lotus 1-2-3.*   **G31**

Lotus 1-2-3 for DOS Advanced   *Superior knowledge of the application.*   **G31**

Lotus 1-2-3 for DOS Intermediate   *Increases Knowledge of Lotus 1-2-3.*   **G31**

Lotus 1-2-3 for Windows - Introduction   *ITec certification.*   **H17**

Lotus 1-2-3 for Windows Version 4 - Advanced   *Advanced knowledge of Lotus for Windows.*   **G31**

Lotus 1-2-3 for Windows Version 4 - Basic   *Basic Knowledge of Lotus for Windows.*   **G31**

Lotus 1-2-3 for Windows Version 4 - Intermediate   *Increased efficiency while using Lotus.*   **G31**

Lotus 1-2-3 Version 2.4 - Introduction   *ITec certification.*   **H17**

Lotus Ami Pro Advanced   *Superior knowledge of Ami Pro. .*   **G31**

Lotus Ami Pro Introductory   *Basic knowledge of Ami Pro.*   **G31**

Lotus Freelance for DOS   *Working knowledge of Lotus Freelance.*   **G31**

Lotus Freelance for Windows   *Working knowledge of Lotus Freelance.*   **G31**

Lotus Symphony   *Basic skills in using Lotus Symphony.*   **G31**

Machine Assembly Processes & Systems - NC   *SCOTVEC/NC in Machine Assembly Processes & Systems.*   **S19**

Management - HNC   *SCOTVEC/HNC in Management.*   **H49 H53**

Mechanical & Computer Aided Engineering - HND   *SCOTVEC/HND in Mechanical & Computer Aided Engineering.*   **F5**

Mechanical C.A.E. Specialising in Mechanics of Materials - MSc   *MSc in Mechanical Computer Aided Engineering.*   **S105**

Mechanical C.A.E. Specialising in Mechanics of Materials - PgD   *PgD in Mechanical Computer Aided Engineering.*   **S105**

Mechanical C.A.E. Specialising in Thermodynamics & Fluid Mechanics - MSc   *MSc in Mechanical Computer Aided Engineering.*
S105

Mechanical C.A.E. Specialising in Thermodynamics & Fluid Mechanics - PgD   *PgD in Mechanical Computer Aided Engineering specialising in Thermodynamics & Fluid Mechanics.*   **S105**

Medical - Computing for Medical Practices   *Skills in medical computing.*   **D5**

Micro Awareness   *College Certificate.*   **L27**

Micro Computers for Beginners   *Basic skills in micro computers.*   **S112**

Microcomputer & Business Applications - Skillseekers/NVQ Level I   *NVQ Level I in Microcomputer & Business Applications.*   **S18**

Microcomputer Awareness   *No formal outcome.*   **L6**

Microcomputer Servicing & Support - HNC   *SCOTVEC/HNC in Microcomputer Servicing & Support.*   **F8**

Microcomputer Servicing & Support - HND   *SCOTVEC/HND in Microcomputer Servicing & Support.*   **F8**

Microcomputer Support - HNC   *SCOTVEC/HNC in Micro Computer Support.*   **C22**

Microcomputers - Introduction   *ITec certification.*   **H17**

Microcomputers - Introduction (C1)   *Basic knowledge of Spreadsheets, Databases, Word Processing.*   **S94**

Microsoft Access for Windows Version 2.0 (User)   *Training to basic & intermediate levels.*   **S117**

Microsoft Access V2 - Advanced   *Skilled use of Microsoft Access.*   **G31**

Microsoft Access V2 Basic & Intermediate   *Basic & intermediate use of Microsoft Access.*   **G31**

Microsoft Excel - Advanced   *ITec certification.*   **H17**

Microsoft Excel - Forecasting & Analysis Techniques   *ITec certification.*   **H17**

Microsoft Excel - Intermediate   *ITec certification.*   **H17**

Microsoft Excel - Introduction   *ITec certification.*   **H17 M8**

Microsoft Excel - Macro Programming   *ITec certification.*   **H17**

Microsoft Excel for Windows Version 5.0 (User)   *Training to basic & intermediate levels.*   **S117**

Microsoft Excel V5 - Advanced   *Skilled use of Microsoft Excel.*   **G31**

Microsoft Excel V5 - Basic   *Basic knowledge of Microsoft Excel.*   **G31**

Microsoft Excel V5 - Intermediate   *Intermediate knowledge of Microsoft Excel.*   **••none**

Microsoft Focpro - Basic   *Basic knowledge of Microsoft Focpro.*   **G31**

Microsoft Focpro - Intermediate/Advanced   *Intermediate & advanced knowledge of Microsoft Focpro.*   **G31**

Microsoft Powerpoint V 4   *Working knowledge of Microsoft Powerpoint.*   **G31**

Microsoft Project   *Working knowledge or Microsoft Project.*   **G31 S149**

Microsoft Windows   *Working knowledge of Microsoft Windows.*   **G31 S112**

Microsoft Windows for Workgroups Version 3.11 (User)   *Training to basic level.*   **S117**

Microsoft Windows Version 3.1 (User)   *Training to basic level.*   **S117**

Microsoft Word for Windows V6 - Advanced   *Superior knowledge of package.*   **G31**

Microsoft Word for Windows V6 - Basic   *Basic knowledge of Word for Windows.*   **G31**

Microsoft Word for Windows V6 - Intermediate   *Intermediate skills in Word for Windows.*   **G31**

Microsoft Word for Windows Version 6.0 (User)   *Training to basic & intermediate levels.*   **S117**

Microsoft Works for Windows   *Company Certificate.*   **S149**

Microsoft Works for Windows Version 3.0 (User)   *Training to basic level.*   **S117**

Multimedia   *MEDC Course Certificate.*   **S151**

Multi Media - HNC   *SCOTVEC/HNC in Multi Media.*   **S91**

Mumaths   *Knowledge of the computer program Mumaths.*   **L27**

Networking - Various Courses Available   *Company Certificate.*   **S149**

Numerical Processing (Spreadsheet) - HN Unit   *1 credit towards a HNC in Computing.*   **C23**

Numerical Processing Using Spreadsheets - HN Unit   *SCOTVEC/HNU.*   **F8**

Numerical Processing Using Spreadsheets- HN Unit   *SCOTVEC/HNU.*   **L5**

Office & Information Studies - SEB S Grade   *SEB S Grade in Office & Information Studies.*   **B11**

Office Administration - HNC   *SCOTVEC/HNC in Office Administration.*   **H49 S11 S14**

Office Information Processing - NC   *SCOTVEC/NC in Office Information Processing.*   **S10**

Office Technology & Administration - NC   *SCOTVEC/NC in Office Technology & Administration.*   **S16**

Office Technology & Administration NC   *SCOTVEC/NC in Office Technology & Administration.*   **S16**

Office Technology - NC   *SCOTVEC/NC in Office Technology.*   **S14**

Office/Secretarial/Administration/ Information - NCMs / HN Units   *Various courses available.*   **H53**

On-Line Communications-CIX COMPUSERVE   *MEDC Certificate Course.*   **S151**

Pagemaker   *Working knowledge of Pagemaker.*   **G31**

Paradox   *MEDC Course Certificate.*   **S151**

Paradox   *Skills gained in the use of Paradox.*   **S6**

Paradox - Intermediate   *ITec certification.*   **H17**

Paradox - Introduction   *ITec certification.*   **H17**

Paradox - Pal Programming   *ITec certification.*
H17

Paradox - Workshop   *ITec certification.*   **H17**

Paradox 3.5 - Introduction   *Introduction to Paradox.*   **M8**

Paradox for Dos   *Working knowledge of Paradox.*
G31

Paradox for Windows   *Working knowledge of Paradox.*   **G31**

Payroll - Sage Popular Payroll   *Certificate of Competence.*   **B6**

Payroll - Sage Sterling Payroll   *Certificate of Competence.*   **B6**

PC Awareness/Introduction to Personal Computing   *Basic skills in personal computing.*
M8

PC Hardware(technical)   *Training to basic & intermediate levels.*   **S117**

Personal Computer Fault Finding Training   *Understanding of the PC & its system.*   **H53**

Powerpoint   *MEDC Course Certificate.*   **S151**

Practical Computing   *Skills in using the computer as a business tool.*   **S57**

Producing Business Documents - HN Units   *2 credits towards a HNC in Office Technology.*
C23

Producing Complex Business Documents - HN Unit   *1 credit towards a HNC in Office Technology.*
C23

Project Management   *MEDC Certificate Course.*
S151

Project Management - PRINCE   *MEDC Course Certificate.*   **S151**

Quality Management   *MEDC Course Certificate.*
S151

Quatro Pro - Advanced   *ITec certification.*   **H17**

Quatro Pro - Forecasting & Analysis Techniques   *ITec certification.*   **H17**

Quatro Pro - Intermediate   *ITec certification.*
H17

Quatro Pro - Introduction   *ITec certification.*   **H17**

Quatro Pro - Macro Programming   *ITec certification.*   **H17**

Quattro Pro 4 - Introduction (C5)   *Basic skills in using Quattro Pro.*   **S94**

Relational Database Methods & Programming - Skillseekers/NVQ Level III   *NVQ Level III in Relational Database Methods & Programming.*
S18

RSA Core Text Processing   *RSA Certificate.*
H54

Sage Accounting - Advanced   *Extended knowledge of Sage Accounting.*   **M8**

Sage Accounting - Introduction   *Introductory skills in Sage Accounting.*   **M8**

Sage Payroll II   *Basic working knowledge of Sage Payroll II.*   **M8**

Sage Popular Accountant   *No formal outcome.*
B6

Sage Popular Accountant Plus   *Certificate of Competence.*   **B6**

Sage Popular Book-Keeping   *Basic skills using the Sage package.*   **B6**

Sage Popular Financial Controller   *Certificate of Competence.*   **B6**

Sage Sterling Accountant   *Basic skills using the Sage Sterling Accountant.*   **B6**

Sage Sterling Accountant Plus   *Certificate of Competence.*   **B6**

Sage Sterling Book-Keeping   *Basic skills using the Sage package.*   **B6**

Sage Sterling Financial Controller   *Certificate of Competence.*   **B6**

Sage Sterling Financial Controller - Computerised Accounting   *Competent use of the Sage package.*
L68

Sage Sterling Payroll - Computerised Accounting   *Competent use of the Sage package.*   **L68**

SCOTVEC Modules in Information Technology   *NCM in word processing, spreadsheet & data base.*   **C47**

Secretarial & Computing Studies - NC   *SCOTVEC/NC.*   **S98**

Secretarial Studies - National Cert   *SCOTVEC/NC in Secretarial Studies.*   **S10**

Secretarial/Administration/Computing - NCMs / HN Units   *Various courses available.*   **H53**

Setting Up a Business Computer   *Basic knowledge of setting up a business computer system.*   **H3**

Short Courses in Business Computing   *College Certificate.*   **L68**

SMART   *Skills gained in the use of SMART.*   **S6**

Software Development - HNC   *Successful students will be awarded the SCOTVEC/HNC in Software Development.*   **H29**

Spreadsheet - NCM (91099)   *SCOTVEC/NCM.*
H29

Spreadsheet Methods 1 - Skillseekers/NVQ Level I   *NVQ Level I in Spreadsheet Methods.*   **S18**

Spreadsheet Methods 2 - Skillseekers/NVQ Level II   *NVQ Level II in Spreadsheets.*   **S18**

Spreadsheets   *Knowledge of how to use spreadsheets to their best advantage.*   **H3 H53**

Spreadsheets & Databases *Training in the use of Spreadsheets & Databases.* **H30**

Spreadsheets - Lotus 123 *SCOTVEC/NCM.* **D5**

Spreadsheets - NCMs *SCOTVEC/NCM.* **L81**

Spreadsheets - Supercalc 5 *SCOTVEC/NCM.* **D5**

Spreadsheets - Various Courses Available *Company Certificate.* **S149**

Spreadsheets - Various Introductory to advanced Levels *No formal outcome.* **S112**

Structural Engineering Computational Technology - MSc/Diploma *MSc Degree/Diploma.* **L6**

Supercalc *Certificate of Competence.* **B6 S6**

Supercalc - Advanced *ITec certification.* **H17**

Supercalc - Forecasting & Analysis Techniques *ITec certification.* **H17**

Supercalc - Macro Programming *ITec certification.* **H17**

Supercalc 5 - Advanced Training Course *Advanced skills using Supercalc 5.* **M8**

Supercalc 5 - Introductory Training Course *Basic skills using Supercalc 5.* **M8**

Supercalc 5.5 - Intermediate *ITec certification.* **H17**

Supercalc 5.5 - Introduction *ITec certification.* **H17**

Support & Opportunity for Adult Returners (S.O.A.R.) *Preparation for employment or further education courses.* **C18**

Teach Yourself Dataease *Knowledge of Dataease.* **H41**

Teach Yourself Dbase 4 *Basic skills in using Dbase 4.* **H41**

Teach Yourself Lotus 1-2-3 *Basic skills in using Lotus 1-2-3.* **H41**

Teach Yourself Lotus 1-2-3, Macros 2.2 *No formal outcome.* **H41**

Teach Yourself Quattro Pro 4.0 *Basic skills in using Quattro Pro.* **H41**

Teach Yourself Supercalc *Basic skills in using Supercalc.* **H41**

Teach Yourself/Understanding Excel for Windows *Basic understanding of Excel.* **H41**

Teach Yourself/Understanding Lotus 1-2-3 for Windows *Basic understanding of Lotus 1-2-3.* **H41**

Telematics in Education *MEDC Course Certificate.* **S151**

Text Processing 1 *SCOTVEC Module.* **H54**

Training in Microsoft Office & Lotus SMART Suite *No formal outcome.* **S111**

Tuition for People with a Disability *LEAD provides advice on educational opportunities for people with a disability.* **H32**

Understanding Paradox *Knowledge of Paradox.* **H41**

Uniplex - Advanced *ITec certification.* **H17**

Uniplex - Forecasting & Analysis Techniques *ITec certification.* **H17**

Uniplex - Intermediate *ITec certification.* **H17**

Uniplex - Introduction *ITec certification.* **H17**

Uniplex - Macro Programming *ITec certification.* **H17**

Uniplex - Workshop *ITec certification.* **H17**

Uniplex Wordprocessing - Introduction *ITec certification.* **H17**

Users of Information Technology *SVQ Level 2.* **C47**

Using a Business Computer *Knowledge of using a business computer system.* **H3**

Using a Microcomputer - Module *SCOTVEC Module.* **F11**

Using Information Technology in Business - HN Unit *SCOTVEC/HNU.* **F8**

Using Information Technology in Business HN Units *2 credits towards a HNC in Office Technology.* **C23**

Using the Internet - Personal & Business (User) *Training to basic level.* **S117**

Utilising the Computer Resource - HN Unit *1 credit towards a HNC in Business Administration or Computing.* **C23 F8**

Women into Technology *Practical skills & knowledge.* **S15**

Women into Work *No formal outcome.* **C48 S147**

Women into Work Programme *Career & Personal Development Action Plan; Course Certification; Project Report.* **C3**

Women Returners Computing Course - ESF *RSA CLAIT Certificate.* **H17**

Women Returners Course *RSA Computer Literacy & Information Technology I.* **H5 H12**

Women Returners Course - Word Processing & Office Computing *RSA Certificate.* **H33**

Word for Windows *MEDC Course Certificate.* **S151**

Word Processing (Evenings) *No formal outcome.* **C48**

Word Processing - Various Courses Available *Company Certificate awarded.* **S149**

Word Processing - Various Introductory to Advanced Levels *No formal outcome.* **S112**

Word Processing Levels 1,2 & 3 *RSA Certificate.* **H54**

Wordperfect 5.1 for DOS Basic *Basic knowledge of Wordperfect.* **G31**

Wordperfect 5.1 for DOS Intermediate
Intermediate skills using Wordperfect.   **G31**

Wordperfect 5.1. for DOS Advanced   *Advanced skills using Wordperfect.*   **G31**

Wordperfect for Windows V6 - Advanced
Advanced skills using Wordperfect.   **G31**

Wordperfect for Windows V6 - Intermediate
Intermediate skills using Wordperfect.   **G31**

Wordperfect for Windows Version - 6 Basic   *Basic knowledge of Wordperfect.*   **G31**

Workplace Education - Computer Applications
Various courses available.   **C16**

Writing for Distance Learning   *MEDC Course Certificate.*   **S151**

Culture, Society & Education

ARCHAEOLOGY

Various Courses available   *No formal outcome.*
S9

Introduction to Field Archaeology   *No formal outcome.*   **B8**

EDUCATION, TEACHING & TRAINING, CAREER GUIDANCE

A Levels & GCSEs   *EEB Certificates.*   **L89**

Access to BEd (Primary)   *Guarantees acceptance to the BEd degree course at Moray House.*   **L28**

Adult Education - BA/BSc Evening Degree Programme   *Accumulation towards a Degree.*   **C42**

Adult Basic Education Programme (For Students with Learning Difficulties)   *Basic skills.*   **S87**

An Introduction in Child Development (SCOTVEC)   *SCOTVEC/NCM in Child Development 0-Puberty.*   **L68**

Applied Linguistics - MSc / Diploma   *MSc Degree / Diploma in Applied Linguistics.*   **L76**

Assessor & Verifier Awards - SCOTVEC   *Accreditation toward TDLB Units D32, D33, D34 & D36.*   **G2**

Assessors & Verifiers - Various   *Qualified to TDLB Standards in appropriate units.*   **G17**

Bachelor of Arts in Educational Studies - BA General   *BA General - Educational Studies.*   **C37**

Career Choices   *No formal outcome.*   **C50**

CEELT Preparation Summer Course   *Cambridge Examination in English for English Language Teachers .*   **L13**

Certificate Course for Exercise Teachers   *Certificate Course for Exercise Teachers.*   **L33**

Certificate in Exercise & Health Studies (PEA/RSA)   *PEA Certificate in Exercise & Health Studies.*   **L5**

Childcare & Education, SVQ Level II   *SCOTVEC, SVQs, SVQ Level II in Childcare & Education.*   **H53**

Childcare & Education, SVQ Level III   *SCOTVEC, SVQs, SVQ Level III in Childcare & Education.*   **H53**

Community Care & Learning Difficulties - BA/Diploma in Professional Studies   *BA in Community Care.*   **G15**

Community Education - MEd/ PgD Certificate   *MEd/Diploma certificate in Community Education.*   **L33**

Continuing Education - Certificate   *Certificate course.*   **G17**

Continuing Education Classes - Vocational   *SCOTVEC Certificate or H Grade Certificate .*   **M2**

Contract Courses in Teacher Education for English As a Foreign Language   *To suit clients' needs.*   **L13**

Drama for Teaching English As a Foreign Language - Summer Course   *Drama as a teaching aid .*   **L13**

Education - (P/T Degree Unit)   *Units can be accumulated towards a degree.*   **C42**

Education - MEd, Diploma or Certificate   *A Certificate, Diploma or Master's Degree in Education.*   **C44**

Education - MSc   *MSc (Education) Degree.*   **L77**

English for TEFL / Applied Linguistics - Summer Course   *Preparation for postgraduate courses in TEFL.*   **L13**

English Studies - BA/BSc Evening Programme   *Accumulation towards a Degree.*   **C42**

English Studies for Overseas Students - Foundation Course   *Preparation for the Examination.*   **G17**

Free-Standing Training Modules & Units   *A greater understanding of all aspects of training.*   **C22**

Further & Adult Education Teachers Certificate   *City & Guilds 7307.*   **G17**

Further & Adult Education Teaching Certificate - CGLI 7307   *City & Guilds 7307 Certificate.*   **L5**

General Education - NC   *Successful students will be awarded the SCOTVEC/NC.*   **S6**

General Education Section Short Course Provision   *College Certificate.*   **L27**

General Vocational Evening Class   *A range of subjects leading to SCE or SCOTVEC certificates.*   **D5**

Grammar & the Communicative Teaching of English - Summer Course   *Skills in teaching English grammar.*   **L13**

Group Work Skills Training   *Participants will be made aware of their individual roles within groups.*   **C13**

Highers   *SEB Certificate.*   **L89**

Hospital Play Specialist Course *Hospital Play Specialist Certificate.* **L68**

Introduction to Play (SCOTVEC) *SCOTVEC/NCM.* **L68**

Introduction to TESOL *College certificate in Basic English Teaching Skills.* **S13**

Introduction to Training *Increased awareness of & improved skills in training.* **C22**

Introduction to Training - NC *SCOTVEC/NC .* **C23**

Leisure & Recreation with Those with Special Needs *How to help special needs clients.* **S87**

Management of Training & Development - HNC *SCOTVEC/HNC in Management of Training & Development.* **S14**

Mathematical Education - MSc/Diploma *MSc Degree / Diploma in Mathematical Education.* **L79**

NC in Training *SCOTVEC/NC.* **C23**

Open University Community Education Course: the Pre-School Child *Development of skills in number work.* **C17**

Organisation of Child Play & Development *2 SCOTVEC/NCMs & a College Certificate.* **L68**

Outreach in Inverclyde & Argyll & Bute *Further Education for people or communities unable to attend College.* **S75**

Outreach in the Community *Further Education for people or communities unable to attend College.* **S75**

Planning Your Route into Higher Education *A better understanding of the higher education system.* **C50**

Pre-School Child Care *Courses are run throughout the Highlands for those involved in pre-school child care.* **H20**

Preparation for Volunteer Tutors *This course will enable lay volunteers to support/befriend/tutor children.* **S140**

Preparing to Work with People with Special Needs *SCOTVEC National Certificate.* **T23**

Psychometric Testing for Educational Choice *Evaluation of suitability for level & method of study.* **C50**

SCE Access for University Entrance *Access to higher education.* **G17**

Seminars in Teaching English As a Foreign Language *To suit individual clients.* **L13**

Short Courses in Teaching English As a Foreign Language *To suit individual clients.* **L13**

Skillstart Course for Adults - Skillstart Level I *Successful students will be awarded the Skillstart Level I.* **S75**

Special Education - HNC *SCOTVEC/HNC in Special Education.* **S81**

Special School Link (For Students with Moderate Learning Difficulties) *Integration into the college community.* **S87**

Specific Learning Difficulties/Dyslexia Awareness Day *Greater awareness of learning difficulties/dyslexia.* **D4**

Supervision Skills *Short courses to help those involved in supervision or instruction.* **H14**

Supervisory Management Skills *Designed to develop knowledge, skills & attitudes.* **H42**

Supervisory Skills - Instructional Techniques *Participants will have gained skills in instructional techniques.* **H35**

Support for Hearing Impaired Students - Consultancy *Students will be better able to reach their personal goals.* **S87**

Support for Physically Disabled Students - Consultancy *Help towards gaining personal goals.* **S87**

Support for Visually Impaired Students - Consultancy *Students will be better able to reach their personal goals.* **S87**

TDLB Assessor (D32 & D33) *Assessor Awards D32 & D33.* **S75**

TDLB Verifier (D34) *Verifier Award D34.* **S75**

Teach English As a Foreign Language to Adults *A grade (Pass, B or A) RSA/UCLES certificate in TEFLA .* **S100**

Teaching & Learning English - Summer Courses
Modern developments in English language
teaching.   L13

Teaching English As a Foreign Language - PgC &
Licentiate Diploma   PgC Certificate awarded.
                                                 G17

Teaching English As a Second Language to Adults
RSA Certificate in teaching English as a second
language.   S13

Teaching English for Medical Purposes - Summer
Course   Introduction to principles & practice.
                                                 L13

Teaching English for Specific Purposes - Summer
Course   Introduction to principles & practice.
                                                 L13

Teaching English to Speakers of Other Languages
(TESOL)   MA/Postgraduate Diploma certificate.
                                                 L33

Teaching English to Speakers of Other Languages
- Introductory   College Certificate awarded.   G17

Teaching of English As a Foreign Language to
Adults - Cambridge Diploma   UCLES Diploma
(Dip TEFLA).   L68

Teaching of English As a Second Language in
Further/Adult/Community Education   RSA (Dip
TESLFACE).   L68

Teaching of English As a Second Language to
Adults (RSA Certificate)   RSA Certificate (Cert.
TESLA).   L68

Teaching of English to Speakers of Other
Languages (TESOL)   College Certificate.   L68

The Institute of Training & Development - Diploma
Diploma of the Institute of Training &
Development.   S79

The Physically Disabled Students Link   Students
will be able to make informed choices for future
courses.   S87

Training & Development - HNC   SCOTVEC/HNC
in Training & Development.   C22

Training & Development - ITD Certificate   ITD
Certificate awarded on successful completion of
course.   G19

Training & Development - SVQ   SCOTVEC, SVQs
(SVQ) in Verifying & Assessing SVQs.   H49

Training & Development - SVQ Level III -IV
SCOTVEC SVQ SVQ Level III-IV in Training &
Development.   C22

Training & Development Lead Body - SVQ Levels
III & IV   SCOTVEC SVQ, SVQ Levels III & IV.
                                                 S75

Training - NC   SCOTVEC/NC in Training &
Development Level III.   C22

Training for Trainers - Modular Programme
Successful students will be awarded the
SCOTVEC/NCMs.   S75

Training Management - Diploma   Diploma in
Training Management.   S14

Training Management - ITD Diploma   Diploma in
Training Management.   F5

Training Needs Analysis   How to specify staff
requirements and training and develop job
descriptions.   G16

Training of Trainers   SCOTVEC SVQs in the
Workplace.   D5 F8 H30 S14 S87

Training of Trainers - NCMs   SCOTVEC/NCMs.
Successful students can apply to the ITD for
Certification.   H53

Training of Trainers Course   Associate
Membership of the Institute of Training
Development.   S2

Various courses available   Company certificate
awarded.   S149

Vocational Skills Course   Basic social & life skills
as well as practical skills.   T1

Volunteer Tutor Training   Development of skills in
helping adults to improve reading & writing skills.
                                                 C17

Working with Groups   Development of group work
skills.   C41 G21

Working with Young Children - NC
SCOTVEC/NC in Working with Young Children.
                                                 C22

Workplace Assessment Awards   First & Second
Line Assessor & Internal Verifier Awards.   C22

Workplace Assessor Training   Skills Assessor
Cert. TDLB D32, Vocational Assessor Cert. TDLB
D32 + D33.   S90

Workplace Education - Communication
Development of skills & the opportunity to gain
SCOTVEC qualifications.   C16

HISTORY

Access to Higher Education - SCE Higher History
Access to Higher Education through SCE H Grade
History.   D5

Alness Local History   The course aims to provide
people with an introduction to the local history of
Alness.   H52

Celtic Church   Knowledge of the history & culture
of the Celtic Church.   C41

Celtic Scotland   A knowledge of Celtic Scotland.
                                                 C41

Certificate in Local Studies   Students will gain a
certificate in local studies.   T13

Civilisation of Persia   An understanding of the
history of Iran.   C41

East - Central Europe - After Communism
Developments in post-communism Eastern
Europe.   C41

East - Central Europe - History in the 20th Century *An appreciation of the history of Eastern Europe.* **C41**

Economic History - SCE Higher *SCE Higher - Economic History.* **F7**

Family History - Advanced *Scottish Records; Legal Sources; Death Records.* **G21**

German, History, Geography - SCE H Grade *Participants will gain a SCE H Grade in one or more of the above subjects.* **M9**

History *SCOTVEC module in History will be awarded on successful completion of this course.* **B1**

History (Alt) Period C - SCE Higher *SCE Higher - History (Alt) Period C.* **F7**

History (Revised) - SCE Higher *SCE Higher - History (Revised).* **F7**

History - H Grade *A SCE H Grade.* **S88**

History - MLitt *Master of Letters Degree in History.* **L76**

History - MSc / Diploma *MSc Degree / Diploma in History.* **L76**

History - S Grade *SCOTVEC/NCM in History.* **S88**

History - SCE CSYS *Scottish Examination Board Certificate of Sixth Year Studies.* **D8**

History - SCE H Grade
B3 B6 C1 C4 C5 C6 C7 C20 C21 C22 C23 C25 C26 C27 C28 C29 C30 C33 C34 C36 C45 C46 F5 F8 S2 S6 S13 S14 S16 S79 S87 S98 T9

History - SCE H Grade (Alternative) *Scottish Examination Board Certificate in History at H Grade.* **D8**

History - SCE H Grade (Revised) *SCE H Grade History.* **L1 L15**

History - SCE H Grade or CSYS *SCE in History Studies at H Grade or Certificate of Sixth Year Studies.* **D3**

History - SCE O Grade *An SCE O Grade certificate in History.* **S14**

History - SCE Revised Higher *SCE Revised Higher - History.* **F10**

History - SCE Standard / SCE H Grade / NCMs *SCE Standard or H Grade or appropriate SCOTVEC modules.* **H13**

History - SCOTVEC *SCOTVEC module in History will be awarded on successful completion of this course.* **B10**

History - SCOTVEC Modules *SCOTVEC Modules in History.* **D8**

History - SEB H Grade *An SEB H Grade in History will be awarded on successful completion of this course.* **B1 B10**

History - SEB Sixth Year Studies *An SEB Certificate of Sixth Year Studies awarded.* **B1**

History H Grade *H grade in History.* **T1**

History: Britain in the World 1850-1914 (P/T Degree Unit) *Units can be accumulated towards a Degree.* **C42**

History: Foundations of Western Political Thought - (P/T Degree Unit) *Units can be accumulated towards a Degree.* **C42**

History: Modern European History 1848-1918 - (P/T Degree Unit) *Units can be accumulated towards a Degree.* **C42**

Local History *There is no formal outcome to this course.* **B3 B6 G13**

Lord of the Isles & Earls of Ross - Local History *An introduction to the history of Inverness & Easter Ross.* **H52**

Modern Studies - SCE H Grade *SCE H Grade in Modern Studies.* **L68**

Northern Studies Courses *These courses are run on a wide variety of subjects for general interest.* **H50**

Revised History - SCE H Grade *The SCE H Grade in Revised History.* **B6**

Roots of Scotland c.400 - 1100 *Knowledge of the history of Scotland.* **C41**

Social Science, History & Politics - BA *BA Degree from Stirling University, taught at Inverness College.* **H53**

Social Sciences - BA *A BA in Social Sciences.* **S27**

Social Sciences - BA (Honours) *A BA (Hons) in Social Sciences.* **S27**

Social Studies & History (SCOTVEC) - O Grade Replacements *SCOTVEC/NCMs.* **L5**

The Early History of North-East Scotland From 560-1560 Ad *The main trends & developments.* **G21**

The Picts & the Scots *A knowledge of Scotland's Heritage.* **C41**

The Silk Route *Knowledge of the great Asian overland trade routes.* **C41**

Travelling Through 4000 Years of History *Ancient Egypt, Peru, Bolivia and Brazil.* **G21**

LITERATURE

20th Century Scottish Literature *A deeper understanding of Twentieth Century Scots Literature.* **C41**

Access to Higher Education - SCE Higher English *Access to Higher Education through SCE H Grade English.* **D5**

American Literature: the 19th Century *A knowledge of American literature.* **C41**

Celtic Church   *Knowledge of the history & culture of the Celtic Church.*   **C41**

Celtic Scotland   *A knowledge of Celtic Scotland.*   **C41**

Chinese Literature in the Modern Age - MSc / Diploma   *MSc / Diploma in Chinese Literature in the Modern Age.*   **L76**

Classical Studies - SCE H Grade   *AN SCE H Grade in Classical Studies.*   **C20 C36**

Communication - Level 3 & 4   *Development of skills in reading, writing, talking & listening.*   **C22**

Comparative & General Literature - MSc   *MSc Degree in Comparative & General Literature.*   **L76**

Conflict in Literature   *In-depth study & discussion of various literary texts.*   **C41**

Contemporary French Studies - MLitt   *A MLitt diploma in Contemporary French Studies.*   **S105**

Contemporary German Studies - MLitt   *A MLitt diploma in Contemporary German Studies.*   **S105**

Contemporary German Studies - PgD   *A PgD in Contemporary German Studies.*   **S105**

Contemporary Latin American Novel   *A knowledge of Latin American literature.*   **C41**

English   *SCOTVEC Certificate will be awarded on successful completion of the module(s).*   **B11**

English (Revised) - SCE H Grade   *The SCE H Grade in English.*   **B6**

English - CSYS   *Scottish Examination Board Certificate of Sixth Year Studies in English.*   **D8**

English - H Grade   *A SCE H Grade.*   **S88**

English - Modular Course 1   *SCOTVEC Module in English, providing entry qualifications for H Grade English.*   **D8**

English - Modular Course 2   *SCOTVEC module in English, providing entry qualifications for English H Grade.*   **D8**

English - SCE H Grade   .
   C1 C4 C5 C6 C7 C20 C21 C22 C23 C25 C26 C27 C28 C29 C30 C33 C34 C36 C45 C46 D8 L68 S16 S98

English - SCE H Grade (Revised)   *SCE at H Grade in English.*   **C45 L1 L15**

English - SCE H Grade Grade   *SCE H Grade in English.*   **M5**

English - SCE H Grade or CSYS   *SCE in English at H Grade or Certificate of Sixth Year Studies.*   **D3**

English - SCE Revised Higher   *SCE Revised Higher - English.*   **F10**

English - SEB H Grade   *SEB H Grade in English.*   **B1 B10 B11**

English - SEB S Grade   *An SEB S Grade in English will be awarded on successful completion of this course.*   **B11**

English - SEB Sixth Year Studies   *An SEB Certificate of Sixth Year Studies in English will be awarded.*   **B1 B11**

English for Drama & Literary Discussion - Summer Course   *Improved command of the English Language.*   **L13**

English for Literary Studies Summer Courses   *Improved command of written English .*   **L13**

English Literature - GCE A Level   *GCE A Level in English Literature.*   **L68**

English Studies - PgD   *A PgD in English Studies.*   **S106**

English Studies - the Novel (P/T Degree Unit)   *Units can be accumulated towards a degree.*   **C42**

Introduction to Literature (SCOTVEC)   *SCOTVEC/NCM.*   **L68 L83**

Introduction to Literature - NC   *SCOTVEC/NC.*   **C23**

Introduction to Literature - Part-Time NC   *SCOTVEC module.*   **L81**

K506: Living Arts Support Group   *Key themes & issues in the arts & their role in contemporary experience.*   **H39**

Literature   *Qualification as studied for.*   **L88**

Literature 1 (SCOTVEC)   *SCOTVEC/NCM in Literature 1.*   **L1 L68**

Literature 1 - Module   *NCM.*   **F8**

Literature 1 - NC   *SCOTVEC/NC.*   **C23**

Literature 1 - Part-Time NC   *SCOTVEC module.*   **L81**

Literature Appreciation   *Participants will have a greater understanding of literature appreciation.*   **C41**

Modern French Literature & Society - MPhil/Diploma   *Master of Philosophy degree in Modern French Literature.*   **C39**

Scottish Studies - MLitt   *Master of Letters Degree in Scottish Studies.*   **L76**

PHILOSOPHY

Introduction to Philosophy   *SCOTVEC module in Philosophy.*   **C22**

Introduction to Philosophy - NC   *SCOTVEC/NC.*   **C23**

Philosophy   *Qualification as studied for.*   **L88**

Philosophy & Morality (SCOTVEC)   *SCOTVEC/NCM 7176031 Philosophy & Morality.*   **L15**

Philosophy & the Environment   *A knowledge of philosophy & ecology.*   **C41**

Philosophy: End or Renewal   *A knowledge of philosophy.*   **C41**

Philosophy: Practical Reasoning   *How to produce more reasoned argument & coherent communication.*   **G21**

Professional & Business Ethics - MSc   *MSc Degree / PgD in Professional & Business Ethics.*   **L65**

RELIGIOUS STUDIES

Buddhism for the Modern West   *An introduction to Buddhism.*   **C41**

Buddhist Meditation   *A practical experience of meditation techniques.*   **C41**

Divinity Access Course   *Admission to Theology and/or Religious Studies courses at Edinburgh University.*   **L80**

Introduction to Community Education   *Prepares participants for work in the community.*   **C22**

Introduction to Religion/Religion & Community/Religion & Politics   *SCOTVEC module in Religion.*   **C22**

Religion & Morality   *SCOTVEC Certificate will be awarded on successful completion of the module(s).*   **B11**

Religious Studies   *SCOTVEC module in Religious Studies will be awarded.*   **B1 L88**

Religious Studies (Revised) - SCE Higher   *SCE Higher - Religious Studies (Revised).*   **F7**

Religious Studies - SCE H Grade
C1 C4 C20 C21 C26 C27 C28 C30 C36 C45 L15

Religious Studies - SCOTVEC Modules   *SCOTVEC Module in Religious Studies.*   **D8**

Religious Studies - SEB H Grade   *SEB H Grade in Religious Studies.*   **B1 B11**

Religious Studies - SEB S Grade   *SEB S Grade in Religious Studies.*   **B11**

SOCIAL, CARE & WELFARE WORK

Ability Awareness Training Course   *Attitudes & misconceptions to the term "Special Needs".*   **C13**

Alcohol & Drug Studies - PgD   *PgD in Alcohol & Drug Studies.*   **S103**

An Introduction in Child Development (SCOTVEC)   *SCOTVEC/NCM in Child Development 0-Puberty.*   **L68**

An Introduction to Basic Counselling Skills in Working with Young People   *Listening & counselling skills.*   **C13**

Applied Social Sciences - MSc   *A MSc in Applied Social Science.*   **S43**

Applied Social Sciences - PgC   *A PgC in Applied Social Science.*   **S43**

Applied Social Sciences - PgD   *A PgD in Applied Social Sciences.*   **S43**

Basic Counselling Skills   *A practical introduction to basic counselling skills.*   **C41**

Bereavement Counselling for Professionals - a Case Study Approach   *See Course Content.*   **S109**

Bereavement, Grief & Loss   *Increased awareness of the Grief Process. Possible SCOTVEC Certification.*   **D5**

Care (Level II) - GSVQ   *SCOTVEC/NC leading to GSVQ Care Level II.*   **G2**

Care - Accreditation of Prior Learning   *SCOTVEC/NCMs in Care.*   **F8**

Care - GSVQ Level II   *GSVQ in Care at Level II.*   **G17**

Care - GSVQ Level II   *GSVQ Level II.*   **F8**

Care - GSVQ Level II/National Certificate   *GSVQ (GSVQ) Level II in Care.*   **S88**

Care - SVQ Levels II & III   *SVQ, SVQ Levels II & III in Care.*   **S75**

Care of People with Dementia - Module   *NCM.*   **F8**

Care:direct Care - YT/SVQ Levels II-III   *SCOTVEC SVQ, SVQ Levels II-III Certificate.*   **S80**

Caring (Short Course)   *SCOTVEC relevant modules tailored to meet the needs of individual employers in the caring sector.*   **D5**

Caring for People - NC   *SCOTVEC/NC & College Certificate.*   **L81**

Caring for the Elderly - NCM   *SCOTVEC/NCM.*   **L81**

Caring Level 3 - GSVQ   *Students can apply for a job in a Caring situation, or enter a more advanced course.*   **G17**

Caring Skills - Bereavement, Grief & Loss   *Improved caring skills - bereavement, grief & loss.*   **D5**

Caring Skills - Counselling   *Improved caring skills - counselling.*   **D5**

Caring Skills - NCMs   *SCOTEC NCs in a variety of caring topics are available.*   **H26 H30**

Caring Skills - the Caring Relationship   *Improved caring skills - the caring relationship.*   **D5**

Certificate in Counselling   *Certificate in Counselling which is recognised & validated by COSCA.*   **L68**

Certificate in Counselling Skills (AEB)   *Certificate in counselling skills awarded by the AEB.*   **F5**

Certificate in Welfare Studies   *Certificate of Welfare Officers.*   **L81**

Child Care & Education - NC   *SCOTVEC/NC in Child Care & Education.*   **C22**

Childcare & Education - SCOTVEC/NC *SCOTVEC Certificate.*   **G17**

Childcare & Education, SVQ Level II   *SCOTVEC, SVQs, SVQ Level II in Childcare & Education.*
H53

Childcare & Education, SVQ Level III   *SCOTVEC, SVQs, SVQ Level III in Childcare & Education.*
H53

Childcare - SCOTVEC Module   *SCOTVEC Module in Childcare.*   **G20**

Childcare, Social Care or Health Care - GSVQ Level 3   *GSVQ in Care at Level 3.*   **G17**

Childminding / Pre-School Child / Childhood 5-10   *An OU Certificate of Completion is issued on completion.*   **H44**

Children with Special Needs - NC   *SCOTVEC/NC listing Modules studied & Learning Outcomes attained will be awarded.*   **C23**

Co-Counselling   *SCOTVEC Certificate & enhanced skills in the workplace.*   **D5**

Combating Drugs Misuse   *Candidates are made aware of drugs issues.*   **C13**

Community & Local Economic Development - HNC *HNC in Community & Local Economic Development.*   **F13**

Community & Local Economic Development - HND *HND in Community & Local Economic Development.*   **F13**

Community & Social Care - GSVQ Levels II & III *SVQ Levels II & III in Community & Social Care.*
B3

Community Care & Learning Difficulties - BA/Diploma in Professional Studies   *BA Degree course.*   **G15**

Community Care in Scotland - NC *SCOTVEC/NC.*   **C23**

Community Caring - NC   *SCOTVEC/NC in Community Caring.*   **S78**

Community Health Studies - BA (Honours)   *BA (Hons) in Community Health Studies.*   **T12**

Community Sports Leadership Course   *6 modules covering various aspects of Sports Leadership.*
C13

Community Welfare - NC   *SCOTVEC/NC & College Certificate.*   **L81**

Community Welfare 2 - NCM   *SCOTVEC/NCM.*
L81

Community Work Assistants - In-Service Training *Details available from contact.*   **S14**

Counselling   *SCOTVEC Certificate & enhanced skills in the workplace.*   **D5 T13**

Counselling - AEB Diploma   *Associated Examination Board Certificate.*   **L5**

Counselling - Introduction to   *Participants will have been introduced to the ideas which lie behind counselling during this course.*   **G21**

Counselling On Alcohol/Drugs   *Insight & skills to be an effective counsellor.*   **H45**

Counselling Psychology - HNC   *SCOTVEC/HNC.*
L5

Counselling Skills   *Level 1-4 of the certificate in counselling skills awarded by COSCA.*   **C22 T9**

Counselling Skills - AEB Certificate   *Associated Examination Board Certificate.*   **L5**

Counselling Skills for Managers   *Understanding of the fundamentals of the counselling relationship & process.*   **S57**

Counselling Theory - AEB Certificate   *Associated Examination Board Certificate.*   **L5**

Counselling Training - Customised Courses *Various. Courses may lead to nationally recognised qualifications.*   **L71**

Crisis Counselling   *SCOTVEC Certificate & enhanced skills in the workplace.*   **D5**

Dealing with Health Emergencies   *Level 1-4 of the certificate in counselling skills awarded by COSCA.*   **C22**

Dealing with Loss, Change & Bereavement   *An understanding of the meaning of loss, change & bereavement.*   **M8**

Dementia Services Development Centre *Development of services used when working with the elderly.*   **C44**

Development of Welfare Services (SCOTVEC) *SCOTVEC/NCM.*   **L5**

Disabilism Is an Educational Issue   *Participants will be made aware of individuals or groups with Special Needs.*   **C13**

Enabling Others to Cope with Loss: an Introduction (1/2 Module)   *SCOTVEC/NC.*   **C23**

First Aid Measures for Carers (SCOTVEC) *SCOTVEC/NCM.*   **L68**

Health Care - HNC/SVQ Level III *SCOTVEC/HNC in Health Care/SVQ in Care Level III.*   **S75**

Health Studies - NC   *SCOTVEC/NC will be awarded on successful completion of this course.*
B3

Home Help Basic Training   *College Certificate.*
L81

Home Help Courses   *Specialised training for home helps.*   **L27**

Human Development - the Older Adult in Need of Care - Module   *SCOTVEC/NCM - 7140830.*   **F8**

Human Development: 0 to Puberty - Module *SCOTVEC/NCM - 96026.*   **F8**

Human Development: the Older Adult in Need of Care - NC   *SCOTVEC/NC.*   **C23**

In-Service in Social Care   *Skills gained in social care.*   **S81**

In-Service Up-Dating for Special Needs Auxiliaries *Up-dated knowledge for special needs auxiliaries.*   **D5**

Introduction to Community Education   *Prepares participants for work in the community.*   **C22**

Introduction to Counselling   *There are 2 courses in counselling available at different levels.*   **H53**

Introduction to Counselling (SCOTVEC) *SCOTVEC/NCM.*   **L5 L31**

Introduction to Counselling - Module *SCOTVEC/NCM.*   **F8**

Introduction to Counselling - NCM *SCOTVEC/NC. Basic principles needed in good counselling/advice work.*   **H26**

Introduction to Counselling - SCOTVEC Module *SCOTVEC/NCM No:76094 'Introduction to Counselling'.*   **L68**

Introduction to Play (SCOTVEC) *SCOTVEC/NCM.*   **L68**

Introduction to Registered Childminding *Childminding & what it entails; can lead towards becoming a Registered Childminder.*   **D5**

Introduction to Working with People with Visual Impairment - HNU   *Higher National Unit.*   **F8**

Managing Violence Courses   *Letter of attendance.*   **S113**

Marketing Products & Services   *City & Guilds & SCOTVEC SVQ/NVQ Level 3.*   **G32**

Mental Health - HNC   *SCOTVEC/HNC in Mental Health.*   **S11**

Mental Health: an Introduction - NC *SCOTVEC/NC.*   **C23**

Moving & Handling for Social Work Staff   *A Certificate will be awarded on successful completion of this course.*   **B4**

Organisation of Child Play & Development   *2 SCOTVEC/NCMs & College Certificate.*   **L68**

People with Special Needs - HN Unit   *2 credits towards a HNC in Social Care.*   **C23**

Practical Caring Skills - NC   *SCOTVEC/NC.*   **L81**

Practical Caring Skills - SCOTVEC/NC   *Safe practice with client groups; personal & social development.*   **T23**

Pre-School Child   *An OU Certificate is issued on completion.*   **H44**

Pre-School Child Care   *Courses are run throughout the Highlands for those involved in pre-school child care.*   **H20**

Preparation for a Child's Admission to & Discharge From Hospital   *SCOTVEC/NC.*   **T23**

Preparing to Work with People with Special Needs - Module   *SCOTVEC/NC half module - 96020.*   **F8**

Preparing to Work with People with Special Needs - NC   *SCOTVEC/NC.*   **C23**

Professional Development Award in Supervisory Care Management   *For care workers involved in staff supervision.*   **C22**

Programme Planning & Administration   *Raised awareness of procedures & processes involved in programme planning.*   **C13**

Provision of Care - SCOTVEC/NC   *Evaluation of the provision of caring services in relation to meeting the needs of clients.*   **T23**

Provision of Community Care - NCM *SCOTVEC/NCM.*   **L81**

Roles of Community Care Personnel - SCOTVEC/NC   *Operation & functions of the major statutory & non-statutory agencies.*   **T23**

Scotland: Society & Politics - MSc/Diploma in Social Sciences   *MSc/Diploma in Social Sciences - Scotland: Society & Politics.*   **L77**

Setting Limits   *SCMA Certificate is issued on completion. Possible progression to SVQ in Childcare & Education.*   **H44**

Short Course Day 1   *Participants have the opportunity to select up to 2 short workshops.*   **C13**

Short Course Day 2   *Participants will have the opportunity to select up to 2 short workshop courses.*   **C13**

Short Courses for Minority Ethnic Women   *A variety of non-certificate courses & courses leading to SCOTVEC certificates.*   **C16**

Social & Public Policy - MSc / Diploma   *MSc Degree / Diploma in Social & Public Policy.*   **L77**

Social Care & Social Work - Short Courses   *To meet the requirements of the client.*   **L68**

Social Care (Revised) - HNC   *Successful candidates will gain SCOTVEC/HNC in Social Care.*   **M7**

Social Care - HNC   *SCOTVEC/HNC in Social Care.*
  C22 D5 F13 S2 S11 S15 S16 S19 S81 S87

Social Care - HNC - SVQ Level III   *HNC in Social Care, SCOTVEC SVQs SVQ Level III.*   **L68**

Social Care - HNC/SVQ Level III   *SCOTVEC/HNC & SVQ Level III.*   **H53**

Social Care - HNC/SVQ Level III   *SCOTVEC/HNC in Social Care/SVQ in Care Level III.*   **S75**

Social Care - NC   *SCOTVEC/NC in Social Care.*
S71

Social Care - NC / GSVQ Level III   *SCOTVEC/NC & GSVQ Level III.*   **H53**

Social Care - SCOTVEC/HNC   *SCOTVEC/HNC will be awarded when the student has gained 12 credits.*   **G17**

Social Service Management - MSc/ PgD Certificate   *MSc/Diploma certificate in Social Service Management.*   **L33**

Social Studies / Caring - NCMs   *SCOTVEC/NC(s) will be awarded to successful students.*   **H53**

Social Work   *Development of skills in social work.*
C44

Social Work - Diploma   *On successful completion of this course students will have a Diploma in Social Work.*   **G12**

Social Work - Post-Qualifying Programme by Individual Study   *According to individual requirements.*   **L77**

Social Work by Distance Learning   *On successful completion students will receive a Diploma in Social Work.*   **G15**

Social Work Management - MSc/Diploma   *A MSc or PgD in Social Work Management.*   **C40**

Social Work Studies - Post-Qualifying (Social Work Practice) - MSc / Dip   *MSc Degree / Dip in Social Work Practice.*   **L77**

Social Work Studies - Post-Qualifying (Social Work Service Planning) - Msc/Dip   *MSc Degree / Dip in Social Work Service Planning.*   **L77**

Sociology & Social Policy: Social Differentiation - (P/T Degree Unit)   *Units can be accumulated towards a Degree.*   **C42**

Sociology & Social Policy: Understanding Social Policy - (P/T Degree Unit)   *Units can be accumulated towards a degree.*   **C42**

Special Care & Education - HNC   *SCOTVEC/HNC in Special Care & Education.*   **S75**

Special Needs & Support Services - Module *SCOTVEC/NCM - 66032.*   **F8**

Supervision of Care Service Management - Advanced Certificate   *AC in Supervision of Care Service Management.*   **S75**

Supervision of Social Care Staff - HN Unit   *1.5 credits towards a HNC in Social Care.*   **C23**

Support & Management of Volunteers - Course 1 *How to manage & make the most effective use of volunteers.*   **C13**

Support & Management of Volunteers - Course 2 *How to make the most effective use of volunteers.*
C13

Supporting Elderly People in the Community - SCOTVEC/NC   *How to identify & support the needs of elderly people.*   **T23**

Supporting the Elderly in the Community - Module *SCOTVEC/NCM - 86029.*   **F8**

Surviving Parenthood   *An insight into the problems of parenting an adolescent & some possible solutions.*   **H31**

The Care of People with Dementia (SCOTVEC) *SCOTVEC/NCM.*   **L68**

The Care of People with Dementia - NC *SCOTVEC/NC.*   **C23**

The Care of People with Dementia - SCOTVEC/NC   *How to meet the needs of people with dementia and alleviate the stresses associated with caring.*   **T23**

The Helping Relationship - NC   *SCOTVEC/NC.*
L81

The Management of Care Services - Diploma   *A Diploma in The Management of Care Services.*
S23

Using Video Equipment Introductory Course *Participants will be able to set up & operate a video system.*   **C13**

Values for Care - SCOTVEC/NC   *On successful completion of this course students will receive a SCOTVEC/NC.*   **T23**

Welfare Provision in Scotland (SCOTVEC) *SCOTVEC/NCM.*   **L5**

Who's Who & What's What   *An introduction to the Resources & Support Agencies within Central Region.*   **C13**

Work with Children (Under 12's) - Course 1 *Support for use in the development of working with younger children.*   **C13**

Work with Children (Under 12's) - Course 2 *Practical methods of working with children.*   **C13**

Working Towards Independent Living - NC *SCOTVEC/NC listing.*   **C23**

Working with Children in Their Early Years - HNC *SCOTVEC/HNC.*   **S8 S15 S75 S87 T9**

Working with Children in Their Early Years - SCOTVEC/HNC   *SCOTVEC/HNC.*   **G17**

Working with Older People - HN Unit   *2 credits towards a HNC in Social Care.*   **C23**

Working with Young Children - NC *SCOTVEC/NC in Working with Young Children.*
C22

SOCIAL & CULTURAL STUDIES

A Taste for Romance: Interpreting the Scottish Historical Novel   *Aspects of writing and how to analyse literature.*   **G21**

Access to Arts & Social Sciences   *Progression to higher education.*   **L96**

Access to Arts & Social Sciences - SCOTVEC/NC & Access *SCOTVEC certificate.* **G17**

Access to Higher Education - SCE GCSE Sociology *Access to Higher Education through GCSE Sociology..* **D5**

Access to Higher Education - SCE Higher Modern Studies *Access to Higher Education through SCE H Grade Modern Studies.* **D5**

Access to Higher Education - SCOTVEC Social Sciences: People & Politics *Access to Higher Education through modules.* **D5**

Access to Technology for Women *Prepares women for further training in new technology related skills.* **F13**

African Studies - MSc / Diploma *MSc Degree / Diploma in African Studies.* **L77**

Applied Social Sciences - MSc *A MSc in Applied Social Science.* **S43**

Applied Social Sciences - PgC *A PgC in Applied Social Science.* **S43**

Applied Social Sciences - PgD *A PgD in Applied Social Sciences.* **S43**

Arts & Social Sciences - Scottish Wider Access *Recognised group of SCOTVEC Modules & University subjects.* **G2**

Basic Applications of Behavioural Science - NC *SCOTVEC/NC.* **C23**

Celtic Church *Knowledge of the history & culture of the Celtic Church.* **C41**

Celtic Scotland *A knowledge of Celtic Scotland.* **C41**

Certificate in Welfare Studies *Certificate of Welfare Officers.* **L81**

Childcare, Social Care or Health Care - GSVQ Level 3 *GSVQ in Care at Level 3.* **G17**

Community & Local Economic Development - HNC *HNC in Community & Local Economic Development.* **F13**

Community & Local Economic Development - HND *HND in Community & Local Economic Development.* **F13**

Current Affairs & Questions of the Hour *Delegates will have an understanding of the topics of Current Concern.* **G21**

Developing Anti-Discriminatory Practice *Enhanced understanding in this area.* **L68**

East - Central Europe - After Communism *A better understanding of developments in post-communism Eastern Europe.* **C41**

Economic Structure of Industry (SCOTVEC) *SCOTVEC/NCM.* **L5**

Environmental Education - Perspectives On the Environment I - (P/T Degree Unit) *Units can be accumulated towards a degree.* **C42**

European & International Politics - MSc/Diploma *MSc/Diploma in Social Sciences - European & International Politics.* **L77**

Gender in Society - MSc/Diploma in Social Sciences *MSc/Diploma in Social Sciences - Gender in Society.* **L77**

Human Development: the Older Adult in Need of Care - NC *SCOTVEC/NC.* **C23**

Introduction to Community Education *Prepares participants for work in the community.* **C22**

Introduction to Religion/Religion & Community/Religion & Politics *SCOTVEC module in Religion.* **C22**

Latin, Life & Language *Contact course provider for full details.* **T13**

Legal Studies MSc/Diploma in Advanced Legal Studies *MSc Degree/Diploma in Advanced Legal Studies.* **L72**

Media & Modern Culture - MA *Master of Arts Degree / PgD in Media & Modern Culture.* **L65**

Modern Studies (Revised) - SCE H Grade *The SCE H Grade in Modern Studies.* **B6**

Modern Studies (Revised) - SCE Higher *SCE Higher - Modern Studies (Revised).* **F7**

Modern Studies - H Grade *A SCE H Grade.* **S88**

Modern Studies - S Grade *SCOTVEC/NCM in Modern Studies.* **S88**

Modern Studies - SCE H Grade *An SCE H Grade in Modern Studies.*
   C1 C4 C6 C7 C20 C22 C23 C25 C26 C2 C29 C30 C33 C34 C36 C45 F5 F8 F11 L68 S2 S6 S13 S14 S16 S79 S98 T9

Modern Studies - SCE H Grade (Revised) *SEB Certificate in Modern Studies at H Grade.* **D8 L1**

Modern Studies - SCE H Grade or CSYS *SCE in Modern Studies at H Grade or CSYS.* **D3**

Modern Studies - SCE Higher *SCE Higher in Modern Studies.* **M3**

Modern Studies - SCE O Grade *An SCE O Grade certificate in Modern Studies.* **S14**

Modern Studies - SCE Revised Higher *SCE Higher - Modern Studies.* **F10**

Modern Studies - SCE Standard / SCE H Grade / NCMs *SCE Standard or H Grade or SCOTVEC modules.* **H13**

Modern Studies - SCOTVEC Modules *SCOTVEC Modules in Modern Studies.* **D8**

Modern Studies - SEB H Grade *An SEB H Grade in Modern Studies will be awarded on successful completion of this course.* **B11**

Modern Studies H Grade *H grade in Modern Studies.* **T1**

Modern Studies, Management & Information Studies, Art & Design - SCE H Grade *SCE H Grade.* **M9**

New Directions for Women   *Delegates will have found out where their strengths lie.*   **G21**

Northern Studies Courses   *These courses are run on a wide variety of subjects for general interest & education.*   **H50**

People & the Environment - British Isles   *SCOTVEC module will be awarded on successful completion of this course.*   **B1**

People & the Environment - British Isles (SCOTVEC)   *SCOTVEC/NCM 7175020 People & the Environment - British Isles.*   **L83**

People & the Environment - Europe/EC (SCOTVEC)   *SCOTVEC/NCM 7175030 People & the Environment - Europe/EC.*   **L83**

People & the Environment - Scotland (SCOTVEC)   *SCOTVEC/NCM 7175050 People & the Environment - Scotland.*   **L83**

People & the Environment - the World (SCOTVEC)   *SCOTVEC/NCM 7175060 People & the Environment - The World.*   **L83**

People in Society - NC   *SCOTVEC/NC.*   **C23**

Plant Identification   *Participants will have a understanding of the principles of plant identification.*   **T13**

Police Studies - HNC   *HNC in Police Studies.*   **L49**

Pre-Entry Course for Arts & Social Studies   *Can lead to BA degree course or entry to an individual Cert. course.*   **S109**

Roots of Scotland c.400 - 1100   *Knowledge of the history of Scotland.*   **C41**

Science & Technology Studies - MSc/Diploma in Social Sciences   *MSc/Diploma in Social Sciences - Science & Technology Studies.*   **L77**

Scotland: Society & Politics - MSc/Diploma in Social Sciences   *MSc/Diploma in Social Sciences - Scotland: Society & Politics.*   **L77**

Scottish Studies - MLitt   *Master of Letters Degree in Scottish Studies.*   **L76**

Social & Political Theory - MSc/Diploma in Social Sciences   *MSc/Diploma in Social Sciences - Social & Political Theory.*   **L77**

Social & Vocational Skills - SEB S Grade   *An SEB S Grade in Social & Vocational Skills.*   **B11**

Social Anthropology - MSc / Diploma   *MSc Degree / Diploma in Social Anthropology.*   **L77**

Social Research - MSc   *A MSc in Social Research.*   **S105**

Social Science & Its Applications - SCOTVEC/NC   *SCOTVEC certificate.*   **G17**

Social Science - SCE H Grade   *SCE H Grade.*   **S13**

Social Science - SCOTVEC/HNC   *SCOTVEC/HNC will be awarded when the student has gained 12 credits.*   **G17**

Social Science, History & Politics - BA   *BA degree from Stirling University, taught at Inverness College.*   **H53**

Social Sciences - BA   *A BA in Social Sciences.*   **S27**

Social Sciences - BA (Honours)   *A BA (Hons) in Social Sciences.*   **S27**

Social Sciences - HNC   *SCOTVEC/HNC will be awarded on successful completion of this course.*   **B6 S71**

Social Studies & History (SCOTVEC) - O Grade Replacements   *SCOTVEC/NCMs.*   **L5**

Sociology   *SCOTVEC module will be awarded on successful completion of this course.*   **B6**

Sociology & Social Policy: Social Differentiation - (P/T Degree Unit)   *Units can be accumulated towards a degree.*   **C42**

Sociology & Social Policy: Understanding Social Policy - (P/T Degree Unit)   *Units can be accumulated towards a degree.*   **C42**

Sociology - GCE A Level   *GCE A Level in Sociology.*   **L68**

Sociology - GCSE   *GCSE in Sociology.*   **L68**

Sociology: Introduction to Human Society   *Some of the ways in which lives may be shaped by society.*   **G21**

The Picts & the Scots   *A knowledge of Scotland's Heritage.*   **C41**

The World About Us Part 2   *Participants will have gained knowledge in a wide range of subjects.*   **T13**

The World in the Twentieth Century Part 2   *Week by week surveys of current national & international issues.*   **T13**

Various Courses Available   *No formal outcome.*   **S137**

Women & Science & Technology   *An introduction to the role of women in science & technology.*   **C41**

Women's Studies - Advanced Certificate   *An Advanced Certificate in Women's Studies.*   **S105**

Women's Studies - Continuing Education Certificate   *Credit bearing for the part-time BA degree in Arts & Social Studies.*   **S109**

Women's Studies - MLitt   *MLitt in Women's Studies.*   **S105**

Women's Studies - PgD   *A PgD in Women's Studies.*   **S105**

Women's Studies Seminar   *Women's history & literature, women & work, women & science/technology.*   **C41**

Women's Workshop   *An analysis of women's roles in society.*   **C41**

Working Towards Independent Living - NC   *SCOTVEC/NC.*   **C23**

Engineering Production & Industrial Design

ENGINEERING & PLANT SAFETY

Abrasive Wheel Regulations   *Certificate of Attendance awarded.*   **C10 H31 T1**

Abrasive Wheels   *A range of courses to meet individual needs.*   **D5 G26 H30**

Abrasive Wheels (Cutting Discs)   *Safe mounting of Cutting Discs & the safe use of Cutting Disc Machines.*   **H53**

Abrasive Wheels - Part-Time NC   *A College Certificate will be issued.*   **L81**

Abrasive Wheels Safety   *Aspects of Abrasive Wheel identification and handling.*   **M8**

Engineering & Building Section Short Course Provision   *College Certificate.*   **L27**

Health, Safety & Hygiene   *Employer's/employee's responsibilities for health & safety.*   **H42**

Industrial & Domestic Gas Safety for Plumbers   *CITB Registration for individuals/CORGI for companies.*   **S141**

Plant Engineering - HNC   *HNC in Plant Engineering which can give partial exemption from HND course.*   **D5**

Safety Awareness Training   *To promote awareness of current safety legislation. CITB approved.*   **H53**

ENGINEERING SYSTEMS & SERVICES

Advanced Certificate in Engineering Practice   *AC in Engineering Practice (Electrical & Electronic).*   **C23**

Business & Manufacturing Management   *Institution of Electrical Engineers (IEE) certificate awarded.*   **L48**

Computer Aided Engineering (Manufacture) - HNC   *SCOTVEC/HNC in Computer Aided Engineering (Manufacture).*   **F8**

Electrical Engineering (Electrical Plant Bias) - NC   *SCOTVEC/NC in Electrical Engineering.*   **L68**

Electrical Plant Installation & Maintenance Stage 3 - NC   *SCOTVEC/NC.*   **G17**

Electrical Plant Installation & Maintenance Stages 1 & 2 - NC   *SCOTVEC/NC.*   **G17**

Engineering & Building Services - Customised Courses   *Various.*   **L71**

Engineering - HNC   *SCOTVEC/HNC in Engineering.*   **L81**

Engineering - NC   *Successful students will be awarded the SCOTVEC/NC in Engineering.*   **S75 S87**

Engineering - Plant Option - Years 1 & 2 - HNC   *SCOTVEC/HNC in Engineering - Plant Option.*   **C22**

Engineering for Plastics Technicians - NC   *SCOTVEC/NC in Engineering for Plastics Technicians.*   **S75**

Engineering Practice (Manufacture & Engineering Support) - AC   *SCOTVEC AC in Engineering Practice.*   **F8**

Engineering Practice (Manufacture & Engineering Support) - HNC   *SCOTVEC/HNC in Engineering Practice.*   **F8**

Engineering Practice - NC   *SCOTVEC/NC in Engineering Practice.*   **S87**

Engineering Systems - BSc   *BSc Degree in Engineering Systems.*   **L59**

Engineering Systems Maintenance Competences - C & G 214 Part II   *C&G Certificate in Engineering Systems Maintenance.*   **C22**

Fault Diagnostics/C.H. for Plumbers   *CITB Registration.*   **S141**

Industrial Measurement & Process Control - HNC   *SCOTVEC/HNC in Industrial Measurement & Process Control.*   **S71**

Industrial Measurement & Process Control - NC   *SCOTVEC/NC in Industrial Measurement & Process Control.*   **S71**

Information Technology (Manufacturing Systems Engineering) - MSc / PgD   *MSc Degree / PgD in Information Technology.*   **L60**

Integrated Engineering & Manufacture - BSc/HND   *BSc/HND in Integrated Engineering & Manufacture.*   **T12**

Maintenance Systems Engineering & Management - MSc   *MSc in Maintenance Systems Engineering & Management.*   **S51**

Maintenance Systems Engineering & Management - PgC   *A PgC in Maintenance Systems Engineering & Management.*   **S51**

Maintenance Systems Engineering & Management - PgD   *A PgD in Maintenance Engineering & Management.*   **S51**

Manufacturing Engineering & Management - HND   *SCOTVEC/HND in Manufacturing Engineering & Management.*   **S8**

Manufacturing Engineering - HNC
SCOTVEC/HNC in Manufacturing Engineering.
S8

Manufacturing Planning & Materials Requirements Planning   *Napier University certificate.*   **L48**

Manufacturing, Planning & Control Systems   *No formal outcome.*   **S87**

Mechanical & Production Engineering (Manufacturing) HNC   *SCOTVEC/HNC.*   **L28**

Mechanical & Production Engineering Yrs 1&2 - NC   *SCOTVEC/NC in Mechanical & Production Engineering.*   **L81**

Mechanical & Production Engineering- Plant Engineering HNC   *SCOTVEC/HNC.*   **L28**

Mechanical Engineering - HNC   *SCOTVEC/HNC in Mechanical Engineering.*   **S94**

Mechanical Engineering Practice - Skillseekers   *Practical skills & knowledge.*   **S15**

Mechanical Engineering Technician   *Mechanical Engineering Technician Certificate.*   **S81**

Mechanical Production Engineering - NC   *SCOTVEC/NC in Mechanical Production Engineering.*   **S15**

Oil-Fired Boilers - Domestic & Industrial   *OFTEC Registration for companies.*   **S141**

Plant Reconditioning - City & Guilds   *City & Guilds Certificate.*   **S91**

Process Control - HNC   *SCOTVEC/HNC in Process Control.*   **F8**

Process Plant Operators - C & G 060 - Levels I, II & III   *Awareness of skills required for process plant operators.*   **C22**

Quantity Surveying - HNC   *HNC in Quantity Surveying.*   **T12**

Robotic Systems Engineering   *On completion of this course participants will be awarded a Napier University certificate.*   **L48**

Siemens Plc Programming   *On completion of this course participants will be awarded a Napier University certificate.*   **L48**

ENGINEERING / TECHNOLOGY / MANUFACTURE (GENERAL)

Advanced Certificate in Engineering Practice, Manufacture & Support   *Advanced Certificate course.*   **S87**

CAD Training for SME's   *No formal outcome.*
S145

Electronic & Electrical Engineering - HNC *SCOTVEC/HNC.*   **H49**

Engineering   *NVQ Level 4.*   **G39**

Engineering (Mechanical Plant) - HNC
SCOTVEC/HNC in Engineering (Mechanical Plant).   **C23**

Engineering (Technician) - NC   *SCOTVEC/NC which gives entry to the HNC or HND in Engineering.*   **S91**

Engineering - Fabrication & Welding - Years 1 & 2 - HNC   *SCOTVEC/HNC in Engineering - Fabrication & Welding option.*   **C22**

Engineering - Foundry Option - Years 1 & 2 - HNC *SCOTVEC/HNC in Engineering - Foundry Option.*   **C22**

Engineering - HNC   *Can lead to SCOTVEC/HND.*
H31 L5 S2 S8 S16 S91

Engineering - HND   *SCOTVEC/HND, which allows access to 3rd year of BSc. or B.Eng degree course.*   **H53 S8**

Engineering - META Course   *META, NVQ & SCOTVEC/NC.*   **G2**

Engineering - NC   *Successful candidates will gain a NC in Engineering.*   **M7 S15 S16 S79**

Engineering - Pre-HNC Course   *Possible entry to HNC in Engineering.*   **L5**

Engineering - SCOTVEC Unit Certificates *SCOTVEC Unit Certificate in Engineering.*   **S8**

Engineering - SCOTVEC/HNC   *On successful completion of this course students will have SCOTVEC/HNC in Engineering.*   **G17**

Engineering - SCOTVEC/NC   *SCOTVEC/NC in Engineering.*   **G2**

Engineering - Short Industrial Training Courses *Skills gained in various fields of engineering.*
S75

Engineering - Skillseekers/NVQ & SVQ Level III *NVQ, NVQ ENTRA Level III Certificate.*   **S93**

Engineering - Welding & Fabrication Craft - NC *NC in Welding & Fabrication. SCOTVEC.*   **L81**

Engineering Construction Industry - NSDS *Certificate indicating units of competence attained issued by ECITB.*   **G2**

Engineering Craft Studies NC   *SCOTVEC/NC.*
L27

Engineering Practice   *SVQ Engineering Manufacture (Foundation) Level II; Group Award in Engineering Practice NN0403301.*   **G2**

Engineering Practice (Craft) - NC   *SCOTVEC/NC in Engineering (Craft).*   **S91**

Engineering Practice (Fabrication & Welding) - HNC   *SCOTVEC/HNC in Engineering Practice (Fabrication & Welding).*   **S19**

Engineering Practice (Manufacture & Engineering Support) - AC.   *SCOTVEC AC in Engineering Practice.*   **F8**

Engineering Practice (Manufacture & Engineering Support) - HNC   *SCOTVEC/HNC in Engineering Practice.*   **F8**

Engineering Practice - AC *Advanced Certificate in Engineering Practice. Gives entry to the HNC in Engineering Practice.* **C22**

Engineering Practice - Fabrication & Welding - HNC *SCOTVEC/HNC in Engineering Practice - Fabrication & Welding.* **D5**

Engineering Practice - HNC *HNC in Engineering.* **S75 S81 S87 S94**

Engineering Practice - NC *NC in Engineering Practice.* **G2 S15 S79**

Engineering Practice - NC (ENTRA) *ENTRA (Engineering Training) Certificate - Parts 1 & 2, Part 3 Specialisation.* **H49**

Engineering Practice - NC (SVQ II) *SCOTVEC/HNC in Engineering Practice.* **S87**

Engineering Practice: Fabrication & Welding - HNC *SCOTVEC/HNC in Engineering Practice: Fabrication & Welding.* **S79**

Engineering Practice: Manufacture or Engineering Support - HNC *SCOTVEC/HNC.* **S79**

Engineering Training (Foundation) - SVQ Level II *SCOTVEC SVQ Level II in Engineering Training.* **C22**

Engineering Training Authority - SVQ Engineering Manufacture *SVQ.* **G2**

Engineering with Electronics - SCOTVEC National Award *SCOTVEC National Award in Engineering.* **G2**

Engineering with Options - BEng (Hons) *A BEng (Hons) in Engineering.* **S44**

Extra Engineering - NC *SCOTVEC/NC in Extra Engineering.* **S15**

Fabrication & Welding Engineering - HNC *SCOTVEC/HNC in Fabrication & Welding Engineering.* **S79**

Fabrication & Welding Engineering Competences Part III - C & G 229 *City & Guilds 229 Certificate.* **C22**

Fabrication & Welding Engineering Practice - HNC *SCOTVEC/HNC in Fabrication & Welding - Engineering Practice.* **S79**

General Engineering & Motor Vehicle Certificate in Quality Assurance *Certificate course.* **C23**

General Engineering - NC *SCOTVEC/NC in General Engineering.* **T9**

Industrial Rope Access Trade Association Training Course: Levels 1 & 2 *IRATA Certification.* **H56**

Joining Materials by Welding *SVQ Level 1 & 2.* **S136**

Manufacturing & Service Industries Supervisory Management - NEBSM *NEBSM Certificate awarded.* **S94**

Manufacturing Technology - Advanced (P2) *Knowledge in advanced manufacturing technology.* **S94**

Mechanical & Production Engineering - Craftsman Level - SCOTVEC *SCOTVEC/NC.* **G17**

Mechanical Engineering - NC *SCOTVEC/NC in Mechanical Engineering.* **F13**

Mechanical Engineering Craft - NC *The SCOTVEC/NC in Mechanical Engineering Craft.* **B6**

Mechanical Engineering Craft Studies (Certificate) - C & G *C & G 205 Certificate Part III.* **G17**

Mechanical Engineering Practice - NC *SCOTVEC/NC in Mechanical Engineering practice (SVQ LEVEL III).* **L81**

Mechanical Engineering Technician - SCOTVEC/NC *SCOTVEC/NC.* **G17**

Mechanical Technicians - NC *SCOTVEC/NC will be awarded on successful completion of this course.* **B6**

Mechanical/Production Engineering - NC *SCOTVEC/NC. Progress to HNC/HND/University possible.* **D5**

Mechatronics - HNC *SCOTVEC/HNC in Mechatronics.* **S87**

Motor Vehicle Studies - BTEC NC *BTEC NC in Motor Vehicle Studies.* **S87**

Multi-Disciplinary Engineering - HNC *SCOTVEC/HNC in Multi-Disciplinary Engineering.* **S87**

Multi-Disciplinary Engineering - HNC *HNC in Multi-Disciplinary Engineering.* **S81**

Plant Operations (Processing) - GSVQ Level I *NVQ in Plant Operations (Processing) at Level I.* **H49**

Properties & Application of Engineering Materials - MSc *A MSc in Properties & Applications of Engineering Materials.* **S105**

Properties & Application of Engineering Materials - PgD *A PgD in Properties & Applications of Engineering Materials.* **S105**

Service Engineering - SCOTVEC/NC *SVQ Level III ; C&G Construction Plant Engineers Certificate (after further study).* **G17**

Single Pitch Supervision *National Certification.* **H56**

Subsea Engineering - MSc/Diploma *MSc Degree/Diploma in Subsea Engineering.* **L6**

Technology - GSVQ Level I *SCOTVEC SVQ GSVQ Level I in Technology.* **C10**

Various Courses Available *Outcome depends on level and subject matter of individual courses.* **S149 T21**

INDUSTRIAL DESIGN

Broad Based Technical - SCOTVEC/NC
SCOTVEC/NC in the modules successfully achieved.   **G2**

Building Technician - NC   *Successful candidates on this course will gain SCOTVEC Certificate for Building Technicians.*   **M7**

Computer Aided Engineering Technology
Achievement of 3.5 credits in Computer Aided Engineering Technology.   **C23**

Conceptual Design Tools Workshop   *On completion of the course participants will be awarded a Napier University certificate.*   **L48**

Drawing Skills: Technical Draughting 1 - NC
SCOTVEC/NC.   **C23**

Electronic Product Design & Manufacture - PgD
PgD in Electronic Design & Manufacture.   **S101**

Engineering (Design Option) - HNC
SCOTVEC/HNC in Engineering (Design Option).
                                                           C22

Engineering - HNC   *SCOTVEC/HNC in Engineering & Incorporated Membership of the Engineering Institutions.*   **L5**

Engineering - Pre-HNC Course   *Possible entry to HNC in Engineering.*   **L5**

Ergonomics: Designing Safe Working
Environments   *Introduction to the basic nature of Ergonomics.*   **G16**

Graphic Communication - SCE H Grade
**C4 C5 C20 C21 C25 C26 C27 C28 C29 C30
C33 C36 C45 C46**

Graphical Communication - SEB S Grade   *An SEB S Grade in Graphical Communication awarded.*   **B11**

Industrial Experimental Design Taguchi Methods
Napier University certificate awarded.   **L48**

Introduction to Computer Aided Draughting - NC
SCOTVEC/NC.   **C23**

Mechanical Engineering - HNC   *SCOTVEC/HNC in Mechanical Engineering.*   **S94**

Mechanical Engineering - NC   *SCOTVEC/NC in Mechanical Engineering.*   **F13**

Mechanical Production Engineering - NC
SCOTVEC/NC in Mechanical Production Engineering.   **S15**

Technical & Graphical Communications -
Skillseekers/NVQ Level I   *NVQ, NVQ Level I in Technical & Graphical Communications.*   **S18**

Technical Drawing - SCE H Grade   *SCE H Grade in Technical Drawing.*   **C6 C7**

Technical Drawing - SCE Higher   *SCE Higher - Technical Drawing.*   **F7 M3**

MECHANICAL ENGINEERING

Acoustics, Vibration & Noise Control-
MSc/Diploma   *MSc Degree/Diploma in Acoustics, Vibration & Noise Control.*   **L6**

Air Conditioning & Refrigeration   *On completion of the course, participants will be awarded a Napier University certificate.*   **L48**

Boiler Operators (CGLI 650)   *City & GuildsCertificate (650).*   **L28**

Broad Based Engineering Practice - NC GSVQ I
SCOTVEC/NC - Broad Based Engineering Practice (GSVQ I).   **F8**

BSc Mechanical Engineering   *Integral to the BSc Mech Eng offered in association with Robert Gordons University.*   **H49**

Building Services: Heating, Ventilating, Air
Conditioning - NC   *SCOTVEC/NC.*   **L5**

Condition Monitoring & Vibration Analysis   *A College Certificate in Condition Monitoring & Vibration Analysis.*   **S71**

Electronic Engineering Practice - NC   *ENTRA Parts 1 & 2 Engineering Training SCOTVEC award.*   **H49**

Electronic/Mechanical Engineering - NC
SCOTVEC/NCs in Electronic Engineering & Mechanical Engineering.   **H49**

Engineering & Building Services - Customised
Courses   *Various.*   **L71**

Engineering (Mechanical Plant) - HNC
SCOTVEC/HNC in Engineering (Mechanical Plant).   **C23**

Engineering - HNC   *HNC in Engineering (with options, Craft or Plant or Fabrication & Welding).*
                                            H49 L81 S91

Engineering - NC   *Successful students will be awarded the SCOTVEC/NC in Engineering.*
                                                 S75 S94

Engineering for Plastics Technicians - NC
SCOTVEC/NC in Engineering for Plastics Technicians.   **S75**

Engineering Mechanical - Part-Time NC   *Modules covering the educational content for Stages I, II & III SVQs.*   **L81**

Engineering Practice - Manufacturing &
Engineering Support - AC   *Advanced Certificate course.*   **H31**

Health, Safety & Hygiene   *Employer's/employee's responsibilities for health & safety.*   **H42**

Heating, Ventilating & Air Conditioning - HNC
SCOTVEC/HNC.   **L5**

Heating, Ventilating & Air Conditioning - Pre HNC
Prepares the students for HNC.   **L5**

Hydraulics   *College Certificate.*   **L28**

Lifting & Handling   *Delegates will have an understanding of lifting & handling techniques.*
G17

Lifting & Handling Skills   *SCOTVEC/NCM is possible.*
D5

Logistics Operation - HNC   *SCOTVEC/HNC in Logistics Operations.*
S8

Mechanical & Computer Aided Engineering - HND   *SCOTVEC/HND in Mechanical & Computer Aided Engineering.*
F5

Mechanical & Production Engineering - HNC   *SCOTVEC/HNC in Mechanical & Production Engineering.*
T1

Mechanical & Production Engineering Yrs 1&2 - NC   *SCOTVEC/NC in Mechanical & Production Engineering.*
L81

Mechanical & Production Engineering- Technician Studies   *SCOTVEC/NC.*
L28

Mechanical Engineering - Bridging Course to HNC   *SCOTVEC.*
S88

Mechanical Engineering - HNC   *HNC In Mechanical Engineering.*   **F5 F13 M7 S79 S94**

Mechanical Engineering - HND   *SCOTVEC/HND in Mechanical Engineering.*
S94

Mechanical Engineering - NC   *SCOTVEC/NC in Mechanical Engineering.*
S88

Mechanical Engineering - Years 1 & 2 - NC   *SCOTVEC/NC in Mechanical Engineering.*   **C22**

Mechanical Engineering Craft Course   *Mechanical Engineering Craft Certificate.*
S81

Mechanical Engineering Craft Studies (CGLI 205 Part 3)   *City & Guilds Certificate 205 Part 3.*   **L27**

Mechanical Engineering Maintenance Craft Studies (CGLI 205 Part 3)   *City & Guilds Certificate 205 Part 3.*
L27

Mechanical Engineering Practice   *Practical skills & knowledge will be gained by successful students.*
S15

Mechanical Engineering Practice (Maintenance or Machining) - ACC   *SCOTVEC Advanced Craft Certificate.*
T1

Mechanical Engineering Practice - Advanced Certificate   *Advanced Certificate in Mechanical Engineering practice.*
S81

Mechanical Engineering Practice - NC   *SCOTVEC/NC in Mechanical Engineering practice (SVQ LEVEL III).*
L81

Mechanical Engineering Practice - Skillseekers   *Practical skills & knowledge will be gained by successful students.*
S15

Mechanical Engineering Practice Part-Time - NC   *Modules cover the educational content for Stages I, II & III SVQ.*
L81

Mechanical Engineering Specialising in Mechanics of Materials - MSc   *MSc in Mechanical Engineering.*
S105

Mechanical Engineering Specialising in Mechanics of Materials - PgD   *PgD in Mechanical Engineering.*
S105

Mechanical Engineering Specialising in Thermodynamics & Fluid Mechanics - MSc   *MSc in Mechanical Engineering.*
S105

Mechanical Engineering Specialising in Thermodynamics & Fluid Mechanics - PgD   *A PgD in Mechanical Engineering .*
S105

Mechanical Engineering Studies - C&G Part 4 (Career Extension Course)   *C&G Certificate Part 4 in Mechanical Engineering Studies.*
S91

Mechanical Engineering Technician   *Mechanical Engineering Technician Certificate.*
S81

Mechanical Maintenance - NC   *SCOTVEC/NC in Mechanical Maintenance.*
C22

Mechanical Production Competencies - C&G Part 3   *C&G Certificate Part 3 in Mechanical Production Competencies.*
S91

Mechanical Production Engineering - NC   *SCOTVEC/NC in Mechanical Production Engineering.*
S15

Mechanical/Production Engineering - NC   *SCOTVEC/NC in Mechanical/Production Engineering. .*
D5

Mechatronic Engineering - HNC   *SCOTVEC/HNC Mechatronic Engineering.*
F5

Multiskill Engineering Technician Programme - NC   *SCOTVEC/NC in Multiskill Engineering.*
F8

Pipework Engineering Craft - NC   *SCOTVEC/NC in Pipework Engineering which leads to the HNC in Engineering.*
S91

Plant Engineering - HNC   *SCOTVEC/HNC will be awarded to successful students.*
S15

Refrigeration & Air Conditioning Mechanics - NVQ C&G 207   *NVQ, NVQ City & Guilds 207 Certificate.*
S88

Refrigeration (SCOTVEC)   *SCOTVEC/NCMs in Refrigeration.*
L68

Refrigeration - NC & SVQ   *SCOTVEC/NC.*   **L5**

Safe Handling of CFCs - C&G 2077   *City & Guilds 2077 Certificate.*
L5

PRODUCTION MANAGEMENT / QUALITY & RELIABILITY

Advanced Statistical Process Control - Low Fraction Defectives *Installation and application of control charts.* **S102**

Advanced Statistical Process Control - Short Run. *Installation and application of Short Run Charts.* **S102**

BPICS - Diploma in Production & Inventory Management *BPICS Diploma in production & inventory management.* **F8**

BS 5750 *How to be a more efficient manager.* **S87**

BS 5750 Quality Systems Management *On completion of this course participants will be awarded a Napier University certificate.* **L48**

BS5750 Audit *This course will improve your knowledge of quality standards.* **S57**

BS5750 Quality Systems *This course will improve your knowledge of quality standards.* **S57**

Business & Manufacturing Management *Institution of Electrical Engineers (IEE) certificate awarded.* **L48**

Certificate in Quality Assurance (C&G 743) Part-Time *City & Guilds 743 Certificate in Quality Assurance.* **L82**

Certificate in Quality Assurance Management *Certificate in Quality Assurance Management.* **C22**

City & Guilds 743 Quality Assurance - Parts 1 & 11 *City & Guilds 743 Quality Assurance.* **L59**

Computer Aided Production Management *Attendance Certificate.* **L10**

Fabrication & Welding - Inspection Quality Control - C&G 219 *City & Guilds 219 Certificate.* **C23**

Fabrication & Welding Inspection & Quality Control - C&G 219 *City & Guilds 219 Certificate.* **C22**

Food Processing & Quality Assurance Management - HND *SCOTVEC/HND.* **S92**

Food Product Development & Quality Management - MSc/PgD *MSc/ PgD in Product Development & Quality Management.* **L65**

General Engineering & Motor Vehicle Certificate in Quality Assurance *Certificate course.* **C23**

Higher Certificate in Quality Assurance *A Higher Certificate in Quality Assurance.* **C22**

Implementing TQM *On completion of the course, participants will be awarded a Napier University certificate.* **L48**

Institute of Quality Assurance Associate Membership Examination Syllabus *Leads to IQA membership.* **F8**

Institute of Quality Assurance Membership *Leads to Membership of the Institute of Quality Assurance.* **L59**

Institute of Quality Management Certificate *Institute of Quality Management Certificate.* **S8**

Instrumental Analytical Chemistry for Environmental Monitoring - MSc *A MSc in Instrumental Analytical Chemistry for Environmental Monitoring & Process Quality Assurance.* **S52**

Instrumental Analytical Chemistry for Environmental Monitoring - PgD *A PgD in Instrumental Analytical Chemistry for Environmental Monitoring & Process Quality Assurance.* **S52**

Internal Audit Course for BS 5750 Quality Systems *Napier University certificate awarded.* **L48**

Introduction to BS5750 *Students will be given a short assessment.* **S70**

Introduction to BS5750:1987 Quality Systems Standard - ISO 9000 Series *Preparation for assessment.* **S102**

Knitwear Quality Control *A College Certificate of Attendance.* **B3**

Management Education & Development - the Scottish Quality Management Centre *Development of quality management skills.* **C44**

Managing Process Improvement for Manufacturability & 6-Sigma Capability *6-Sigma, and the use of process cabability indices.* **S102**

Manufacturing Planning & Materials Requirements Planning *Napier University certificate awarded.* **L48**

Materials Management - MSc/Pgd *MSc/Postgraduate Diploma in Marketing.* **S101**

Mechanical Production Competencies - C&G Part 3 *C&G Certificate Part 3 in Mechanical Production Competencies.* **S91**

Organisation & Quality Issues - HN Unit *SCOTVEC HNU - 2400070.* **F8**

Printing Production & Quality Control - HNC *SCOTVEC/HNC in Printing Production & Quality Control.* **S68**

Production & Inventory Management - BPICS *Professional Diploma in Production & Inventory Management.* **S5**

Production & Inventory Management - BPICS Diploma *British Production & Inventory Control Society Diploma.* **S15**

Production Control with Management - HNC *SCOTVEC/HNC in Production Control with Management.* **S87**

Quality & Reliability Management - MSc *MSc in Quality & Reliability Management.* **T12**

Quality Assurance *Participants will learn about the principles of quality assurance.* **T1**

Quality Assurance - C & G 743   *City & Guilds 743 in Quallity Assurance.*   **F8**

Quality Assurance - Certificate   *SCOTVEC Certificate in Quality Assurance, Associate Membership of IQA.*   **F5**

Quality Assurance - CGLI Certificate 743   *City & Guilds 743 Certificate - Quality Assurance.*   **L59**

Quality Assurance - Diploma   *Diploma from the Institute of Quality Assurance (IQA).*   **F8**

Quality Assurance - HNC   *SCOTVEC/HNC.*
H53 S8 S75 S91

Quality Assurance Management   *This is a two credit SCOTVEC Higher National Unit.*   **S8**

Quality Assurance Management - A3 Part-Time   *IQA Quality Assurance Management - A3 Certificate.*   **L82**

Quality Assurance Management A3   *A3 Quality Assurance Management.*   **L59**

Quality Control - C & G 743   *Certificate from City & Guilds (743).*   **F8**

Quality Control Inspection - C & G   *C & G in Quality Control Inspection.*   **S87**

Quality Engineering - PgD   *PgD in Quality Engineering.*   **S102**

Quality Management - HND   *SCOTVEC/HND in Quality Management.*   **S8**

Quality Management - MSc   *MSc degree in Quality Management.*   **S102**

Quality Management Systems - Lead Assessor   *IQM Certificate course.*   **L48**

Quality System Documentation   *Documentation requirements for quality systems.*   **S102**

Quality Systems Management - MSc/Postgraduate Diploma   *MSc/Postgraduate Diploma.*   **L59**

Reducing Quality Costs   *How to assess quality costs & decide where improvements may be made.*   **S102**

Software Quality Engineering - MSc   *MSc in Software Quality Engineering.*   **S28**

Software Quality Engineering - PgD   *PgD in Software Quality Engineering.*   **S28**

Statistical Process Control for Supervisors & Operators   *Statistical Process Control and its applications.*   **S102**

Statistical Quality Control - HND   *SCOTVEC/HND.*   **L28**

Taguchi Approach to Quality   *Experimental design & the Taguchi method.*   **S102**

The Principles & Techniques of Quality Assurance - HN Unit   *SCOTVEC Higher National Unit - 2400109.*   **F8**

Total Quality Management   *TQM Needs Analysis and its applications.*   **G16 S87 S102**

Various Courses Available   *Company Certificate awarded.*   **S149**

PRODUCTION PROCESS WORK

Abrasive Wheels   *A variety of courses are available. These courses are for interest only.*   **H30**

Appreciation of Welding   *Knowledge of various welding skills.*   **L81**

Basic Welding   *Students will be able to weld using both gas & electric welding equipment.*   **T1**

Basic Welding (Introduction)   *Basic Welding Skills.*   **L68**

Basic Welding (SCOTVEC)   *SCOTVEC/NCM(s).*   **L68**

Basic Welding Skills - (MMA, MAGS, TAGS)   *A knowledge of basic welding techniques.*   **S87**

CNC Machining I (SCOTVEC)   *SCOTVEC/NCM.*   **L27**

CNC Machining II (SCOTVEC)   *SCOTVEC/NCM.*   **L27**

CNC Part Programming I (SCOTVEC)   *SCOTVEC/NCM leading to CNC Part Programming II.*   **L27**

Certificate in Welding Craft Studies - C & G   *C & G 215 Certificate in Welding Engineering Craft Studies part III.*   **G17**

CNC & CAM - NC   *SCOTVEC/NC.*   **B6**

CNC Machining/Programming   *Students will be able to write programmes & run them on CNC machines.*   **T1**

CNC Part Programming - NC   *SCOTVEC/NC.*   **C23**

Coded Welding   *ASME IX Company Welding Procedure or a Welding Qualification.*   **G17**

Craft & Design - SCE H Grade
C4 C5 C20 C25 C26 C27 C28 C29 C30 C33 C34 C36 C45

Design & Make (SCOTVEC)   *SCOTVEC/NCM.*   **L5**

Engineering & Building Section Short Course Provision   *College Certificate.*   **L27**

Engineering & Building Services - Customised Courses   *Various.*   **L71**

Engineering - Fabrication & Welding - Years 1 & 2 - HNC   *SCOTVEC/HNC in Engineering - Fabrication & Welding option.*   **C22**

Engineering - Foundry Option - Years 1 & 2 - HNC
SCOTVEC/HNC in Engineering - Foundry Option.
C22

Engineering - NC   *SCOTVEC/NC in Engineering
(Technician Level).*   **S79**

Engineering - Welding & Fabrication Craft - NC
SCOTVEC NC in Welding & Fabrication.   **L81**

Engineering Manufacture - SVQ Level 2   *SVQ
Level 2.*   **L5**

Engineering Manufacture, Fabrication & Welding -
SVQ Level II   *SCOTVEC SVQ Level II.*   **C10**

Engineering Practice (Fabrication & Welding) -
HNC   *SCOTVEC/HNC.*   **S19 S91**

Engineering Practice (Fabrication/ Welding) - HNC
SCOTVEC/HNC.   **F8**

Engineering Practice (Welding/ Fabrication) - AC
*SCOTVEC AC in Engineering Practice (Welding/
Fabrication).*   **F8**

Engineering Practice - Fabrication & Welding - AC
Consists of 6 SCOTVEC HNUs.   **H31**

Engineering Practice - Fabrication & Welding -
HNC   *SCOTVEC/HNC in Engineering Practice -
Fabrication & Welding.*   **D5**

Engineering Practice - HNC   *SCOTVEC/HNC in
Engineering. The course will develop skills needed
by higher technicians.*   **H31**

Engineering Practice - Manufacturing &
Engineering Support - AC   *Consists of 6
SCOTVEC HNUs.*   **H31**

Engineering Practice - NC   *SCOTVEC/NC in
Engineering Practice (Mechanical or Plant).*   **S79**

Engineering Practice - Fabrication & Welding - AC
Advanced Certificate course.   **S87**

Engineering Practice: Fabrication & Welding -
HNC   *SCOTVEC/HNC in Engineering Practice:
Fabrication & Welding.*   **S79**

Engineering Toolmaking - NC   *SCOTVEC/NC in
Engineering Toolmaking.*   **S15**

European Welding Coordinator   *Participants will
meet with the Weld Coordination Standard 719
requirements.*   **C23**

Fabrication & Welding - HNC   *SCOTVEC/HNC in
Fabrication & Welding.*   **F5**

Fabrication & Welding - Inspection Quality Control
- C & G 219   *C & G 219 Certificate awarded.*
C23

Fabrication & Welding - NC   *Successful
candidates will gain SCOTVEC/NC in Fabrication
& Welding.*   **M7**

Fabrication & Welding - NC SVQ Level III
*SCOTVEC/NC in Fabrication & Welding (SVQ
Level III in Engineering Practice).*   **F8**

Fabrication & Welding - Skillseekers/ SVQ
*SCOTVEC modules for Fabrication/Welding
apprentices.*   **S19**

Fabrication & Welding Competencies - NVQ C & G
229   *NVQ, NVQ C & G 229 in Fabrication &
Welding.*   **S88**

Fabrication & Welding Craft Studies NC
SCOTVEC/NC.   **L27**

Fabrication & Welding Engineering - HNC
SCOTVEC/HNC in Fabrication & Welding.
F13 H53 S79 S91

Fabrication & Welding Engineering - META Course
META,. NVQ & SCOTVEC/NC.   **G2**

Fabrication & Welding Engineering - NC   *NC in
Fabrication & Welding Engineering Studies.*
F5 F13 H53 S87

Fabrication & Welding Engineering Competences
Part III - C & G 229   *C & G 229 Certificate.*   **C22**

Fabrication & Welding Engineering Practice (Craft)
- NCMs   *SCOTVEC/NCMs in Fabrication &
Welding Engineering Practice.*   **S91**

Fabrication & Welding Engineering Practice - HNC
*SCOTVEC/HNC in Fabrication & Welding -
Engineering Practice.*   **S79**

Fabrication & Welding Engineering Practice - NC
*SCOTVEC/NC in Fabrication & Welding
Engineering Practice.*   **S79**

Fabrication & Welding Inspection & Quality Control
- C & G 219   *A City & Guilds 219 Certificate.*
C22

Fabrication & Welding Practice - NC
SCOTVEC/NC in Fabrication & Welding Practice.
S87

Fabrication   *NVQ Level 3.*   **G39**

Fabrication - YT/SVQ Level II   *SCOTVEC SVQ,
SVQ Levels I-III Certificate.*   **S79**

Fabrication Welding - HNC   *SCOTVEC/HNC in
Fabrication & Welding.*   **S75**

Fabrication/Welding - NC   *SCOTVEC/NC in
Fabrication/Welding.*   **C22 S16**

Fish Industry Welding Course   *Students will have
improved their basic welding techniques.*   **H37**

Foundry/Patternmaking - NC   *SCOTVEC/NC in
Foundry/Patternmaking.*   **C22**

Introduction to Machining Skills   *SCOTVEC/NCM.*
L5

Introductory Welding   *Introduction to welding of
ferrous & non ferrous metals using gas, arc & MIG
welding.*   **B2 B6**

Machine Woodworking/Lathe & Drillwork - NC   *On
successful completion of this course students will
have a NC.*   **G17**

Machining Skills (SCOTVEC)   *SCOTVEC/NCM.*
L5

Manual Metal Arc Welding Practice 1 - NC
SCOTVEC/NC.   **C23**

Mechanical Engineering Practice   *Practical skills
& knowledge will be gained by successful
students.*   **S15**

Metal Arc Gas Shielded Welding 1 (SCOTVEC) *SCOTVEC/NCM.*   **L5**

Metal Joining Skills (Thermal) (SCOTVEC) *SCOTVEC/NCM.*   **L5**

Metal Joining Skills - Thermal - NC *SCOTVEC/NC.*   **C23**

Metal Sculpture (SCOTVEC) *SCOTVEC/NCM.*   **L5**

Metalwork *Participants will have gained metalwork skills.*   **H31 M3**

MIG Welding *The SCOTVEC Module 64748.*   **B2 B6**

Oxy/Fuel Gas Cutting *Skills & knowledge required to operate oxy/fuel gas cutting equipment.*   **D5**

Oxy/Fuel Gas Cutting Equipment *Safe practice & efficient use of oxy/ fuel gas cutting equipment.*   **D5**

Practical Welding Skills *Participants will have gained skills in welding.*   **H31**

Quality Control Inspection - C & G *C & G in Quality Control Inspection.*   **S87**

Sheetmetal Craft Studies NC *SCOTVEC/NC.*   **L27**

Shielded Arc Welding Practice 1 & 2 - NC *SCOTVEC/NC.*   **C23**

TIG Welding Process *Participants will acquire the skills associated with tungsten inert gas welding process.*   **T1**

Tool & Cutter Grinding Techniques NC - Part-Time *A College Certificate will be issued.*   **L81**

Toolmaking/Polymer Moulds - HNC *SCOTVEC/HNC will be awarded to successful students.*   **S15**

Tungsten Arc Gas Shielded Practice - TIG/TAG Welding (SCOTVEC) *SCOTVEC/NCM.*   **L5**

Welding *NVQ Level 3.*   **G39**

Welding *SCOTVEC/NCs will be gained on successful completion. See course content for details.*   **H53**

Welding & Ancillary Skills (SCOTVEC) *SCOTVEC/NCM.*   **L27**

Welding & Fabrication - NC *SCOTVEC/NC in Welding & Fabrication.*   **S19**

Welding & Fabrication Engineering - HNC *SCOTVEC/HNC in Welding & Fabrication; membership of the Welding Institute.*   **S87**

Welding & Fabrication Engineering - HND *SCOTVEC/HND in Fabrication & Welding Engineering.*   **S87**

Welding & Fabrication Level I & II - ENTRA *Recognition of achievement by ENTRA and by award of NVQ.*   **G2**

Welding & Metal Fabrication (ENTRA) *SCOTVEC course validated by ENTRA in Welding & Metal Fabrication.*   **S87**

Welding (Broad Based) - SCOTVEC/NC *SCOTVEC/NC in the modules successfully achieved.*   **G2**

Welding - Broad Based Welding *Year 1: ENTRA NVQ Welding & Fabrication; Year 2: SCOTVEC/NC in Broad Based Welding.*   **G2**

Welding Courses *Courses on offer include SCOTVEC modules, ASME IX, Heating & Ventilation Pipe Welding.*   **S88**

Welding Craft Studies - NC *SCOTVEC/NC in Welding Craft Studies.*   **S75**

Welding Engineering - NCMs *SCOTVEC/NCs will be awarded to successful students.*   **H53**

Welding Fabrication & Non Destructive Testing - HNC *SCOTVEC/HNC in Welding Fabrication & Non Destructive Testing.*   **F5**

Welding Fabrication Practice - Advanced Craft Certificate *SCOTVEC AC Certificate leading to HN in Engineering Practice.*   **T1**

Welding SCOTVEC/NC *SCOTVEC/NC:- Oxy-Acetylene Welding, MMA Welding I & II, TAG Welding I & II, MAG Welding I.*   **T9**

Welding/Fabrication Work - NC *Modules allow entry to advanced C & G courses or SCOTVEC/HNC Practice.*   **D5**

TESTING MEASUREMENT & PRECISION ENGINEERING

Condition Monitoring by Vibration Analysis *A College Certificate in Condition Monitoring by Vibration Analysis.*   **S71**

Dye Penetrant Inspection *Basic theory & practice of testing & inspection of industrial components. Accredited to ASNT level 1 & 2, & PCN level 1 & 2.*   **F5**

Geometric Dimensioning & Tolerancing *Knowledge gained in Geometric Dimensioning & Tolerancing.*   **S8**

Hydraulic Circuits & Fault Finding *Use of circuits to control sequences with various control systems & to fault find existing circuits.*   **F8**

Industrial Measurement & Process Control - HNC *SCOTVEC/HNC in Industrial Measurement & Process Control.*   **S71**

Instrumentation with Applied Physics - BSc *A BSc in Instrumentation with Applied Physics.*   **S53**

Instrumentation with Applied Physics - BSc (Hons) *A BSc in Instrumentation with Applied Physics.*   **S53**

Interpretation of Radiographs - Level 2 *Radiographic interpretation. Training is accredited to ASNT & PCN level 2.*   **F5**

Introduction to Fracture Mechanics for Engineers *Napier University Certificate awarded.* **L48**

Magnetic Particle Inspection *Basic theory & practical work. Accredited to ASNT level 1 & 2, & PCN level 1 & 2.* **F5**

Measurement & Control - SCOTVEC/NC *SCOTVEC/NC.* **G17**

NDT Appreciation Course *Candidates will gain knowledge of the four main methods of Non Destructive Testing.* **F5**

Pneumatic Circuits & Fault Finding *Use of circuits to control sequences with various control systems.* **F8**

Practical Ultrasonic Inspection - Level 1 *Theory & practice of ultrasonic testing of welds. Accredited to ASNT & PCN level 1.* **F5**

Practical Ultrasonic Inspection - Level 2 *Theory & practice of ultrasonic testing of welds. Accredited to ASNT & PCN level 2.* **F5**

Product Technology *Candidates will gain a basic knowledge of product technology.* **F5**

Radiation Safety *Theory to meet the requirements of PCN for the level 2 radiation safety endorsement.* **F5**

Supervised Practical Ultrasonic Inspection (Nozzle & Node Welds) *Practical preparation for PCN & ASNT level 1 & 2 exams.* **F5**

Supervised Practical Ultrasonic Inspection (Plate & Pipe Butt Welds) *Practical preparation for PCN & ASNT level 1 & 2 exams.* **F5**

Welding *SCOTVEC/NCs will be gained on successful completion. A variety of welding types is on offer.* **H53**

Welding Fabrication & Non Destructive Testing - HNC *SCOTVEC/HNC in Welding Fabrication & Non Destructive Testing.* **F5**

Environment, Security, Health & Safety

ENVIRONMENT SECURITY, HEALTH & SAFETY

Various Courses Available   *No formal outcome.*
S9

CLEANSING

Accommodation & Cleaning Technology - NC   *NC in Accommodation & Cleaning Technology.*   **S70**

Cleaning Science   *Training for staff in the cleaning industry.*   **H53 S81**

Cleaning Science 2   *Supervision certificate & City & Guilds certificate in Cleaning Science.*   **S81**

Cleaning Science 2 - NC   *SCOTVEC/NC in Cleaning Science 2.*   **G17**

Cleaning Technology (Part 1) - NC   *SCOTVEC/NCMs in Cleaning Technology.*   **F13**

Cleaning Technology (Part II) - NC   *SCOTVEC/NCMs in Cleaning Technology.*   **F13**

Cleaning Technology 2 - NC   *SCOTVEC/NC.*   **L5**

Cleaning Technology I - NC   *SCOTVEC/NC.*   **L5**

Waste Management - NEBSM   *National Examining Board in Supervisory Management Certificate.*   **S94**

ENVIRONMENTAL CONSERVATION

Applied Environmental Science - HNC   *SCOTVEC/HNC.*   **H53**

Chemical Analysis with Environmental Science - Advanced Diploma   *Leads to Licentiateship of the Royal Society of Chemistry.*   **S79**

Countryside Recreation & Conservation Management - HNC   *SCOTVEC/HNC in Recreation & Conservation Management.*   **S92**

Countryside Recreation & Conservation Management - HND   *SCOTVEC/HND in Recreation & Conservation Management.*   **S92**

Draught Proofing & Loft Insulation   *No formal outcome.*   **T14**

Energy & Environmental Systems - MSc   *MSc in Energy & Environmental Systems.*   **S46**

Energy & Environmental Systems - PgC   *A PgC in Energy & Environmental Systems.*   **S46**

Energy & Environmental Systems - PgD   *A PgD in Energy & Environmental Systems.*   **S46**

Energy Awareness   *No formal outcome.*   **T14**

Environmental Education BA/BSc Evening Degree Programme   *Accumulation towards a Degree.*   **S42**

Environmental Management - Advanced Diploma   *Advanced Diploma in Environmental Management.*   **S8 S79**

Environmental Management Systems BS 7750   *Napier University certificate awarded.*   **L48**

Environmental Science - GCE Advanced Supplementary Level   *Higher SCE Grades.*   **F5**

Environmental Science - MSc   *MSc in Environmental Science.*   **S105**

Environmental Science - NC   *SCOTVEC/HNC in Environmental Science.*   **S16**

Environmental Studies   *Practical skills & knowledge will be gained by successful students.*   **S15**

Environmental Study - PgD   *A PgD in Environmental Study.*   **S105**

Exhaust Emission & the Environment   *College based certificate in Exhaust Emission & the Environment.*   **S88**

Gamekeeping & Wildlife Conservation - Accreditation of Prior Learning   *SCOTVEC/NCMs & SVQs.*   **F4**

Gamekeeping & Wildlife Conservation - NC   *NC in Gamekeeping & Wildlife Conservation.*   **F3**

Gamekeeping & Wildlife Management - APL   *SCOTVEC/NC in Gamekeeping & Wildlife Management.*   **F4**

Gamekeeping & Wildlife Management - Diploma   *SCOTVEC/NC in Gamekeeping & Wildlife Management.*   **F3**

Gamekeeping & Wildlife Management - HNC   *SCOTVEC/HNC.*   **B2**

Instrumental Analytical Chemistry for Environmental Monitoring - MSc   *MSc degree course.*   **S52**

Instrumental Analytical Chemistry for Environmental Monitoring - PgD   *PgD course.*   **S52**

Integrated Rural Land Use - APL   *SCOTVEC/NC. Knowledge & skills associated with rangers, wardens & countryside technicians.*   **F4**

Integrated Rural Land Use - NC   *SCOTVEC/NC. Knowledge & skills associated with rangers, wardens & countryside technicians.*   **F3**

Managing Urban Environments - HNC   *SCOTVEC/HNC in Urban Environmental Management.*   **C22 C23**

Marine Resource Development & Protection - MSc/Diploma   *MSc Degree/Diploma in Marine Resource Development & Protection.*   **L8**

Recycling Materials   *Napier University certificate course.*   **L48**

Rural Recreation & Tourism - HNC   *SCOTVEC/HNC in Recreation & Tourism.*   **S92**

Rural Recreation & Tourism - HND   *SCOTVEC/HND in Rural Recreation & Tourism.*   **S92**

The Urban Environment   *SCOTVEC module will be awarded on successful completion of this course.*   **B1**

FIRE PREVENTION & FIRE FIGHTING

Basic Sea Safety Courses   *Students will have the basic minimum qualification to go to sea.*   **H36**

Breathing Apparatus   *Participants will have gained knowledge of Breathing Apparatus and Search & Rescue techniques.*   **H23**

Breathing Apparatus Wearers' Course   *Course completion certificate.*   **T17**

Fire Fighting   *No formal outcome.*   **G33**

Fire Safety - HNC   *SCOTVEC/HNC in Fire Safety.*   **S68**

Gas Fire Fighting Course   *Course completion certificate.*   **T17**

Helicopter Fire Course (OPITO Approved)   *Course completion certificate.*   **T17**

Initial Training in Hydrocarbon Fire Fighting   *Course completion certificate.*   **T17**

Introduction to Oil Industry Fire Fighting & Emergencies   *Course completion certificate.*   **T17**

Management of Major Emergencies Course   *Course completion certificate.*   **T17**

Offshore Basic Fire Course (OPITO Approved)   *Course completion certificate.*   **T17**

Offshore Basic Fire Refresher Course (OPITO Approved)   *Course completion certificate.*   **T17**

Offshore Basic Fire Teamwork Course (OPITO Approved)   *Course completion certificate.*   **T17**

Offshore Company Specific Special Fire Team Training   *Course completion certificate.*   **T17**

Offshore Fire Leaders' Course (OPITO Approved)   *Course completion certificate.*   **T17**

Offshore One-Day Fire Course   *Course completion certificate.*   **T17**

Offshore Rescue Course   *Course completion certificate.*   **T17**

Offshore Two-Day Fire Course   *Course completion certificate.*   **T17**

Sea Survival, Fire Fighting, First Aid (Basic)   *DoT approved certificates for all courses.*   **G2**

Staff Fire Safety Training   *Participants will have gained knowledge of fire safety matters relative to their place of work.*   **H23**

When you contact a Provider for further information, you may wish to make mention of **PART-TIME CLASSES & COURSES in Scotland.**

OCCUPATIONAL HEALTH & SAFETY

Abrasive Wheels *College Certificate in Abrasive Wheels safety procedures & regulations.*   **D5**

ACOPS Gas Safety *Knowledge of ACOPS Gas Safety gained.*   **S6**

Approved Code of Practice: Domestic Gas Safety *SNIPEF Gas Safety Certificate.*   **T9**

Asbestos *BEBOH Preliminary Certificate.*   **L93**

Basic Offshore Safety Induction *Certificate for Offshore Workers.*   **G25**

BPEC Gas Safety *Knowledge of BPEC Gas Safety gained.*   **S6**

BS 7750 Environmental Systems *Implementation of BS 7750.*   **S135**

Confined Space Entry *Training to SVQ standards.*   **T19**

CORGI Gas Safety Registration *CORGI Gas Safety Registration.*   **L5**

Customised Short Courses in Science & Technology *Nationally recognised or College/Company certificate can be issued.*   **L68**

Developing Flexibility *The participant will further his/her effectiveness as a coach.*   **B9**

Environmental Auditing *EARA Registration.*   **S135**

First Aid *No formal outcome.*   **G33**

First Aid At Work - Revision (S2) *Allows updating of Certificate which is valid for 3 years.*   **S94**

First Aid Certificate (HASW) *First aid training (HASW) to comply with recent amendments to the act.*   **F8**

First Aid Course (HSE) Four Day *Certificate.*   **G25**

Fish Industry Safety Courses *Short courses in a variety of subjects to increase safety awareness.*   **H14**

Freefall Lifeboat Coxswain & Passenger *Certificate.*   **G25**

Further Emergency Training *Refresher Certificate for Offshore Workers.*   **G25**

Gas Installation Inspection - Domestic *Knowledge gained in Gas Installation Inspection.*   **S68**

Gas Safety (Installation & Use) *Knowledge gained in Gas Installation inspection & use.*   **S68**

HSE Health & Safety Regulations *Training to SVQ standards.*   **T19**

Hazardous Substances *BEBOH (Module).*   **L93**

Health & Safety *Health & Safety Executive Certificate in Health & Safety in the workplace.*   **D5 H30**

Health & Safety - (M11) *Skills gained in Health & Safety.*   **S94**

Health & Safety / COSHH / First Aid Courses for Industry *Skills for work situations. Courses may be certificated.*   **H31 H49**

Health & Safety / COSHH Courses for Industry *Skills for work situations. Courses may be certificated.*   **H46 H53**

Health & Safety At Work - a Basic Introduction *Trainees will receive a Certificate at the end of the course.*   **G14**

Health & Safety for Safety Representatives Stage 1 *Non-certificated.*   **L67**

Health & Safety for Safety Representatives Stage 2 *Non-certificated.*   **L67**

Health & Safety Management *No formal outcome.*   **S87**

Health & Safety Management - Diploma *Membership of the Institution of Occupational Health & Safety.*   **S25**

Health, Safety & Hygiene *Raises awareness of employer's/employee's responsibilities for health & safety. H5 Hoisting & Rigging T019 Training to SVQ standards.*   **H42**

Introduction to Health & Safety Management *Delegates will gain knowledge of HSE Regulations.*   **M8**

Measurement of Hazardous Substances *BEBOH (Module).*   **L93**

Merchant Vessel Deckhand *SVQ Level II Deck Hand.*   **G2**

National Diploma in Occupational Safety & Health (NEBOSH) *NEBOSH Diploma in Occupational Safety & Health.*   **L68**

NC in Occupational Safety & Health (NEBOSH) *NEBOSH General Certificate in Occupational Safety & Health.*   **C22**

NEBOSH - National General Certificate in Health & Safety *NEBOSH National General Certificate in Health & Safety.*   **F8**

NEBOSH Diploma (Block Release). *Nationally recognised Diploma awarded.*   **G42**

NEBOSH Certificate (Block Release) *Nationally recognised certificate awarded.*   **G42**

NEBOSH NC *Award of NEBOSH Certificate.*   **S124**

Noise & Vibration *BEBOH Preliminary Certificate.*   **L93**

Occupational Hygiene Foundation *BEBOH (Module).*   **L93**

Occupational Safety & Health (NEBOSH) Certificate *NEBOSH NC in Occupational Safety & Health.*   **L68 S9**

Occupational Safety & Health - General Certificate *NEBOSH certificate course.*   **S15**

Occupational Safety & Health - National Examination Board   *NEBOSH Certificate course.*   **D5**

Occupational Safety & Health - NEB   *National Examination Board certificate in Occupational Safety & Health.*   **S75**

Occupational Safety & Health - NEBOSH   *The National General Certificate in Occupational Safety & Health.*   **S87**

Occupational Safety & Health - NEBOSH General Certificate   *NEBOSH National General Certificate course.*   **M8**

Physical Agents   *BEBOH (Module).*   **L93**

Power Cut Off Saw   *College certificate. This course can also be studied on your own premises.*   **T9**

Prevention & Treatment of Injury   *Greater awareness of prevention & treatment of sports injuries.*   **B9**

Radiation Safety   *Theoretical knowledge to meet the requirements of PCN for the level 2 radiation safety endorsement.*   **F5**

Radiation Safety Practice - C & G 741 (Stage 1)   *City & Guilds 741 Stage 1 Radiation Safety Practice Certificate.*   **H49**

Radiation Safety Practice - City & Guilds (741) Stage II   *City & Guilds 741 Stage II Radiation Safety Practice Certificate.*   **H49**

Risk Assessment   *BEBOH (Module).*   **L93 M8**

Safe Use of Ballistic Tools   *College certificate. This course can also be studied on your own premises.*   **T9**

Safety Awareness   *Students will gain training in Safety Awareness.*   **H30**

Safety for Supervisors   *Training to SVQ standards.*   **T19**

Scaffolding   *Training to SVQ standards.*   **T19**

Site Management Safety Certificate   *Certificate course.*   **S146**

Trade Union Studies: Health & Safety (Stage 2)   *A working knowledge of health & safety regulations.*   **C22**

Trade Union Studies: Introductory (Stage 1)   *Increased skills & awareness of the Union Representative's job.*   **C22**

TUC Course - European Health & Safety Legislation   *Increased skills & awareness of Health & Safety legislation.*   **C22**

Various Courses Available   *Outcome depends on level and subject matter of individual courses.*   **S149 T21**

Workplace Control   *BEBOH (Module).*   **L93**

POLLUTION CONTROL

Exhaust Emission & the Environment   *College based certificate in Exhaust Emission & the Environment.*   **S88**

Marine Resource Development & Protection - MSc/Diploma   *MSc Degree/Diploma in Marine Resource Development & Protection.*   **L8**

PUBLIC HEALTH & SAFETY

Elementary Food Hygiene Certificate   *REHIS Elementary Hygiene Certificate awarded.*   **B3**

Environmental Health - MSc / Diploma   *MSc Degree / Diploma in Environmental Health.*   **L75**

Environmental Health - REHIS   *The Royal Environment Health Institute of Scotland award in Environmental Health.*   **S87**

Health & Safety for Manual Staff   *Aspects of Health & Safety law for manual staff.*   **M8**

Health & Safety for Office Staff   *Aspects of Health & Safety law in an office environment.*   **M8**

Royal Institute of Public Health & Hygiene Certificate for Food Handlers   *Certificate for Food Handlers.*   **F5**

SECURITY, POLICE, ARMED SERVICES

Police Studies - BA   *Bachelor of Arts in Police Studies.*   **S8**

Police Studies - Diploma   *Diploma in Police Studies.*   **S8**

Police Studies - HNC   *HNC in Police Studies.*   **L49 S8**

PUBLISHERS' NOTE

Because of local government re-organisation, details of providers for some courses, in particular for leisure pursuits, cannot be confirmed as we go to print. Libraries and other local sources should be consulted and the Community Education contacts on pages 24 to 26 may also be of assistance.

Food, Catering, Leisure & Tourism

COOKING, FOOD & DRINK PREPARATION

Advanced Cookery 706/3 - City & Guilds of London Institute *City & Guilds Certificate course.* **G17**

Advanced Pastry *Advanced Pastry.* **S70**

Bakery & Food Management Studies - NVQ C & G 127 Certificate *NVQ, NVQ City & Guilds 127 Certificate.* **S70**

Bakery Supervisory Management *SCOTVEC/HNC for those interested in bakery management.* **H53**

Baking - NC/SVQ Level III *SVQ, SVQ Level III NC in Baking.* **S70**

Basic Cookery Skills (Italian Cookery) *SCOTVEC/NCMs in Cookery Skills (Italian Cookery).* **D6**

Basic Craft Cookery - NC *SCOTVEC/NC in Basic Craft Cookery.* **S6**

Biscuit Technology - NVQ City & Guilds 130 Certificate *NVQ, NVQ City & Guilds 130 Certificate in Biscuit technology.* **S70**

Broadbased Catering Course *SCOTVEC/NC in Broadbased Catering.* **S78**

Cake Decoration *No formal outcome, although participants will gain further knowledge in this subject.* **B8**

Cake Decoration - NC *On successful completion of the course students will be awarded the SCOTVEC/NC in Cake Decoration.* **S70**

Cake Decoration - NCMs *SCOTVEC/NCMs if required.* **L81**

Cake Decoration - Sugar Paste - NC *SCOTVEC/NC.* **C23**

Cake Decoration Course - Advanced *No formal qualification, but students will extend their knowledge of cake decoration.* **S70**

Cake Decoration Techniques (SCOTVEC) *SCOTVEC/NCM 3230913 Cake Decoration Techniques.* **L83**

Cake Decoration Techniques - Module *SCOTVEC/NCM - 3230913.* **F8**

Cake Decoration Techniques - NC *SCOTVEC/NC.* **C23**

Cake Decoration: Gateaux Finishing Processes - Module *SCOTVEC/NCM - 3230943.* **F8**

Catering & Hospitality: Food Preparation & Cooking - SVQ Level I & Level II *SVQ Level I (SE0704208) & Level II (SF0704205). .* **M7**

Catering - NC *NCMs in Catering leading to the award of GSVQ Hospitality Level II.* **H49**

Catering Section Short Course Provision *College Certificate.* **L27**

Christmas Cookery *Participants will have learned some of the skills of Christmas cookery.* **H53**

City & Guilds 706/3 Advanced Cookery for Catering Industry *City & Guilds 706/3.* **T9**

Community Day Classes *Improved personal, social & learning skills.* **L68**

Community Evening Class *Improved personal, social & learning skills.* **L68**

Cookery *There is no formal outcome to this course.* **B2 H53**

Cookery - NC *SCOTVEC/NC in Cookery which gives entry to the HNC Hospitality Operations (Professional Cookery).* **S91**

Cookery for the Catering Industry (Kitchen & Larder) - NVQ C & G 706 Pt III *C & G 706 Part III.* **S87**

Cookery for the Catering Industry - (Year 1) - NC *SCOTVEC/NC in Cookery for the Catering Industry.* **C22**

Cookery for the Catering Industry - NVQ City & Guilds 706 Part III Certificate *NVQ, NVQ C & G 706 Certificate Part III.* **S70**

Cookery for the Catering Industry Stages I - III *Students will be eligible for progress to C & G 706 III certificate.* **S87**

Cookery Processes 1 - Module *SCOTVEC/NC half module 97600.* **F8**

Cooking for All Occasions *Experience in Christmas Cookery.* **C16**

Cooking for Men *Students will be able to prepare a range of dishes.* **T9**

Cooking for Pleasure Part One *Those participating will gain knowledge in preparation & presentation of selected dishes.* **L27**

Cooking for Pleasure Part Two *An extension of part 1 for those interested in extending their knowledge & skills.* **L27**

Cooking for the Catering Industry - NC *SCOTVEC/NC.* **C23**

Cooking with Flair *There is no formal outcome to this course.* **B3**

Craft Bakery Production - HNC *SCOTVEC/HNC in Craft Bakery Production.* **L5**

Craft Baking - NC *SCOTVEC/NC in Craft Baking. Guaranteed access to the HNC in Craft Bakery Production.* **L5**

Craft Baking - SCOTVEC/NC *SCOTVEC/NC in Craft Baking.* **G17**

Craft Baking Technology - NC/SVQ Level II *SVQ, SVQ Level II NC in Baking.* **S70**

Craft Cookery - NC *SCOTVEC/NC in Craft Cookery.* **S6**

Creative Cake Decoration *Skills & techniques for production and decoration of traditional and celebration cakes.* **H31**

Creative Studies for Sugarcraft - City & Guilds 7900 *City & Guilds 7900 certificate.* **L27**

Essential Food Hygiene Course - REHIS *REHIS Intermediate Food Hygiene Certificate. Progression is possible.* **H49**

Fish & Shellfish - Module *SCOTVEC/NC half module 97410.* **F8**

Food Preparation & Cooking - SVQ Level II & III *SCOTVEC SVQ Level II & Level III in Food Preparation & Cooking.* **S6**

Food Service - SVQ Level II & III *SCOTVEC SVQ Level II & Level III in Food Service.* **S6**

Food Technology for Non-Food Technologists *Candidates will increase their practical skills & knowledge.* **S70**

Food, Hospitality & Tourism - Customised Courses *Various.* **L71**

Gateaux Finishing Techniques NC *SCOTVEC/NC.* **C23**

Gourmet Cookery *Participants will have gained experience in gourmet cookery.* **H31**

Great Scottish Food *The participant will know about the origins & development of food in Scotland.* **S57**

Healthy Cooking for Chefs *No formal qualification, however knowledge gained in the preparation of healthy food.* **S70**

Hospitality (Professional Cookery) - HNC *SCOTVEC/HNC in Hospitality (Professional Cookery).* **M7**

Hospitality - GSVQ Level III *SCOTVEC SVQ GSVQ Level III in Hospitality.* **C10**

Hospitality - SVQ Level II *SCOTVEC SVQ SVQ Level II in Hospitality.* **C10**

Hospitality Operations (Professional Cookery) - HND *SCOTVEC/HNC in Hospitality Operations (Professional Cookery).* **S91**

Hotel & Catering Courses *The outcome of courses will depend on the nature of the course & the needs of the client.* **H53**

Hotel & Catering Courses for Industry *Courses are designed around the needs of a particular client group.* **H31**

International Cookery - Masterclass Series *Improved cookery skills.* **L5**

Introduction to Cake Decoration *Improved cake decorating skills.* **L5**

Introduction to Cookery Processes *SCOTVEC Module.* **H54**

Introduction to Eastern Cookery *Participants will have the opportunity to learn how to prepare Chinese food.* **H53**

Introduction to Food Preparation Techniques *SCOTVEC Module.* **H54**

Modular Foods *Skills gained in food preparation.* **S81**

New Opportunities in Catering *NCMs towards SVQ Level 1 in Serving Food & Drink (counter) or in Food Preparation.* **L5**

Pastry - Module *SCOTVEC/NC half module 97604.* **F8**

Patisserie *SCOTVEC/NCM in Patisserie.* **D6**

Patisserie - Module *SCOTVEC/NCM.* **F8**

Practical Catering for Christmas *This course is for interest only.* **H49**

Practical Designer Christmas Cakes *This course is for interest only.* **H49**

Practical Vegetarian Cooking *This course is for interest only.* **H49**

Professional Cake Decoration - NC *SCOTVEC/NC in Cake Decoration Techniques.* **C22**

Professional Cookery *SCOTVEC/NC in Professional Cookery.* **S78**

Professional Cookery - HNC *SCOTVEC/HNC in Professional Cookery.* **F5 S6 S75**

Professional Cookery - NC *SCOTVEC/NC in Professional Cookery.* **F3 F13 L27 S15 S75 S91**

Professional Cookery - Skillseekers *SCOTVEC/NC in Professional Cookery.* **S78**

Professional Cookery - SVQ Level I *SCOTVEC SVQ, SVQ level I in Professional Cookery.* **S11**

Professional Cookery - SVQ Level II *SCOTVEC SVQ, SVQ level II in Professional Cookery.* **S11**

Professional Cookery - Training for Work *SCOTVEC/NC in Professional Cookery.* **S78**

Professional Cookery Part I - NC *SCOTVEC/NC in Professional Cookery Part I.* **S70**

Professional Cookery Part II - NC *NC in Professional Cookery Part II.* **S70**

Professional Cookery, Part 2 - NC *SCOTVEC/NC in Professional Cookery.* **D5**

Professional Culinary Arts (Culinary Arts Option) - HNC *SCOTVEC/HNC in Professional Culinary Arts.* **L5**

Professional Culinary Arts (Culinary Arts Option) - HND *SCOTVEC/HND in Professional Culinary Arts.* **L5**

Professional Culinary Arts (Professional Patisserie Option) - HNC *SCOTVEC/HNC in Professional Culinary Arts.* **L5**

Professional Culinary Arts (Professional Patisserie Option) - HND   *SCOTVEC/HND in Professional Culinary Arts.*   **L5**

Professional Culinary Arts - NC   *SCOTVEC/NCMs.*   **L5**

Speciality Chocolate & Sugarcraft Course   *There is no formal qualification, however students will extend their knowledge.*   **S70**

Sugarcraft   *Experience in sugarcraft.*   **C16**

Sugarcraft Course   *There is no formal qualification, however students will extend their knowledge.*   **S70**

Sugarcraft Skills - C & G   *City & Guilds certificate in Sugarcraft Skills.*   **S81**

Sweets, Pastries & Breadmaking   *Skills & techniques used by confectioners and breadmakers.*   **H31**

The Wine & Spirit Education Trust Ltd - Certificate   *Certificate of the Wine & Spirit Education Trust Ltd.*   **S70**

The Wine & Spirit Education Trust Ltd - Higher Certificate   *Higher Certificate of the Wine & Spirit Education Trust Ltd.*   **S70**

Vegetarian Cookery   *Participants will have the opportunity to learn how to prepare Vegetarian meals.*   **H53**

Wine & Spirit Education Trust - Higher Certificate in Wines & Spirits   *Higher Certificate in Wines & Spirits.*   **L59**

Wine & Spirit Education Trust Certificate   *Wine & Spirit Education Trust (WSET) in London Certificate.*   **S91**

Wine Appreciation   *There is no formal outcome to this course.*   **B3 S57 T9**

Wine Appreciation Course   *Improved knowledge of wines.*   **L5**

Wired Sugar Flowers   *Techniques for producing wired sugar flowers and leaves.*   **M8**

FOOD MANUFACTURE, SALES, DISTRIBUTION

Butchery   *Participants will have gained skills in butchery.*   **H31**

Counter Service   *SCOTVEC Module.*   **H54**

Data Processing & Computing   *Participants will have learned basic computing skills.*   **H14**

Finance   *Non-certificated course to help those involved in financial operations.*   **H14**

First Aid   *Participants will have gained skills in First Aid.*   **H14**

Fish Industry Safety Courses   *Short courses in a variety of subjects to increase safety awareness.*   **H14**

Fish Industry Short Courses   *Short courses in a variety of subjects relating to fishing/fisheries are available.*   **H14**

Food Hygiene Courses - REHIS   *Courses are run at all levels of hygiene skills. See course content for details.*   **H14**

Food Manufacture Introduction   *Up to 9 SCOTVEC Modules.*   **S144**

Food Processing with Quality Assurance - HNC   *SCOTVEC/HNC in Food Processing with Quality Assurance.*   **S92**

Food Product Development & Quality Management - MSc/Pgdip   *MScs Degree / PgD. REHIS qualification.*   **L65**

Fork-Lift Truck   *Participants will have improved their skills in operating a Fork-Lift truck.*   **H14**

Interviewing Techniques   *Non-certificated course to help those involved in interviewing staff.*   **H14**

Management Skills   *Participants will have improved their management skills.*   **H14**

Meat Processing YT/SVQ Level II   *SVQ, SVQ Level II (SF0502113) in Meat Processing.*   **L84**

Motivation & Communication   *Non-certificated course to improve managerial skills in the fishing trade.*   **H14**

Performance Appraisal   *Participants will have learned skills needed to appraise performance.*   **H14**

FOOD SCIENCE

Advanced Food Hygiene - REHIS Diploma   *REHIS Diploma in Advanced Food Hygiene.*   **S87**

Advanced Food Hygiene Diploma (REHIS)   *Diploma in Food Hygiene by REHIS.*   **L5**

Catering for Therapeutic Dietary Needs   *SCOTVEC module in catering for therapeutic dietary needs.*   **S70**

Certificate for Food Handlers - Elementary   *Royal Society of Health Certificate for Food Handlers.*   **S70**

Certificate in Food Hygiene (REHIS)   *Certificate in Food Hygiene by the REHIS.*   **L5**

Certificate in Food Hygiene - Royal Society of Health   *Royal Society of Health Certificate in Food Hygiene.*   **D6**

Cold Preparations - Module   *SCOTVEC/NCM - 97603.*   **F8**

Community Nutrition - MSc   *MScs Degree / PgD / PgC in Community Nutrition.*   **L65**

Customised Short Courses in Science & Technology *National and/or College/Company certificate can be issued.*   **L68**

Dietetics - MSc *MSc Degree / PgD / PgC in Dietetics.*   **L65**

Elementary Food Hygiene (REHIS) *The Royal Environmental Health Institute For Scotland Certificate.*   **F8 F13 L5**

Elementary Food Hygiene - REHIS Certificate *Participants will have gained knowledge of hygienic practices.*   **H30**

Elementary Food Hygiene - Royal Society for Health *REHIS Certificate.*   **H53**

Elementary Food Hygiene Certificate *REHIS Elementary Hygiene Certificate awarded.*   **B3 C22**

Elementary Food Hygiene Certificate - REHIS & RIPHH *REHIS or RIPHH Elementary Food Hygiene Certificate.*   **L81**

Elementary Food Hygiene Course *Elementary Certificate (by examination).*   **B3 C10 G36 M9 S111 T1**

Essential Food Hygiene - RSH Certificate *Royal Society of Health Certificate - basic principles of food hygiene.*   **H31**

Essential Food Hygiene Course - REHIS *REHIS Intermediate Food Hygiene Certificate. Progression is possible.*   **H49**

Focus On Clean Food *Trainees will receive a Certificate at the end of the course.*   **G14**

Food & Nutrition - SCE H Grade *An SCE H Grade in Food & Nutrition.*   **C4 C33**

Food Hygiene & the Handling of Food Certificate *RIPHH Certificate in Food Hygiene & the Handling of Food.*   **S70**

Food Hygiene - Diploma *Royal Institute of Public Heath & Hygiene Diploma in Food Hygiene.* **S70**

Food Hygiene - Elementary *Elementary Food Hygiene Certificate as endorsed by REHIS.*   **G2**

Food Hygiene - Elementary Course *Elementary Certificate of REHIS.*   **L68**

Food Hygiene - Focus *Trainees will receive a Certificate at the end of the course.*   **G14**

Food Hygiene - Intermediate Course *Intermediate Certificate of REHIS.*   **L68**

Food Hygiene - REHIS *REHIS Intermediate Certificate in Food Hygiene.*   **D5**

Food Hygiene - REHIS Advanced Diploma *REHIS Advanced Diploma in food hygiene.*   **T9**

Food Hygiene - REHIS Certificate *Royal Environmental Health Institute of Scotland Certificate.*   **H53**

Food Hygiene - REHIS Certificates *Introductory & Intermediate courses will lead to REHIS Certification.*   **H37**

Food Hygiene - REHIS Intermediate Certificate *REHIS Intermediate Certificate in food hygiene.*   **T9**

Food Hygiene Courses - REHIS *Courses are run at all levels of hygiene skills. See course content for details.*   **H14**

Food Hygiene Courses for Industry *Introductory, intermediate & advanced courses are run.*   **H46**

Food Hygiene Management - Focus *Trainees will receive a Certificate at the end of the course.*   **G14**

Food Hygiene Practices *College will supply a record of completion where appropriate.*   **L68**

Food Laboratory Microbiology *SAC Certificate.*   **S122**

Food Preparation Skills *Can lead to REHIS Elementary Food Hygiene Certificate. Particularly suitable for B&B establishments.*   **H6**

Food Preparation Techniques - Module *SCOTVEC/NCM - 97500.*   **F8**

Food Processing & Quality Assurance Management - HND *SCOTVEC/HND.*   **S92**

Food Product Development & Quality Management - MSc/PgD *MSc/ PgD in Product Development & Quality Management.*   **L65**

Food Science HNC *SCOTVEC/HNC.*   **L28**

Food Science NC *SCOTVEC/NC (Includes GSVQ level 2).*   **L28**

Food Technology - NC *NC in Food Technology.*   **S70**

Hands On Hygiene *Understanding of: Bacteria; Food Poisoning; Cross Contamination; Personal Hygiene; Food Storage.*   **T23**

Highlighting Hygiene in the Food Industry *Trainees will receive a Certificate at the end of the course.*   **G14**

Hygiene Training for Food Handlers *REHIS qualification - Elementary Food Hygiene Course.*   **S57**

Intermediate Food Hygiene (REHIS) *Royal Environmental Health Institute For Scotland Intermediate Certificate is awarded.*   **F13**

Intermediate Food Hygiene Certificate *REHIS Intermediate Food Hygiene Certificate.*   **C22**

Intermediate Food Hygiene Certificate - REHIS & RIPHH *REHIS or RIPHH- Intermediate Food Hygiene Certificate.*   **L81**

Intermediate Food Hygiene Course *Intermediate Food Hygiene Certificate.*   **G36**

Introduction to Hazard Analysis - Critical Control Points in Food Industry *SAC Certificate.*   **S122**

Meat Inspection - Distributive Trade Course *Certificate in Inspection of Meat & other Foods from REHIS.*   **S69**

Professional Cookery - SVQ Level I *SCOTVEC SVQ, SVQ level I in Professional Cookery.*   **S11**

REHIS Intermediate Food Hygiene Course
REHIS Intermediate Certificate in Food Hygiene.
M8

REHIS Elementary Food Hygiene Course
*Delegates will have an understanding of Food
Safety Awareness.*   **M8**

REHIS - Elementary Certificate   *REHIS
Elementary Certificate.*   **S87**

REHIS - Food Hygiene Certificate   *REHIS
Intermediate Certificate in Food Hygiene.*   **S87**

REHIS Elementary Food Hygiene   *REHIS
Certificate.*   **L27**

REHIS Food Hygiene Course   *Skills gained in
food hygiene.*   **S81**

REHIS Intermediate Certificate in Food Hygiene
REHIS Certificate.   **L27**

RIPHH Certificate for Food Handlers   *Basic Skills
are gained in food handling & hygiene.*   **F5**

Science Section Short Course Provision   *College
Certificate.*   **L27**

Tourism Winter Training   *Numerous topics of
interest to those whose businesses are concerned
with tourism.*   **H8**

HOME ECONOMICS

Care in the Community - College Programme
*Participants can gain skills required to live more
safely at home.*   **F8**

Home Economics   *SCOTVEC Certificate will be
awarded on successful completion of the
module(s).*   **B11**

Home Economics (Revised) - SCE Higher   *SCE
Higher - Home Economics (Revised).*   **F7**

Home Economics - HNC   *Students will be
awarded SCOTVEC/HNC in Home Economics.*
S75

Home Economics - SCE H Grade   *SCE H Grade
in Home Economics.*
C1 C25 C28 C34 C36 C45 C46 D8 S16 S79

Home Economics - SCE H Grade/ CSYS/ module
*SCE H Grade or Certificate of Sixth Year Studies
or SCOTVEC Module.*   **D3**

Home Economics - SCOTVEC Modules
SCOTVEC Modules in Home Economics.   **D8**

Home Economics - SEB S Grade   *SEB S Grade in
Home Economics course.*   **B11**

HOTELS, COMMERCIAL
CATERING

Accommodation Servicing - NC   *SCOTVEC/NC in
Accommodation Servicing.*   **C22**

Advance Food Hygiene   *SAC Certificate.*   **S122**

Advanced Craft Kitchen & Larder - C & G 706/3
*City & Guilds 706/3 Advanced Craft Kitchen &
Larder.*   **F5**

Bakery Supervisory Management
*SCOTVEC/HNC for those interested in bakery
management.*   **H53**

Bar Management   *Practical skills & knowledge will
be gained by students.*   **S15**

Basic Food Hygiene   *SAC Certificate.*   **S122**

Basic Marketing   *A Certificate of Attendance will
be awarded to participants.*   **B6**

Broadbased Catering Course   *SCOTVEC/NC in
Broadbased Catering.*   **S78**

Catering & Hospitality - SVQ Levels I-IV   *SVQ,
SVQ Levels I-IV Certificates in Catering &
Hospitality.*   **S70**

Catering & Hospitality - SVQs At Level 1 & 2
SVQs in Catering & Hospitality at Levels 1 & 2.
L5

Catering & Hospitality - SVQs At Level 3   *SVQs at
Level 3.*   **L5**

Catering & Hospitality Supervision - NC GSVQ
Level 3   *SCOTVEC/NC in Catering & Hospitality
Supervision (GSVQ level III).*   **F13**

Catering & Hospitality: Food Preparation &
Cooking - SVQ Level I & Level II   *SVQ Level I
(SE0704208) & Level II (SF0704205).*   **M7**

Catering (Craft) - SCOTVEC/NC   *SCOTVEC/NC
and/or City & Guilds of London Institute.*   **G2**

Catering (General) - SCOTVEC/NC
*SCOTVEC/NC and/or City & Guilds of London
Institute.*   **G2**

Catering - NC   *NCMs in Catering leading to the
award of GSVQ Hospitality Level II.*   **H49**

Catering Basic Craft Programme (Part 1) - YT/NC
SCOTVEC/NC Basic Craft Catering (Part 1). .
D6

Catering Hospitality - GSVQ Level I   *SCOTVEC
GSVQ Level I in Catering Hospitality.*   **S79**

Catering Section Short Course Provision   *College
Certificate.*   **L27**

Catering Supervision   *Practical skills & knowledge
will be gained by all successful students.*   **S15**

Catering Technician - SCOTVEC/NC
*SCOTVEC/NC and/or City & Guilds of London
Institute.*   **G2**

Certificate of Excellence for Bed & Breakfast Operators   *SCOTVEC Modules - SCOTVEC Tailored Award.*   **G32**

Certificate of Ships' Cooks   *Successful students will gain the Higher General Cookery Certificate of Ships' Cooks.*   **S70**

Cold Preparations - Module   *SCOTVEC/NCM - 97603.*   **F8**

Cookery for the Catering Industry Stages I - III   *Students will be eligible for progress to C & G 706 III certificate.*   **S87**

Cookery Processes 1 - Module   *SCOTVEC/NC half module 97600.*   **F8**

Cooking for the Catering Industry - NC   *NC.*   **F5**

Craft Catering (Basic) - SCOTVEC/NC   *SCOTVEC/NC in Basic Craft Catering.*   **G17**

Craft Catering 1 - NC   *On successful completion of this course students will have a NC.*   **G17**

Craft Catering 2 - NC   *On successful completion of this course students will have a NC.*   **G17**

Craft Trainer Award (TSI)   *Certificate awarded.*   **G36**

Day Release in Catering   *Students will gain knowledge of food preparation techniques & insight into reception & food service.*   **T1**

Elementary Food Hygiene Certificate   *REHIS Elementary Hygiene Certificate will be awarded.*   **B3**

Facilities Management (Support Services) - HNC   *SCOTVEC/HNC.*   **L5**

Fish & Shellfish - Module   *SCOTVEC/NC half module 97410.*   **F8**

Food & Beverage Service   *A Certificate in Food & Beverage Service will be awarded to successful students.*   **S70**

Food & Beverage Service - NC Part I   *SCOTVEC/NC in Food & Beverage Service Part I.*   **D5**

Food & Beverage Service Management - HNC   *SCOTVEC/HNC in Food Beverage Service Management.*   **S91**

Food & Beverage Service NC   *SCOTVEC/NC.*   **L27**

Food & Drink Service - NC Part 2   *SCOTVEC/NC in Food & Beverage Service Part 2. .*   **D5**

Food Hygiene   *REHIS certificate in Food Hygiene at Elementary - Intermediate level will be awarded.*   **S15**

Food Hygiene - Elementary (REHIS)   *Students will be awarded the REHIS Elementary Food Hygiene Certificate.*   **S75**

Food Hygiene - Intermediate (REHIS)   *Students will be awarded the REHIS Intermediate Food Hygiene Certificate.*   **S75**

Food Preparation & Cooking - SVQ Level I   *SCOTVEC SVQ Level I in Food Preparation & Cooking.*   **S79**

Food Preparation Skills   *Can lead to REHIS Elementary Food Hygiene Certificate. Suitable for B&B establishments.*   **H6**

Food Preparation Techniques - Module   *SCOTVEC/NCM - 97500.*   **F8**

Food Purchasing & Cooking for Bed & Breakfast Guest House Operators   *This course is for interes only.*   **H49**

Food, Hospitality & Tourism - Customised Courses   *Various.*   **L71**

French for Hotel Reception   *Practical language: words & phrases which occur in every day situations.*   **M9**

Function Waiting (Half Module) - NC   *SCOTVEC/NC. .*   **C23**

Group Training Techniques (TS2)   *Certificate awarded.*   **G36**

HCIMA Professional Certificate   *The HCIMA Professional\Certificate.*   **F13**

HNC in Hospitality Operations SCOTVEC   *SCOTVEC/HNC.*   **L27**

Hospitality - GSVQ Level III   *SCOTVEC SVQ GSVQ Level III in Hospitality.*   **C10**

Hospitality - HNC   *Successful candidates will gain a HNC in Hospitality.*   **M7 S15**

Hospitality - SVQ Level II   *SCOTVEC SVQ SVQ Level II in Hospitality.*   **C10 S19**

Hospitality - SVQ Level III   *SVQ, SVQ Level III in Hospitality.*   **S19**

Hospitality Management - C & G 491   *City & Guilds 491 in Establishment Management.*   **D6**

Hospitality Management - MSc   *A MSc in Hospitality Management.*   **S60**

Hospitality Management - PgC   *A PgC in Hospitality Management.*   **S60**

Hospitality Management - PgD   *A PgD in Hospitality Management.*   **S60**

Hospitality Management Practice - MSc   *A MSc in Hospitality Management Practice.*   **S62**

Hospitality Management Practice - PgC   *A PgC in Hospitality Management Practice.*   **S62**

Hospitality Management Practice - PgD   *A PgD in Hospitality Management Practice.*   **S62**

Hospitality Operations (Front Office) - HNC   *SCOTVEC/HNC for those interested in Reception.*   **H53**

Hospitality Operations (Professional Cookery) - HND   *SCOTVEC/HND in Hospitality Operations (Professional Cookery).*   **S91**

Hospitality Operations - HNC   *SCOTVEC/HNC in Hospitality Operations.*
C10 C22 F13 H53 L5 S6 S11 S19 S75 S91

Hospitality Operations - SCOTVEC/HNC *HNC Level II and III in Hospitality.* **G17**

Hospitality Operations - Skillseekers/ HNC *On successful completion trainees can gain an HNC in Hospitality Operations.* **S20**

Hospitality Operations Professional Cookery - HNC *SCOTVEC/HNC in Hospitality Operations (Professional Cookery).* **S87**

Hotel & Catering - NCMs *Students gain further skills relating to the hotel & catering trade.* **H53**

Hotel & Catering Courses *The outcome of courses will depend on the nature of the course & the needs of the client.* **H53**

Hotel & Catering Courses for Industry *Courses are designed around the needs of a particular client group.* **H31**

Hotel Housekeeping *Practical skills & knowledge will be gained by successful students.* **S15**

Hotel Law for Front Office Staff (SCOTVEC) *SCOTVEC/NCM.* **L5**

Hotel Reception *Practical skills & knowledge in hotel reception.* **S15**

Hotel Reception - NC *SCOTVEC/NC in Hotel Reception.* **S10 S91**

Hotel Receptionists - NC *SCOTVEC/NC. Skills required to work as a Receptionist in the Hotel or Hospitality Industry.* **H49**

Hotel Skills *Practical skills & knowledge will be gained by successful students.* **S15**

Menu Planning for Bed & Breakfast Guest House Operators *This course is for interest only.* **H49**

New Opportunities in Catering *NCMs towards SVQ Level 1 in Serving Food & Drink (counter) or in Food Preparation.* **L5**

Non-Advanced Vocational Courses for Adults *Skills in chosen subject.* **S75**

Office Administration & Technology NC *SCOTVEC/NC in Office Administration & Technology.* **L81**

Organisation of Practical Skills 2 - Module *SCOTVEC/NCM - 97652.* **F8**

Organisation of Practical Skills 3 - Module *SCOTVEC/NCM - 97653.* **F8**

Organisation of Practical Skills 4 - Module *SCOTVEC/NCM - 97654.* **F8**

Professional Catering Management - HNC *SCOTVEC/HNC in Catering Management.* **S70**

Professional Certificate - HCIMA *Hotel, Catering & Institutional Management Association Professional Qualification.* **S70**

Professional Cookery *SCOTVEC/NC in Professional Cookery.* **S78**

Professional Cookery - NC *SCOTVEC/NC in Professional Cookery.* **F3**

Professional Cookery - Training for Work *SCOTVEC/NC in Professional Cookery.* **S78**

Professional Cookery, Part 1 - NC *SCOTVEC/NC in Professional Cookery.* **D5**

Professional Cookery, Part 2 - NC *SCOTVEC/NC in Professional Cookery.* **D5**

Professional Food & Beverage Service - (Year 1) - NC *SCOTVEC/NC in Food & Beverage Services.* **C22**

Ships' Cooks Certificate of Competency - Part I *Ships' Cooks Certificate of Competency Part I.* **S70**

Ships' Cooks Certificate of Competency - Part II *Ships' Cooks Certificate of Competency Part II.* **S70**

Short Courses for Guest House Owners *Participants will learn to analyse their business performance.* **H31**

Stock & Sauces - Module *SCOTVEC/NCM - 97602.* **F8**

Supervision of Catering & Accommodation Services - NC *SCOTVEC/NC.* **S6 S70**

Table Service *Students will gain training in the service of food at the table.* **H30**

Tourism - NC *SCOTVEC/NC in Tourism. Possible progression to HNC or HND level courses.* **C10**

Tourism / Hotel & Catering Courses for Industry *Skills appropriate to the needs of work situations. May be certificated.* **H46**

Tourism Winter Training *Numerous topics of interest to those whose businesses are concerned with tourism.* **H8**

United Kingdom Bartenders' Guild (UKBG) *The award of a United Kingdom Bartenders Guild certificate.* **S6**

Use of Borders Produce to Promote You *A Certificate of Attendance will be awarded to participants.* **B6**

Wine & Spirit Education Trust Certificate Course *WSET Certificate in Wines, Spirits & Associated Beverages.* **C23**

Wine Appreciation *There is no formal outcome to this course.* **B3**

Wines & Spirits Education Trust *Improved knowledge of the wine & spirit trade.* **D6**

SPORTS, LEISURE & ARTS MANAGEMENT

Arts Management - HNC *SCOTVEC/HNC in Arts Management.* **S19 S87**

Arts Management - HND *SCOTVEC/HND in Arts.* **S87**

Countryside Recreation & Conservation Management - HNC *SCOTVEC/HNC in Recreation & Conservation Management.* **S92**

Countryside Recreation & Conservation Management - HND   *SCOTVEC/HND in Recreation & Conservation Management.*   **S92**

Cultural Services Management - MSc/ PgD   *MSc/Diploma/Certificate in Cultural Services Management.*   **L33**

Leisure & Recreation - NC   *SCOTVEC/NC will be awarded on successful completion of this course.*   **B6**

Leisure & Recreation with Those with Special Needs   *How to help special needs clients with their leisure & recreation.*   **S87**

Leisure Management - HNC   *SCOTVEC/HNC in Leisure Management.*   **C22 L5 S8 S75 S87 S94**

Leisure Management - HND   *SCOTVEC/HND in Leisure Management.*   **S8 S94**

Leisure Management - MSc   *MSc in Leisure Management.*   **S61**

Leisure Management - NC   *Successful students will be awarded with SCOTVEC/NC.*   **S75**

Leisure Management - PgC   *A PgC in Leisure Management.*   **S61**

Leisure Management - PgD   *A PgD in Leisure Management.*   **S61**

Sport & Leisure - Customised Courses   *Various.*   **L71**

Sport & Leisure - YT/SVQ Level II   *SCOTVEC SVQ, SVQ Level II Certificate.*   **S79**

TRAVEL & TOURISM

Business Administration (Travel & Tourism) - HNC   *HNC in Business Administration (Travel & Tourism).*   **C22 F5 S13 S75 S91**

Business Administration (Travel & Tourism) - HND   *HND in Business Administration (Travel & Tourism).*   **B6 F5 S15**

Business Studies (Travel & Tourism) - NC   *SCOTVEC/NC in Business Studies (Travel & Tourism).*   **S14**

Entering the Tourism Business   *Participants will gain knowledge in various aspects of the Tourism Business.*   **T9**

Food, Hospitality & Tourism - Customised Courses   *Various.*   **L71**

Languages & Tourism Studies - NC (SCOTVEC)   *SCOTVEC/NC in Languages & Tourism Studies.*   **L68**

Leisure & Tourism - GSVQ SCOTVEC/NC Level 2   *GSVQ SCOTVEC/NC in Leisure & Tourism.*   **G17**

Local Knowledge   *Local Knowledge gained of the Glasgow area.*   **S70**

Making Your Tourism Business More Successful   *Enables tourism businesses to operate more efficiently & profitably.*   **T9**

Rural Recreation & Tourism - HNC   *SCOTVEC/HNC in Recreation & Tourism.*   **S92**

Rural Recreation & Tourism - HND   *SCOTVEC/HND in Rural Recreation & Tourism.*   **S92**

Specialist Tourist Guide   *Shetland Islands Tourism Guide Badge awarded upon successful completion of the course.*   **H46**

Sustainable Tourism - MSc   *MSc Degree / PgD in Sustainable Tourism.*   **L65**

Tourism - HNC   *SCOTVEC/HNC in Tourism. Progress to HND in Travel & Tourism possible.*   **C10 D5 L5 S13**

Tourism - NC   *SCOTVEC/NC in Tourism. Possible progression to HNC or HND level courses.*   **C10**

Tourism - PgD   *A PgD in Tourism.*   **S105**

Tourism / Hotel & Catering Courses for Industry   *Participants will gain skills appropriate to the needs of their work situation.*   **H46**

Tourism Management - MSc   *A MSc in Tourism Management.*   **S59**

Tourism Management - PgC   *A PgC in Tourism Management.*   **S59**

Tourism Management - PgD   *A PgD in Tourism Management.*   **S59**

Tourism Training for Industry   *Various courses are on offer.*   **H31**

Tourism Winter Training   *Numerous topics of interest to those whose businesses are concerned with tourism.*   **H8**

Travel & Tourism   *SCOTVEC/NCMs.*   **T14**

Travel & Tourism - NC   *SCOTVEC/NC in Travel & Tourism.*   **S88**

Travel - NC   *Successful students will be awarded the SCOTVEC/NC in Travel.*   **S75 S91**

Travel Industry Geography: British Isles (SCOTVEC)   *SCOTVEC/NCM 92404 Travel Industry Geography: British Isles.*   **L83**

Travel Industry Geography: European & Mediterranean Area (SCOTVEC)   *SCOTVEC/NCM 92405 Travel Industry Geography: European & Mediterranean Area.*   **L83**

Travel Industry Geography: Popular Longhaul Destinations (SCOTVEC)   *SCOTVEC/NCM 5110460 Travel Industry Geography: Popular Longhaul Destinations.*   **L83**

Visitor Attraction Operations   *City & Guilds Certificate.*   **S144**

Visitor Attraction Operations - C & G 489   *C & G 489 Certificate in Visitor Attraction Operations.*   **S70**

Health & Personal Care

DENTAL, OPHTHALMIC & AUDIOLOGY SERVICES

Anomalies of Binocular Vision & Orthoptics *Specialist qualification from the British College of Optometrists.* **S32**

Community Dental Health - MSc / Diploma *MSc Degree / Diploma in Community Dental Health.* **L75**

Dental Nursing - NC *SCOTVEC/NC.* **L5**

Dental Surgery Assistants *DSA Examination Board Certificate.* **L5 S81**

Dental Surgery Assistants - NC *SCOTVEC/NC including all modules recommended for Dental Nurses.* **S16**

Dental Technician Course *Skills gained in crown & bridge technology, prosthodontics & orthodontics.* **S81**

Dental Technicians - NC *SCOTVEC/NC.* **L5**

Dental Technology - HNC *SCOTVEC/HNC.* **L5 S81**

Dental Technology - NC *SCOTVEC/NC in Dental Technology.* **S81**

Dental Technology Year 1 - HNC *HNC in Dental Technology.* **G17**

Dental Technology Year 1 - NC *On successful completion of this course students will have a NC.* **G17**

Oral Health Education *Certificate in Oral Health Education.* **S81**

Oral Health Education - RSH Certificate *Training in the techniques required to teach Dental Health Education. RSH Certificate.* **L5**

Orthodontics - Frankel Appliances *College Certificate.* **L5**

Principles of Contact Lens Practice *A Post Graduate Diploma in Contact Lens Practice.* **S33**

HEALTH (GENERAL) & HEALTH ADMIN.

Anatomy, Physiology & Health - SCE H Grade *AN SCE H Grade in Anatomy, Physiology & Health.* **C4 F5**

Causes & Prevention of Disease - Module *SCOTVEC/NCM - 7310091.* **F8**

Certificate in Health Management Studies *Certificate in Health Management Studies.* **L65**

Childcare, Social Care or Health Care - GSVQ Level 3 *GSVQ in Care at Level 3.* **G17**

Clinical Reception - SCOTVEC/NC *SCOTVEC/NC indicating the modules gained.* **G17**

Community Health - BA/BA (Hons) *Bachelor of Arts (Honours) Degree in Community Health.* **L65**

Community Health - MSc / Diploma *MSc Degree / Diploma in Community Health.* **L75**

Computing for Medical Practices *How particular computer programmes operate.* **D5**

Deaf Unit *Students will study for entry qualifications to specific college courses.* **S75**

Dealing with Health Emergencies *Level 1-4 of the certificate in counselling skills awarded COSCA.* **C22**

Diploma in Practice Management - AMSPAR *Diploma Diploma in Practice Management.* **L68**

Exercise & Health Science - MSc *An MSc in Exercise & Health Science.* **S108**

Health & Gender *How gender affects health, illness & medical provision.* **G21**

Health Care - HNC *SCOTVEC/HNC in Health Care.* **S16**

Health Care - HNC/SVQ Level III *SCOTVEC/HNC in Health Care/SVQ in Care Level III.* **S75**

Health Care Management - MSc *MSc Degree / PgD in Health Care Management Ethics.* **L65**

Health Management Studies - Certificate *Certificate in Health Management Studies.* **S8**

Health Promotion - MSc *MSc Degree / PgD in Health Promotion.* **L65**

Health Promotion - NC *SCOTVEC/NC.* **C23**

Health Sciences - MSc / Diploma *MSc Degree / Diploma in Health Sciences.* **L75**

Health Studies - BA *BA degree in Health Studies.* **S101**

Health Studies - BA (Hons) *BA (Hons) in Health Studies.* **S42**

Health Studies - BSc (Hons) *BSc (Hons) in Health Studies.* **G15 L65 S42**

Health Studies - Dip HE *Diploma of Higher Education in Health Studies.* **S101**

Health Studies - MSc *MSc in Health Studies.* **S66**

Health Studies - PgC *PgC in Health Studies.* **S66**

Health Studies - PgD   *PgD in Health Studies.*
S66

International Health - MSc   *MSc Degree / PgD in International Health.*   **L65**

Law & Ethics in Medicine   *A course certificate will be awarded.*   **S82**

Managing Budgets (For NHS Managers)   *How to understand financial procedures.*   **S57**

Medical - Computing for Medical Practices   *How to use the type of programme operated in most medical practices.*   **D5**

Medical - Financial Management of Practices   *How to manage the financial system of a medical practice.*   **D5**

Medical - Practice Managers Course   *How to manage a medical practice.*   **D5**

Medical - Practice Receptionists' Course   *How to work in a medical reception area.*   **D5**

Medical Reception & Administration NC   *SCOTVEC/NC.*   **L27**

Medical Reception - NC   *SCOTVEC/NCM Medical Reception.*   **S11**

Office Administration & Technology NC   *SCOTVEC/NC in Office Administration & Technology.*   **L81**

Prevention of Infection - Module   *SCOTVEC/NCM - 96053.*   **F8**

Professional & Business Ethics - MSc   *MSc Degree / PgD in Professional & Business Ethics.*
L65

MEDICAL TECHNOLOGY & PHARMACOLOGY

Clinical Imaging - MSc / Diploma   *MSc / PgD in Clinical Imaging.*   **L75**

Clinical Oncology - MSc / Diploma   *MSc Degree / Diploma in Clinical Oncology.*   **L75**

Clinical Pharmacy - MSc   *MSc in Clinical Pharmacy.*   **S105**

Clinical Pharmacy - PgD   *A PgD in Clinical Pharmacy.*   **S105**

Customised Short Courses in Science & Technology   *National and/or College/Company certificate can be issued.*   **L68**

Laboratory Science Technology Course - NC (SCOTVEC)   *SCOTVEC/NC in Laboratory Science Technology. .*   **L68**

Medical Terminology (SCOTVEC)   *SCOTVEC/NCM in Medical Terminology (Double Module).*   **L68**

Pharmaceutical Sciences - HNC   *SCOTVEC/HNC in Pharmaceutical Sciences.*   **L5 S75**

Pharmaceutical Sciences - NC   *On successful completion of this course the student will gain SCOTVEC/NC.*   **S75**

Pharmacology - MSc   *MSc in Pharmacology.*
S105

Pharmacy Technicians - NC   *SCOTVEC/NC.*   **L5**

Prosthetics & Orthotics - MSc   *MSc in Prosthetics & Orthotics.*   **S105**

MEDICINE, SURGERY, COMPLEMENTARY MEDICINE

Clinical Oncology - MSc / Diploma   *MSc Degree / Diploma in Clinical Oncology.*   **L75**

Community Health - MSc / Diploma   *MSc Degree / Diploma in Community Health.*   **L75**

Complementary Medicines   *Delegates will have an understanding of Complementary Medicines.*
G21

Health Sciences - MSc / Diploma   *MSc Degree / Diploma in Health Sciences.*   **L75**

Medical Aid Course - Advanced   *Advanced emergency medical aid for survivors from offshore oil & gas installations.*   **G11**

Medical Aid Course - Advanced (Refresher Course)   *Refresher course for 5 Day Advanced Medical Aid Course.*   **G11**

Medical Aid Course - Basic   *Emergency medical Aid for survivors from offshore oil & gas installation evacuations.*   **G11**

Medical Sciences - NC   *SCOTVEC/NC in Medical Sciences.*   **S94**

NURSING

Access to Nursing - SCOTVEC/NC & Access Course   *SCOTVEC/NC in Nursing.*   **G17**

Advanced Nursing - BSc/BSc (Hons)   *BSc Degree/Honours Degree in Advanced Nursing.*
L65

Childcare & Education, SVQ Level II   *SCOTVEC, SVQs, SVQ Level II in Childcare & Education.*
H53

Childcare & Education, SVQ Level III   *SCOTVEC, SVQs, SVQ Level III in Childcare & Education.*
H53

Community Health - BA/BA (Hons)   *Bachelor of Arts (Honours) Degree in Community Health.*
L65

Community Health Nursing (Health Visiting) - BA
BA in Community Health Nursing.   **G15**

Community Health Nursing (Occupational Health) -
BA *BA in Community Health Nursing
(Occupational Health).*   **G15**

Community Health Nursing (Option Two) - BA *BA
in Community Health Nursing.*   **G15**

Community Health Nursing - Professional Studies
Diploma *Diploma in professional studies in
Community Health Nursing.*   **S40**

Community Health Nursing in District Nursing - BA
BA in Community Health Nursing.   **G15**

Community Health Studies - BA (Honours) *BA
(Hons) in Community Health Studies.*   **T12**

Community Nurses - Assessors Course
Extension of assessment techniques.   **S23**

Creche Work   *College Certificate.*   **L81**

Diploma in Advanced Nursing   *Diploma in
Advanced Nursing.*   **L65**

District Nurses - Continuing Education   *Extension
of knowledge & skills.*   **S23**

Family Planning Course   *Statement of
Competence from the National Board for Nursing,
Midwifery & Health Visiting.*   **S41**

Health Studies - NC   *SCOTVEC/NC will be
awarded on successful completion of this course.*
                                            B3

Health Visitors - Continuing Education Courses
Extension of knowledge & skills.   **S23**

HIV, Aids & Hepatitis B (1/2 Module) - NC
SCOTVEC/NC.   **C23**

HIV, Aids & Hepatitis B - SCOTVEC/NC   *Routes
of infection for HIV & Hepatitis B & how infection
may be prevented.*   **T23**

HIV, Related Illnesses & Hepatitis B (SCOTVEC)
SCOTVEC/NCM.   **L68**

HIV/Aids - 'Understanding the Issues'
*Participants will be made aware of the issues
concerned with HIV/AIDS.*   **C13**

Hospital Play Specialist Course   *Hospital Play
Specialist Certificate.*   **L68**

Medical - Screening & Motivating Change for
Practice Nurses   *Improved ability to screen &
motivate change.*   **D5**

Mental Health - HNC   *SCOTVEC/HNC in Mental
Health.*   **S75**

Midwifery - BSc (Honours)   *A BSc Hons in
Midwifery.*   **T12**

Midwifery- BSc (Honours)   *BSc Degree (Honours)
in Midwifery.*   **L65**

Nursing   *Participants will gain a basic knowledge
of home nursing.*   **S129**

Nursing, Psychiatry & Psychology - HNC/NC
SCOTVEC/HNC/NC.   **S9**

Nursing & Education - MSc/Diploma   *MSc Degree
/ Diploma in Nursing & Education.*   **L77**

Nursing & Health Studies MSc/Diploma   *MSc
Degree/ Diploma in Nursing & Health Studies.*
                                            L77

Nursing - BA/Diploma in Professional Studies
BA/Diploma in Nursing.   **G15**

Nursing - BSc (Honours) (UCAS - B700 Nursing)
BSc Hons Degree in Nursing.   **T12**

Nursing - Diploma   *Diploma in Nursing.*   **S8**

Nursing - Diploma in Professional Studies
Diploma in Professional Studies in Nursing.   **S42**

Nursing for Qualified Nurses- BSc (Hons)   *BSc
Degree (Honours) in Nursing.*   **L65**

Nursing Studies - BA   *Bachelor of Arts in Nursing
Studies.*   **S8**

Post Certificate Nursery Nurse Course - SNNB
Scottish Nursery Nurse Board Post Certificate.
                                            L68

Practice Nurse Course   *Statement of Competence
from National Board for Nursing, Midwifery &
Health Visiting.*   **S39**

Pre Nursing - Course   *Progress to Nurse Training
College/ HNC level/ employment within the field of
caring.*   **M7**

Pre-Nursing - NC   *SCOTVEC/NCs which are
recognised as a pre-entry qualification to Colleges
of Nursing.*   **H53**

Preparation for Caring - NC   *SCOTVEC/NCMs &
SCE H Grades which may allow entry to RGN or
RMN training.*   **C10**

Training in Elderly Care   *SCOTVEC/NCMs.*   **S81**

PERSONAL CARE, HAIR, BEAUTY

Advanced Epilation   *International Health & Beauty
Council Diploma awarded.*   **S14**

Advanced Epilation - HN Unit   *Improved skills in
epilation & SCOTVEC HNU.*   **H53**

Advanced Hairdressing   *Practical skills &
knowledge will be gained by successful students.*
                                            S15

Advanced Styling   *Basic skills & experience in
styling.*   **S14**

Aromatherapy   *Practical experience in
aromatherapy.*   **C41 H53**

Aromatherapy - Higher National Unit   *SCOTVEC
Higher National Unit in Aromatherapy.*   **L5**

Aromatherapy - HNUs   *3 SCOTVEC HNUs in
Aromatherapy. Possible progression to
HNC/HND course.*   **C10**

Aromatherapy - Introduction   *Basic skills & experience in aromatherapy.*   **S14**

Aromatherapy for Women   *Practical experience in aromatherapy.*   **C41**

Basic Beauty Skills   *Student will have the basic knowledge required to enter the beauty care & therapy business.*   **S10**

Beautician - NC   *Successful students will be awarded SCOTVEC certificate which will record their achievements.*   **S75**

Beauty Care   *SCOTVEC/NCMs in Beauty Care for those working in the Industry.*   **D5 L27**

Beauty Care - NC   *SCOTVEC/NC in Beauty Care.*   **S16**

Beauty Care NC   *SCOTVEC/NC.*   **L27**

Beauty Therapy & Electrical Epilation - NVQ   *NVQ (2/3) - endorsed by the Health & Beauty Therapy Training Board.*   **G17**

Beauty Therapy & Health Care - NC   *SCOTVEC/NC in Beauty Therapy & Health Care.*   **S19**

Beauty Therapy - City & Guilds   *C & G 304 - 305 Beauty Therapy Examination & Electrolysis Examination.*   **G2**

Beauty Therapy - City & Guilds 3028   *NVQ (2/3) - endorsed by the Health & Beauty Therapy Training Board.*   **G17**

Beauty Therapy - HND   *SCOTVEC/HND in Beauty Therapy.*   **S16**

Beauty Therapy - NCMs   *C & G Certificates/NC modules are awarded to successful students.*   **H53**

Beauty/Cosmetic Skills Course   *SCOTVEC/NC in Beauty/Cosmetic Skills Course.*   **S77**

Cosmetic Camouflage   *Intended for professionals, the course gives an insight into the art of Cosmetic Camouflage.*   **H53**

Cosmetic Make-Up & Manicure - SCOTVEC Module   *SCOTVEC Certificate for successfully completed module.*   **H53**

Cosmetic Make-Up - Beauty Workshop   *College certificate awarded on successful completion of the course.*   **F8**

Cosmetic Make-Up - NC   *NC Cosmetic Make-Up.*   **F5 S14**

Cosmetic Make-Up - Part-Time NC   *SCOTVEC/NC cosmetic Make-up.*   **L81**

Cosmetic Make-Up 1 - SCOTVEC/NC   *On successful completion of this course students will have SCOTVEC/NC.*   **G17**

Dressing Long Hair   *After training delegates will be able to dress long hair to produce a range of styles.*   **M8**

Electrical Epilation   *SCOTVEC Unit in Electrical Epilation will be awarded on successful completion of the course.*   **S14**

Facial Care - HN Unit   *Participants will gain the Higher National Unit in Facial Care.*   **H49**

Gents Haircutting   *Trainees can gain skills in graduation techniques. Module number 3313.*   **L27**

Gents Hairdressing   *Students will gain updated skills in Gents Hairdressing.*   **F5**

Gents Hairdressing (SCOTVEC) NCM   *SCOTVEC/NCM.*   **L5**

Hair Extensions - Short Course   *College Certificate.*   **L81**

Hairdressing   *Participants will improve their skills in hairdressing.*   **H53 T1**

Hairdressing & Beauty Therapy - Customised Courses   *Various.*   **L71**

Hairdressing & Salon Organisation - HN Units   *SCOTVEC HNUs in Hairdressing & Salon Organisation.*   **C10**

Hairdressing & Salon Organisation - HNC   *SCOTVEC/HNC.*   **D5 G2 L5 M7 S10 S14 S16 S75 S79**

Hairdressing - HNC   *SCOTVEC/HNC in Hairdressing.*   **S14 S91**

Hairdressing - Level III SVQ Part-Time   *SCOTVEC/HTB Level III Hairdressing.*   **L81**

Hairdressing - NC   *A NC in a Hairdressing Programme.*   **S14 S16 S75 S79 S91 T9**

Hairdressing - NCMs   *SCOTVEC/NC(s) will be awarded to successful students.*   **H53**

Hairdressing - Refresher Course   *Knowledge gained in new hairdressing techniques.*   **S14**

Hairdressing - SCOTVEC/HTB Level II SVQ - Part-Time   *SCOTVEC/HTB Level II SVQ.*   **L81**

Hairdressing - SVQ   *SVQ in Hairdressing.*   **G2**

Hairdressing - SVQ Level II   *SVQ Level II awarded (endorsed by the Hairdressing Training Board).*   **G17**

Hairdressing - SVQ Level II   *SVQ Level II in Hairdressing.*   **B3 M7 S15**

Hairdressing - SVQ Level III   *SCOTVEC Hairdressing - SVQ Level III.*   **L5 S15**

Hairdressing - YT/SVQ Level II   *SCOTVEC, SVQ Level II (SF0703201) in Hairdressing .*   **D5**

Hairdressing Programme - NC/SVQ Level II   *SCOTVEC/NC/SVQ in Hairdressing. .*   **H53**

Hairdressing Refresher Course   *The knowledge & skills to keep up to date on recent changes in the profession.*   **D6**

Hairdressing Studies - SVQ Level III   *SVQ Level III which provides entry to HNC or C & G Advanced Programme.*   **H53**

Hairdressing SVQ Level II NC   *SCOTVEC/NC.*   **L27**

Hairdressing/Beauty Culture   *SCOTVEC/NC in Hairdressing/Beauty Culture.*   **S77**

Holistic Therapeutic Massage   *Practical experience in therapeutic massage.*   **C41**

Introduction to Aromatherapy   *Participants will gain basic knowledge of Aromatherapy & Massage techniques.*   **H53 S14**

Introduction to Holistic Therapeutic Massage   *Practical experience in therapeutic massage.*   **C41**

Ladies Hairdressing - NC   *SCOTVEC/NC in Ladies Hairdressing.*   **L5 S79**

Long Hair Styling - Certificate   *A Certificate in Long Hair Styling.*   **S14**

Make-Up & Skin Care   *There is no formal outcome to this course.*   **B3**

Management Skills   *D32 & D33.*   **G37**

Manicure   *Experience & skills in manicure & artificial nails.*   **S14**

Manicure - Part-Time NC   *SCOTVEC 63371.*   **L81**

Nail Extensions - Part-Time   *College Certificate.*   **L81**

Non-Advanced Vocational Courses for Adults   *Skills in chosen subject.*   **S75**

Personal Care (SCOTVEC)   *SCOTVEC/NCM in Personal Care.*   **L5**

Personal Presentation (SCOTVEC)   *SCOTVEC/NCM.*   **L5**

Reflexology - Certificate   *A Certificate in Reflexology.*   **S14**

Refresher Course in Hairdressing   *Participants will gain an update of information & skills in hairdressing.*   **L27**

Women's Health Courses (Various)   *No formal outcome.*   **S137**

PERSONAL HEALTH CARE & FITNESS, FIRST AID

4 Day Health & Safety (Certificated)   *Health & Safety Qualification in First Aid.*   **G29**

Anatomy, Physiology & Body Massage   *CIBTAC Certificate.*   **T9**

Basic First Aid   *Participants will gain a basic knowledge of first aid.*   **S129**

Basic Sea Safety Courses   *Students will have the basic minimum qualification to go to sea.*   **H36**

Cardio-Pulmonary Resuscitation   *Basic essentials of life-saving resuscitative measures (uncertificated).*   **D5**

Certificate Course for Exercise Teachers   *Certificate Course for Exercise Teachers.*   **L33**

Certificate in Exercise & Health Studies (PEA/RSA)   *PEA Certificate in Exercise & Health Studies.*   **L5**

Childminding / Pre-School Child / Childhood 5-10   *An OU Certificate issued on completion.*   **H44**

Citizen CPR (Heart Start)   *Participants will gain ability to restart heart & provide resuscitation for casualties.*   **H35**

Community Based Adult Education   *The Local Collaborative Programme organises classes for local groups.*   **H7**

Community Day Classes   *Improved personal, social & learning skills.*   **L68**

Community Health - MSc / Diploma   *MSc Degree / Diploma in Community Health.*   **L75**

Customised Short Courses in Science & Technology   *National and/or College/Company certificate can be issued.*   **L68**

Emergency First Aid   *St. Andrew's Ambulance Association HSE approved Certificate, valid for 3 years awarded.*   **H35**

Emergency First Aid - (S3)   *Participants will learn the basic fundamentals of First Aid.*   **S94**

Emergency First Aid Courses   *Certificate - HSE Approved.*   **S113**

Emergency First Aid or 'Appointed Persons' First Aid   *Basic essentials of Life-Saving (uncertificated).*   **D5**

First Aid   *There is no formal outcome to this course.*   **B2 C10 G26 H14 H30 H49 S15 T18**

First Aid - Community Education Adult Classes   *St Andrews Ambulance Association Certificate in First Aid.*   **F17 F19**

First Aid - Practice & Update   *The opportunity for Certificate Holders to practice & update their First Aid skills.*   **H35**

First Aid - Refresher Programme for HSE Regulations   *To obtain renewal of Certification for First Aid.*   **D5**

First Aid At Sea Courses   *First Aid at Sea certificate or RYA equivalent.*   **L20**

First Aid At Work   *Successful students will be awarded a Health & Safety Executive Certificate in First Aid.*   **S75**

First Aid At Work - HSE   *Health & Safety Executive Nominated First Aid.*   **H49**

First Aid At Work - Revision (S2)   *Revision and updating of 3-year Certificate.*   **S94**

First Aid Certificate (HASW)   *First aid training (HASW) qualification to comply with recent amendments to the act.*   **F8**

First Aid Certificate - Community Education Adult Classes   *St Andrews Ambulance Association Certificate.*   **F9 F18 F23**

First Aid Certificate - Health & Safety   *HSE & St Andrews Ambulance Association First Aid Certificate.*   **D5**

First Aid Certificate - HSE (Recognised Course)   *First Aid Certificate - valid for three years & approved by the HSE.*   **L68**

First Aid Certificate - St Andrew's Ambulance Association   *St Andrew's Ambulance Association First Aid Certificate.*   **D5**

First Aid Certificate Approved by the HSE   *First Aid Certificate of the HSE.*   **D5**

First Aid Courses   *Development of first aid skills.*   **C22**

First Aid in the Work Place   *Health & Safety Executive approved certificate.*   **S113**

First Aid Measures - NC   *SCOTVEC/NC.*   **C23**

First Aid Measures for Carers (SCOTVEC)   *SCOTVEC/NCM.*   **L68**

First Aid Refresher Course   *St. Andrew's Ambulance Association HSE approved Certificate, valid for 3 years.*   **H35**

First Aid Training   *Basic life-saving procedures. The course can be tailored to the client group.*   **H2 S79**

First Aid Training for Industry (Refresher Course)   *Renewal of the Standard First Aid Course.*   **H2**

First Aid, personal Health Care & Fitness   *First Aid Certificate & SCOTVEC/NC modules in Health & Fitness.*   **T14**

Health & Fitness - HNC   *SCOTVEC/HNC in Health & Fitness.*   **L5**

Health & Safety / COSHH / First Aid Courses for Industry   *Skills appropriate to the needs of work situations.*   **H31 H49**

Health Education - Certificate   *On completion of the course students may gain a certificate in health education.*   **S64**

Health Education - Diploma   *Students will be awarded SCOTVEC Professional Development Award at HND Level.*   **S75**

Health Promotion & Health Education - MSc / Diploma   *MSc Degree / Diploma in Health Promotion & Health Education.*   **L75**

Health Promotion - MSc   *MSc Degree / PgD in Health Promotion.*   **L65**

Health Promotion - NC   *SCOTVEC/NC.*   **C23**

Health Studies - BA (Hons)   *BA (Hons) in Health Studies.*   **S42**

Health Studies - BSc (Hons)   *BSc (Honours) in Health Studies.*   **S42**

Health Studies - MSc   *MSc in Health Studies.*   **S66**

Health Studies - PgC   *PgC in Health Studies.*   **S66**

Health Studies - PgD   *PgD in Health Studies.*   **S66**

Health, Safety & Hygiene   *Employer's/employee's responsibilities for health & safety and a safe working environment.*   **H42**

Introduction to Alexander Technique   *Participants will gain experience in the Alexander Technique.*   **C41 C43**

Keep Fit   *Delegates will understand that Keep Fit can be fun!.*   **G13**

Men's Aerobic Classes   *Delegates will have developed fitness, strength, muscle tone & flexibility.*   **G13**

Nursing & Education - MSc/Diploma   *MSc Degree / Diploma in Nursing & Education.*   **L77**

One Day First Aid Course   *Emergency First Aid Attendance Certificate.*   **G29**

Personal Presentation   *Improved personal appearance & presentation.*   **D6**

Planning Personal Fitness (SCOTVEC)   *SCOTVEC/NCM 80002 Planning Personal Fitness.*   **L83**

Practical First Aid   *Participants will gain knowledge of practical application of first aid.*   **S129**

Refresher First Aid Courses (2 day)   *Renewed first aid certificate, HSE Approved.*   **S113**

Sea Survival, Fire Fighting, First Aid (Basic) *Department of Transport approved certificates for all courses.*   **G2**

Short Courses for Minority Ethnic Women   *A variety of non-certificate courses & SCOTVEC certificate courses.*   **C16**

Standard First Aid   *Theoretical/practical knowledge of first aid.*   **S129**

Teaching Exercise to Music - RSA Basic Certificate   *RSA Basic Certificate in Teaching Exercise to Music.*   **L5**

The Alexander Technique   *Participants will acquire a knowledge of this stress reducing technique.*   **S109**

Women & Health   *This course aims to give women an understanding of women's issues & women's health issues.*   **H52**

PHYSIOTHERAPY, OCCUPATIONAL & SPEECH THERAPY

Anatomy, Physiology & Body Massage   *CIBTAC Certificate awarded.*   **T9**

Dramatherapy - PgD   *PgD in Dramatherapy.*   **L65**

Holistic Therapeutic Massage   *Practical experience in therapeutic massage.*   **C41**

Hospital Play Specialist Course   *Hospital Play Specialist Certificate.*   **L68**

Introduction to Art Therapy   *Practical experience in art therapy.*   **C41**

Introduction to Holistic Therapeutic Massage *Practical experience in therapeutic massage.*   **C41**

Occupational Therapy - BSc/Bsc (Hons) UCAS Code: B970   *BSc in Occupational Therapy.*   **G15**

Occupational Therapy for Qualified Occupational Therapists - BSc   *BSc Degree in Occupational Therapy.*   **L65**

Occupational Therapy Support - HNC   *HNC.*   **F8 L5 S81**

Physiotherapy - BSc (Hons)   *BSc Degree (Honours) in Physiotherapy.*   **L65**

Physiotherapy Studies - MSc   *An MSc in Physiotherapy Studies.*   **S65**

Physiotherapy Studies - PgC   *A PgC in Physiotherapy Studies.*   **S65**

Physiotherapy Studies - PgD   *A PgD in Physiotherapy Studies.*   **S65**

PSYCHIATRY, PSYCHOLOGY

Access to Higher Education - SCOTVEC Psychology (SCE O/S Equivalent)   *Part-time SCOTVEC modules.*   **D5**

An Introduction to Psychology   *An introduction to psychology.*   **C41**

An Introduction to Psychology Part 2   *Participants will learn more about their own and others' behaviour.*   **T13**

Basic Applications of Behavioural Science - NC *SCOTVEC/NC.*   **C23**

Behavioural Science - SCE H Grade   *SCE H Grade.*   **S13**

Certificate in Welfare Studies   *Certificate of Welfare Officers.*   **L81**

Counselling Psychology - HNC   *SCOTVEC/HNC.* **L5**

Diploma in Counselling & Supervision   *PgD validated by Glasgow Caledonian University.*   **D9**

Handwriting Analysis   *Basic understanding of what makes people tick.*   **T9**

Human Development : Infancy to Old Age - Module *SCOTVEC/NCM - 7140800.*   **F8**

Introduction to Community Education   *Prepares participants for work in the community.*   **C22**

Introduction to Psychology   *SCOTVEC module in Psychology.*   **C22**

Introduction to Psychology - NC   *SCOTVEC/NC.* **C23**

Mental Health - HNC   *SCOTVEC/HNC in Mental Health.*   **S75**

Nursing - Psychiatry & Psychology - HNC/NC *SCOTVEC/HNC/NC.*   **S9**

Psychiatry - MPhil / Diploma   *Master of Philosophy / Diploma in Psychiatry.*   **L75**

Psychological Testing   *Basics of psychological testing & its value in staff selection, appraisal and development.*   **G16**

Psychology - GCSE   *GCSE in Psychology.*   **L68**

Psychology - Introduction - NC   *On successful completion of this course students will have a NC.* **G17**

Psychology: Introduction to Human Behaviour II *Introduction to a variety of interesting areas.*   **G21**

The Use of the Myers-Briggs Type Indicator   *The use of the MBTI and the role of type in group settings.*   **G16**

Transactional Analysis: a Guide to Self & Relationships   *Basic ideas and applications of Transactional Analysis.*   **G16**

Language, Communication & Self-Help

AUDIO & VISUAL MEDIA

Access to Photography - SCOTVEC/NC *SCOTVEC NC Awarded.* **G17**

Advanced Colour Photography *Knowledge gained in advanced colour photography.* **S68**

Advanced Photography *Improved photographic skills.* **L68**

Advanced Studio Photography *Knowledge gained in advanced studio photography.* **S68**

Audio Visual Technology - HNC *SCOTVEC/HNC in Audio Visual Technology.* **L68**

Audio Visual Technology - NC *SCOTVEC/NC in Audio Visual Technology.* **L68**

Audio/Video Production Technology - NC *SCOTVEC/NC in Audio & Video Production Technology.* **S16**

Basic Video Camera Techniques *Participants will learn to use the video recorder effectively.* **H53**

BBC & Public Service Broadcasting: Cultural Asset or Expensive Luxury? *No formal outcome.* **C41**

Broadcasting Analysis & Production - SCOTVEC/HNC *SCOTVEC/HNC in Broadcasting, Analysis & Production.* **G17**

Camcorder Techniques *Participants will have gained skills in video production.* **H31**

Community Media Skills *6 months work experience for those unemployed over a year.* **G28**

Electronic Editing - Audio Visual Technology Evening Class (SCOTVEC) *SCOTVEC/NCM in AVT Electronic Editing.* **L68**

Film & Media Studies - (P/T/ Degree Unit) *Units completed can be accumulated towards Degree.* **C42**

Film Production - Audio Visual Technology Evening Class (SCOTVEC) *SCOTVEC/NCM in AVT Film Production.* **L68**

Foundation Photography *Non-certificated (see course content).* **L68**

Home Recording *SCOTVEC 4 Track Module (1).* **T9**

Intermediate Studio Photography *Knowledge gained in intermediate studio photography.* **S68**

Introduction to Photography (SCOTVEC) *SCOTVEC/NCM in Introduction to Photography.* **L1 L31**

Introduction to Photography - Module *SCOTVEC/NCM - 91844.* **F8**

Introduction to Photography - NC *SCOTVEC/NC listing Modules studied & Learning Outcomes attained.* **C23**

K506: Living Arts Support Group *No formal outcome.* **H39**

Media Studies: Film (SCOTVEC) *SCOTVEC/NCM in Media Studies: Film.* **L1**

Multimedia Computing - Diploma *Successful students will be awarded a Diploma Post Degree/HND in Multimedia Computing.* **S75**

Music Technology - HNC *SCOTVEC/HNC in Music Technology.* **S94**

Part-Time Integrated Photography/Audio Visual Technology -National Certificate *SCOTVEC/NC.* **L68**

Photography *There is no formal outcome to this course.* **B3 C16 D5 S87 S119**

Photography & Audio Visual Technology - NC *SCOTVEC/NC in Photography & Audio Visual Technology.* **S68**

Photography & Video Techniques - NC *SCOTVEC/NC in Photography & Video Techniques.* **C22**

Photography (Introduction) - SCOTVEC *SCOTVEC/NC.* **G17**

Photography - GCSE *GCSE Photography.* **L81**

Photography - HNC *SCOTVEC/HNC in Photography.* **L68 S68**

Photography - NC *SCOTVEC/NC in Photography.* **L68**

Photography - SCOTVEC/HNC *HNC in Photography.* **G17**

Photography 1 - HN Unit *SCOTVEC Higher National Unit.* **L5**

Photography 1 Package - NCMs *SCOTVEC/NCMs.* **L5**

Photography 2 Package - NCMs *SCOTVEC/NCMs.* **L5**

Photography Evening Class - Basic Studio (SCOTVEC) *SCOTVEC/NCM in Basic Studio Techniques.* **L68**

Photography Evening Class - Camera Techniques (SCOTVEC) *SCOTVEC/NCM in Camera Techniques.* **L68**

Photography Evening Class - Monochrome Film Process & Print (SCOTVEC) *SCOTVEC/NCM in Monochrome Film Process & Print.* **L68**

Photography Evening Class - Portraiture (SCOTVEC) *SCOTVEC/NCM in Photography Portraiture.* **L68**

Photography Evening Class - Product (SCOTVEC) *SCOTVEC/NCM in Photography Product.*   **L68**

Photography Evening Class - Scientific - (SCOTVEC) *SCOTVEC/NCM in Photography Scientific.*   **L68**

Photography/Art & Design - Part-Time NC *SCOTVEC certificate.*   **L81**

Portraiture - NC *SCOTVEC/NC listing Modules studied & Learning Outcomes attained will be awarded at the end of session.*   **C23**

Radio Interviewing & Reporting - HN Unit *HNU.*   **F8**

Radio Presentation - HN Unit *SCOTVEC Higher National Unit - 8480612.*   **F8**

Radio Scripting & Presentation - HN Unit *HNU.*   **F8**

Radio, Television & the Constructive Use of Leisure *A greater understanding of the facilities offered by broadcasting companies.*   **C41**

Short Course in Colour Photography (Tape Slide Production) *Working knowledge of producing a tape slide programme.*   **L68**

Short Course in Colour Processing & Printing *Working knowledge of colour processing & printing.*   **L68**

Studio Recording *SCOTVEC Module Hi-Tech One.*   **T9**

Tape Slide Production - Audio Visual Technology Evening Class (SCOTVEC) *SCOTVEC/NCM in AVT Tape Slide Production.*   **L68**

Technical Operations & Editing for Radio Broadcasting - HN Unit *SCOTVEC Higher National Unit - 8480572.*   **F8**

Television/Video Production - NC *SCOTVEC/NC in Television/Video Production.*   **S68**

Using Video Equipment Introductory Course *Participants will be able to set up & operate a video system.*   **C13**

Video - Editing - HNU   *HNU.*   **F8**

Video - Single Camera - HNU   *HNU.*   **F8**

Video Production (Editing) *Non-certificated (see course content).*   **L68**

Video Production (Portable Equipment) *Non-certificated (see course content).*   **L68**

Video Production - Audio Visual Technology Evening Class (SCOTVEC) *SCOTVEC/NCM in AVT Video Production.*   **L68**

Video Production Skills - HNC *SCOTVEC/HNC in Video Production Skills.*   **F8**

Video Production Technology: Basic Skills (SCOTVEC) *SCOTVEC/NCM in Video Production Technology: Basic Skills.*   **L1**

Video Skills *Experience in video filming.*   **C16**

Video Skills - Module *SCOTVEC Module - Video Skills.*   **F9**

Video Skills: Single Camera - HN Unit *SCOTVEC Higher National Unit - 8480562.*   **F8**

BASIC SKILLS, READING, WRITING, ARITHMETIC, SOCIAL

Adult Basic Education *Improved literacy, numeracy, social & independent living skills.*   **C22**

Adult Basic Education & Learning Support *Preparation for education or employment.*   **L5**

Adult Basic Education/Communication Skills - Special Needs *Improved reading & communication skills & confidence to use them.*   **C12**

Arithmetic for Adults *Participants will be able cope with everyday arithmetical problems.*   **T4**

Brush Up On English *Improved English skills & confidence to use them.*   **C12**

Brush Up Your English *Delegates will have confidence in Written English & will have developed Writing Skills.*   **G21**

Business Numeracy - 81053 - SCOTVEC/NC *On successful completion of this course learners will have SCOTVEC/NCM.*   **T23**

Career Extension Course - C & G *Licentiateship of the C & G of London Institute.*   **S87**

Communication 1: Spoken Communication (SCOTVEC) *SCOTVEC/NCM in Communication 1: Spoken Communication.*   **L1**

Communication 1: Written Communication (SCOTVEC) *SCOTVEC/NCM in Communication 1: Written Communication.*   **L1**

Community Day Classes *Improved personal, social & learning skills.*   **L68**

Community Evening Class *Improved personal, social & learning skills.*   **L68**

English - S Grade *SCE at S Grade in English.*   **D3**

English - S Grade - SCE *SCE awarded on successful completion of this course.*   **T23**

English - SCE H Grade *SCE awarded on successful completion of this course.*   **T23**

English, Arithmetic & Computers *At the end of the course participants will have gained a higher level of Arithmetic & English.*   **T5**

Essential Skills *Essential Skills is for those who want to brush up on e.g. reading, writing, everyday maths, form-filling.*   **H7**

Extension Programme (For Students with Learning Difficulties) *No formal outcome.*   **S87**

Fresh Opportunities Course   *Each student will receive a college certificate indicating the topics covered.*   **S88**

Learning Support (For Students Experiencing Learning Difficulties)   *The course is designed to support students & trainees.*   **S87**

Life / Social Skills - NCMs   *SCOTVEC modules for people with moderate learning difficulties, to prepare them for work.*   **H53**

Literacy & Numeracy   *City & Guilds Certificate.*   **S155**

Local Investigation   *SCOTVEC/NC units.*   **S153**

Maths & Business Numeracy   *The SCOTVEC Module 81053 in Maths/ Business Numeracy.*   **B6**

Numeracy 1 (SCOTVEC)   *SCOTVEC/NCM in Numeracy 1.*   **L1**

Numeracy 2   *SCOTVEC/NC Units.*   **S153**

Numeracy I - NCM (Reflex Learning Unit)   *SCOTVEC/NCM in Numeracy.*   **S2**

Numeracy: Levels Foundation, 1 & 2   *City & Guilds Certificate.*   **H54**

Open University Community Education Course: the Pre-School Child   *Development of skills in number work.*   **C17**

Options & Choices - NC   *SCOTVEC/NC will be awarded to successful participants who complete a series of modules.*   **T4**

Outlook   *Students will gain confidence & various SCOTVEC modules.*   **S20**

Outreach Further Education Services   *Some students may attain various appropriate SCOTVEC modules.*   **S16**

Pathways   *SCOTVEC/NCM.*   **L68**

Practical Writing Skills (SCOTVEC)   *SCOTVEC/NCM in Practical Writing Skills.*   **L5**

Practical Writing Skills - Part-Time NC   *SCOTVEC module.*   **L81**

Pre-Access   *Success will provide a route into higher education.*   **S87**

Punctuation & Grammar for Adults   *Participants will be able understand punctuation & grammar.*   **T4**

Refresher English   *Improved reading & writing skills & confidence to use them.*   **C19**

Resource Centre Link Course   *No formal outcome.*   **T1**

Skillstart - GSVQ Level I   *When you complete the course you will be awarded the Skillstart 1 award.*   **G17**

Skillstart 1   *Students will gain confidence & various SCOTVEC modules.*   **S20**

Skillstart 2   *Students will gain confidence & various SCOTVEC modules.*   **S20**

Social & Vocational Skills - SEB S Grade   *An SEB S Grade in Social & Vocational Skills awarded.*   **B11**

Special Education Bridgework (Special Needs)   *No formal outcome.*   **F3**

Special Educational Needs   *Students will gain a more confident approach to their daily life.*   **S14**

Special Needs Adult Link Programme   *Skills gained in personal development.*   **S13**

Special Needs for Dalgairn Centre, Cupar   *Skills gained include basic help with literacy, numeracy & self advocacy.*   **F3**

Special Needs Schools Link Foundation Course   *Skills gained in personal development.*   **S13**

Special Needs Youth Enterprise Skills Course   *Skills gained in personal development.*   **S13**

Steps to Independence   *Students will gain confidence & various SCOTVEC modules.*   **S20**

Support & Opportunity for Adult Returners (S0AR)   *Preparation for employment or further education courses.*   **C18**

Tuition for Adults   *Participants will be able to work on their own with someone who can give help in what they need.*   **T4**

Tuition in Basic Skills & English for Speakers of Other Languages   *No formal outcome.*   **H58**

Various Courses Available   *No formal outcome.*   **S137**

Vocational Skills Course   *No formal outcome.*   **T1**

Volunteer Tutor Training   *Development of skills in helping adults to improve reading & writing skills.*   **C17**

Workplace Education - Communication   *Development of relevant skills & the opportunity to gain SCOTVEC qualification.*   **C16**

Workplace Education - Numeracy   *Development of relevant skills & the opportunity to gain SCOTVEC qualification.*   **C16**

Writing for Study   *Delegates will have an understanding of the skills needed for essays & pieces of work.*   **G21**

CAREER CHANGE, JOB SEARCH, RETIREMENT

Access for Women   *SCE subjects & SCOTVEC vocational modules.*   **L5**

Access to Business Administration   *Entry to Higher National & Degree Courses.*   **S3**

Access to Higher Education - SCE GCSE Sociology   *Access to Higher Education through GCSE Sociology.*   **D5**

Access to Higher Education - SCE Higher Biology *Access to Higher Education through SCE H Grade Biology.*   **D5**

Access to Higher Education - SCE Higher Chemistry *Access to Higher Education through SCE H Grade Chemistry.*   **D5**

Access to Higher Education - SCE Higher English *Access to Higher Education through SCE H Grade English.*   **D5**

Access to Higher Education - SCE Higher Geography *Access to Higher Education through SCE H Grade Geography.*   **D5**

Access to Higher Education - SCE Higher History *Access to Higher Education through SCE H Grade History.*   **D5**

Access to Higher Education - SCE Higher Modern Studies *Access to Higher Education through SCE H Grade Modern Studies.*   **D5**

Access to Higher Education - SCE Higher Physics *Access to Higher Education through SCE H Grade Physics.*   **D5**

Access to Higher Education - SCOTVEC Biology (SCE O/S Equivalent) *SCOTVEC modules in Biology.*   **D5**

Access to Higher Education - SCOTVEC Chemistry (SCE O/S Equivalent) *SCOTVEC modules in Chemistry.*   **D5**

Access to Higher Education - SCOTVEC Computing (SCE O/S Equivalent) *SCOTVEC modules in Computing.*   **D5**

Access to Higher Education - SCOTVEC French (SCE O/S Equivalent) *SCOTVEC modules in French.*   **D5**

Access to Higher Education - SCOTVEC German (SCE O/S Equivalent) *SCOTVEC modules in German.*   **D5**

Access to Higher Education - SCOTVEC Italian (SCE O/S Equivalent) *SCOTVEC modules in Italian.*   **D5**

Access to Higher Education - SCOTVEC Maths (SCE Higher Equivalent) *SCOTVEC modules in Maths.*   **D5**

Access to Higher Education - SCOTVEC Maths (SCE O/S Equivalent) *SCOTVEC modules in Maths.*   **D5**

Access to Higher Education - SCOTVEC Physics (SCE O/S Equivalent) *SCOTVEC modules in Physics.*   **D5**

Access to Higher Education - SCOTVEC Psychology (SCE O/S Equivalent) *SCOTVEC modules in Psychology.*   **D5**

Access to Higher Education - SCOTVEC Social Sciences: People & Politics *SCOTVEC modules.*   **D5**

Access to Information Technology *SCOTVEC/NCMs in Science, Technology & Maths.*   **S11**

Access to Information Technology (Beginners Course) *Applicants will learn how to handle computers with confidence.*   **L5**

Access to Science & Technology *SCOTVEC/NCMs.*   **S16 S87**

Access to Technology for Women *Prepares women for further training in new technology related skills.*   **F13**

Adult Basic Education & Learning Support *Preparation for education or employment.*   **L5**

Basic Programme for People with Hearing Impairments *Experience of a range of NCMs.*
                                                 L5

Career Change - Choice & Methods for Success *No formal outcome.*   **S142**

Career Change Options Workshop *No formal outcome.*   **F21**

Career Counselling *No formal outcome.*
                                            L97 S148

Career Extension Course - C & G *Licentiateship of the C & G of London Institute.*   **S87**

Career Guidance *No formal outcome.*
                                            L97 S148

Careers Beyond Redundancy *No formal outcome.*   **C50**

Choices *Identification of skills, abilities, interests etc. Broadening knowledge of options available.*
                                                 L68

Community Based Adult Education *No formal outcome.*   **H7**

Day Release From Special Schools *Prepares students for possible employment or transference to full-time SEN course.*   **T9**

Divinity Access Course *Admission to Theology and/or Religious Studies degree courses at University of Edinburgh.*   **L80**

Engineering Practice: Electrical & Electronic - Advanced Certificate *Advanced Certificate in Engineering Practice.*   **L68**

Essential Skills *No formal outcome.*   **H7**

General Modular - SCOTVEC/NC *At the end of the course successful students will receive the SCOTVEC/NC.*   **G17**

General Vocational Evening Class *A range of Academic Subjects leading to SCE examinations or Certification by SCOTVEC.*   **D5**

Goal Setting & Career Planning *No formal outcome.*   **S142**

Headway - NC *Vocational modules/SCOTVEC NC.*   **L68**

Interview Techniques *No formal outcome.*   **F21**

Interviewing Skills *No formal outcome.*   **C50**

Interviewlink *Participants will gain skills required for successful job searching, interview techniques, c.v. preparation etc.*   **H4**

Into Employment *Participants gain work skills &
job search techniques. Certified courses
Independent life skills training.* **T11**

Job Search *No formal outcome.* **G28**

Job Search & Interview Techniques *No formal
outcome.* **S142**

Job Search Techniques *No formal outcome.*
C50

Jobsearch Skills *No formal outcome.* **F21**

Learning Skills (SCOTVEC) *SCOTVEC/NCM
7351423 (half module).* **L5**

Learning Support (For Students Experiencing
Learning Difficulties) *No formal outcome.* **S87**

Link Courses (Multi-Disciplinary) *A large variety
of modules offered.* **T1**

New Horizons *There is no formal outcome to this
course.* **B7**

New Horizons for Women *No formal outcome.*
S109

New Moves *No formal outcome.* **T9**

New Opportunities - Return to Study *No formal
outcome.* **T13**

Options & Choices *SCOTVEC/NCM.* **L5**

Pathways *SCOTVEC/NCM.* **L68**

Pre Access Science - GSVQ Level II *SCOTVEC
module may be awarded.* **L68**

Pre-Access Course *Preparation for Access
courses & consideration of various routes to
Higher Education.* **L68**

Pre-Entry Course for Arts & Social Studies
Access to full/part time BA/ Certificate courses.
S109

Pre-Retirement Course *Prepares participants for
retirement.* **C22 S15 S75**

Pre-Retirement Planning *No formal outcome.*
S142

Pre-Retirement Workshop *No formal outcome.*
F21

Pre-Training Programme - Women Returners
Training for Work *No formal outcome.* **S72**

Preparation for Caring - NC *SCOTVEC/NCMs &
SCE H Grades may allow entry for RGN or RMN
training.* **C10**

Preparation for Retirement *No formal
qualification, however prepares people nearing
retirement.* **S1**

Prospects Training - Customised Training
*Training caters for those seeking training/re-
training in an occupational area.* **C31**

Psychometric Testing for Occupational Choice
Evaluation of suitability for work choices. **C50**

Resource Centre Link Course *No formal
outcome.* **T1**

Restart *Aims to help unemployed people build up
their skills.* **T9**

Retirement Course *See Course Content.* **L68**

SCE / GCE & H Grades (Part-Time) *SCE
Highers/GCE A Levels/GCSE.* **L81**

SCE / GCE & H Grades (Day Release) *SCE
Highers/GCE A Levels/GCSE.* **L81**

SCE / GCE & H Grades (Evening Classes) *SCE
Highers/GCE A Levels/GCSE.* **L81**

Special Education Bridgework (Special Needs)
No formal outcome. **F3**

Springboard - a Course for Women *Skills of
assertiveness, confidence building & a formulated
action plan for the future.* **D6**

Step Link (Support for Learning) *No formal
outcome.* **S75**

Stepping Stones: Job Ideas Generator *No formal
outcome.* **S144**

Vocational Skills Course *No formal outcome.*
T1

Women into Work Programme *A Career &
Personal Development Action Plan; Course
Certification; Project Report.* **C3**

Women Returners Computing Course *May lead
to RSA Certificate courses.* **H17**

Workplace Education - Redundancy Counselling
*Development of relevant skills/appropriate
SCOTVEC qualification.* **C16**

Women Returners Course *RSA Computer
Literacy & Information Technology I.* **H5 H12**

COMMUNICATION FOR AND WITH DISABLED PEOPLE

Basic Programme for People with Hearing
Impairments *Experience of a range of NCMs.*
L5

Communication for & with Disabled People - Short
Course *No formal outcome.* **S9**

Introduction to Lip-Reading *Participants will gain
an understanding of the practice of lip reading.*
H53

Introduction to Signs & Fingerspelling - NC
*SCOTVEC/NC listing Modules studied & Learning
Outcomes attained.* **C23**

Sign Language *On successful completion of this
course students will have gained SCOTVEC
Module.* **G7**

Sign Language for the Deaf *Council for
Advancement for Communication with Deaf
People award.* **F8**

COMMUNICATION, WRITING, JOURNALISM, SPEAKING, MASS MEDIA

Adult Basic Education/Communication Skills - Special Needs *No formal outcome.*   **C12**

Advertising Copywriting - HNC *SCOTVEC/HNC in Advertising Copywriting.*   **S75**

Communicate for Profit *No formal outcome.*   **T8**

Communication - HNC *SCOTVEC/HNC.*   **L5 S8**

Communication - NC *SCOTVEC/NC Level 1 or 2.*   **T4**

Communication - SCE H Grade *A SCE H Grade.*   **S16**

Communication - SCOTVEC/HNC *HNC in Communication.*   **G17**

Communication 1-4 *SCOTVEC/NC units.*   **S153**

Communication 1: Spoken Communication (SCOTVEC) *SCOTVEC/NCM in Communication 1: Spoken Communication.*   **L1**

Communication 1: Written Communication (SCOTVEC) *SCOTVEC/NCM in Communication 1: Written Communication.*   **L1**

Communication 2 & 3 - NC *SCOTVEC/NC listing Modules studied & Learning Outcomes attained.*   **C45**

Communication 2 (SCOTVEC) *SCOTVEC/NCM in Communication 2.*   **L1 L68 L83**

Communication 2,3 or 4 - Module *NCM.*   **F8**

Communication 3 *SCOTVEC module will be awarded on successful completion of this course.*   **B1**

Communication 3 (SCOTVEC) *SCOTVEC/NCM in Communication 3.*   **L1 L68 L83**

Communication 3 - Module *SCOTVEC module 7110041 - Communication 3.*   **F15**

Communication 3 - NC *SCOTVEC/NC listing Modules studied & Learning Outcomes attained.*   **C23**

Communication 3 - NCM *SCOTVEC/NC. This is widely accepted as an equivalent to S Grade English.*   **H53**

Communication 3 - Part-Time NC *SCOTVEC module.*   **L81**

Communication 4 - Double Module - NC *SCOTVEC/NC listing Modules studied & Learning Outcomes attained will be awarded.*   **C23**

Communication 4 - NCM *SCOTVEC/NC. Communication 4 plus Literature 1 may be accepted as an SCE H Grade English.*   **H53**

Communication for Business - HNC *SCOTVEC/HNC in Communication for Business.*   **M7**

Communication for Managers *No formal outcome.*   **S57**

Communication in Europe - HNC *SCOTVEC/HNC.*   **L5**

Communication Level 4 (SCOTVEC) *SCOTVEC/NCM in Communication 4 (Double Module).*   **L68**

Communication Levels 2,3 & 4 *SCOTVEC in Communications 2,3 or 4 depending on which course was followed.*   **H30**

Communication Skills *Improved communication skills.*   **C22**

Communication Skills - Customised Courses *Various.*   **L71**

Communication Skills: Levels Foundation, 1 & 2 *City & Guilds Certificate.*   **H54**

Communication Studies (CAM Certificate) *Communication, Advertising & Marketing Foundation (CAM) Certificate.*   **L68**

Communication Studies - Certificate *Certificate in Communication Studies.*   **S14**

Communication Studies - SCOTVEC/NC *Successful completion guarantees entry to HND in Communication Studies.*   **G17**

Communication, Advertising & Marketing Education Foundation - Certificate *Certificate awarded & progression to Diploma.*   **S14**

Communication, Advertising & Marketing Education Foundation - Diploma *Diploma in Communication, Advertising & Marketing.*   **S14**

Communications - NC *SCOTVEC/NC listing the modules studied & learning outcomes achieved.*   **S98**

Communications - SCOTVEC Module *SCOTVEC Module in Communications.*   **G18**

Communications 2 - Module *SCOTVEC Module - Communications 2.*   **F10**

Communications 3 *The SCOTVEC Module 7010041 in Communications 3.*   **B3**

Communications 3 - Module *SCOTVEC Module - Communications 3.*   **F10**

Communications Skills (M10) *Participants will have improved their Communication skills.*   **S94**

Communications Skills - HN Unit *SCOTVEC Higher National Unit.*   **L5**

Creative Communications - NC *SCOTVEC/NC in a Creative Communications.*   **S14**

Creative Writing *There is no formal outcome to this course.*   **B6**

Creative Writing 1 (SCOTVEC) *SCOTVEC/NCM in Creative Writing 1.*   **L5**

Creative Writing 1 - NC *SCOTVEC/NC listing Modules studied & Learning Outcomes attained.*   **C45**

Creative Writing 1 or 2 - Module *SCOTVEC/NCM.*   **F8**

Creative Writing 2 (SCOTVEC)   *SCOTVEC/NCM 7110411 Creative Writing 2.*   **L83**

Creative Writing 2 - SCOTVEC Module *SCOTVEC certificate is awarded on successful completion.*   **T9**

Creative Writing Part 2   *No formal outcome.*   **T13**

Customer Care   *No formal outcome.*   **H42**

Editing for Everyone   *No formal outcome.*   **T23**

Effective Speaking   *At the end of the course participants will be able to speak & write more effectively.*   **T13**

English   *SCOTVEC Certificate will be awarded on successful completion of the module(s).*   **B11**

English - SCE Higher   *Can lead to SCE H Grade Certificate in English.*   **H49**

English - SCE Standard / SCE H Grade / NC Communication Modules   *SCE Standard or H grade or SCOTVEC modules.*   **H13**

Film & Media Studies - (P/T Degree Unit)   *Units completed can be accumulated towards Degree.*   **C42**

General Education Section Short Course Provision   *College Certificate.*   **L27**

General Media Studies (SCOTVEC) *SCOTVEC/NCM in General Media Studies.*   **L1**

General Media Studies - NC   *SCOTVEC/NC listing Modules studied & Learning Outcomes attained.*   **C23**

Introduction to Media Studies (SCOTVEC) *SCOTVEC/NCM 7112010 Introduction to Media Studies.*   **L83**

Introduction to Transactional Analysis *Development of effective communication skills.*   **C41**

Journalism - Certificate   *Certificate in Journalism and an opportunity to sit formal exams.*   **L39**

Languages & Communication - HNC *SCOTVEC/HNC.*   **L5**

Listening Skills   *No formal outcome but SCOTVEC 40 hour option can be chosen.*   **D5**

Media & Modern Culture - MA   *Master of Arts Degree / PgD in Media & Modern Culture.*   **L65**

Media Culture - MLitt   *A MLitt diploma in media culture.*   **S106**

Media Education - MSc   *MSc in Media Education.*   **S67**

Media Education - PgC   *A PgC in Media Education.*   **S67**

Media Education - PgD   *A PgD in Media Education.*   **S67**

Media Presentation Skills   *Improved communication & presentation skills.*   **C22**

Media Studies - NC   *Successful students will be credited with the SCOTVEC/NC.*   **B3**

Media Studies - NCMs   *SCOTVEC/NC(s) will be awarded.*   **H53**

Multimedia Computing - Diploma   *Successful students will be awarded a Diploma Post Degree/HND in Multimedia Computing.*   **S75**

Non-Verbal Communication   *No formal outcome.*   **H42**

Office Administration (Day Release) - HNC   *HNC in Office Administration.*   **T9**

Oral Presentation (SCOTVEC)   *SCOTVEC/NCM in Oral Presentation.*   **L5**

Practical Talking Skills (SCOTVEC) *SCOTVEC/NCM in Practical Talking Skills.*   **L5**

Practical Talking Skills - Part-Time NC *SCOTVEC module.*   **L81**

Practical Writing Skills (SCOTVEC) *SCOTVEC/NCM in Practical Writing Skills.*   **L5**

Presentation Skills   *Participants by the end of the course will have increased their confidence in front of an audience.*   **S57**

Public Speaking   *No formal outcome.*   **L6**

Public Speaking, Vocal Confidence/Presentation Technique, Speech Writing   *No formal outcome.*   **S121**

Quality System Documentation   *No formal outcome.*   **S102**

Radio Interviewing & Reporting - HN Unit   *HNU.*   **F8**

Radio Scripting & Presentation - HN Unit   *HNU.*   **F8**

Reception Skills   *No formal outcome.*   **H42**

Self Presentation & Public Speaking   *No formal outcome.*   **G16**

Short Courses in Communications & Languages *Experience & knowledge of the subject studied will be gained.*   **T1**

Support & Opportunity for Adult Returners (SOAR) *Preparation for employment or further education courses.*   **C18**

Write-On - Gaelic Writing Course   *No formal outcome.*   **H31**

Writing Creatively II   *Delegates will have an understanding of Creative Writing.*   **G21**

Writing Creatively III   *Delegates will have an understanding of Creative Writing.*   **G21**

ENGLISH & UK 'ETHNIC' LANGUAGES

Academic English   *Improved English language & study skills.*   **L13**

Access to Higher Education - SCE Higher English
Access to Higher Education through SCE H Grade
English. **D5**

Advanced English Use Summer Courses *No formal outcome.* **L13**

Advanced Text Study & Translation Summer Courses *Advanced translation & text analysis skills.* **L13**

Beginners Gaelic *Development of Gaelic language skills.* **C41**

Business English *College Certificate. Entry to LCC English for Business/Commerce exam.* **L68**

Business English - Advanced *Improved comprehension & fluency in English in a variety of business contexts.* **L13**

Business English - Intermediate *Improved comprehension & fluency in English in a variety of business contexts.* **L13**

CEELT Preparation Summer Course *Cambridge Examination in English for English Language Teachers (CEELT).* **L13**

Certificates in Teaching English As a Foreign Language to Adults *RSA/UCLES Certificate.* **L89**

Communication - Level 3 & 4 *Development of skills in reading, writing, talking & listening.* **C22**

Communication 2 & 3 - NC *SCOTVEC/NC listing Modules studied & Learning Outcomes attained will be awarded.* **C45**

Communication 2 (SCOTVEC) *SCOTVEC/NCM Communication 2.* **L68 L83**

Communication 3 (SCOTVEC) *SCOTVEC/NCM Communication 3.* **L68 L83**

Communication 3 - NC *SCOTVEC/NC listing Modules studied & Learning Outcomes attained will be awarded.* **C23**

Communication 3 - NCM *SCOTVEC/NC. This is widely accepted as an equivalent to S Grade English.* **H53**

Communication 4 - Double Module - NC *SCOTVEC/NC listing Modules studied & Learning Outcomes attained.* **C23**

Communication 4 - NCM *SCOTVEC/NC. Communication 4 plus Literature 1 may be accepted as an SCE H Grade English.* **H53**

Communication Level 4 (SCOTVEC) *SCOTVEC/NCM in Communication 4 (Double Module).* **L68**

Communication Levels 2,3 & 4 *SCOTVEC in Communications 2,3 or 4.* **H30**

Communications 3 *The SCOTVEC Module 7010041 in Communications 3.* **B3 B6**

Communications in Gaelic - SCOTVEC HN Unit *Delegates will have developed their Reading & Writing skills.* **H58**

Contract Courses in English Language Training *Improved command of the English language to suit clients' needs.* **L13**

Conversation for Overseas Students *There is no formal qualification.* **S70**

Conversational Gaelic *Participants will have gained knowledge of Gaelic.* **H31**

Courses in English As a Second Language *SCOTVEC or RSA certificates; progress to ILBS or CIC certificates.* **L70**

English *SCOTVEC Certificate will be awarded on successful completion of the module(s).* **B11**

English & UK Languages *Standard & H Grades.* **L95**

English (Revised) - SCE H Grade *A SCE H Grade in English will be awarded on successful completion of this course.* **B2 B6**

English (Revised) - SCE Higher *SCE Higher - English (Revised).* **F7**

English - CSYS *Scottish Examination Board Certificate of Sixth Year Studies in English.* **D8**

English - H Grade *A SCE H Grade.* **S88**

English - H Grade (SCE) *On successful completion of the course candidates gain a SCE H Grade in English.* **M1**

English - Modular Course 1 *SCOTVEC Module in English, providing entry qualifications for H Grade English.* **D8**

English - Modular Course 2 *SCOTVEC module in English, providing entry qualifications for English H Grade.* **D8**

English - S Grade *SCOTVEC/NCM in English.* **S88**

English - S Grade (SCE) *On successful completion of the course candidates gain a SCE S Grade in English.* **M1**

English - SCE (Revised) H Grade *SCE - Higher English (Revised).* **F11**

English - SCE H Grade .
B3 B4 B6 C1 C4 C5 C6 C7 C20 C21 C2 C23 C25 C26 C27 C28 C29 C30 C33 C34 C36 C45 C46 D8 F5 F8 F9 F19 L31 L68 S2 S6 S13 S14 S16 S79 S87 S98 T9

English - SCE H Grade (Revised) *SCE at H Grade in English.* **C45 L1 L15**

English - SCE H Grade Grade *On successful completion of this course candidates will have a SCE H Grade in English.* **M5**

English - SCE H Grade or CSYS *SCE in English at H Grade or Certificate of Sixth Year Studies.* **D3**

English - SCE Higher   *Can lead to SCE H Grade Certificate in English.*   **H49**

English - SCE O Grade   *An SCE O grade certificate in English.*   **S14**

English - SCE Revised H Grade   *SCE - Higher English.*   **F12**

English - SCE Revised Higher   *SCE Revised Higher - English.*   **F10**

English - SCE S Grade   *SCE S Grade English on successful completion of the course.*   **T9**

English - SCE Standard / SCE H Grade / NC Communication Modules   *SCE Standard or H Grade or SCOTVEC modules.*   **H13**

English - SEB H Grade   *A SEB H Grade in this subject will be awarded on successful completion of this course.*   **B1 B10 B11**

English - SEB S Grade   *An SEB S Grade in English will be awarded on successful completion of this course.*   **B11**

English - SEB Sixth Year Studies   *An SEB Certificate of Sixth Year Studies in English will be awarded.*   **B1 B11**

English As a Foreign Language   *Cambridge examination, JMB, RSA examination.*   **S6 S114**

English As a Second Language   *Gives access to further or higher education.*   **S15 S79 S87**

English As a Second or Foreign Language College Certificate. *Students may also enter for external exams set by the Cambridge Exams Syndicate, Joint Matriculation Board, RSA, LCC & Oxford Exams Board.*   **L68**

English for Academic Purposes (EAP)   *JMB exam, which is acceptable for University or Polytechnic entry.*   **L68**

English for Advanced Learners   *Increased fluency & accuracy in English.*   **L68**

English for Business Studies Summer Courses   *Improved command of the English language for use in studying business studies.*   **L13**

English for Drama & Literary Discussion - Summer Course   *No formal outcome.*   **L13**

English for Ecology & Resource Management   *No formal outcome.*   **L13**

English for General Academic Purposes Summer Courses   *No formal outcome.*   **L13**

English for Legal Studies Summer Courses   *No formal outcome.*   **L13**

English for Literary Studies Summer Courses   *Improved command of written English for the purposes of literary study.*   **L13**

English for Medicine - Advanced Classes   *Improved comprehension & fluency in English for a medical environment.*   **L13**

English for Medicine - Intermediate Classes   *Improved comprehension & fluency in English for a medical environment.*   **L13**

English for Medicine Individual Courses- Advanced   *Improved comprehension & fluency in English for a medical environment.*   **L13**

English for Medicine Individual Courses- Intermediate   *Improved comprehension & fluency in English for a medical environment.*   **L13**

English for Medicine Individual Courses- Post-Elementary   *Improved comprehension & fluency in English.*   **L13**

English for Medicine Summer Course   *Improved command of English for use in a medical context.*   **L13**

English for Natural & Applied Sciences/ English for the Humanities   *Improved English as preparation for academic courses.*   **L13**

English for Non-English Speakers   *Certificate awarded.*   **T9**

English for Non-Native Speakers   *Participants will have improved their command of English.*   **H53**

English for Overseas Students   *Proficiency Certificates can be awarded.*   **S70**

English for Speakers of Other Languages   *No formal outcome.*   **C22 S2 S13 S81**

English for Speakers of Other Languages (ESOL)   *ESOL 1, 2 or 3 SCOTVEC module.*   **C16**

English for Special Purposes   *Students improve their written & spoken English for special purposes like business, medicine etc.*   **S81**

English for University Studies - Upper-Intermediate to Advanced Summer Courses   *Improved English language & study skills.*   **L13**

English H Grade   *H grade in English.*   **T1**

English Language Summer Programme   *Enhanced knowledge of English. Course Certificate.*   **L68**

Gaelic   *Increased knowledge of the Gaelic language.*   **C16 S2**

Gaelic - Module   *SCOTVEC Module - Gaelic.*   **F9**

Gaelic - NCMs   *Students will have gained some knowledge of Gaelic.*   **H26**

Gaelic - SCE H Grade   *SCE H grade in Gaelic.*   **S2 S16**

Gaelic - SCE H Grade Grade   *On successful completion of this course candidates will have a SCE H Grade in Gaelic.*   **M5**

Gaelic - SCE S Grade   *The SCE S Grade in Gaelic will be awarded on successful completion of this course.*   **B6**

Gaelic - SCE S Grade / SCE H Grade / NCMs   *SCE Standard or H Grade or the appropriate SCOTVEC modules will be awarded.*   **H13**

Gaelic - Tourist (Beginner)   *Basic skills & knowledge in Gaelic.*   **S2**

Gaelic - Tourist (Intermediate)   *Increased skills & knowledge in Gaelic.*   **S2**

Gaelic 1 (SCOTVEC)   *SCOTVEC/NCM in Gaelic 1.* **L5**

Gaelic 2 (SCOTVEC)   *SCOTVEC/NCM in Gaelic 2.* **L5**

Gaelic for Beginners - 2 SCOTVEC/NCMs   *On completion of this course students will receive SCOTVEC/NCM.* **H58**

Gaelic Language - Various Courses Available   *No formal outcome.* **H60**

Gaelic Level 1 - Module   *NCM Level 1. Skills are gained in communicating in Gaelic.* **F8**

General English - Advanced   *Improvement in ability to understand & communicate in English.* **L13**

General English - Intermediate   *Improvement in ability to understand & communicate in English.* **L13**

General English - Intermediate Summer Course   *Improvement in ability to understand & communicate in English.* **L13**

General English - Post Elementary   *Improvement in ability to understand & communicate in English.* **L13**

General English - Post-Elementary Summer Courses   *Improvement in ability to understand & communicate in English.* **L13**

General English As a Second or Foreign Language   *Cambridge FCE/CPE & other EFL exams can be taken.* **L68**

General English with Options - Advanced   *Option to study for Cambridge First Certificate, Advanced & Proficiency exams.* **L13**

General English with Options - Intermediate   *Option to study for Cambridge First Certificate, Advanced & Proficiency exams.* **L13**

Initiating Rural Development in the Gaidhealtachd - SCOTVEC HN   *Delegates will have gained SCOTVEC HN Unit.* **H58**

Language - Gaelic I (SCOTVEC)   *SCOTVEC/NCM 7340041 Language - Gaelic I.* **L31**

Language - Gaelic II (SCOTVEC)   *SCOTVEC/NCM 7340341 Language - Gaelic II.* **L31**

Language 1: Gaelic (SCOTVEC)   *SCOTVEC/NCM in Language 1: Gaelic.* **L1**

Language 2: Gaelic (SCOTVEC)   *SCOTVEC/NCM in Language 2: Gaelic.* **L1**

Language 3: Gaelic (SCOTVEC)   *SCOTVEC/NCM in Language 3: Gaelic.* **L1**

Legal English - Advanced   *Improved comprehension & fluency in English in a legal context.* **L13**

Legal English - Intermediate   *Improved comprehension & fluency in English in a legal context.* **L13**

Living Gaelic - Introductory Part 2   *Students will gain an understanding of Gaelic.* **T13**

Maths, English, French - SCE H Grade   *Participants will gain a SCE H Grade in one or more of the above subjects.* **M9**

Practical English for Work & Study   *RSA ESOL profile certificate.* **L68**

Short Courses for Minority Ethnic Women   *A variety of non-certificate courses & courses leading to SCOTVEC certificates.* **C16**

Speaking our Language - Short Course   *No formal outcome.* **H59**

Speaking our Language: Home Study for Beginners - Intermediate Level   *No formal outcome.* **H59**

Speaking our Language for Businesses   *No formal outcome.* **H59**

Spoken English - Advanced Summer Courses   *Improvement in ability to understand & communicate in English.* **L13**

Spoken English - Upper-Intermediate Summer Courses   *Improvement in ability to understand & communicate in English.* **L13**

Teaching & Learning English - Summer Courses for English Language Teachers   *No formal outcome.* **L13**

Workplace Education - Communication   *The development of relevant skills & the opportunity to gain a SCOTVEC.* **C16**

Write-On - Gaelic Writing Course   *No formal qualification.* **H31**

FOREIGN LANGUAGES

Access to Higher Education - SCOTVEC French (SCE O/S Equivalent)   *SCOTVEC modules in French.* **D5**

Access to Higher Education - SCOTVEC German (SCE O/S Equivalent)   *SCOTVEC modules in German.* **D5**

Access to Higher Education - SCOTVEC Italian (SCE O/S Equivalent)   *SCOTVEC modules in Italian.* **D5**

Additional Languages   *No formal outcome.* **S114**

Advanced French Diploma Classes   *Preparation for DELF & DALF Exams & Alliance Francaise Diplomas.* **S115**

Advanced German   *Participants will have a greater understanding of German.* **C41**

Advanced Italian   *Development of Italian language skills.* **C41**

Advanced Urdu   *A GCSE Advanced Level in Urdu.* **C16**

Arabic - Part 2   *Students will gain an insight into Arab life & learn basic conversational Arabic.*   **T13**

Arabic Foreign Language Training   *Development of foreign language skills.*   **L29**

Basic Communication in French - HN Unit   *SCOTVEC Higher National unit.*   **L5**

Basic Communication in German - HN Unit   *SCOTVEC Higher National unit.*   **L5**

Basic Communication in Spanish - HN Unit   *SCOTVEC Higher National unit.*   **L5**

Beginners Arabic   *Improved Language Skills.*   **L68**

Beginners Dutch   *A knowledge of the Dutch language.*   **C41**

Beginners French   *Skills necessary to cope with everyday situations in France.*   **C41 L34 M9**

Beginners German   *German speaking skills.*   **C41 L34 M9**

Beginners Italian   *Development of Italian language skills.*   **C41 L34 M9**

Beginners Japanese   *An introduction to the Japanese language.*   **C41 L68**

Beginners Language Open Learning with Cd Rom - ESF   *Students will gain skills in French at appropriate level.*   **H17**

Beginners Modern Greek   *Improved Language Skills.*   **L68**

Beginners Portuguese   *Development of Portuguese language skills.*   **C41**

Beginners Spanish   *An introduction to Spanish vocabulary, pronunciation, grammar & conversation.*   **C15 C41 L34 M9**

Business French   *No formal outcome.*   **S114**

Business French - European Social Fund   *No formal outcome.*   **H18**

Business German   *No formal outcome.*   **S114 S120**

Business Italian   *No formal outcome.*   **S114**

Business Japanese   *No formal outcome.*   **S114**

Business Language Open Learning with Cd Rom - ESF   *No formal outcome.*   **H17**

Business Languages   *No formal outcome.*   **C22**

Business Languages - NCMs   *Students will have developed basic language skills & may gain SCOTVEC qualifications.*   **H26**

Business Russian   *No formal outcome.*   **S114**

Business Spanish   *No formal outcome.*   **S114**

Chinese Literature in the Modern Age - MSc / Diploma   *MSc Degree / Diploma in Chinese Literature in the Modern Age.*   **L76**

Classes for Children 3 to 18 Years Old   *No formal outcome.*   **S115**

Classical Studies/Latin - SCE O Grade   *An SCE O grade certificate in Classic Studies/Latin.*   **S14**

Community Languages - Urdu & Mandarin   *Development of skills in the Urdu or Mandarin languages.*   **C16**

Conversational French   *There is no formal outcome to this course.*   **B8 S114**

Conversational French for Absolute Beginners   *Participants will have gained skills in French.*   **H31**

Conversational German   *No formal outcome.*   **S114**

Conversational German for Beginners   *Participants will have gained conversational skills in German.*   **H31**

Conversational Greek   *No formal outcome.*   **S114**

Conversational Holiday Spanish for Beginners   *Participants will have gained skills in Spanish.*   **H31**

Conversational Italian   *There is no formal outcome to this course.*   **B8 S114**

Conversational Italian Beginners   *There is no formal outcome to this course.*   **B8**

Conversational Japanese   *No formal outcome.*   **S114**

Conversational Portuguese   *No formal outcome.*   **S114**

Conversational Russian   *No formal outcome.*   **S114**

Conversational Spanish   *No formal outcome.*   **S114**

Customised Language Training Courses - Advanced   *Language skills for business purposes to suit clients' needs.*   **L13**

Customised Language Training Courses - Beginners & Elementary   *Language skills for business purposes to suit clients' needs.*   **L13**

Customised Language Training Courses - Intermediate   *Language skills for business purposes to suit clients' needs.*   **L13**

Danish Conversation   *Students will have a conversational knowledge of Danish.*   **T9**

Dutch - Group Session   *A Certificate of Attendance will be awarded on completion of this course.*   **B6**

Dutch - Individual Tuition   *Certificate of Attendance.*   **B6**

Eurospeak   *No formal outcome.*   **T9**

Everyday Arabic   *This course will build on the students knowledge of the Arabic language.*   **T13**

Foreign Language Training for Business Use   *No formal outcome.*   **C10**

Foreign Languages   *Standard & H Grades.*
L95 T18

French   *SCOTVEC module will be awarded on successful completion of this course.*
B1 B3 L88

French (Revised) - SCE Higher   *SCE Higher - French (Revised).*
F7

French - Advanced   *Communication skills in French.*
L12 T9

French - Advanced C Part 2   *Certificate awarded (optional).*
T13

French - Beginners   *Introduction to the French language.*
L12

French - Beginners Summer Course   *Communication skills in French.*
L12

French - Elementary & Intermediate Summer Courses   *Communication skills in French.*   **L12**

French - GCE A Level Course   *GCE A Level in French.*
L68

French - Group Session   *A Certificate of Attendance will be awarded on completion of this course.*
B6

French - Higher Elementary   *Communication skills in French.*
L12

French - Higher Intermediate   *Communication skills in French.*
L12

French - Individual Tuition   *Can lead to LCC or SCOTVEC Certificate depending on individual requirements.*
B6

French - Intermediate C Part 2   *Certificate awarded (optional).*
T13

French - Introductory I C Part 2   *Certificate awarded (optional).*
T13

French - Introductory II C Part 2   *Certificate awarded (optional).*
T13

French - Lower Elementary   *Communication skills in French.*
L12

French - Lower Intermediate   *Communication skills in French.*
L12

French - Lower Intermediate C Part 2   *Certificate awarded (optional).*
T13

French - Module   *A vocational SCOTVEC module in French.*
D3

French - Modules 1, 2 or 3   *SCOTVEC Module French at Level 1, 2 or 3.*
M3

French - SCE H Grade   .
B3 B6 C1 C4 C5 C6 C7 C20 C21 C22 C23 C25 C26 C27 C28 C29 C30 C33 C34 C36 C45 C46 F5 F8 H53 S2 S6 S13 S14 S16 S79 T9 T23

French - SCE H Grade (Revised)   *SCE H Grade French.*
L1

French - SCE H Grade Course (Revised Syllabus)   *SCE H Grade in French (revised).*
L68

French - SCE H Grade Grade   *On successful completion of this course candidates will have a SCE H Grade in French.*
M5

French - SCE H Grade or CSYS   *SCE in French at H Grade or Certificate of Sixth Year Studies.*
D3

French - SCE O Grade   *An SCE O grade certificate in French.*
S14

French - SCE Revised Higher   *SCE Revised Higher - French.*
F10

French - SCE Standard / SCE H Grade / NCMs   *SCE Standard or H Grade or SCOTVEC modules will be awarded.*
H13

French - SCOTVEC   *The SCOTVEC Module in French will be awarded on successful completion of this course.*
B6

French - SCOTVEC 1   *On successful completion, this module will count towards the SCOTVEC/NC.*
B6

French - SCOTVEC 2   *On successful completion, this module will count towards the SCOTVEC/NC.*
B6

French - SCOTVEC 3   *On successful completion, this module will count towards the SCOTVEC/NC.*
B6

French - SCOTVEC 4   *On successful completion, this module will count towards the SCOTVEC/NC.*
B6

French - SEB H Grade   *A SEB H Grade in this subject will be awarded.*   **B1 B10**

French - SEB H Grade (Revised)   *An SEB H Grade in French will be awarded.*   **B11**

French - SEB S Grade   *An SEB S Grade in French will be awarded on successful completion of this course.*
B11

French - SEB Sixth Year Studies   *An SEB Certificate of Sixth Year Studies in French will be awarded.*   **B1 B11**

French - Telephone Receptionists   *A Certificate of Attendance.*
B6

French - Upper Intermediate C Part 2   *Certificate awarded, optional.*
T13

French 1 (Introductory Mainly Spoken)   *SCOTVEC Module Certificate.*
T1

French 1 (SCOTVEC)   *SCOTVEC/NCM French 1.*
L5

French 1 - (P/T Degree Unit)   *Units completed can be accumulated towards the award of a Degree.*
C42

French 1 - Module   *SCOTVEC/NCM - 7340034.*
F8 F9 F11 F12

French 1 - NC   *SCOTVEC/NC listing Modules studied & Learning Outcomes attained.*   **C45**

French 1 - NCM   *SCOTVEC Module will be gained.*
H53

French 1 - NCM (SCOTVEC) *SCOTVEC/NCM French 1.* **L68**

French 1 - SCOTVEC Module *SCOTVEC certificate in Language - French 1.* **T9**

French 2 (SCOTVEC) *SCOTVEC/NCM French 2.* **L5**

French 2 - Module *SCOTVEC/NCM - 7340334.* **F8 F9 F11 F12**

French 2 - NC *This is SCOTVEC Modular course.* **G17**

French 2 - NCM (SCOTVEC) *SCOTVEC/NCM French 2.* **L68**

French 2, 3, 4, 5 - NCMs *These courses lead to SCOTVEC modules.* **H53**

French 3 (SCOTVEC) *SCOTVEC/NCM.* **L5 L68**

French 3 - (P/T Degree Unit) *Units completed can be accumulated towards the award of a Degree.* **C42**

French 3 - Module *SCOTVEC/NCM - 7340634.* **F8**

French 3 - NCM (SCOTVEC) *SCOTVEC/NCM French 3.* **L68**

French 4 (SCOTVEC) *SCOTVEC/NCM French 4.* **L5**

French 4 - Module *SCOTVEC/NC (Double) Module - 7340934.* **F8**

French Classes At All Levels for Adults *Internal certificates.* **S115**

French Conversation *There is no formal outcome to this course.* **B2 B6 C16 C17**

French Conversation II *There is no formal outcome to this course.* **B6**

French for Beginners *Participants will gain basic knowledge of the French language at a beginners level.* **H49**

French for Business *Improved language skills in French for Business.* **D6 S115**

French for Business - Module *NCM. Skills are gained in communicating in Business French.* **F8**

French for Distillery Guides *Candidates will be able to show French Tourists/Business People around a Distillery.* **M9**

French for Hotel Reception *No formal outcome.* **M9**

French for the Tourist Industry *Participants will receive an Open Learning Centre Certificate. SCOTVEC accreditation is possible.* **M9**

French Foreign Language Training *Development of foreign language skills.* **L29**

French Language Classes *A working knowledge of French.* **S14**

French Level 1 - Module *NCM Level 1. Skills are gained in communicating in French.* **F8**

French Level 2 - Module *NCM Level 2. Skills are gained in communicating in French.* **F8**

French Level 3 - Module *NCM Level 3. Skills are gained in communicating in French.* **F8**

French Level 5 - Module *NCM Level 5. Skills are gained in communicating in French.* **F8**

French Modules 1 & 2 *SCOTVEC modular certificate after successful completion of course.* **T9**

French/German - CSYS *Scottish Examination Board Certificate of Sixth Year Studies in French/German.* **D8**

General Education Section Short Course Provision *College Certificate.* **L27**

German *SCOTVEC module will be awarded on successful completion of this course.* **B1 B3 L88**

German (Revised) - SCE Higher *SCE Higher - German (Revised).* **F7**

German (Revised) - SEB H Grade *An SEB H Grade in German will be awarded.* **B11**

German - Advanced *Communication skills in German.* **L12**

German - All Levels *Non-vocational.* **S120**

German - Beginners *Communication skills in German.* **L12**

German - Beginners Summer Course *Communication skills in German.* **L12**

German - Elementary & Intermediate Summer Courses *Communication skills in German.* **L12**

German - GCE A Level Course *GCE A Level in German.* **L68**

German - Group Session *A Certificate of Attendance will be awarded on completion of this course.* **B6**

German - Higher Elementary *Communication skills in German.* **L14**

German - Higher Intermediate *Communication skills in German.* **L12**

German - Individual Tuition *Can lead to LCC or SCOTVEC Certificate depending on individual requirements.* **B6**

German - Introductory C Part 2 *Certificate awarded (optional).* **T13**

German - Lower Elementary *Communication skills in German.* **L12**

German - Lower Intermediate *Communication skills in German.* **L12**

German - Lower Intermediate *C Part 2 Certificate awarded (optional).* **T13**

German - SCE Grade *SCE, H Grade.* **S13**

German - SCE H Grade *AN SCE H Grade in German.*
C1 C4 C5 C6 C7 C20 C21 C22 C23 C25 C26 C27 C28 C29 C30 C34 C36 C45 C46 F5 F8 H53 S14 S16 T9

German - SCE H Grade (Revised) *SCE H Grade German.* **L1**

German - SCE H Grade Course (Revised Syllabus) *SCE H Grade in German (Revised).* **L68**

German - SCE H Grade or CSYS *SCE in German at H Grade or Certificate of Sixth Year Studies.* **D3**

German - SCE O Grade *An SCE O Grade certificate in German.* **S14**

German - SCE Revised Higher *SCE Higher - German.* **F10**

German - SCE Standard / SCE H Grade / NCMs *SCE Standard or H Grade or SCOTVEC modules awarded.* **H13**

German - SCOTVEC 1 *On successful completion, this module will count towards the SCOTVEC/NC.* **B6**

German - SCOTVEC 2 *On successful completion, this module will count towards the SCOTVEC/NC.* **B6**

German - SCOTVEC 3 *On successful completion, this module will count towards the SCOTVEC/NC.* **B6**

German - SCOTVEC 4 *On successful completion, this module will count towards the SCOTVEC/NC.* **B6**

German - SEB H Grade *A SEB H Grade in this subject will be awarded on successful completion of this course.* **B1 B10**

German - SEB S Grade *An SEB S Grade in German will be awarded on successful completion of this course.* **B11**

German - SEB Sixth Year Studies *An SEB Certificate of Sixth Year Studies in German will be awarded.* **B1 B11**

German - Standard & Highers *Non-vocational.* **S120**

German - Telephone Receptionists *A Certificate of Attendance.* **B6**

German - Upper Intermediate C Part 2 *Certificate awarded (optional).* **T13**

German 1 (Introductory) Mainly Spoken *SCOTVEC Module Certificate.* **T1**

German 1 (SCOTVEC) *SCOTVEC/NCM German 1.* **L5**

German 1 - (P/T Degree Unit) *Units completed can be accumulated towards the award of a degree.* **C42**

German 1 - Module *SCOTVEC/NCM - 7340054.* **F8 F9 F11**

German 1 - NC *SCOTVEC/NC listing Modules studied & Learning Outcomes attained will be awarded.* **C45**

German 1 - NCM *This course leads to SCOTVEC Module.* **H53**

German 1 - NCM (SCOTVEC) *SCOTVEC/NCM German 1.* **L68**

German 1 - SCOTVEC Module *SCOTVEC certificate in Language - German 1.* **T9**

German 2 (SCOTVEC) *SCOTVEC/NCM German 2.* **L5**

German 2 - Module *SCOTVEC/NCM - 7340634.* **F8 F9**

German 2 - NCM (SCOTVEC) *SCOTVEC/NCM German 2.* **L68**

German 2, 3, 4, 5 - NCMs *These courses lead to SCOTVEC modules.* **H53**

German 3 (SCOTVEC) *SCOTVEC/NCM German 3.* **L5 L68**

German 3 - (P/T Degree Unit) *Units completed can be accumulated towards the award of a Degree.* **C42**

German 3 - Module *SCOTVEC/NC (Double) Module - 7340654.* **F8**

German 3 - NCM (SCOTVEC) *SCOTVEC/NCM German 3.* **L68**

German 4 - Module *SCOTVEC/NC (Double) Module - 7340954.* **F8**

German Beginners *There is no formal outcome to this course.* **B8**

German Conversation *There is no formal outcome to this course.* **B6 C15 C16**

German for Bed & Breakfast Providers *No formal outcome.* **M9**

German for Beginners *Participants will gain basic knowledge of the German language at a beginners level.* **H49 S120**

German for Business *Improved language skills in German for Business.* **D6 F8**

German for Distillery Guides *Candidates will be able to show German Tourists/Business People around a Distillery.* **M9**

German for Hotel Reception *No formal outcome.* **M9**

German for the Tourist Industry *Participants will receive an Open Learning Certificate. SCOTVEC accreditation is possible.* **M9**

German for Tourism *Improved language skills in German for Tourism.* **D6**

German Foreign Language Training *Development of foreign language skills.* **L29**

German I - Module *SCOTVEC Module - German I.* **F1**

German Language *A working knowledge of German.* **S14**

German Level 1 - Module   *NCM Level 1. Skills are gained in communicating in German.*   **F8**

German Level 2 - Module   *NCM Level 2. Skills are gained in communicating in German.*   **F8**

German Level 3 - Module   *NCM Level 3. Skills are gained in communicating in German.*   **F8**

German Level 5 - Module   *NCM Level 5. Skills are gained in communicating in German.*   **F8**

German, History, Geography - SCE H Grade *Participants will gain a SCE H Grade in one or more of the above subjects.*   **M9**

Greek   *You will be able to have conversations in Greek.*   **T9**

Holiday Language Course in French (Intermediate Level - Conversation)   *No formal outcome.*   **L68**

Holiday Language Course in German (Beginners) *Basic Language Skills for Holidays in German Speaking Countries.*   **L68**

Holiday Language Course in Greek (Beginners) *Basic Language Skills for Holidays in Greece (Beginners).*   **L68**

Holiday Language Course in Italian (Beginners) *Basic Language Skills for Holidays in Italy.*   **L68**

Holiday Language Course in Spanish (Beginners) *Basic Language Skills for Holidays in Spanish Speaking Countries.*   **L68**

Holiday Languages - French, Italian & Spanish *No formal outcome.*   **H53**

Holiday Languages - German   *No formal outcome.*   **H53**

Intermediate French   *Development of French vocabulary & conversational skills.*   **C41 L34**

Intermediate German   *Development of German language skills.*   **C41 L34**

Intermediate Italian   *Development of Italian language skills.*   **C41 L34**

Intermediate Spanish   *Intermediate speaking & writing skills in the Spanish language.*
C41 H53 L34

Intermediate/Advanced French   *Development of spoken & written French skills.*   **C41**

Intermediate/Conversational French   *A knowledge of the French language.*   **C41**

Introduction to Everyday Russian   *Participants will have gained an introduction to Russian language & culture.*   **H31**

Introduction to French   *Conversational French skills.*   **C41**

Introduction to German   *Development of German skills.*   **C41**

Introduction to Italian   *Conversational Italian skills.*
C41

Introduction to Spanish   *Participants will have a greater understanding of Spanish.*   **C41**

Italian (Trad) - SCE Higher   *SCE Higher - Italian (Trad).*   **F7**

Italian - Advanced   *Communication skills in Italian*
L12

Italian - Beginners   *Communication skills in Italian*
L12

Italian - Beginners Summer Course *Communication skills in Italian.*   **L12**

Italian - Elementary & Intermediate Summer Courses   *Communication skills in Italian.*   **L12**

Italian - GCE A Level Course   *GCE A Level in Italian.*   **L68**

Italian - Group Session   *A Certificate of Attendance will be awarded on completion of this course.*   **B6**

Italian - Higher Elementary   *Communication skills in Italian.*   **L12**

Italian - Higher Intermediate   *Communication skills in Italian.*   **L12**

Italian - Individual Tuition   *Can lead to LCC or SCOTVEC Certificate depending on individual requirements.*   **B6**

Italian - Intermediate   *Communication skills in Italian.*   **L12**

Italian - Introductory Part 2   *No formal outcome.*
T13

Italian - Lower Elementary   *Communication skills in Italian.*   **L12**

Italian - Lower Intermediate Part 2   *No formal outcome.*   **T13**

Italian - SCE H Grade   *The SCE H Grade in Italian.*
B3 B6 C6 C23 C33 L1 S13 S14 S16 T9

Italian - SCE H Grade Course (Revised Syllabus) *SCE H Grade in Italian (revised).*   **L68**

Italian - SCE O Grade   *SCE O Grade Certificate in Italian.*   **S14**

Italian - SCOTVEC 1   *On successful completion, this module will count towards the SCOTVEC/NC.*
B6

Italian - SCOTVEC 2   *On successful completion, this module will count towards the SCOTVEC/NC.*
B6

Italian - SCOTVEC 3   *On successful completion, this module will count towards the SCOTVEC/NC.*
B6

Italian - SCOTVEC 4   *On successful completion, this module will count towards the SCOTVEC/NC.*
B6

Italian - Telephone Receptionists   *Certificate of Attendance awarded.*   **B6**

Italian 1 (SCOTVEC)   *SCOTVEC/NCM Italian 1.*
L5

Italian 1 - Module   *SCOTVEC/NCM - 7340064.*
F8 F9

talian 1 - NCM (SCOTVEC)   *SCOTVEC/NCM*
Italian 1.   **L68**

Italian 2 (SCOTVEC)   *SCOTVEC/NCM Italian 2.*
                                               L5

Italian 2 - NCM (SCOTVEC)   *SCOTVEC/NCM*
Italian 2.   **L68**

Italian 3 (SCOTVEC)   *SCOTVEC/NCM Italian 3.*
                                          L5 L68

Italian 3 - NCM (SCOTVEC)   *SCOTVEC/NCM*
Italian 3.   **L68**

Italian Conversation   *There is no formal outcome
to this course.*   **B6 C15**

Italian Foreign Language Training   *Development
of foreign language skills.*   **L29**

Italian I - Module   *SCOTVEC Module - Italian I.*
                                               F1

Italian Language   *A working knowledge of Italian.*
                                               S14

Italian Level 1 - Module   *NCM Level 1. Skills are
gained in communicating in Italian.*   **F8**

Italian Level 2 - Module   *NCM Level 2. Skills are
gained in communicating in Italian.*   **F8**

Italian Modules 1 & 2   *SCOTVEC certificate on
successful completion of course.*   **T9**

Japanese - Beginners   *Communication skills in
Japanese.*   **L12**

Japanese - Higher Elementary   *Communication
skills in Japanese.*   **L12**

Japanese - Intermediate   *Communication Skills in
Japanese.*   **L12**

Japanese - Introductory Part 2   *Participants will
become familiar with the Japanese language.*
                                               T13

Japanese - Lower Elementary   *Communication
skills in Japanese.*   **L12**

Japanese 1 - Module   *SCOTVEC/NCM - 71439.*
                                               F8

Japanese 2 - Module   *SCOTVEC/NCM -
7341522.*   **F8**

Japanese Continuation   *Participants will increase
knowledge of the Japanese language at an
intermediate level.*   **H49**

Japanese Etiquette for the Businessman   *No
formal outcome.*   **M8**

Japanese for Beginners   *Participants will gain
basic knowledge of the Japanese language at a
beginners level.*   **H49**

Japanese Introductory Day   *An introduction to the
Japanese language.*   **C41**

Japanese Language & Culture   *Development of
skills in Japanese language & culture.*   **C44**

Japanese Level 1 - Module   *NCM Level 1. Skills
are gained in communicating in Japanese.*   **F8**

Keep Up Your French   *Advanced skills in
conversational French.*   **L5**

Keep Up Your German   *Advanced skills in
conversational German.*   **L5**

Keep Up Your Spanish   *Advanced skills in
conversational Spanish.*   **L5**

Language - French 1 (SCOTVEC)
SCOTVEC/NCM 7340034 Language - French 1.
                                               L3

Language - French 2 (SCOTVEC)
SCOTVEC/NCM 7340334 Language - French 2.
                                               L83

Language - French I (SCOTVEC)
SCOTVEC/NCM 7340031 Language - French I.
                                               L31

Language - German 1 (SCOTVEC)
SCOTVEC/NCM 7340054 Language - German 1.
                                               L3

Language - German I (SCOTVEC)
SCOTVEC/NCM 7340051 Language - German I.
                                               L31

Language - Italian 1 (SCOTVEC)
SCOTVEC/NCM 7340064 Language - Italian 1.
                                               L3

Language 1 - French - NC   *SCOTVEC/NC listing
Modules studied & Learning Outcomes attained.*
                                               C23

Language 1 - German - NC   *SCOTVEC/NC listing
Modules studied & Learning Outcomes attained.*
                                               C23

Language 1 - Italian - NC   *SCOTVEC/NC listing
Modules studied & Learning Outcomes attained.*
                                               C23

Language 1 - Russian - NC   *SCOTVEC/NC listing
Modules studied & Learning Outcomes attained.*
                                               C23

Language 1 - Spanish - NC   *SCOTVEC/NC listing
Modules studied & Learning Outcomes attained.*
                                               C23

Language 1: Dutch (SCOTVEC)   *SCOTVEC/NCM
in Language 1: Dutch.*   **L1**

Language 1: French (SCOTVEC)
SCOTVEC/NCM in Language 1: French.   **L1**

Language 1: German (SCOTVEC)
SCOTVEC/NCM in Language 1: German.   **L1**

Language 1: Italian (SCOTVEC)   *SCOTVEC/NCM
in Language 1: Italian.*   **L1**

Language 1: Modern Greek (SCOTVEC)
SCOTVEC/NCM in Language 1: Modern Greek.
                                               L1

Language 1: Spanish (SCOTVEC)
SCOTVEC/NCM in Language 1: Spanish.   **L1**

Language 2 - French - NC   *SCOTVEC/NC listing
Modules studied & Learning Outcomes attained.*
                                               C23

Language 2 - German - NC   *SCOTVEC/NC listing
Modules studied & Learning Outcomes attained.*
                                               C23

Language 2 - Italian - NC   *SCOTVEC/NC listing
Modules studied & Learning Outcomes attained.*
C23

Language 2 - Spanish - NC   *SCOTVEC/NC listing
Modules studied & Learning Outcomes attained.*
C23

Language 2: French (SCOTVEC)
SCOTVEC/NCM in Language 2: French.   **L1**

Language 2: German (SCOTVEC)
SCOTVEC/NCM in Language 2: German.   **L1**

Language 2: Italian (SCOTVEC)   *SCOTVEC/NCM
in Language 2: Italian.*   **L1**

Language 2: Modern Greek (SCOTVEC)
SCOTVEC/NCM in Language 2: Modern Greek.
L1

Language 2: Spanish (SCOTVEC)
SCOTVEC/NCM in Language 2: Spanish.   **L1**

Language 3 - French - NC   *SCOTVEC/NC listing
Modules studied & Learning Outcomes attained.*
C23

Language 3 - German - NC   *SCOTVEC/NC listing
Modules studied & Learning Outcomes attained.*
C23

Language 3 - Italian - NC   *SCOTVEC/NC listing
Modules studied & Learning Outcomes attained.*
C23

Language 3 - Spanish - NC   *SCOTVEC/NC listing
Modules studied & Learning Outcomes attained.*
C23

Language 3: French (SCOTVEC)
SCOTVEC/NCM in Language 3: French.   **L1**

Language 3: German (SCOTVEC)
SCOTVEC/NCM in Language 3: German.   **L1**

Language 3: Spanish (SCOTVEC)
SCOTVEC/NCM in Language 3: Spanish.   **L1**

Language 4 - French - NC   *SCOTVEC/NC listing
Modules studied & Learning Outcomes attained.*
C23

Language 4: German (SCOTVEC)   *Introduction to
SCOTVEC/NC in Language 4: German.*   **L1**

Language Courses for Business   *Development of
basic skills necessary for business
communication.*   **C2**

Language Training - Customised Courses
Various.   **L71**

Languages & Communication - HNC
SCOTVEC/HNC.   **L5**

Languages & Tourism Studies - NC (SCOTVEC)
SCOTVEC/NC in Languages & Tourism Studies.
L68

Languages - Business French   *Languages -
improved ability to use the French language in a
business context.*   **D5**

Languages - Business German   *Languages -
improved ability to use the German language in a
business context.*   **D5**

Languages for Employment   *No formal outcome.*
T22

Languages - French   *Languages - improved ability
to use the French language.*   **D5**

Languages - German   *Languages - improved
ability to use the German language.*   **D5**

Languages - Italian   *Languages - improved ability
to use the Italian language.*   **D5**

Languages - Spanish   *Languages - improved
ability to use the Spanish language.*   **D5**

Languages for Business - French, German, Italian
& Spanish   *No formal outcome.*   **L81**

Languages for Industry & Business   *Basic skills &
knowledge in French, German or Spanish.*   **S79**

Languages for the European Market   *A knowledge
of a European language for business purposes.*
L28

Languages/Tourism Courses for Industry (French)
College certificate if required.   **L69**

Languages/Tourism Courses for Industry
(German)   *College certificate if required.*   **L69**

Languages/Tourism Courses for Industry (Italian)
College certificate if required.   **L69**

Languages/Tourism Courses for Industry
(Spanish)   *College certificate if required.*   **L69**

Languages/Tourism Courses for Industry Any
Language Version   *College certificate if required.*
L69

Latin (Revised) - SCE Higher   *SCE Higher - Latin
(Revised).*   **F7**

Latin - SCE H Grade   *AN SCE H Grade in Latin.*
C20   C25   C26   C28   C30   C34   C45

Latin, Life & Language   *Contact course provider
for full details.*   **T13**

LCC - French   *LCC Certificate Level 1.*   **B6**

LCC - German   *LCC Certificate Level 1.*   **B6**

LCC - Italian   *LCC Certificate Level 1.*   **B6**

Maths, English, French - SCE H Grade
*Participants will gain a SCE H Grade in one or
more of the above subjects.*   **M9**

Modern European Languages   *SCOTVEC
modules levels I-II in modern European languages.*
S2

Modern European Languages - SCE H Grades
*SCE H grade in various modern European
languages.*   **S2**

Modern European Languages - Tourist (Beginner)
*Basic knowledge & understanding of modern
European languages.*   **S2**

Modern Greek - Beginners Part 2   *No formal
outcome.*   **T13**

Modern Language - SCOTVEC Modules
SCOTVEC Module in French or Italian.   **D8**

Modern Languages   *An understanding of the French, German, Italian or Spanish language at Levels 1-4.*   **C22**

Modern Languages - H Grade   *A SCE H Grade.*   **S88**

Modern Languages - General   *Outcome depends on level of individual courses.*   **G41**

Modern Languages - SCE H Grade (Revised) French/German   *SEB Certificate in Modern Languages at H Grade.*   **D8**

New Testament Greek (SCOTVEC) SCOTVEC/NCM in New Testament Greek.   **L1**

Phonetic Skills Project   *No formal outcome.*   **T22**

Polish 1 - Module   *SCOTVEC/NCM - 7340094.*   **F8**

Polish 2 - Module   *SCOTVEC/NCM - 7340394.*   **F8**

Polish Level 1 - Module   *NCM Level 1. Skills are gained in communicating in Polish.*   **F8**

Polish Level 2 - Module   *NCM Level 2. Skills are gained in communicating in Polish.*   **F8**

Portuguese - Beginners   *Communication skills in Portuguese.*   **L12**

Portuguese - Group Session   *There is no formal outcome to this course.*   **B6**

Portuguese - Higher Elementary / Intermediate   *Communication skills in Portuguese.*   **L12**

Portuguese - Individual Tuition   *There is no formal outcome to this course.*   **B6**

Portuguese - Introductory Part 2   *Participants will learn how to communicate in every day situations.*   **T13**

Portuguese - Post-Beginners / Lower Elementary   *Communication skills in Portuguese.*   **L12**

Portuguese Conversation   *There is no formal outcome to this course.*   **B6**

Post Beginners French   *Development of French speaking skills.*   **C41**

Post Beginners German   *Participants will have greater understanding of German.*   **C41**

Post Beginners Italian   *Development of Italian language skills.*   **C41**

Post Beginners Japanese   *An introduction to the Japanese language.*   **C41**

Russian - Individual Tuition   *Can lead to LCC or SCOTVEC Certificate depending on individual requirements.*   **B6**

Russian - Introductory Part 2   *Participants will learn to take part in basic conversations in a wide range of everyday situations.*   **T13**

Russian - SCE H Grade   *AN SCE H Grade in Russian.*   **C29   S14   S16**

Russian - SCE O Grade   *SCE O Grade Certificate in Russian.*   **S14**

Russian 1 - Module   *SCOTVEC/NCM - 7340114.*   **F8**

Russian Conversation   *There is no formal outcome to this course.*   **B6**

Russian Foreign Language Training   *Development of foreign language skills.*   **L29**

Russian Language   *A working knowledge of Russian.*   **S14**

Russian Level 1 - Module   *NCM Level 1. Skills are gained in communicating in Russian.*   **F8**

Secretarial Section Short Course Provision   *College Certificate.*   **L27**

Short Course in Modern Language - French   *Students will improve their communication skills.*   **S70**

Short Course in Modern Language - Italian   *Students will improve their communication skills.*   **S70**

Short Course in Modern Language - Russian   *Students will improve their communication skills.*   **S70**

Short Course in Modern Language - Spanish   *Students will improve their communication skills.*   **S70**

Spanish   *There is no formal outcome to this course.*   **B3   B11   L88   T1**

Spanish (Revised) - SCE Higher   *SCE Higher - Spanish (Revised).*   **F7**

Spanish (Revised) - SEB H Grade   *An SEB H Grade in Spanish will be awarded.*   **B11**

Spanish - Advanced   *Communication skills in Spanish.*   **L12**

Spanish - Beginners Summer Course   *Communication skills in Spanish.*   **L12**

Spanish - Elementary & Intermediate Summer Courses   *Communication skills in Spanish.*   **L12**

Spanish - GCE A Level Course   *GCE A Level in Spanish.*   **L68**

Spanish - Group Session   *A Certificate of Attendance will be awarded on completion of this course.*   **B6**

Spanish - Higher Elementary   *Communication skills in Spanish.*   **L12**

Spanish - Higher Intermediate   *Communication skills in Spanish.*   **L12**

Spanish - Individual Tuition   *Can lead to LCC or SCOTVEC Certificate depending on individual requirements.*   **B6**

Spanish - Intermediate   *Communication skills in Spanish.*   **L12**

Spanish - Introductory C Part 2   *Students will gain an introduction to the Spanish language.*   **T13**

Spanish - Lower Elementary   *Communication skills in Spanish.*   **L12**

Spanish - Lower Intermediate   *Communication skills in Spanish.*   **L12**

Spanish - Lower Intermediate C Part 2   *No formal outcome.*   **T13**

Spanish - New Beginners   *Communication skills in Spanish.*   **L12**

Spanish - SCE Grade   *SCE, H Grade.*   **S13**

Spanish - SCE H Grade   *AN SCE H Grade in Spanish.*   **C34 L1 S2 S14 S16 T9**

Spanish - SCE H Grade Course (Revised Syllabus)   *SCE H Grade in Spanish (revised).*   **L68**

Spanish - SCE O Grade   *SCE O Grade Certificate in Spanish.*   **S14**

Spanish - Upper Intermediate C Part 2   *No formal outcome.*   **T13**

Spanish 1 (SCOTVEC)   *SCOTVEC/NCM Spanish 1.*   **L5**

Spanish 1 - Module   *SCOTVEC/NCM - 7340124.*   **F8 F11 F12**

Spanish 1 - NC   *SCOTVEC/NC listing Modules studied & Learning Outcomes attained.*   **C45**

Spanish 1 - NCM (SCOTVEC)   *SCOTVEC/NCM Spanish 1.*   **L68**

Spanish 2 (SCOTVEC)   *SCOTVEC/NCM Spanish 2.*   **L5**

Spanish 2 - Module   *SCOTVEC/NCM - 7340424.*   **F8 F11**

Spanish 2 - NCM (SCOTVEC)   *SCOTVEC/NCM Spanish 2.*   **L68**

Spanish 3 (SCOTVEC)   *SCOTVEC/NCM Spanish 3.*   **L5 L68**

Spanish 3 - (P/T Degree Unit)   *Units completed can be accumulated towards the award of a Degree.*   **C42**

Spanish 3 - NCM (SCOTVEC)   *SCOTVEC/NCM Spanish 3.*   **L68**

Spanish Conversation   *There is no formal outcome to this course.*   **B2 B6 C16**

Spanish for Beginners   *Participants will gain basic knowledge of the Spanish language at a beginners level.*   **H49**

Spanish Foreign Language Training   *Development of foreign language skills.*   **L29**

Spanish Language   *A working knowledge of Spanish.*   **S14**

Spanish Level 1 - Module   *NCM Level 1. Skills are gained in communicating in Spanish.*   **F8**

Spanish Level 2 - Module   *NCM Level 2. Skills are gained in communicating in Spanish.*   **F8**

Survival Language for Business Persons Abroad (French & German)   *No formal outcome.*   **M8**

Telephone Skills in the Foreign Language (French or German)   *No formal outcome.*   **M8**

The German Club   *Further development of German language skills.*   **C41**

Workplace Education - Foreign Languages   *Development of relevant skills & the opportunity to gain SCOTVEC qualification.*   **C16**

LANGUAGE STUDIES

Advanced Text Study & Translation Summer Courses   *Advanced translation & text analysis skills.*   **L13**

Applied Linguistics - MSc / Diploma   *MSc Degree / Diploma in Applied Linguistics.*   **L76**

English - SCE (Revised) H Grade   *SCE - Higher English (Revised).*   **F11**

English - SCE H Grade   *SCE - Higher English.*   **F9**

English for TEFL / Applied Linguistics - Summer Course   *Preparation for postgraduate courses.*   **L13**

Gaelic - SCE H Grade Grade   *On successful completion of this course candidates will have a SCE H Grade.*   **M5**

Language 1 - French - NC   *SCOTVEC/NC listing Modules studied & Learning Outcomes attained.*   **C23**

Language 1 - Italian - NC   *SCOTVEC/NC listing Modules studied & Learning Outcomes attained.*   **C23**

Language 1 - Spanish - NC   *SCOTVEC/NC listing Modules studied & Learning Outcomes attained.*   **C23**

Language 2 - French - NC   *SCOTVEC/NC listing Modules studied & Learning Outcomes attained.*   **C23**

Language 2 - German - NC   *SCOTVEC/NC listing Modules studied & Learning Outcomes attained.*   **C23**

Language 2 - Italian - NC   *SCOTVEC/NC listing Modules studied & Learning Outcomes attained.*   **C23**

Language 2 - Spanish - NC   *SCOTVEC/NC listing Modules studied & Learning Outcomes attained.*   **C23**

Language 3 - French - NC   *SCOTVEC/NC listing Modules studied & Learning Outcomes attained.*   **C23**

Language 3 - German - NC   *SCOTVEC/NC listing Modules studied & Learning Outcomes attained.*   **C23**

Language 3 - Italian - NC   *SCOTVEC/NC listing Modules studied & Learning Outcomes attained.*   **C23**

PRINT & PUBLISHING

Electronic Publishing - HNC *SCOTVEC/HNC in Electronic Publishing.*   **S68 S75**

Fine Bookbinding & Book Restoration - HNC *SCOTVEC/HNC in Fine Bookbinding & Book Restoration.*   **S68**

Graphic Design & Illustration - HNC *SCOTVEC/HNC. Possible progression to HND level course.*   **C10**

In-House Publishing - HNC *SCOTVEC/HNC in In-house Publishing.*   **C22**

Information Technology - Customised Courses *Various.*   **L71**

Information Technology Courses *SCOTVEC or RSA Certificates in relevant modules.*   **H46**

Introduction to Computer Programming - Pascal & Desktop Publishing 1 (SCOTVEC) *SCOTVEC/NCMs 91115 & 91128.*   **L83**

Introduction to Desktop Publishing *There is no formal outcome to this course.*   **B6 T9**

Introduction to Desktop Publishing - NCM *SCOTVEC/NCM.*   **L81**

Introduction to Gem Applications *College Certificate.*   **L27**

Lithography *Participants will have learned some lithograpghy techniques.*   **H19**

Magazine Design 1 - HN Unit *SCOTVEC Higher National Unit.*   **L5**

Pagemaker - Introduction *ITec certification is given on completion of course.*   **H17**

Pagemaker - Introduction (C11) *Students will know the basics of Desktop publishing using Pagemaker.*   **S94**

Pagemaker - Workshop *ITec certification is given on completion of course.*   **H17**

Pagemaker 4 *Skills gained in the use of Pagemaker 4.*   **S6**

Print Sales & Marketing - HNC *SCOTVEC/HNC in Print Sales & Marketing.*   **S68**

Print Technology 1 - HN Unit *SCOTVEC Higher National Unit.*   **L5**

Printing *No formal outcome.*   **S119**

Printing (Administration) - NC *SCOTVEC/NC in Printing (Administration).*   **S68**

Printing (Origination, Machine Printing, Print Finishing) - NC *SCOTVEC/NC in Printing.*   **S68**

Printing (Reprographics) - NC *SCOTVEC/NC in Printing (Reprographics).*   **S68**

Printing - NC (SCOTVEC) *SCOTVEC/NC in Printing This course replaces the C & G 523 Certificate in Printing.*   **L44**

Printing - Screen/Textile *Participants will have gained skills required for successful screen-printing.*   **H19**

Printing Management with Production - HNC *SCOTVEC/HNC in Printing Management with Production.*   **S6**

Printing Production & Quality Control - HNC *SCOTVEC/HNC in Printing Production & Quality Control.*   **S6**

Printing Techniques *Participants will have gained practical skills in Printmaking techniques at a suitable level.*   **H19**

Publishing *Participants will learn all aspects of the publishing process.*   **S109**

Reprographic Techniques - NC *SCOTVEC/NC.*   **L5**

Screen Process Printing - NC *SCOTVEC/NC in Screen Process Printing.*   **S68**

Secretarial/Administration/Computing - NCMs / HN Units *SCOTVEC/NC(s) or Higher National Units awarded.*   **H53**

Teach Yourself Lotus Freelance Plus *Participants will gain a knowledge of the computer package of their choice.*   **H41**

Teach Yourself Pagemaker *Participants will gain a knowledge of the computer package of their choice.*   **H41**

Typography 1 - HN Unit *SCOTVEC Higher National Unit.*   **L5**

Understanding Ami Professional *Participants will gain a knowledge of the computer package of their choice.*   **H41**

Uniplex - Introduction *ITec certification is given on completion of course.*   **H17**

Word Perfect/Desk Top Publishing *Skills gained in Word Perfect/desk top publishing.*   **S81**

Word Processing & Text Processing - NCMs. *SCOTVEC/NCMs.*   **L68**

SELF-HELP, COUNSELLING, PERSONAL DEVELOPMENT

A Taste for Study *Delegates will have a flavour of studying with support in a small group situation.*   **G21**

Assertiveness *Delegates will have developed Confidence & Self-Awareness through Assertiveness.*   **G21**

Assertiveness Training *Development of assertiveness skills.*   **C41**

Assertiveness Training & Confidence Building *No formal outcome.*   **F8**

Assertiveness, Communication & Rapport Skills *Participants will learn effective communication & influencing skills.* **S111**

Basic Programme for People with Hearing Impairments *Experience of a range of NCMs.* **L5**

Be More Confident *Non-certificated.* **L68**

Buddhist Meditation *A practical experience of meditation techniques.* **C41**

Caring Skills - Co-Counselling *Improved caring skills - co-counselling.* **D5**

Caring Skills - Springboard Women's Development Course *Improved skills - development for women.* **D5**

Certificate in Counselling *Advanced counselling skills (SCOTCAT accredited course).* **S125**

Classes for Physically Disabled Adults *Development of skills & creative ability.* **S81**

Community & Social Care - GSVQ Levels II & III *SVQ Levels II & III in Community & Social Care.* **B3**

Community Evening Class *Improved personal, social & learning skills.* **L68**

Confidence & Self Belief *No formal outcome.* **S142**

Coping with Stressful Situations - Module *NCM.* **F8**

Counselling On Alcohol/Drugs *No formal outcome.* **H45**

Crisis Counselling *SCOTVEC Certificate & enhanced skills in the workplace. Part of Modular Programme.* **D5**

Dealing with Loss, Change & Bereavement *No formal outcome.* **M8**

Health & Stress (S4) *Participants will learn strategies to avoid heart disease.* **S94**

HIV & Aids - Awareness Course *Helps delegates to understand the nature & characteristics of HIV & Aids - Awareness Course.* **M8**

HIV, Aids & Hepatitis B (1/2 Module) - NC *SCOTVEC/NC listing Modules studied & Learning Outcomes attained.* **C23**

Into Employment *Participants gain work skills & job search techniques. Certified courses Independent life skills training.* **T11**

Introduction to Alexander Technique *Development of self awareness.* **C41**

Listening Skills *Can result in SCOTVEC certificate if the 40 hour option is chosen.* **D5**

Life / Social Skills - NCMs *SCOTVEC modules designed for people with moderate learning difficulties.* **H53**

Living with Stress *Awareness of effects of stress in self and others & development of coping strategies.* **S125**

Meditation & Stress Management *Participants will learn how to manage stress.* **S109**

Mindstore for Business *Two day course developing right brain creativity & focus.* **S130**

Mindstore for Life *Two day course developing right brain creativity & focus.* **S130**

New Horizons *There is no formal outcome to this course.* **B7**

New Horizons for Women *No formal outcome.* **S109**

New Opportunities - Return to Study *Preparation for higher education.* **T13**

Parent Link Part 1 *No formal outcome.* **L87**

Personal & Professional Development *No formal outcome.* **S133**

Personal Presentation *Improved personal appearance & presentation.* **D6**

Practical Caring Skills - NC *SCOTVEC/NC.* **L81**

Self Help Project *Confidence building work experience.* **S126**

Self Help, Counselling & Personal Development *SCOTVEC/NCMs.* **T14**

Self-Development - Buddhist Approach *Delegates will have been introduced to the principles of Buddhism.* **G21**

Social & Vocational Skills - SEB S Grade *An SEB S Grade in Social & Vocational Skills awarded.* **B11**

Special Needs Adult Link Programme *Skills gained in personal development.* **S13**

Special Needs for Dalgairn Centre, Cupar *Skills gained include basic help with literacy, numeracy & self advocacy.* **F3**

Special Needs Schools Link Foundation Course *Skills gained in personal development.* **S13**

Special Needs Youth Enterprise Skills Course *Skills gained in personal development.* **S13**

Speed Reading for Managers *Improved reading speed & time management with possible SCOTVEC Certification.* **D5**

Springboard - a Course for Women *Skills of assertiveness, confidence building & a formulated action plan for the future.* **D6**

Steps to Excellence for Personal Success *Certificate of completion.* **C49**

Stress Management *Participants will learn new strategies to cope with stress.* **S111**

Study Skills Course *Preparation for employment or further education courses.* **C17**

Surviving Parenthood *No formal outcome.* **H31**

The Art of Spontaneity in Art *Knowledge of the art of spontaneity.* **C41**

The Assertive Woman At Work *Development of assertiveness skills.* **C41**

The Positive Woman *Development of positive attitudes.* **C41**

The Psychology of Human Relations *No formal outcome.* **T13**

Tuition for People with a Disability *Advice on educational opportunities for people with a disability or health problem.* **H32**

Understanding Grief & Loss *Awareness of grieving process, appropriate for private individuals & professional carers.* **S125**

Various Courses Available *Company Certificate awarded.* **S149**

Women & Health *No formal outcome.* **H52**

Women Returning to the Workplace *No formal outcome.* **S142**

Workplace Education - Personal Development *Development of relevant skills & opportunity to gain SCOTVEC.* **C16**

Workplace Education - Redundancy Counselling *Development of relevant skills & opportunity to gain SCOTVEC.* **C16**

Law, Politics & Economics

ECONOMICS

Business Economics - BA / BA (Hons)   *Bachelor of Arts Degree / Hons Degree in Business Economics.*   **L52**

Business Economics - MSc   *An MSc in Business Economics.*   **S105**

Community & Local Economic Development - HNC   *HNC in Community & Local Economic Development.*   **F13**

Community & Local Economic Development - HND   *HND in Community & Local Economic Development.*   **F13**

Contemporary Macro Economic Issues (SCOTVEC)   *SCOTVEC/NCM.*   **L5**

Domestic Economic Environment - HN Unit   *SCOTVEC Higher National Unit.*   **L5**

Economic History - SCE Higher   *SCE Higher - Economic History.*   **F7**

Economic Structure of Industry (SCOTVEC)   *SCOTVEC/NCM.*   **L5**

Economics   *SCOTVEC Certificate in this subject be awarded on successful completion of this course.*   **B1 L88**

Economics (Revised) - SCE H Grade   *The SCE H Grade in Economics.*   **B6**

Economics (Revised) - SCE Higher   *SCE Higher - Economics (Revised).*   **F7**

Economics - H Grade   *A SCE H Grade.*   **S88**

Economics - SCE H Grade   *AN SCE H Grade in Economics.*
   C1 C4 C5 C6 C21 C25 C26 C27 C28 C29 C30 C33 C34 C36 C45 D8 F5 L5 S6 S13 S14 S16 S79

Economics - SCE H Grade (Day)   *SCE H Grade in Economics.*   **L68**

Economics - SCE H Grade (Evening Class)   *SCE H Grade in Economics.*   **L68**

Economics - SCE H Grade (Revised)   *A SCE at H Grade in Economics.*   **C45 L1**

Economics - SCE Higher   *On successful completion of this course candidates will have a SCE Higher in Economics.*   **M3**

Economics - SCE O Grade   *An SCE O Grade Certificate in Economics.*   **S14**

Economics - SCE Standard / SCE H Grade / NCMs   *SCE Standard or H Grade or appropriate SCOTVEC module.*   **H13**

Economics - SCOTVEC Module (O Grade Replacement)   *SCOTVEC/NCM in Economics.*   **L68**

Economics - SEB H Grade   *A SEB H Grade in this subject will be awarded.*   **B1 B10 B11**

Economics - BA/BSc Evening Programme   *Accumulation towards a Degree.*   **C42**

Economics of the Market (SCOTVEC)   *SCOTVEC/NCM.*   **L5**

Economics of the Market - 6120120 - SCOTVEC/NC   *SCOTVEC/NC.*   **T23**

Home Economics - SCE H Grade   *A SCE H grade certificate in Home Economics.*   **S87**

Logistics - MSc   *An MSc in Logistics.*   **S48**

Logistics - PgD   *A PgD in Logistics.*   **S48**

Social Sciences - BA   *A BA in Social Sciences.*   **S27**

Social Sciences - BA (Honours)   *A BA (Hons) in Social Sciences.*   **S27**

The Individual in the Economy - SCOTVEC/NC   *SCOTVEC/NC.*   **T23**

The World This Week Part 2   *This class will provide an analysis of issues of the day.*   **T13**

Urban Development - MSc   *An MSc in Urban Development.*   **S105**

Urban Development- PgD   *A PgD in Urban Development.*   **S105**

LAW

Arbitration/Construction Law & Arbitration - PgC/Pgd/MSc   *PgC/PgD/ MSc in Construction Law & Arbitration.*   **G15**

Business Administration - HND   *SCOTVEC/HND in Business Administration.*   **L5**

Business Law   *This course forms part of the Chartered Institute of Marketing's Certificate in Marketing.*   **F8**

Business Law - HN Unit   *SCOTVEC Higher National Unit.*   **L5**

Business Law I - (P/T Degree Unit)   *Units completed can be accumulated towards the award of a degree.*   **C42**

Business Studies Evening Classes (SCOTVEC)   *SCOTVEC/NCMs.*   **L68**

Child Law   *A course certificate will be awarded.*   **S82**

Civil Advocacy & Pleading   *A course certificate will be awarded.*   **S82**

Compulsive Competitive Tendering   *A course certificate will be awarded.*   **S82**

Computer & Information Technology Law - LLM   *A MLL in Computer & Information Law.*   **S105**

Computer & Information Technology Law - PgD   *A PgD in Computer & Information Technology Law.*   **S105**

Construction Law - LLM   *A LLM in Construction Law.*   **S105**

Construction Law - PgD   *A PgD in Construction law.*   **S105**

Consumer & Mercantile Law - Short Course   *A knowledge of Consumer & Mercantile Law.*   **L81**

Contract Law   *Attendance Certificate.*   **L10**

Contract Law (SCOTVEC)   *SCOTVEC/NCM.*   **L5**

Contract Law - Short Course   *A knowledge of Contract Law.*   **L81**

Debt Recovery   *A course certificate will be awarded.*   **S82**

Discipline Procedures & Dismissal   *This course will up-date participants on the changes introduced in the Employment Act 1990.*   **L6**

Discrimination At Work   *This course will up-date participants on the changes introduced in the Employment Act 1990.*   **L6**

Employment Law   *No formal outcome.*   **M8 S82**

Employment Law & Practice - PgD/MSc   *PgD/MSc in Employment Law & Practice.*   **G15**

Employment Law - LLM   *A LLM in Employment Law.*   **S105**

Employment Law - PgD   *A PgD in Employment Law.*   **S105**

Employment Law - Short Course   *A knowledge of Employment Law.*   **L81**

Employment Law for Personnel Professionals   *No formal outcome.*   **L6**

Environmental Law   *A course certificate will be awarded.*   **S82**

Equal Pay for Equal Work   *This course will up-date participants on the changes introduced in the Employment Act 1990.*   **L6**

European Law - BA (Honours) [UCAS Code M375]   *A BA with Hons in European Law.*   **S105**

European Law - LLM   *A LLM in European Law.*   **S105**

European Law - PgD   *A PgD in European Law.*   **S105**

Hotel Law for Front Office Staff (SCOTVEC)   *SCOTVEC/NCM.*   **L5**

Housing Law (SCOTVEC)   *SCOTVEC/NCM.*   **L5**

Insolvency Practice   *A course certificate will be awarded.*   **S82**

Intellectual Property Law   *A course certificate will be awarded.*   **S82**

Introduction to Administrative Law (SCOTVEC)   *SCOTVEC/NCM.*   **L5**

Introduction to Scots Law - Short Course   *Introduction to Scots Law.*   **L81**

Law & Ethics in Medicine   *A course certificate will be awarded.*   **S82**

Law in Employment (SCOTVEC)   *SCOTVEC/NCM.*   **L5**

Law LLM/Diploma in Advanced Legal Studies   *Master of Laws Degree / Diploma in Advanced Legal Studies.*   **L72**

Law of the Tenement   *A course certificate will be awarded.*   **S82**

Law with Administrative Studies - BA   *A BA in Law with Administrative Studies.*   **S37**

Law with Administrative Studies - Certificate   *A Certificate in Law with Administrative Studies.*   **S37**

Law with Administrative Studies - Diploma   *A Diploma in Law with Administrative Studies.*   **S37**

Legal Services - HNC   *SCOTVEC/HNC in Legal Services.*   **S8 S14**

Legal Services - SCOTVEC/HNC   *The SCOTVEC/HNC in Legal Services will be awarded.*   **G17**

Legal Services - SCOTVEC/HND   *SCOTVEC/HND in Legal Services will be awarded.*   **G17**

Legal Services - SCOTVEC/NC   *At the end of the course students will gain the Scottish NC awarded by SCOTVEC.*   **G17**

Legal Studies - NC   *A NC in a Legal Studies Programme.*   **S14**

Legal Studies MSc/Diploma in Advanced Legal Studies   *MSc Degree in Legal Studies Diploma in Advanced Legal Studies.*   **L72**

Liquor Licensing Law   *A course certificate will be awarded.*   **S82**

Property Law   *A course certificate will be awarded.*   **S82**

The Employment Contract   *This course will up-date participants on the changes introduced in the Employment Act 1990.*   **L6**

The Law & Industrial Action   *This course will up-date participants on the changes introduced in the Employment Act 1990.*   **L6**

The Legal Framework (SCOTVEC)   *SCOTVEC/NCM.*   **L5**

The Scottish Legal Framework - 92351 - SCOTVEC/NC   *No formal outcome.*   **T23**

Trading Standards - Diploma   *Diploma in Trading Standards.*   **S63**

TUC Course - European Health & Safety Legislation   *Increased skills & awareness of Health & Safety legislation.*   **C22**

Young People & the Law - 92350 - SCOTVEC/NC   *No formal outcome.*   **T23**

POLITICS

Access to Higher Education - SCOTVEC Social Sciences: People & Politics *SCOTVEC modules.* **D5**

African Studies - MSc / Diploma *MSc Degree / Diploma in African Studies.* **L77**

Central Government (SCOTVEC) *SCOTVEC Double Module.* **L5**

European & International Politics - MSc/Diploma in Social Sciences *MSc/Diploma in Social Sciences - European & International Politics.* **L77**

Government & Political Studies - GCE A Level *GCE A Level in Government & Political Studies.* **L68**

International Health - MSc *MScs Degree / PgD in International Health.* **L65**

Introduction to Administrative Law (SCOTVEC) *SCOTVEC/NCM.* **L5**

Introduction to Religion/Religion & Community/Religion & Politics *SCOTVEC module in Religion.* **C22**

Introductory Course for Trade Union Representatives Stage 1 *Non-certificated.* **L67**

Introductory Course for Trade Union Union Representatives Stage 2 *Non-certificated.* **L67**

Local Authorities (SCOTVEC) *SCOTVEC/NCM.* **L5**

Local Government Administration - SCOTVEC/NC *SCOTVEC/NC in Local Government Administration.* **G17**

Modern Studies *Qualification as studied for.* **L88**

Modern Studies - SCE H Grade *SCE H Grade in Modern Studies.* **L68**

Political Studies - Political Ideas (P/T Degree Unit) *Units completed can be accumulated towards Degree.* **C42**

Political Studies - Politics of the British Isles - (P/T Degree Unit) *Units can be accumulated towards degree.* **C42**

Political Studies - Politics of the European Union - (P/T Degree Unit) *Units can be accumulated towards Degree.* **C42**

Politics *Qualification as studied for.* **L88**

Politics/Current Affairs *A knowledge of Politics/Current Affairs.* **C41**

Scotland: Society & Politics - MSc/Diploma in Social Sciences *MSc/Diploma in Social Sciences - Scotland: Society & Politics.* **L77**

Social & Political Theory - MSc/Diploma in Social Sciences *MSc/Diploma in Social Sciences - Social & Political Theory.* **L77**

Social Science, History & Politics - BA *BA from Stirling University, taught at Inverness College.* **H53**

The World This Week Part 2 *This class will provide an analysis of issues of the day.* **T13**

Trade Union Course - Introductory Stage One *TUC validated Union Rep. Stage One. Health & Safety Stage One.* **F8**

Trade Union Studies *Can lead to full time Union Official posts and/or TUC sponsored training at Ruskin College.* **D5 S14**

Trade Union Studies - Short Course Provision *Non-certificated.* **L67**

Minerals, Materials & Fabrics

CHEMICAL ENGINEERING & TECHNOLOGY

Chemical Engineering - HNC *SCOTVEC/HNC. Successful students can proceed to Year 2 BEng Hons Degree.* **H49**

Chemical Engineering - Years 1 & 2 - HNC *SCOTVEC/HNC in Chemical Engineering.* **C22**

Pharmaceutical Sciences - NC *SCOTVEC/NC in Pharmaceutical Sciences.* **S94**

Process Systems Engineering - MSc / Diploma *MSc Degree / Diploma in Process Systems Engineering.* **L79**

FURNITURE MANUFACTURE

Furniture Production & Design - NC *SCOTVEC/NC in Furniture Production & Design.* **F5**

Furniture Re-Upholstery Training *SCOTVEC Modules.* **S126**

MATERIALS ENGINEERING, METALLURGY & TECHNOLOGY

Composite Materials *On completion of the course, participants will be awarded a Napier University certificate.* **L48**

Composite Materials Technology - MSc/PgD *MSc/Postgraduate Diploma in Composite Materials Technology.* **S101**

Concrete Technology & Construction - NVQ C & G 629 Certificate *NVQ, NVQ City & Guilds of London Institute, 629 Certificate.* **S68**

Engineering for Plastics Technicians - NC *SCOTVEC/NC in Engineering for Plastics Technicians.* **S75**

Failure Mechanisms in Materials *Napier University certificate awarded.* **L48**

Glass Reinforced Plastics *SCOTVEC/NCM in Glass Reinforced Plastics.* **L68**

Materials Engineering - MSc *MSc in Materials Engineering.* **S105**

Materials Engineering - PgD *A PgD in Materials Engineering.* **S105**

Materials Technology - HNC *SCOTVEC/HNC in Materials Technology.* **S8**

Materials Technology - HND *SCOTVEC/HND in Materials Technology.* **S8**

Materials Technology - MSc /Postgraduate Diploma *MSc Degree / PgD in Materials Technology.* **L38**

Mechanical CAE Specialising in Mechanics of Materials - MSc *MSc in Mechanical Computer Aided Engineering.* **S105**

Mechanical CAE Specialising in Mechanics of Materials - PgD *A PgD in Mechanical Computer Aided Engineering.* **S105**

Mechanical Engineering Specialising in Mechanics of Materials - MSc *MSc in Mechanical Engineering.* **S105**

Mechanical Engineering Specialising in Mechanics of Materials - PgD *A PgD in Mechanical Engineering.* **S105**

Plastics Moulding Technology - MSc / PgD & Advanced Diploma *SCOTVEC Unit Certificate or SCOTVEC Advanced Diploma or MSc PgD in Plastics Moulding Technology.* **L46**

Polymer Technology - HNC *SCOTVEC/HNC in Polymer Technology.* **L46**

Strengthening Metallic Structures *Napier University certificate awarded.* **L48**

Toolmaking/Polymer Moulds - HNC *SCOTVEC/HNC will be awarded to successful students.* **S15**

MINING OIL & MINERALS TECHNOLOGY

Basic Rigging *Training to SVQ standards.* **T19**

Crane Operating Training *Training to SVQ standards.* **T19**

Drilling Calculations *Training to SVQ standards.* **T19**

Drilling Operations & Techniques Course *Training to SVQ standards.* **T19**

Drilling Problems *Training to SVQ standards.* **T19**

Drilling Rig Safety *Training to SVQ standards.* **T19**

Fork-Lift Training *Training to SVQ standards.* **T19**

H2S *Training to SVQ standards.* **T19**

Hoisting & Rigging *Training to SVQ standards.* **T19**

Operational Safety At Rig Site *Training to SVQ standards.* **T19**

Part IV Air Diving: First Aid (HSE Regulation 7(1)(b)) *R.G.I.T. Part IV Air Diving: First Aid Certificate.* **H37**

Petroleum, Oil and Gas Courses. *Certificate awarded.* **G42**

Refresher Courses for Diver Inspectors *Refresher Course to meet the requirements of 3.1U or 3.2U exams.* **F5**

Rigging, Slinging *Training to SVQ standards.* **T19**

Shotfiring - Certificate *Shotfiring Certificate from the Quarry Products Training Council.* **S6**

PAPER & BOARD

Coating Paper & Board - Paper & Board SVQ Level 2 *SVQ level 2 - Coating Paper & Board.* **F8**

Finishing Paper & Board - Paper & Board SVQ Level 2 *SVQ level 2 - Finishing Paper & Board.* **F8**

Make Paper & Board - Paper & Board SVQ Level 2 *SVQ level 2 - Making Paper & Board Stock.* **F8**

Making Paper & Board Stock - Paper & Board SVQ Level 2 *SVQ level 2 - Making Paper & Board Stock.* **F8**

Packaging Principles & Practice - (S8) *Skills gained in packaging.* **S94**

Paper & Board *SVQ level I.* **F8**

Paper & Board (Introduction) *No formal outcome.* **F8**

Paper & Board Making - C & G 512 *Parts I & II City & Guilds 512.* **F8**

Paper & Board Making Part 1 - C & G 512 *City & Guilds Certificate in Paper & Board Making Part 1.* **F8**

Paper & Board Technical Training *No formal outcome.* **F8**

TEXTILES FASHION & FURNISHINGS

Clothing Machine Technicians - NVQ C & G 469 *SCOTVEC/NCMs & NVQ C & G 469 Certificate.* **S88**

Clothing Machine Technicians - NVQ C & G 469-3 *NVQ, NVQ City & Guilds 469-3 Certificate.* **S88**

Clothing Technology - NC *SCOTVEC/NC in Clothing Technology.* **S13**

Creative Studies Fashion Part I - NVQ C & G 7900 *NVQ, NVQ City & Guilds.* **S2**

Creative Studies Fashion Part II - NVQ C & G 7900 *NVQ, NVQ City & Guilds 030 Research for Craft Skills, 035 Design for Hand Craft Production - Fashion, 036 Extended Fashion Skills.* **S2**

Fashion Influences *This unit will be accredited towards the HNC in Knitwear Design & Production.* **B3**

Fashion Marketing *This unit will be accredited towards the HNC in Knitwear Design & Production.* **B3**

Fashion Merchandising - NC *SCOTVEC/NC in Fashion Merchandising.* **S14**

Fashion Studies - NC *SCOTVEC/NC will be awarded on successful completion of this course.* **B3**

Fashion Technology - NC *SCOTVEC/NC in Fashion Technology.* **S13**

Floorcovering - SVQ Level II *On completion of this course students will have gained a SVQ Level II in Floorcovering.* **G5**

Furniture Production & Design - NC *SCOTVEC/NC in Furniture Production & Design.* **F5**

Garment Assembly & Applied Decoration *This unit will be accredited towards the HNC in Knitwear Design & Production.* **B3**

Garment Design *This unit will be accredited towards the HNC in Knitwear Design & Production.* **B3**

Garment Development & Knitting *This unit will be accredited towards the HNC in Knitwear Design & Production.* **B3**

Knitwear Quality Control *A College Certificate of Attendance.* **B3**

Knitwear Technicians' Course - NC *SCOTVEC/NC will be awarded on successful completion of this course.* **B3**

Millinery Class *There is no formal outcome to this course.* **B8**

Printing - Screen/Textile *Participants will have gained skills required for successful screen-printing.* **H19**

Printing Techniques *No formal outcome.* **H19**

Soft Furnishings *Experience in soft furnishings.* **C16**

Stitched Textiles & Fashion Design - HNC *SCOTVEC/HNC.* **L5**

Textile Craft - SCOTVEC *SCOTVEC module in Textile Craft will be awarded.* **B10**

Textile Fashions & Furnishings *Sewing machine & overlocker training, work experience.* **S126**

Textile Production - ET/SVQ Levels I-Ii *SCOTVEC SVQ, SVQ Levels I-II Certificate.* **S79**

Textile Production - YT/SVQ Levels I- Ii *SCOTVEC SVQ, SVQ Levels I-II Certificate.* **S79**

Yarn Sourcing & Selection *This unit will be accredited towards the HNC in Knitwear Design & Production.* **B3**

Music & Performing Arts

DANCE

Adult Ballet Dancing Course   *No formal outcome.*
S154

Adult Tap Dancing Course   *No formal outcome.*
S154

Adult Tap Dancing - 6 Levels of Graded Classes for 18 to 80 year olds   *No formal outcome.*   **L98**

Ballet, Tap & Jazz to Advanced Level   *British Ballet Organisation Exams.*   **L98**

Dance   *No formal outcome.*   **S119**

Highland Dancing   *Graded Classes leading to Associate of UKADTD.*   **L98**

Pre-professional Dance Course   *Allows entry to full-time Professional Dancer's Course.*   **S154**

Professional Dancer/Dance Teachers Course   *No formal outcome.*   **S154**

MUSIC HISTORY & THEORY

Continuing Education   *No formal outcome.*
S134

History of Piobaireachd   *No formal outcome.*
S143

Introduction to Reading Music   *There is no formal outcome to this course.*   **B2**

Music (Revised) - SCE Higher   *SCE Higher - Music (Revised) - A.*   **F7**

Music (Revised) - SEB H Grade   *An SEB H Grade in Music will be awarded on successful completion of this course.*   **B1**

Music - CSYS   *Scottish Examination Board Certificate of Sixth Year Studies in Music.*   **D8**

Music - GCE A Level   *GCE A Level in Music.*
L69

Music - MMus/Diploma   *Master of Music Degree OR Diploma in Music.*   **L73**

Music - SCE H Grade   *SCE H Grade in Music.*
C1   C4   C5   C6   C7   C20   C21   C25   C26   C C28   C29   C30   C33   C34   C36   C45   C46   D8 L69

Music - SCE H Grade or CSYS   *SCE in Music at H Grade or Certificate of Sixth Year Studies.*   **D3**

Music - SCOTVEC Modules   *SCOTVEC Modules in Music.*   **D8**

Music - SEB H Grade   *An SEB H Grade in Music will be awarded on successful completion of this course.*   **B11**

Music - SEB S Grade   *An SEB S Grade in Music will be awarded on successful completion of this course.*   **B11**

Music Technology - HNC   *SCOTVEC/HNC in Music Technology.*   **S94**

Music Technology for Leisure - (E9)   *Skills gained in the proper use of electronic studio equipment.*
S94

Music Technology for Music Teachers (E10)   *No formal outcome.*   **S94**

MUSIC PERFORMANCE

Classical String Ensemble   *Experience in Classical String Ensemble.*   **C43**

Electronic Keyboard Course (1 & 2)   *Participants will have gained the ability to play & read music.*
L90

Electronic Organ Course (1 - 8)   *From beginner to professional – optional exams.*   **L90**

Guitar   *SCOTVEC Module Solo One (Strings).*
T9

Guitar Workshop - Improve Your Guitar Playing Skills   *SCOTVEC Module Solo Two (Strings).*
T9

How to Break into Show Business   *No formal outcome.*   **G40**

Improve your Vocal Presentation   *No formal outcome.*   **G40**

Midi Music   *No formal outcome.*   **S119**

Music (Revised) - SEB H Grade   *An SEB H Grade in Music will be awarded on successful completion of this course.*   **B1**

Music - CSYS   *Scottish Examination Board Certificate of Sixth Year Studies in Music.*   **D8**

Music - GCE A Level   *GCE A Level in Music.*
L69

Music - SCE H Grade   *SCE H Grade in Music.*
L69

Music - SEB H Grade   *An SEB H Grade in Music will be awarded on successful completion of this course.*   **B11**

Music - SEB S Grade   *An SEB S Grade in Music will be awarded on successful completion of this course.*   **B11**

Music Making (Solo Keyboard 1) - Module   *SCOTVEC Module - Music Making (Solo Keyboard 1).*   **F9**

Music Making (Solo Keyboard 2) - Module   *SCOTVEC Module - Music Making (Solo Keyboard 2).*   **F9**

Music Making (Solo Keyboard 3) - Module   *SCOTVEC Module - Music Making (Solo Keyboard 3).*   **F9**

Music Making - Keyboard   *Successful students will be awarded SCOTVEC/NCM/s.*   **S87**

Music Making : Solo 1 Keyboard (SCOTVEC)   *SCOTVEC/NCM 71621 Music Making : Solo 1 (Keyboard).*   **L3**

Music Making : Solo 1 Percussion (SCOTVEC)   *SCOTVEC/NCM 71623 Music Making : Solo 1 (Percussion).*   **L3**

Music Making: Solo Keyboard 4 - Module   *SCOTVEC module 81642 - Music Making: Solo Keyboard 4.*   **F15**

Musical Keyboard   *There is no formal outcome to this course.*   **B2**

Musical Keyboarding   *There is no formal outcome to this course.*   **B6**

Piping   *No formal outcome.*   **S143**

Private Keyboard Tuition   *No formal outcome.*   **G40**

Strum for Fun   *There is no formal outcome to this course.*   **B2**

MUSIC OF SPECIFIC CULTURES

Music Making - Keyboard   *Successful students will be awarded SCOTVEC/NCM/s.*   **S87**

Scottish Studies - MLitt   *Master of Letters Degree in Scottish Studies.*   **L76**

MUSIC OF SPECIFIC KINDS

Home Recording   *SCOTVEC 4 Track Module (1).*
T9

Music of Specific Kinds   *No formal outcome.*
T18

Music Technology for Leisure - (E9)   *Skills gained in the proper use of electronic studio equipment.*   **S94**

Music Technology for Music Teachers (E10)   *Participants will know how to include electronic equipment in their instruction.*   **S94**

THEATRE & DRAMATIC ARTS

Community Theatre - PgD   *PgD in Community Theatre.*   **L65**

Creative Drama 1 (SCOTVEC)   *SCOTVEC/NCM.*
L5

Creative Drama 1 - NC   *SCOTVEC/NC listing Modules studied & Learning Outcomes attained.*   **C23**

Creative Drama 2 (SCOTVEC)   *SCOTVEC/NCM.*
L5

Drama   *Successful Candidates will gain a SCE Higher in Drama or SCOTVEC Modules - Studio Production, Lighting, Acting.*   **M3**

Drama - SCE H Grade   *SCE H Grade in Drama.*
L5

Drama Audition Techniques   *The course helps students to develop the skills & techniques required for audition standard.*   **S87**

Drama for Teaching English As a Foreign Language - Summer Course   *Ability to use drama as a teaching aid.*   **L13**

How to Break into Show Business   *No formal outcome.*   **G40**

SCE Higher Drama   *SCE/Higher in Drama.*   **L68**

Speech, Drama, Acting.   *No formal outcome.*
S121

Theatre Arts - Module   *SCOTVEC/NCM - 61284.*
F8

Various Informal Courses (Throughout the Year)   *No formal outcome.*   **S128**

PUBLISHERS' NOTE

Because of local government re-organisation, details of providers for some courses, in particular for leisure pursuits, cannot be confirmed as we go to print. Libraries and other local sources should be consulted and the Community Education contacts on pages 24 to 26 may also be of assistance.

Sciences & Mathematics

ASTRONOMY

Astronomy & Meteorology   *SCOTVEC module 78663.*   **L28**

Astronomy - Introduction   *No formal outcome.*   **G21**

Exploring the Universe   *No formal outcome.*   **T13**

CHEMISTRY

Access to Higher Education - SCE Higher Chemistry   *SCE H Grade Chemistry taken part-time to gain qualifications.*   **D5**

Access to Higher Education - SCOTVEC Chemistry (SCE O/S Equivalent)   *SCOTVEC modules in Chemistry.*   **D5**

Analytical Chemistry - Advanced Diploma Licentiateship of Royal Society of Chemistry   *Advanced Diploma in Chemistry (Licentiateship of the Royal Society of Chemistry).*   **S8**

Analytical Chemistry - PgD   *A PgD in Advanced Analytical Chemistry.*   **G23**

Applied Chemistry - BSc / BSc (Honours)   *BSc Degree / Hons Degree in Applied Chemistry.*   **L40**

Applied Chemistry - HNC   *HNC in Applied Chemistry.*   **G15**

Applied Chemistry - HNC/HND (UCAS - O11F HND App Chem)   *HNC/HND in Applied chemistry.*   **T12**

Applied Chemistry - HND UCAS Code: 011F   *HND in Chemistry.*   **G15**

Biological Sciences - NC   *SCOTVEC/NC in Biological Sciences.*   **S75**

Biomedical Sciences - MSc   *MSc in Biomedical Science.*   **S26**

Biomedical Sciences - PgD   *On successful completion of the course students will be awarded a PgD in Biomedical Science.*   **S26**

Chemical Analysis with Environmental Science - Advanced Diploma   *An advanced diploma in Chemical Analysis with Environmental Science & the Licentiateship of the Royal Society of Chemistry.*   **S79**

Chemistry   *Qualification as studied for.*   **L88   L95**

Chemistry (Revised) - SCE Higher   *SCE Higher - Chemistry (Revised).*   **F7**

Chemistry - CSYS (Revised)   *Certificate of Sixth Year Studies in Chemistry.*   **D8**

Chemistry - GCE A Level Course   *GCE A Level in Chemistry.*   **L68**

Chemistry - GRSC (Part 1)   *Graduateship (part 1) of the Royal Society of Chemistry [GRSC].*   **F5**

Chemistry - HNC   *SCOTVEC/HNC in Chemistry. This course meets the academic requirements for the Graduateship (Part 1) of the Royal Society of Chemistry (GRSC).*   **F5   H49   L46   S8   S79**

Chemistry - NC   *SCOTVEC/NC in Chemistry.*   **F5   S79**

Chemistry - S Grade   *SCOTVEC/NCM in Chemistry.*   **S88**

Chemistry - SCE H Grade   *AN SCE H Grade in Chemistry.*   **C1   C4   C5   C6   C7   C20   C21   C22   C23   C C26   C27   C28   C29   C30   C33   C34   C36   C45 C46   D8   F5   F9   L5   L68   S6   S13   S16   S79   S87 T23**

Chemistry - SCE H Grade (Evening)   *SCE H Grade in Chemistry.*   **L68**

Chemistry - SCE H Grade or CSYS   *SCE in Chemistry at H Grade or Certificate of Sixth Year Studies.*   **D3**

Chemistry - SCE O Grade   *SCE O Grade Certificate in Chemistry.*   **S87**

Chemistry - SCE Standard / SCE H Grade / NCMs   *Can lead to SCE Standard or H Grade or SCOTVEC modules.*   **H13**

Chemistry - Science Modules   *SCOTVEC/NCMs. May be used for entry to higher level courses & University entrance.*   **S8**

Chemistry - SCOTVEC Module   *Participants will gain SCOTVEC Certificate in Chemistry.*   **T9**

Chemistry - SCOTVEC Module (O Grade Replacement)   *SCOTVEC/NCM in Chemistry.*   **L68**

Chemistry - SCOTVEC Modules   *SCOTVEC Modules in chemistry (series 1 or series 2).*   **D8**

Chemistry - SEB H Grade   *A SEB H Grade in this subject will be awarded on successful completion of this course.*   **B1   B10   B11**

Chemistry - SEB S Grade   *An SEB S Grade in Chemistry will be awarded on successful completion of this course.*   **B11**

Chemistry - SEB Sixth Year Studies   *An SEB Certificate of Sixth Year Studies in Chemistry will be awarded.*   **B1   B11**

Chemistry - Years 1 & 2 - HNC   *SCOTVEC/HNC in Chemistry.*   **C22**

Chemistry - Years 1 & 2 - NC   *SCOTVEC/NC in Chemistry. Gives entry to the HNC courses.*   **C22**

Chemistry SCE H Grade (Revised)   *SCE H Grade Chemistry.*   **L15**

Chemistry Stage I - NCMs   *Successful completion leads to SCOTVEC/NCMs in Chemistry.*   **S87**

Chemistry with Information Technology & Instrumentation - BSc   *BSc in Chemistry with Information Technology & Instrumentation.*   **S55**

Chemistry with Information Technology & Instrumentation - BSc (Hons)   *BSc (Hons) in Chemistry.*   **S55**

Chemistry with Instrumental Analysis - BSc   *BSc in Chemistry with Instrumental Analysis.*   **S8**

Chemistry with Instrumental Analysis - BSc (Honours)   *BSc in Chemistry with Instrumental Analysis.*   **S8**

Chemistry/Chemistry with Instrumental Analysis - HNC (Access Course)   *SCOTVEC/HNC.*   **S8**

Chemistry: Introducing Fundamentals of Chemistry - NC   *SCOTVEC/NC listing Modules studied & Learning Outcomes attained.*   **C45**

Customised Short Courses in Science & Technology   *Certification can be organised.*   **L68**

Foundation Course in Chemistry - NC   *SCOTVEC/NC listing Modules studied & Learning Outcomes attained.*   **C23**

Graduate Membership - the Royal Society of Chemistry Part 1   *Graduate Membership of the Royal Society of Chemistry.*   **H49**

Instrumental Analytical Chemistry for Environmental Monitoring - MSc   *MSc in Instrumental Analytical Chemistry.*   **S52**

Instrumental Analytical Chemistry for Environmental Monitoring - PgD   *A PgD in Instrumental Analytical Chemistry.*   **S52**

Instrumental Analytical Sciences - PgD/MSc   *PgD in Instrumental Analytical Sciences.*   **G15**

Introducing Chemical Reactions (SCOTVEC)   *SCOTVEC/NCM 3181011 Introducing Chemical Reactions.*   **L15**

Introducing Fundamentals of Chemistry (SCOTVEC)   *SCOTVEC/NCM 3181001 Introducing Fundamentals of Chemistry.*   **L15**

Introducing Metals & Electrochemistry (SCOTVEC)   *SCOTVEC/NCM 3181011.*   **L15**

Introduction to Chemistry (SCOTVEC)   *SCOTVEC/NCM 3181213 Introduction to Chemistry.*   **L83**

Laboratory Science Technology Course - NC   *SCOTVEC/NC in Laboratory Science Technology.*   **L68**

Physics, Chemistry & Biology - SCE H Grade   *Participants will gain a SCE H Grade in one or more of the above subjects.*   **M9**

Science & Technology - NC   *SCOTVEC/NC in Science & Technology.*   **S15**

EARTH SCIENCES

Access to Higher Education - SCE Higher Geography   *SCE H Grade Geography.*   **D5**

Astronomy & Meteorology   *SCOTVEC module 78663.*   **L28**

Central Region's Environment, Geology & Scenery   *Development of knowledge of geology & the local environment.*   **C41**

Discovering Scottish Geology Part 2   *No formal outcome.*   **T13**

Geography (Revised) - SCE H Grade   *The SCE H Grade in Geography.*   **B6**

Geography - CSYS - Revised   *A Certificate of Sixth Year Studies in Geography.*   **D8**

Geography - H Grade   *SCE H Grade.*   **S88**

Geography - Higher (Revised)   *Scottish Examination Board Certificate in Geography at H Grade.*   **D8**

Geography - S Grade   *SCOTVEC/NCM in Geography.*   **S88**

Geography - SCE H Grade   *SCE H Grade in Geography.*
C1 C4 C5 C6 C7 C20 C21 C25 C26 C C28 C29 C30 C33 C34 C36 C45 L5 L68 S2 S6 S13 S14 S16 S79 T9

Geography - SCE H Grade (Revised)   *SCE H Grade Geography.*   **L1**

Geography - SCE H Grade or CSYS   *SCE in Geography at H Grade or Certificate of Sixth Year Studies.*   **D3**

Geography - SCE Higher   *SCE Higher - Geography.*   **F7**

Geography - SCE O Grade   *An SCE O Grade certificate in Geography.*   **S14**

Geography - SCE Standard / SCE H Grade / NCMs   *SCE Standard or H Grade or SCOTVEC modules.*   **H13**

Geography - SCOTVEC Modules   *SCOTVEC Modules in Geography.*   **D8**

Geography - SEB H Grade   *An SEB H Grade in Geography will be awarded.*   **B1 B10 B11**

Geography - SEB S Grade   *An SEB S Grade in Geography will be awarded.*   **B11**

Geography - SEB Sixth Year Studies   *SEB Certificate of Sixth Year Studies in Geography.*   **B1 B11**

Geology   *Participants will have gained an understanding of geology.*   **H31**

Geology & Scenery   *SCE recording all short course passes.*   **C45**

Geology - SCE H Grade   *An SCE H Grade certificate in Geology.*   **S14**

Geology - SCE O Grade   *An SCE O Grade certificate in Geology.*   **S14**

Geology - SEB Short Courses   *Scottish Examination Board Short Course in Geology.*   **D8**

Geology, People & Environment   *SCE recording all short course passes.*   **C45**

Geology: the Study of the Earth   *SCE recording all short course passes.*   **C45**

German, History, Geography - SCE H Grade   *SCE H Grade in one or more of the above subjects.*   **M9**

Meteorology   *Successful participants will have acquired skills in meteorology.*   **H15**

People & the Environment - British Isles   *SCOTVEC module will be awarded.*   **B1**

People & the Environment - British Isles (SCOTVEC)   *SCOTVEC/NCM 7175020 People & the Environment - British Isles.*   **L83**

People & the Environment - Europe/Ec (SCOTVEC)   *SCOTVEC/NCM 7175030 People & the Environment - Europe/EC.*   **L83**

People & the Environment - Scotland (SCOTVEC)   *SCOTVEC/NCM 7175050 People & the Environment - Scotland.*   **L83**

People & the Environment - the World (SCOTVEC)   *SCOTVEC/NCM 7175060 People & the Environment - The World.*   **L83**

Shorebased Yachtmaster Ocean (RYA)   *RYA Shorebased Yachtmaster Ocean Certificate.*   **L20**

Shorebased Yachtmaster Offshore/Coastal Skipper (RYA)   *RYA Shorebased Yachtmaster Offshore/ Coastal Skipper Certificate.*   **L20**

The Urban Environment   *SCOTVEC module will be awarded on successful completion of this course.*   **B1**

MATHEMATICS, STATISTICS

Access to Higher Education - SCOTVEC Maths (SCE Higher Equivalent)   *SCOTVEC modules in Maths.*   **D5**

Access to Higher Education - SCOTVEC Maths (SCE O/S Equivalent)   *SCOTVEC modules in Maths.*   **D5**

Algebra (Boolean A) - 91061 - SCOTVEC/NC   *SCOTVEC/NCM.*   **T23**

Algebra, Analysis & Numerical Methods - HN Unit   *1 credit towards a HNC in Electronic & Electrical Engineering.*   **C23**

Analysis/Algebra 1 (SCOTVEC)   *SCOTVEC/NCM.*   **T23**

Analysis/Algebra 1 - 810589 - SCOTVEC/NC   *On successful completion of this course students will have gained SCOTVEC/NC.*   **T23**

Analysis/Algebra 2 (SCOTVEC)   *SCOTVEC/NCM in Analysis/Algebra 2.*   **L5**

Analysis/Algebra 2 - 81059 - SCOTVEC/NC   *On successful completion of this course learners will have SCOTVEC/NCM.*   **T23**

Analysis/Algebra 3 - 81060 - SCOTVEC/NC   *On successful completion of this course learners will have SCOTVEC/NCM.*   **T23**

Arithmetic - Modular Course   *SCOTVEC Module in Arithmetic will be awarded on successful completion of this course.*   **B6**

Arithmetic - NC   *SCOTVEC/NC listing the modules studied & learning outcomes achieved.*   **S98**

Arithmetic - SCE O Grade   *An SCE O grade Certificate in Arithmetic.*   **S14**

Arithmetic Skills   *No formal outcome.*   **L86**

Business Statistics - NC   *On successful completion of this course students will have a NC.*   **G17**

Calculus 1 - SCOTVEC Module   *SCOTVEC Module in Calculus.*   **H31**

Calculus 1(A) - 81062 - SCOTVEC/NC   *No formal outcome.*   **T23**

Calculus 1(B) - 81068 - SCOTVEC/NC   *On successful completion of this course learners will have SCOTVEC/NCM.*   **T23**

Calculus 2 - 81071 - SCOTVEC/NC   *On successful completion of this course learners will have SCOTVEC/NCM.*   **T23**

Collection & Analysis of Numerical Data - HN Unit   *SCOTVEC Higher National Unit - 7400160.*   **F8 L5**

Combinational Logic - Module   *SCOTVEC/NCM - 2150010.*   **F8**

Core Maths 1/2 - SCOTVEC Module   *SCOTVEC Module in Core Maths.*   **G18**

Core Maths 2 (SCOTVEC)   *SCOTVEC/NCM in Core Maths 2.*   **L1 L3 L5 L83**

Core Maths 2 - 7180311 - SCOTVEC/NC   *On successful completion of this course learners will have SCOTVEC/NCM.*   **T23**

Core Maths 3 (SCOTVEC)   *SCOTVEC/NCM in Core Maths 3.*   **L1 L5 L83**

Core Maths 3 - 7180321 - SCOTVEC/NC   *On successful completion of this course learners will have SCOTVEC/NCM.*   **T23**

Core Maths 3 - Module   *SCOTVEC Module - Core Maths 3.*   **F10 F11**

Core Maths 3 - NC   *SCOTVEC/NC listing Modules studied & Learning Outcomes attained.*   **C23 C45**

Core Maths 4 (SCOTVEC)   *SCOTVEC/NCM in Core Maths 4.*   **L1 L5 L83**

Core Maths 4 - 7180331 - SCOTVEC/NC   *On successful completion of this course learners will have SCOTVEC/NCM.*   **T23**

Core Maths 4 - Module   *SCOTVEC Module - Core Maths 4.*   **F10 F11**

Core Maths 4 - NC   *SCOTVEC/NC listing Modules studied & Learning Outcomes attained.*   **C23 C45**

Engineering Calculus - HN Unit   *SCOTVEC Higher National Unit - 7400039.*   **F8**

Engineering Maths - HN Unit   *SCOTVEC Higher National Unit - 7400190.*   **F8**

Foundation Course in Maths (SCOTVEC)   *SCOTVEC/NCMs.*   **L68**

Industrial Maths - MSc   *A MSc in Industrial Maths.*   **S47 S105**

Industrial Maths - PgD   *A PgD in Industrial Maths.*   **S47 S105**

Logistics - MSc   *An MSc in Logistics.*   **S48**

Logistics - PgD   *A PgD in Logistics.*   **S48**

Management Science/Mathematics & Its Applications - BSc Hons [UCAS GINI]   *BSc Hons.*   **C37**

Mathematical Education - MSc/Diploma   *MSc Degree / Diploma in Mathematical Education.*   **L79**

Maths   *SCOTVEC module in Maths will be awarded on successful completion of this course.*   **B1 B11 L88 L95 T1**

Maths & Business Numeracy   *The SCOTVEC Module 81053 in Maths/ Business Numeracy.*   **B6**

Maths (Revised) - SCE H Grade   *The SCE H Grade in Maths.*   **B6**

Maths (Revised) - SCE Higher Higher   *SCE Higher - Maths (Revised).*   **F7**

Maths - Analysis Algebra 1 - NC   *SCOTVEC/NC listing Modules studied & Learning Outcomes attained.*   **C23**

Maths - Core 3 SCOTVEC Module   *Participants will gain a Core 3 SCOTVEC module in Maths.*   **T9**

Maths - Core 4 SCOTVEC Module   *Participants will gain a Core 4 SCOTVEC module in Maths.*   **T9**

Maths - CSYS Paper 1 (General)   *Scottish Examination Board Certificate of Sixth Year Studies in Maths.*   **D8**

Maths - H Grade   *A SCE H Grade.*   **S88**

Maths - Higher National Units   *SCOTVEC modules will be awarded awarded on successful completion.*   **H53**

Maths - NC   *NC - equivalent to SCE O Grade Maths.*   **F8 S98**

Maths - NCMs   *SCOTVEC modules will be awarded awarded on successful completion.*   **H53**

Maths - NCMs Core 3 & 4   *Successful students will be awarded the appropriate SCOTVEC/NC.*   **H53**

Maths - S Grade   *SCOTVEC/NCM in Maths.*   **S88**

Maths - SCE (Revised) H Grade   *SCE - Higher English Maths (Revised).*   **F11**

Maths - SCE H Grade   *SCE H Grade in Maths.*   **B3 B6 C1 C4 C5 C6 C7 C20 C21 C22 C23 C25 C26 C27 C28 C29 C30 C33 C34 C36 C45 C46 F5 F8 F9 L3 L5 L31 S2 S6 S13 S14 S16 S79 T23**

Maths - SCE H Grade (Revised)   *Scottish Examination Board Certificate in Maths at H Grade.*   **D8 L1**

Maths - SCE H Grade Intensive Upgrade   *Upgrade in SCE H Grade Maths.*   **L5**

Maths - SCE H Grade or CSYS or Core Maths Module   *SCE H Grade or Certificate of Sixth Year Studies or SCOTVEC.*   **D3**

Maths - SCE O Grade   *An SCE O Grade certificate in Maths.*   **S14**

Maths - SCE Revised H Grade   *SCE - Revised Higher Maths.*   **F12**

Maths - SCE Standard / SCE H Grade / NCMs   *SCE Standard or H Grade or the appropriate SCOTVEC modules.*   **H13**

Maths - SCOTVEC Modules   *SCOTVEC Modules in Maths.*   **D8**

Maths - SEB H Grade   *An SEB H Grade in Maths will be awarded.*   **B1 B10 B11**

Maths - SEB S Grade   *An SEB S Grade in Maths will be awarded on successful completion of this course.*   **B11**

Maths - SEB Sixth Year Studies   *An SEB Certificate of Sixth Year Studies in Maths will be awarded.*   **B1 B11**

Maths 1   *SCOTVEC/NC units.*   **S153**

Maths 1 (SCOTVEC)   *SCOTVEC/NCM.*   **L5**

Maths Grade 3   *The SCOTVEC Module 81059 in Maths Grade 3.*   **B6**

Maths H Grade   *H grade in Maths.*   **T1**

Maths of Nonlinear Models - Diploma/MSc   *MSc / Diploma in Maths of Nonlinear Models.*   **L78**

Maths, English, French - SCE H Grade   *SCE H Grade in one or more of the above subjects.*   **M9**

Maths/Arithmetic - SCE H Grade   *SCE H Grade in Maths/Arithmetic.*   **M5**

Maths/Statistics Modular Courses - SCE H Grade   *Relevant certificate.*   **T9**

Maths: Analysis/Algebra 1 *SCOTVEC/NCM in
Maths: Analysis/Algebra 1.*   **L1**

Maths: Analysis/Algebra 1 (SCOTVEC)
*SCOTVEC/NCM 7180401 Maths:
Analysis/Algebra 1.*   **L83**

Maths: Analysis/Algebra 3 (SCOTVEC)
SCOTVEC/NCM.   **L5**

Maths: Calculus 1 (SCOTVEC) *SCOTVEC/NCM.*
                                                     L5

Maths: Calculus 2 (SCOTVEC) *SCOTVEC/NCM.*
                                                     L5

Quantitative Methods - HN Unit *SCOTVEC
Higher National Unit (x3) - 6400059.*   **F8**

Statistics - SCE O Grade *An SCE O Grade
certificate in Statistics.*   **S14**

Statistics 1 (SCOTVEC) *SCOTVEC/NCM.*   **L5**

Statistics 1 - 91063 - SCOTVEC/NC
SCOTVEC/NC.   **T23**

Statistics 2 - 91064 - SCOTVEC/NC
SCOTVEC/NC.   **T23**

Using Arithmetic Skills - SCOTVEC/NC *On
successful completion of this course students will
have gained SCOTVEC/NC.*   **T23**

Workplace Education - Numeracy *The
development of relevant skills & opportunity to
gain SCOTVEC.*   **C16**

NATURAL HISTORY, LIFE
SCIENCES

Access to Higher Education - SCE Higher Biology
*SCE H Grade Biology taken part-time to gain
qualifications.*   **D5**

Access to Higher Education - SCOTVEC Biology
(SCE O/S Equivalent) *SCOTVEC modules in
Biology.*   **D5**

Anatomy, Physiology & Health - SCE H Grade *A
SCE H grade in Anatomy Physiology & Health.*
                                                     S79

Anatomy, Physiology & Health - SCE Higher *SCE
Higher - Anatomy Physiology & Health.*   **F7**

Anatomy, Physiology & Body Massage *CIBTAC
Certificate.*   **T9**

Anatomy, Physiology & Health - SCE H Grade
SCE H Grade in Anatomy, Physiology & Health.
                                     C4 F5 S14 S16

Anatomy, Physiology & Health - SCE H Grade /
NCMs *SCE H GRADE or appropriate SCOTVEC
module(s).*   **H13**

Applied Biological Sciences - HNC
SCOTVEC/HNC in Applied Biological Sciences.
                                                     S8

Applied Biosciences - BSc *A BSc degree in
Applied Biosciences.*   **S26**

Applied Biosciences - BSc (Honours) *A BSc
(Honours) degree in Applied Biosciences.*   **S26**

Applied Chemistry - HNC/HND (UCAS - O11F
HND App Chem) *HNC/HND in Applied chemistry.*
                                                     T12

Aquaculture *Development of skills in aquaculture.*
                                                     C44

Bioengineering - MSc *MSc in Bioengineering.*
                                                     S105

Bioengineering - PgD *A PgD in Bioengineering.*
                                                     S105

Biological Cells (Introducing) - SCOTVEC/NC
SCOTVEC/NC.   **T23**

Biological Sciences - HNC *SCOTVEC/HNC in
Biological Sciences. May lead to HND or degree
course.*   **S101**

Biological Sciences - HNC/HND (UCAS -
021C/HND Biol Sci) *HNC/HND in Biological
Sciences.*   **T12**

Biological Sciences - NC *SCOTVEC/NC in
Biological Sciences.*   **S75 S94**

Biological Sciences - SCOTVEC/NC *On
successful completion of the course students will
have SCOTVEC/NC.*   **G17**

Biology *SCOTVEC Certificate will be awarded on
successful completion of the module(s).*
                                                 B11 L88

Biology (Revised) - SCE H Grade *The SCE H
Grade in Biology will be awarded on successful
completion of this course.*   **B3**

Biology (Revised) - SCE Higher *SCE Higher -
Biology (Revised).*   **F7**

Biology - an Introduction to the Human Body - NC
*SCOTVEC/NC listing Modules studied & Learning
Outcomes attained.*   **C45**

Biology - CSYS *SCE SYS in Biology which can
provide entry to further studies at FE College or
University.*   **D7 D8**

Biology - GCE A Level (Evening) *GCE A Level in
Biology.*   **L68**

Biology - GCE A Level Course *GCE A Level in
Biology.*   **L68**

Biology - S Grade *SCOTVEC/NCM in Biology.*
                                                     S88

Biology - SCE H Grade *AN SCE H Grade in
Biology.*
  **C1 C4 C5 C6 C7 C20 C21 C22 C25 C
C27 C28 C29 C30 C33 C34 C36 C45 C46
D7 F5 F9 F12 F19 L5 L31 L68 S2 S6 S13
S16 S79 S87 T9 T23**

Biology - SCE H Grade (Evening) *SCE H Grade
in Biology.*   **L68**

Biology - SCE H Grade (Revised) *A SCE Revised
H Grade in Biology.*   **B6 D8 H53 L1**

Biology - SCE H Grade or CSYS   *SCE in Biology at H Grade or Certificate of Sixth Year Studies.*
D3

Biology - SCE Higher   *On successful completion of this course candidates will have a SCE Higher in Biology.*   **M3**

Biology - SCE O Grade   *A SCE O grade Certificate in Biology.*   **S87**

Biology - SCE S Grade   *SCE at S Grade in Biology.*   **D7**

Biology - SCE Standard / SCE H Grade / NCMs   *SCE Standard or H Grade or appropriate SCOTVEC modules.*   **H13**

Biology - SCOTVEC Module (Evening)   *SCOTVEC/NCM in Biology.*   **L68**

Biology - SCOTVEC Module (O Grade Replacement)   *SCOTVEC/NCM in Biology.*   **L68**

Biology - SCOTVEC Modules   *SCOTVEC Modules in Biology.*   **D8**

Biology - SCOTVEC Stage 1   *SCOTVEC Stage 1 in Biology.*   **B6**

Biology - SEB H Grade   *A SEB H Grade in this subject will be awarded.*   **B1 B10 B11**

Biology - SEB S Grade   *An SEB S Grade in Biology will be awarded.*   **B11**

Biology - SEB Sixth Year Studies   *SEB Certificate of Sixth Year Studies in Biology.*   **B1 B11**

Biology or Human Biology - SCE Higher   *Successful candidates will be awarded the SCE H Grade.*   **H49**

Biology Stage I - NCMs   *Successful completion leads to SCOTVEC/NCMs in Biology.*   **S87**

Biomedical Sciences - BSc   *A BSc in Biomedical Sciences.*   **S26**

Biomedical Sciences - MSc   *On successful completion of the course students will be awarded a MSc in Biomedical Science.*   **S26**

Biomedical Sciences - PgD   *On successful completion of the course students will be awarded a PgD in Biomedical Science.*   **S26**

Biotechnology - HND   *SCOTVEC/HND in Biotechnology.*   **S92**

Central Region's Environment, Geology & Scenery   *No formal outcome.*   **C41**

Customised Short Courses in Science & Technology   *Certification can be organised.*   **L68**

Exploring the North East   *No formal outcome.*
G21

Horticulture - NC   *SCOTVEC/NC will be awarded. Students will have gained practical skills in horticulture.*   **S15**

Human Biology - SCE H Grade   .
B3 B6 C20 C22 C23 C26 C28 C30 C36 F19 L1 L5 L68 S2 S87 T9

Human Biology - SCE H Grade (Evening)   *SCE H Grade in Human Biology.*   **L68**

Human Biology - SCE Higher   *SCE Higher - Human Biology.*   **F7**

Human Biology - SCOTVEC Module (O Grade Replacement)   *SCOTVEC/NCM in Human Biology.*   **L68**

Human Biology - SEB H Grade   *The SEB H Grade in Human Biology.*   **B6**

Human Biology Stage I - NCMs   *Successful completion leads to SCOTVEC/NCMs in Human Biology.*   **S87**

Human Biology/Biology - SCE H Grade   *SCE H Grade Human Biology or SCE H Grade Biology.*   **L15**

Human Development: Infancy to Old Age - (Introduction) SCOTVEC National Cert.   *SCOTVEC/NC.*   **T23**

Introducing Inheritance (1/2 Module) - NC   *SCOTVEC/NC listing Modules studied & Learning Outcomes attained.*   **C45**

Introducing the Human Body - SCOTVEC/NC   *On successful completion of this course learners will have SCOTVEC/NCM.*   **T23**

Laboratory Science Technology Course - NC (SCOTVEC)   *SCOTVEC/NC in Laboratory Science Technology.*   **L68**

Life Sciences - BSc / BSc (Honours)/ Diploma/Certificate   *Certificate/Diploma/Degree/Honours Degree.*
L35

Microbiology Course for School Science Technicians (Level 3)   *No formal outcome.*   **S8**

Physics, Chemistry & Biology - SCE H Grade   *SCE H Grade in one or more of the above subjects.*   **M9**

Physiological Measurement - HNC   *SCOTVEC/HNC in Physiological Measurement.*
S94

Physiological Measurement - NC   *SCOTVEC/NC in Physiological Measurement.*   **S94**

Structure of the Body   *The participant will further his/her knowledge of body structure.*   **B9**

Teacher Training Course in Microbiology   *Knowledge gained in Microbiology.*   **S8**

PHYSICS

Access to Higher Education - SCE Higher Physics   *SCE H Grade Physics taken part-time to gain qualifications.*   **D5**

Access to Higher Education - SCOTVEC Physics (SCE O/S Equivalent) *SCOTVEC modules in physics.* **D5**

Acoustics, Vibration & Noise Control- MSc/Diploma *MSc Degree/Diploma in Acoustics, Vibration & Noise Control.* **L6**

Applied Physics with Microcomputing - BSc / BSc (Honours) *BSc Degree / Hons Degree.* **L41**

Bulk Solids Handling Technology - MSc *An MSc in Bulk Solids Handling Technology.* **S56**

Bulk Solids Handling Technology - PgD *A PgD in Bulk Solids Handling Technology.* **S56**

Customised Short Courses in Science & Technology *Certification can be organised .* **L68**

Electromagnetism - Module *SCOTVEC/NCM - 3171302.* **F8**

Experimental Stress Analysis *No formal outcome.* **S109**

Foundation Course in Physics - NC *SCOTVEC/NC listing Modules studied & Learning Outcomes attained.* **C23**

Hydraulic Circuits & Fault Finding *SCOTVEC module certificate is available if required.* **F8**

Instrumentation with Applied Physics - BSc *A BSc in Instrumentation with Applied Physics.* **S53**

Instrumentation with Applied Physics - BSc (Hons) *A BSc in Instrumentation with Applied Physics.* **S53**

Intro to Hydraulics *Skills will be gained in the basic principles of hydraulics equipment, circuitry & control.* **F8**

Intro to Hydraulics Circuit Computer Simulation *Skills are gained in the use of a computer simulation package.* **F8**

Intro to Pneumatics *Skills will be gained in the basic principles of pneumatics equipment, circuitry & control.* **F8**

Intro to Pneumatics Circuit Computer Simulation *Skills are gained in the use of a computer simulation package.* **F8**

Introducing Mechanics - 3171031 - SCOTVEC/NC *SCOTVEC/NCM.* **T23**

Introduction to Physics *SCOTVEC/NCM in Introduction to Physics.* **L1**

Introduction to Physics (SCOTVEC) *SCOTVEC/NCM 3171223 Introduction to Physics.* **L3**

Introductory to Building Craft Science - NCM *SCOTVEC/NCM.* **L81**

Mechanical CAE Specialising in Thermodynamics & Fluid Mechanics - MSc *MSc in Mechanical Computer Aided Engineering.* **S105**

Mechanical CAE Specialising in Thermodynamics & Fluid Mechanics - PgD *PgD in Mechanical Computer Aided Engineering.* **S105**

Mechanical Engineering Specialising in Thermodynamics & Fluid Mechanics - MSc *A MSc in Mechanical Engineering.* **S105**

Mechanical Engineering Specialising in Thermodynamics & Fluid Mechanics - PgD *A PgD in Mechanical Engineering.* **S105**

Motor Vehicle Mechanics - NC *SCOTVEC/NC - Motor Vehicle Engineering.* **S87**

Physics *Qualification as studied for.* **L88 L95**

Physics (Revised) - H Grade *An SEB H Grade in Physics will be awarded.* **B1**

Physics (Revised) - SCE Higher *SCE Higher - Physics (Revised).* **F7**

Physics - CSYS *Scottish Examination Board Certificate of Sixth Year Studies in Physics.* **D8**

Physics - GCE A Level Course *GCE A Level in Physics.* **L68**

Physics - S Grade *SCOTVEC/NCM in Physics.* **S88**

Physics - SCE H Grade *AN SCE H Grade in Physics.*
C1 C4 C5 C6 C7 C20 C21 C22 C23 C C26 C27 C28 C29 C30 C33 C34 C36 C46 F9 L5 L68 S2 S6 S13 S16 S79 S87 T9

Physics - SCE H Grade (Evening) *SCE H Grade in Physics.* **L68**

Physics - SCE H Grade (Revised) *Scottish Examination Board Certificate in Physics at H Grade.* **D8 L1**

Physics - SCE H Grade or CSYS *SCE in Physics at H Grade or Certificate of Sixth Year Studies.* **D3**

Physics - SCE Standard / SCE H Grade / NCMs *SCE Standard or H Grade or the appropriate SCOTVEC module.* **H13**

Physics - SCOTVEC Module (O Grade Replacement) *SCOTVEC/NCM in Physics.* **L68**

Physics - SCOTVEC Modules *SCOTVEC Modules in Physics.* **D8**

Physics - SEB H Grade *An SEB H Grade in Physics will be awarded.* **B10 B11**

Physics - SEB S Grade *An SEB S Grade in Physics will be awarded.* **B11**

Physics - SEB Sixth Year Studies *An SEB Certificate of Sixth Year Studies in Physics will be awarded.* **B1 B11**

Physics Stage I - NCMs *Successful completion leads to SCOTVEC/NCMs in Physics.* **S87**

Physics, Chemistry & Biology - SCE H Grade *SCE H Grade in one or more of the above subjects.* **M9**

Physics-Introducing Mechanics & Physics Introducing Electricity SCOTVEC Modules *SCOTVEC Modules.* **T9**

Physics: Introducing Mechanics - NC *SCOTVEC/NC listing Modules studied & Learning Outcomes attained.* **C45**

Pneumatic & Hydraulic Systems *An introduction to circuit construction & fault finding.* **T1**

Pneumatic Circuits & Fault Finding *SCOTVEC module certificate is available if required.* **F8**

Science & Technology - NC *SCOTVEC/NC in Science & Technology.* **S15**

Small Engine Maintenance *Participants will improve their skills in small engine maintenance.* **H31**

SCIENCE & TECHNOLOGY (GENERAL)

Access to Higher Education in Science *College Certificate.* **L5**

Access to Science & Engineering *Progression to higher education.* **L96**

Access to Science & Technology *SCOTVEC/NCMs.* **S16 S87**

Access to Technology for Women *Prepares women for further training in new technology related skills.* **F13**

Animal Technology - HNC *SCOTVEC/HNC in Animal Technology.* **L68**

Automotive Management with Technology - HNC *SCOTVEC/HNC in Automotive Management with Technology.* **S88**

Chemistry - Years 1 & 2 - HNC *SCOTVEC/HNC in Chemistry.* **C22**

Chemistry - Years 1 & 2 - NC *SCOTVEC/NC in Chemistry.* **C22**

General Sciences - SCOTVEC/HNC *The SCOTVEC/HNC in General Sciences.* **G17**

Introducing Science (SCOTVEC) *SCOTVEC/NCM 3161001 Introducing Science.* **L83**

Introducing Science Investigation Skills (SCOTVEC) *SCOTVEC/NCM 3161121.* **L83**

Laboratory Science Technology Course - NC (SCOTVEC) *SCOTVEC/NC.* **L68**

Laboratory Technology - HNC *HNC in Science Laboratory Technology.* **F5**

Local Investigations 2 (SCOTVEC) *SCOTVEC/NCM 81213.* **L5**

Master of Technology Management *A Master of Technology Management.* **S105**

Northern Studies Courses *These courses are run on a wide variety of subjects for general interest & education.* **H50**

Nursing & Health Studies MSc/Diploma *MSc Degree in Nursing & Health Studies Diploma in Nursing & Health Studies.* **L77**

Physiological Measurement - HNC *SCOTVEC/HNC in Physiological Measurement.* **S94**

Physiological Measurement - NC *SCOTVEC/NC in Physiological Measurement.* **S94**

Pre Access Science - GSVQ Level II *SCOTVEC module may be awarded if work is assessed.* **L68**

Process Plant Operations - GSVQ Level I *GSVQ Level I.* **H49**

Science & Technology - NC *SCOTVEC/NC in Science & Technology.* **F5 S15**

Science & Technology - NCMs *SCOTVEC/NC(s) will be awarded for module(s) successfully completed.* **H53**

Science (Swap Access) *Success on this Access programme guarantees place on a Degree or Diploma Course.* **G2**

Science - GSVQ Level II *GSVQ in Science at Level II, Biology Option.* **G17**

Science - NC *SCOTVEC/NC. Progression to HNC,HND or Degree Level courses.* **H53 S94**

Science - SEB S Grade *An SEB S Grade in Science will be awarded.* **B11**

Science Laboratory Technicians - NC *SCOTVEC/NC for Science Laboratory Technicians.* **S16**

Science Stage I - NCMs *Successful completion leads to SCOTVEC/NCMs.* **S87**

Science with Management Studies - HNC *SCOTVEC/HNC in Science with Management Studies.* **L5**

Sciences - H Grade *A SCE H Grade.* **S88**

Sciences - NC *SCOTVEC/NC. Will give entry to science courses at degree level or to HND & HNC courses.* **H49**

Technological Studies - SCE Higher *SCE Higher - Technological Studies.* **F7**

Technological Studies - SEB S Grade *An SEB S Grade in Technological Studies awarded.* **B11**

Technology *There is no formal outcome to this course.* **B10**

Technology - GSVQ Level I *SCOTVEC SVQ GSVQ Level I in Technology.* **C10**

Technology - SEB Short Course *Scottish Examination Board Short Course in Technology.* **D8**

Various Courses Available *Outcome depends on level and subject matter of individual courses.* **T21**

Women & Science & Technology   *An introduction to the role of women in science & technology.*   **C41**

SURVEYING & CARTOGRAPHY

Computer Aided Landscape Technology - HNC   *SCOTVEC/HNC in Computer Aided Landscape Technology.*   **F3**

Computer Aided Landscape Technology - HND   *SCOTVEC/HND in Computer Aided Landscape Technology.*   **F3**

General Surveying Foundation   *A Certificate in General Surveying Foundation.*   **S68**

Land Economics - Diploma   *Diploma in Land Economics leading examination of the RICS (General Practice Division).*   **S101**

Map Reading & Hill Safety   *SCOTVEC/NCM in Map Reading (half module).*   **L68**

Surveying & Levelling   *Participants will receive a College Certificate in surveying & levelling.*   **T9**

Topographic Studies - HNC   *SCOTVEC/HNC in Topographic Studies.*   **S68**

Topographic Studies - NC   *SCOTVEC/NC in Topographic Studies.*   **S68**

Urban Property Appraisal - MSc/PgD   *MSc/Postgraduate Diploma Urban Property Appraisal, approved by RICS.*   **S101**

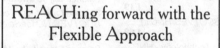

Sports, Games & Recreation

AIR SPORTS

Club Pilot's Course　*Course leads to the full Club Pilot's Exam.*　**T20**

Hang Gliding - Starter Pack　*No formal outcome.*　**T20**

Paragliding - Beginners Pack　*No formal outcome.*　**T20**

ATHLETICS, GYMNASTICS, FITNESS TRAINING, COMBAT SPORTS

Developing Endurance　*The participant will further his/her effectiveness as a coach.*　**B9**

Sport & Leisure - Customised Courses　*Various.*　**L71**

BALL & RELATED GAMES

Golf Course Management - HNC　*SCOTVEC/HNC in Golf Course Management.*　**F3**

INDOOR, COMPUTER & CARD GAMES

Indoor, Computer & Card Games　*No formal outcome.*　**T18**

OUTDOOR & ANIMAL SPORTS

Associate Instructor Training (3 Modules of 2 Days)　*Associate Instructor & progress towards VQ at Level 2.*　**H59**

Clay Pigeon Shooting - Part 1　*This course forms the first part of a three part syllabus for SCOTVEC Module 78402.*　**B5**

Clay Pigeon Shooting - Part 2　*This course forms the second part of a three part syllabus for SCOTVEC Module 78402.*　**B5**

Clay Pigeon Shooting - Part 3　*This course forms the third part of a three part syllabus for SCOTVEC Module 78402.*　**B5**

Falconry　*Participants will have gained sufficient experience to train & maintain own hawk.*　**T15**

Game Fishing Course - Part 1　*A Certificate of Attendance.*　**B5**

Game Fishing Course - Part 2　*A Certificate of Attendance.*　**B5**

Horse Riding Classes (Novice, Adult or Advanced)　*An ability to ride a Horse.*　**G10**

Horse Riding Courses - Various Levels　*No formal outcome.*　**L94**

Instructor's Course - 5 Days　*Recommendation & progress towards VQ Level 2 & Ski Instructor Licence.*　**H59**

Leisure & Recreation　*SCOTVEC module will be awarded on successful completion of this course.*　**B1**

Leisure - Outdoor Recreation - SCOTVEC/HND *HND in Outdoor Recreation.*   **G17**

Map Reading & Hill Safety   *SCOTVEC/NCM in Map Reading (half module).*   **L68**

Mountain Leader Training   *SMLTB Awards.*   **M12**

Rural Recreation & Tourism - HNC *SCOTVEC/HNC in Recreation & Tourism.*   **S92**

Rural Recreation & Tourism - HND *SCOTVEC/HND in Rural Recreation & Tourism.*   **S92**

Ski Instructor's Course - 10 Days   *Ski Instructor's Licence & continuation towards VQ levels 2 & 3.*   **H59**

Telemark Ski Instructor's Course - 6 Day S *Telemark Ski Instructor's Licence.*   **H59**

Workplace Education - Outdoor Pursuits   *The opportunity to gain an appropriate SCOTVEC qualification.*   **C16**

SPORTS STUDIES & COMBINED SPORTS

Analysing Performance   *The participant will further his/her effectiveness as a coach.*   **B9**

Coaching Children   *The participant will develop a better understanding in coaching children.*   **B9**

Community Sports Leader Award   *CCPR Certificate.*   **F8**

Community Sports Leadership Course   *6 modules covering various aspects of Sports Leadership.*   **C13**

Delivering the Goods   *The participant will gain further knowledge in effective coaching.*   **B9**

Developing Endurance   *The participant will further his/her effectiveness as a coach.*   **B9**

Developing Flexibility   *The participant will further his/her effectiveness as a coach.*   **B9**

Developing Strength & Speed   *The participant will further his/her effectiveness as a coach.*   **B9**

Health & Fitness - HNC   *SCOTVEC/HNC in Health & Fitness.*   **L5 S75**

Introduction to Sports Mechanics   *The participant will further his/her awareness of the mechanics of sport.*   **B9**

Leisure & Recreation - NC   *SCOTVEC/NC will be awarded on successful completion of this course.*   **B6**

Mental Preparation for Performance   *The participant will further his/her effectiveness as a coach.*   **B9**

Motivating Your Athlete   *The participant will further his/her effectiveness as a coach.*   **B9**

National Coaching Foundation Course in Developing Endurance   *National Coaching Foundation Level II qualification.*   **F6**

Nutrition & Sports Performance   *The participant will further his/her effectiveness as a coach.*   **B9**

Physical Education   *SCOTVEC Certificate will be awarded on successful completion of the module(s).*   **B11**

Physical Education - SCE H Grade   *SCE H Grade.*   **C5 C7 C20 C21 C25 C26 C28 C30 C34 C36 C46**

Physical Education - SCE H Grade or CSYS   *SCE in Physical Education at H Grade or Certificate of Sixth Year Studies.*   **D3**

Physical Education - SCOTVEC Modules *SCOTVEC Modules in Physical Education.*   **D8**

Physical Education - SEB S Grade   *SEB S Grade in Physical Education will be awarded.*   **B11**

Planning Your Programme   *The participant will further his/her effectiveness as a coach.*   **B9**

Prevention & Treatment of Injury   *No formal outcome.*   **B9**

Sport & Leisure - Customised Courses   *Various.*   **L71**

Sport & Leisure - YT/SVQ Level II   *SCOTVEC SVQ, SVQ Level II Certificate.*   **S79**

Sport & Recreation - NC   *A variety of awards can be included on this course.*   **F6 G2**

Sports & Recreation Services - NC *SCOTVEC/NC in Sports & Recreation.*   **C22**

Sports Coaching & Development - HNC *SCOTVEC/HNC / Opportunity to do National Governing Body Awards.*   **L5 M7 S71**

Sports Coaching Courses   *There are a variety of courses on offer in various districts throughout Highland Region.*   **H53**

Sports Technology 2000 - NC   *SCOTVEC/NC in Sports Technology 2000.*   **S71**

Structure of the Body   *The participant will further his/her knowledge of body structure.*   **B9**

Teaching Exercise to Music - RSA Basic Certificate   *RSA Basic Certificate in Teaching Exercise to Music.*   **L5**

Understanding & Improving Skill   *The participant will further his/her effectiveness as a coach.*   **B9**

WATER SPORTS

Canoe & Kayak Instructor Training   *SCA/BCU Awards.* **M12**

Coastal Skipper/Yachtmaster Offshore   *RYA Coastal Skipper/Yachtmaster Offshore Shorebased Certificate.* **G2**

Crew & Day Skipper/Watch Leader Certificate - (RYA Competent)   *RYA Course Completion Certificate.* **G2**

Leisure & Recreation   *SCOTVEC module will be awarded on successful completion of this course.* **B1**

Lifesaving - RLSS Bronze Medallion   *RLSS Bronze Medallion Lifesaving Award.* **H10**

Royal Life Saving Society - Pool Lifeguard Award   *Royal Life Saving Society - Pool Lifeguard Award.* **F15**

RYA Day Skipper   *On successful completion of this course candidates will have a RYA in Yachting.* **M6**

RYA Shore Based Coastal/Off Shore Yachtmaster *No formal outcome.* **S71**

RYA Shore Based Day Skipper   *No formal outcome.* **S71**

RYA Shore Based Ocean Yachtmaster   *No formal outcome.* **S71**

RYA Yachtmaster Ocean   *On successful completion of this course candidates will have a RYA in Yachtmaster Ocean.* **M6**

Workplace Education - Outdoor Pursuits   *The opportunity to gain an appropriate SCOTVEC qualification.* **C16**

Yachtmaster Ocean   *RYA Yachtmaster (Ocean) Shorebased Certificate.* **G2**

WINTER SPORTS

Leisure & Recreation   *SCOTVEC module will be awarded on successful completion of this course.* **B1**

Ski Instructor Training   *BASI/SNSC Awards.* **M12**

Workplace Education - Outdoor Pursuits   *The opportunity to gain an appropriate SCOTVEC qualification.* **C16**

Transport Services & Vehicle Engineering

AVIATION

Aeronautical Engineering - Factory Processes & Procedures (C&G 208)   *City & Guilds Certificate 208 Part III.*   **S6**

Aeronautical Engineering - HNC   *SCOTVEC/HNC in Aeronautical Engineering.*   **S6**

Aeronautical Engineering - NC   *SCOTVEC/NC in Aeronautical Engineering.*   **M7 S6**

Aeronautical Engineering Practice - Advanced Certificate   *Successful students will be awarded the Advanced Certificate.*   **S6**

Aeronautical Engineering Practice - NC   *Successful students will be awarded the SCOTVEC/NC in Aeronautical Engineering.*   **S6**

DRIVING & ROAD SAFETY

Certificate of Professional Competence (CPC)   *RSA Certificate of Competence (Modules A & B).*   **L68**

Health, Safety & Hygiene   *No formal outcome.*   **H42**

Young Heavy Goods Vehicle Drivers Associated Knowledge Certificate - RSA   *Certificate awarded.*   **S87**

FREIGHT HANDLING

Certificate of Professional Competence (CPC)   *RSA Certificate of Competence (Modules A & B).*   **L68**

Diploma in Distribution Studies   *Diploma in Distribution Studies.*   **S87**

Driver of Vehicles Carrying Dangerous Goods Regulations   *No formal outcome.*   **S87**

Fork-Lift Driving   *Students will have an understanding of the skills needed to drive a Fork-Lift truck.*   **H31**

Fork-Lift Truck   *Participants will have improved their skills in operating a Fork-Lift truck.*   **H14**

Fork-Lift Truck Driver Course - HSE Approved   *ATB Group 1 Fork-Lift Truck Operators Certificate.*   **H37**

Fork-Lift Truck Operation 1 & 2   *ATB Fork-Lift Truck Operator's Certificate.*   **H30**

Fork-Lift Truck Operations   *SCOTVEC module 'Forklift Truck Operations' or Agricultural Training Board certification.*   **T1**

Fork-Lift Truck Operations - Improver   *Participants will have improved their skills & gained a Certificate.*   **H35**

Fork-Lift Truck Operations - Refresher   *One day refresher course.*   **H35**

Fork-Lift Truck Operations - Safety   *A one day safety course for supervisors & managers.*   **H35**

Fork-Lift Truck Operator Courses   *A Certificate of Competence will be awarded.*   **G17**

Fork-Lift Trucks   *A College Certificate of Attendance.*   **B2**

Health, Safety & Hygiene   *No formal outcome.*   **H42**

Industrial Fork-Lift Trucks   *CITB Certificate.*   **G26**

Industrial Rider/Operator Counter Balance Truck Drivers' Course   *Licence to operate industrial Fork-Lift truck awarded.*   **G26**

Lift Truck Driver Training   *A knowledge of Lift Fork Driver operations.*   **S87**

Ride On Rollers   *CITB Certificate.*   **G26**

Rough Terrain Fork-Lift Trucks   *CITB Certificate.*   **G26**

RTITB Fork-Lift Truck Course - 5 Days   *Road Transport Industry Training Board (RTITB) Licence.*   **S118**

Safety Operation for Supervisors of Fork-Lift Truck Operation   *Participants will have gained relevant skills.*   **H35**

Telescopic Handlers   *CITB Certificate.*   **G26**

Tractor & Fork-Lift Truck Operation & Maintenance   *SCOTVEC/NC. Fork-Lift Truck Operators Certificate.*   **F3**

Transportation of Dangerous Goods   *Certificate awarded.*   **G42**

Various Courses Available   *Company Certificate awarded.*   **S149**

MARINE & WATERWAY TRANSPORT

Basic Fire Fighting & Fire Prevention At Sea   *Successful completion can lead to Dept. of Transport Certificate.*   **H15**

Basic Fire Fighting At Sea   *Successful completion can lead to Dept. of Transport Certificate.*   **H31**

Basic First Aid At Sea *Successful completion will lead to a Department of Transport Certificate.*
H15

Basic Navigation *Successful participants will have learned basic navigation skills.* **H15**

Basic Sea Safety Courses *Students will have the basic minimum qualification to go to sea.* **H36**

Basic Sea Survival *Successful completion will lead to a Dept. of Transport Certificate.*
H15 H31 S71

Boat Handling *Participants will have become competent boat handlers.* **H15**

Coastal Navigation *Participants will have gained skills in coastal navigation.* **H31**

Coastal Navigation I - SCE *SCE - Coastal Navigation 1.* **F10**

Deckmanship Courses *These courses explore various skills.* **H15**

Elect & Electronic Engineering Section Short Course Provision *College Certificate.* **L21**

Engine Maintenance for Yachtsmen *Details available from contact.* **S71**

Fast Rescue Craft Coxswain Refresher Course *No formal outcome.* **G11**

Fish Industry Welding Course *Students will have improved their basic welding techniques.* **H37**

Fisheries Patrol Boat Coxswain Course *Delegates will have been trained to an acceptable level of competence.* **G11**

International Transportation of Dangerous Goods by Sea-IMDG Code *Certificate awarded.* **L85**

Liferaft/Survival Course for Yachtpersons & Others *College Certificate.* **L20**

Liferaft/Survival Courses *Department of Transport Certificate or RYA Certificate.* **L20**

Management of Ship Operations (By Distance Learning) *Diploma:Dip MSO.* **L85**

Marine Maintenance Courses *Contact Provider for a list of course titles.* **H15**

Marine Navigation Equipment Operation *A knowledge of marine navigation equipment operation.* **L20**

Marine Technology - MSc *A MSc in Marine Technology.* **S105**

Marine Technology - PgD *A PgD in Marine Technology.* **S105**

Meteorology *Successful participants will have acquired skills in meteorology.* **H15**

Nautical Studies Short Courses *Various courses are available.* **H37**

Navigators & Sounders *Successful participants will have been given an introduction to electronic aids.* **H15**

Ongoing Board Rescue & Care Operations (Part B) *No formal outcome.* **G11**

Outboard Engine/Ancillary Systems Maintenance Course *No formal outcome.* **G11**

Outboard Motor Maintenance *Participants will have gained skills in outdoor motor maintenance.*
H31

Pilotage *Successful participants will have learned the International Rules of Pilotage.* **H15**

Radar & Electronic Navigation for Yachtpersons. *College Certificate.* **L20**

Radiotelex *College Certificate.* **L22**

Rapid Interception Craft Coxswain Course *No formal outcome.* **G11**

Restricted Radiotelephony Certificate Course *DTI Certificate of Competence in Radiotelephony Restricted.* **L22**

Rural Skills Courses *Short courses in a variety of subjects relating to rural skills.* **H27**

RYA Coastal/Offshore *A RYA Coastal/Offshore Certificate.* **S71**

RYA Day Skipper *A RYA Day Skipper Qualification.* **S71**

RYA Ocean Yachtmaster *A RYA Ocean Yachtmaster Certificate.* **S71**

Sea Survival *No formal Outcome.* **G33**

Search & Rescue Lifeboat Coxswain Course *No formal outcome.* **G11**

Ship Production Technology - MSc *A MSc in Ship Production Technology.* **S105**

Ship Production Technology - PgD *A PgD in Ship Production Technology.* **S105**

Shipbuilding - C & G 242 *City & Guilds 242 Shipbuilding Advanced.* **F5**

Shipbuilding - HNC *SCOTVEC/HNC in Shipbuilding.* **F5**

Shipbuilding - NC *NC in Shipbuilding. Enables entry to HNC in Shipbuilding.* **F5**

Shipbuilding Craft Studies - C & G 241 *City & Guilds 241 Shipbuilding Craft Studies Part 3.*   **F5**

Shorebased Day Skipper/Watch Leader (RYA) *RYA Certificate.*   **L20**

Shorebased Yachtmaster Ocean (RYA) *RYA Shorebased Yachtmaster Ocean Certificate.*   **L20**

Shorebased Yachtmaster Offshore/Coastal Skipper (RYA) *RYA Certificate.*   **L20**

Small Engine Maintenance *Participants will improve their skills in small engine maintenance.*   **H31**

Subsea Engineering - MSc/Diploma *MSc Degree/Diploma in Subsea Engineering.*   **L6**

Transportation of Dangerous Goods by Sea (By Distance Learning) *Certificate awarded.*   **L85**

VHF Radio Operation *Preparation for the Dept. of Transport's 'Restricted Certificate of Competence, VHF.*   **H15**

Yacht & Boatbuilding - NC *Successful students will be awarded SCOTVEC/NC in Yacht & Boatbuilding.*   **S75**

Yacht & Boatbuilding Skills - NVQ C & G *NVQ, NVQ City & Guilds Certificate.*   **S75**

ROAD TRANSPORT: PASSENGER, FREIGHT, INSPECTION, LEGISLATION

Certificate of Professional Competence (CPC) *RSA Certificate of Competence (Modules A & B).*   **L68**

Certificate of Professional Competence (Goods National) - CPC *Award of the RSA Certificate.*   **L81**

Certificate of Professional Competence - RSA *RSA Certificate of Professional Competence.*   **S16**

Competence in Road Transport (CPC) *Certificate of Professional Competence (Royal Society of Arts).*   **S87**

CPC International Freight *RSA Certificate of Professional Competence in Road Transport Operation.*   **H49**

CPC International Passenger *RSA Certificate of Professional Competence (Road Transport).*   **H49**

Institute of Road Transport Engineers (IRTE) - Final Certificate *IRTE Section C - Final Exam.*   **L68**

Preparation Course for Ministry of Transport Testers (M.O.T.) *Prepares participants to sit the Dept.of Transport test.*   **H53**

Road Haulage - Professional Competence Certificate *RSA Certificate in Professional Competence.*   **T9**

Road Passenger Transport/Road Freight Transport Certificate - RSA *RSA Certificates.*   **S14**

Road Transport Industry - Certificate of Professional Competence *Certificate of Professional Competence.*   **S88**

Road Transport Operation - Certificate of Professional Competence *Certificate of Professional Competence.*   **F3**

Road Transport Operations - HNC *SCOTVEC/HNC in Road Transport Operations.*   **S87**

RSA - Certificate in Professional Competence - Road Transport *RSA Certificate in Professional Competence.*   **C23**

TRANSPORT (GENERAL)

Automotive Management with Technology - HNC *SCOTVEC/HNC .*   **S88**

Engineering - HNC *Can lead to SCOTVEC/HNC.*   **H31**

Engineering - HND *SCOTVEC/HND, which prepares the student for registration as an Incorporated Engineer or allows access to 3rd year of a Degree course of a BSc. or B.Eng.*   **H53**

Engineering - Short Industrial Training Courses *Skills gained in various fields of engineering.*   **S75**

Exhaust Emission & the Environment *College based certificate in Exhaust Emission & the Environment.*   **S88**

Institute of Motor Industry - Certificate of Management *Institute of Motor Industry Certificate of Management.*   **S88**

Institute of the Motor Industry (IMI) Certificate of Management *IMI Certificate of Management.*   **L81**

Institute of the Motor Industry (IMI) Higher Certificate of Management *IMI Higher Certificate of Management.*   **L81**

Institute of Transport - Administration Graduate/Associate Membership Courses *Membership of the ITA.*   **S14**

Management (IMI) - Certificate *Learners will gain a Certificate in Management.*   **T23**

Road Transport Operation - Certificate of Professional Competence *Certificate of Professional Competence.*   **F3**

RSA Certificate of Professional Competence in Road Transport *The RSA Certificate of Professional Competence.* **B6**

Transportation Engineering - MSc/ Postgraduate Degree *MSc Degree in Transportation Engineering.* **L59**

Warehousing & Transportation - 63106 - SCOTVEC/NC *SCOTVEC/NC awarded.* **T23**

VEHICLE MAINTENANCE & REPAIR

2nd Level Vehicle Painting - C & G 3980 Part 2 *City & Guilds 398 Part 2.* **L68**

3rd/4th Year Motor Mechanic *SCOTVEC qualifications enabling progress to craftsman level & NCC/HNC.* **D5**

Airbrush Art *Basic airbrush techniques.* **L68**

Anti Lock Braking *Students will have updated their knowledge in Anti Lock Braking.* **D5**

Auto Electrician/Electronics - NC *SCOTVEC/NC - Auto Electrician/Electronics.* **S87**

Auto Electricians (1st Year) - NC *SCOTVEC/NC course in Auto Electrics.* **S88**

Auto Electricians (2nd Year) - NC *SCOTVEC/NC course in Auto Electrics.* **S88**

Auto-Electronics - NC *SCOTVEC/NC leading toward SVQ.* **L69**

Basic Car Maintenance *There is no formal outcome to this course.* **B2**

Basic Spray Painting Techniques (DIY) *Basic spray painting skills.* **L68**

Basic Welding (SCOTVEC) *SCOTVEC/NCM(s).* **L68**

Car Care & Maintenance *Participants will gain a basic knowledge of how to care & maintain a car. This course is for interest only.* **H49**

Charging System Fault Finding & Repair *A knowledge of charging systems & fault finding repair.* **S87**

Diesel Engine Injection Systems *A knowledge of Diesel Engine Injection Systems.* **S87**

Electronic Engine Management Systems *There is no formal outcome to this course.* **B6**

Electronic Fuel Injection *Students will have updated their knowledge in Electronic Fuel Injection Systems.* **D5**

Electronic Ignition *Enhanced knowledge of modern ignition systems.* **D5**

Engine Diagnostics *A knowledge of Engine Diagnostics.* **S87**

Engine Management Systems *A knowledge of Engine Management Systems.* **S87**

Glass Reinforced Plastics *SCOTVEC/NCM in Glass Reinforced Plastics.* **L68**

Heavy Vehicle Maintenance - YT/NVQ C & G Level II *NVQ, NVQ City & Guilds Level II Certificate.* **S79**

Know Your Car *There is no formal outcome to this course.* **B6**

Light Vehicle Maintenance *No formal outcome.* **H53 S136**

Light Vehicle Maintenance - YT/NVQ C & G Level II *NVQ, NVQ City & Guilds Level II Certificate.* **S79**

Mechanical & Electronic Systems Maintenance & Repair (Heavy Vehicles) *NVQ.* **G27**

Mechanical & Electronic Systems Maintenance & Repair (Light Vehicles) *NVQ.* **G27**

Motor Cycle Mechanics - NC *SCOTVEC/NC in Motor Cycle Mechanics.* **S87**

Motor Cycle, Scooter & Moped Users Maintenance (Basic) (SCOTVEC) *SCOTVEC/NCM.* **L68**

Motor Vehicle Body Fitting - NVQ Level II *A NVQ NVQ Level II in Vehicle Body Fitting.* **C11**

Motor Vehicle Bodywork Studies - NC *SCOTVEC/NC in Motor Vehicle Bodywork Studies.* **S88**

Motor Vehicle Craft - NVQ C & G 381/3 *NVQ, NVQ City & Guilds 383/3 Certificate.* **S15**

Motor Vehicle Craft Studies (CGLI 381 Part 3) *City & Guilds Certificate 381 Part 3.* **L27**

Motor Vehicle Craft Studies - NVQ C & G (383,1,2,3) *NVQ, NVQ City & Guilds 383 (1,2,3) Certificate.* **S15**

Motor Vehicle Craft Studies - NVQ C & G 381 Part III *NVQ, NVQ City & Guilds 381 Part III Certificate.* **S75**

Motor Vehicle Craft Studies C & G 381 Part 3 (Advanced) *City & Guilds 381 Part 3 (advanced).* **T9**

Motor Vehicle Craft Studies NC *SCOTVEC/NC.* **L27**

Motor Vehicle Craft Studies Part III C & G 381 *A City & Guilds 381 Certificate.* **C22**

Motor Vehicle Electricians Part II Year 1 - C & G 3810 *A City & Guilds 381 Certificate.* **C22**

Motor Vehicle Electrics - SCOTVEC/NC *SCOTVEC/NC in Motor Vehicle Electrics.* **G17**

Motor Vehicle Engineering - NC *SCOTVEC/NC in Motor Vehicle Engineering.* **S15 S16**

Motor Vehicle Engineering Craft - NC *SCOTVEC/NC for Motor Vehicle Engineering Mechanics.* **F3**

Motor Vehicle Engineering Technician - Accreditation of Prior Learning   *SCOTVEC/NC.*   **F4**

Motor Vehicle Maintenance   *Participants will have learned some vehicle maintenance skills.*   **H31**

Motor Vehicle Maintenance Skills - YT/ET   *Training & appropriate work placement allows further progress.*   **D5**

Motor Vehicle Mechanics - NC   *SCOTVEC/NC in Motor Vehicle Mechanics.*   **L81**

Motor Vehicle Painting - NC   *SCOTVEC/NC in Motor Vehicle Painting.*   **S88**

Motor Vehicle Parts   *NVQ.*   **G27**

Motor Vehicle Refinishing - NVQ Level III   *A NVQ NVQ Level III in Vehicle Refinishing.*   **C11**

Motor Vehicle Servicing   *Skills & knowledge required to maintain & service a car at a basic level.*   **D6**

Motor Vehicle Studies - NC   *SCOTVEC National Craft Certificate in Light Vehicle Mechanics.*   **F13 S19**

Motor Vehicle Studies - Skillseekers   *SCOTVEC modules in Motor Vehicle engineering for Motor trade apprentices.*   **S19**

Motor Vehicle Subjects - Specialised Courses   *SCOTVEC/NC, or College Certificate, or appropriate skills.*   **L69**

Motor Vehicle Technician - NVQ/C&G 309   *NVQ, NVQ City & Guilds 309 Certificate.*   **S15**

Owner/Driver Motor Maintenance   *Participants will be able to carry out the small repairs.*   **T1**

Repair & Servicing of Road Vehicles - NVQ C & G 383   *NVQ, NVQ City & Guilds 383 Certificate.*   **S79**

Repair & Servicing of Road Vehicles C & G 383   *A City & Guilds 383 Certificate.*   **C22**

Road Vehicle Repair & Servicing - C & G   *The City & Guilds in Road Vehicle Repair & Servicing.*   **B6**

Small Engine Maintenance   *Participants will improve their skills in small engine maintenance.*   **H31**

Specialist Vehicle Paint Application   *Vehicle painting Techniques.*   **S87**

Steering & Suspension Geometry   *A knowledge of Steering & Suspension Geometry.*   **S87**

Tyre Fitting: Car/Van Tyres - NVQ Levels I-Ii   *A NVQ NVQ Level I-II in Tyre Fitting (Car/Van).*   **C11**

Vehicle (Car) Maintenance   *Vehicle car maintenance.*   **S88**

Vehicle Body Craft Studies C & G 398   *398 City & Guilds in Vehicle Body Repair.*   **T9**

Vehicle Body Jig Work   *A knowledge of Vehicle Body Jig Work.*   **S87**

Vehicle Body Repair   *NVQ.*   **G27**

Vehicle Body Repair - NC   *SCOTVEC/NC in Vehicle Body Repair.*   **S87 S88**

Vehicle Body Repair - NVQ Level III   *A NVQ NVQ Level III in Vehicle Body Repair.*   **C11**

Vehicle Body Repair/Refinishing   *LEVELS I,II,III in Body Repair or Vehicle Painting by C & G 398 scheme or level 3 NVQ C & G.*   **T9**

Vehicle Body Trades - YT/SVQ Level II   *SCOTVEC SVQ, SVQ Level II Certificate.*   **S79**

Vehicle Mechanical & Electronic System Unit Replacement (Light Vehicle) - NVQ   *A NVQ NVQ Level II in Vehicle Mechanical & Electronic Systems Unit Replacement.*   **C22**

Vehicle Mechanical & Electronic Systems - City & Guilds NVQ Levels II & III   *City & Guilds NVQ, NVQ Level II in Vehicle Mechanical & Electronic Systems.*   **S91**

Vehicle Mechanics & Systems for Vehicle Mechanics - National Craft Certificate   *National Craft Certificate.*   **S75**

Vehicle Minor Damage Repair   *Various skills needed for repair of minor damage to vehicles.*   **L68**

Vehicle Petrol Injection Systems   *A knowledge of Vehicle Petrol Injection Systems.*   **S87**

Vehicle Refinishing   *NVQ.*   **G27**

Vehicle Restoration   *Various skills needed for restoration of body parts from vintage or veteran vehicles.*   **L68 S88**

Vehicle Trimming/Upholstery - NC   *SCOTVEC/NC in Vehicle Trimming/Upholstery.*   **S87**

Vehicle, Mechanical & Electronic Systems Maintenance & Repairs - NVQ Level III   *A NVQ NVQ Level III.*   **C11**

Vehicle, Mechanical & Electronic Systems Unit Replacement - NVQ Level II   *A NVQ NVQ Level II.*   **C11**

VEHICLE MANUFACTURE, MOTOR TRADE & SALES

Automotive Engineering & Management HND   *HND in Automotive Engineering & Management.*   **L68**

Automotive Engineering - Advanced Craft Course NVQ C & G 381 Part III   *Advanced Craft Course C & G 381 part III.*   **S88**

Automotive Engineering - HNC   *HNC in Automotive Engineering.*   **L68**

Automotive Management & Technology - HNC
SCOTVEC/HNC in Automotive Management &
Technology. **S75**

Automotive Management - HNC   HNC in
Automotive Management. **T9**

Automotive Management with Technology -
Accreditation of Prior Learning   SCOTVEC/HNC.
F4

Automotive Management with Technology - HNC
SCOTVEC/HNC.
C22 C23 F3 L69 S16 S19 S87

Automotive Management with Technology -
SCOTVEC/HNC   SCOTVEC/HNC. **G17**

Certificate of Management (IMI)   Institute of Motor
Industry Certificate of Management. **L68**

Certificate of Professional Competence (CPC)
The knowledge required for the RSA Exam for
CPC Holder. **D5**

Engineering (Basic) - SCOTVEC/NC   At the end
of the course students will be awarded the
SCOTVEC/NC. **G17**

Financial Control Systems for the Vehicle Industry
SCOTVEC HN Unit will be awarded on successful
completion. **H53**

General Engineering & Motor Vehicle Certificate in
Quality Assurance   A Certificate in Quality
Assurance awarded. **C23**

Institute of the Motor Industry (IMI) Certificate of
Management   Institute of the Motor Industry (IMI)
Certificate. **L81**

Institute of the Motor Industry (IMI) Higher
Certificate of Management   IMI Higher Certificate
of Management. **L81**

Motor Cycle Mechanics - NC   SCOTVEC/NC in
Motor Cycle Mechanics. **S87**

Motor Cycle, Scooter & Moped Users Maintenance
(Basic) (SCOTVEC)   SCOTVEC/NCM. **L68**

Motor Vehicle Craft Studies NC   SCOTVEC/NC.
L27

Motor Vehicle Engineering - HNC
SCOTVEC/HNCMs in Motor Vehicle Engineering.
S88

Motor Vehicle Engineering - SCOTVEC/NC
SCOTVEC/NC in Motor Vehicle Engineering.
G2 G17

Motor Vehicle Engineering Craft - NC
SCOTVEC/NC & possible progression a more
advanced level. **F3**

Motor Vehicle Engineering Technician -
Accreditation of Prior Learning   SCOTVEC/NC.
F4

Motor Vehicle Mechanics (Year I) - NC
SCOTVEC/NC in Motor Vehicle Mechanics I.
S88

Motor Vehicle Mechanics (Year II) - NC
SCOTVEC/NC in Motor Vehicle Mechanics II.
S88

Motor Vehicle Mechanics (Year III) - NC
SCOTVEC/NC in Motor Vehicle Mechanics III.
S88

Motor Vehicle Mechanics - NC   SCOTVEC/NC in
Motor Vehicle Mechanics. **L81**

Motor Vehicle Parts Personnel - NVQ Level I-II   A
City & Guilds of London   Craft 384 Certificate.
C11

Motor Vehicle Parts Personnel C & G 384   384
City & Guilds in Garage Parts Personnel. **T9**

Motor Vehicle Studies   A wide range of motor
vehicle skills gained. **S81**

Motor Vehicle Studies - BTEC NC   BTEC NC in
Motor Vehicle Studies. **S87**

Motor Vehicle Studies - NC   SCOTVEC National
Craft Certificate in Light Vehicle Mechanics.
F13 S19

Vehicle Mechanical & Electronic Systems - NVQ
NVQ in Vehicle Mechanical & Electronic Systems.
G2

Vehicle Mechanics & Systems for Vehicle
Mechanics - National Craft Certificate   Certificate
awarded. **S75**

Vehicle Parts & Distribution - NC   SCOTVEC/NC
in Vehicle Parts & Distribution. **S88**

Vehicle Parts Personnel - NC   SCOTVEC/NC in
Vehicle Parts Personnel. **S87**

PUBLISHERS' NOTE

Whilst every care has been taken to ensure that the information
contained in this book is accurate, the Publishers and the Network
of TAP Agencies cannot accept responsibility for errors, omissions
or changes which may have taken place after passing for press.

IT'S ALL ON TAP!

Looking for information on Classes and Courses: Full-Time and Part-Time? Find out about your nearest Training Access Point from these regional TAP agencies!

STEPahead
381 Union Street
ABERDEEN AB1 2BX
Tel: 01224 210300

TAYSIDE TAP AGENCY
New Directions (Tayside) Ltd
88 Commercial Street
DUNDEE DD1 2AP
Tel: 01382 206116

LOTHIAN TAP AGENCY
8 St Mary's Street
EDINBURGH EH1 1SU
Tel: 0131 557 5822

MORAY, BADENOCH & STRATHSPEY TAP
Elgin Business Centre
Maisondieu Road
ELGIN IV30 1RH
Tel: 01343 551858

TAP TRAINING INFORMATION
Scottish Borders Enterprise
Bridge Street,
GALASHIELS TD1 1SW
Tel: 01896 758991

STRATHCLYDE TAP AGENCY (inc. LANTRACS)
Network Scotland
57 Ruthven Lane
GLASGOW G12 9JQ
Tel: 0141 357 1774

FIFE TRAINING INFORMATION SERVICES
9–10 Flemington Road
GLENROTHES KY7 5OW
Tel: 01592 611231

HIGHLANDS & ISLANDS TAP
Inverness Business Centre
Seafield Road
INVERNESS IV1 1SJ
Tel: 01463 710019

DUMFRIES & GALLOWAY TAP AGENCY
The Penninghame Centre
Auchendoon Road
NEWTON STEWART DG8 6HD
Tel: 01671 403530

CAREERS CENTRAL LTD
TAP Training Information Service
Cape Unicentre, Kerse Road
STIRLING FK7 7RW
Tel: 01786 446150

For general enquiries, contact:

SCOTTISH TAP NETWORK AGENCY

Room 1M1, 1 Parliament Square,
EDINBURGH EH1 1RF
Tel: 0131 469 3464

Part-time Classes and Courses

IN SCOTLAND 1995–96

PART TWO

Classes & Courses

Providers

The section which follows contains the contact details for the organisations which provide the classes and courses listed in the preceding section. Each 'provider' has an individual code and these are listed numerically under the region of Scotland where the provider is located. The regions and their codes are as follows:

Borders	**B**
Central	**C**
Dumfries and Galloway	**D**
Fife	**F**
Highlands & Islands	**H**
Lothian	**L**
Moray, Badenoch & Strathspey	**M**
Strathclyde	**S**
Tayside	**T**

There is also a short section for *'Distance Learning'* coded '**X**'.

Where a provider has more than one class or course – as in the case of many colleges and universities – and where the information has been supplied, we have given a separate code reference for each entry. This should enable the reader to make contact with the most suitable department or subject adviser.

The information is as accurate as we can establish at the time of going to press.

To use the Provider Section, simply look up the code/number (**B1, C8, S78** etc) listed against the appropriate entry in the Classes & Courses Section. Where more than one reference is given, you can use the code to find the Provider most convenient to where you wish to attend.

You will find additional useful addresses on pages 219-220 as well as the Community Education Department addresses on pages 25-6, the TAP's on pages 29 and 194, and the Local Enterprise addresses on pages 30-32.

When you contact a Provider for further information,
you may wish to make mention of
PART-TIME CLASSES & COURSES in Scotland.

BORDERS

B1 Berwickshire High School
DUNS
Berwickshire TD11 3QQ
Tel: 01361 83710

B2 Borders College
Duns Building
Newtown Street
DUNS TD11 3AE
Tel: 01361 883738

B3 Borders College
Henderson Building
Commercial Road
HAWICK TD9 7AW
Tel: 01450 374191

B4 Borders College
Training Studio 19b
Eastgate
PEEBLES EH45 8AD
Tel: 01721 723905

B5 Borders College
Agricultural Building
NEWTOWN ST
BOSWELLS
Roxburghshire TD6 0SJ
Tel: 01835 823023

B6 Borders College
Queens Building
Melrose Road
GALASHIELS TD1 2AF
Tel: 01896 757755

B7 Community Education Services
Borders College
Melrose Road
GALASHIELS TD1 2AF
Tel: 01896 755110

B8 Community Education Services
Chambers Institution
High Street
PEEBLES EH45 8AP
Tel: 01721 720123

B9 Community Education Services
Queens Centre
Melrose Road
GALASHIELS TD1 2AR
Tel: 01835 823301

B10 Eyemouth High School
The High School
EYEMOUTH
Berwickshire TD14 5BY
Tel: 01890 750363

B11 Kelso High School
Bowmont Street
KELSO
Roxburghshire TD5 7ED
Tel: 01573 224444

CENTRAL

C1 Alloa Academy
Claremont
ALLOA FK10 2EQ
Tel: 01259 214979

C2 Alloa Clackmannan Enterprise Ltd
Alloa Business Centre
Alloa Business Park
Whins Road
ALLOA FK10 3SA
Tel: 01259 721454

C3 Alloa Women's Technology Centre
14 Bank Street
ALLOA FK10 1HP
Tel: 01259 211180

C4 Alva Academy
Park Street
ALVA FK12 5LY
Tel: 01259 760342

C5 Balfron High School
Cotton Street
BALFRON G63 OPW
Tel: 01360 40469

C6 Bannockburn High School
Broomridge
Bannockburn Road
STIRLING FK7 OHQ
Tel: 01786 813519

C7 Bo'ness Academy
Academy Road
BO'NESS EH51 9QD
Tel: 01506 822260

C8 Business Management Enterprises Ltd
Old Anchor Works
Grangepans Industrial Estate
BO'NESS
West Lothian EH51 8SB
Tel: 01506 826910

C9 Central Scotland Chamber of Commerce
Suite A
Haypark Business Centre
Marchmont Avenue
POLMONT FK2 OPW
Tel: 01324 716868

C10 Clackmannan College
Branshill Road
ALLOA
Clackmannanshire FK10
3BT
Tel: 01259 215121

C11 Clackmannan College
Branshill Road
ALLOA
Clackmannanshire FK10
3BT
Tel: 01259 722506

**C12 CRC Community
Education Service**
Adult Education Base
Grangemouth High School
Tinto Drive
GRANGEMOUTH FK3 OHW
Tel: 01324 484817

**C13 CRC Community
Education Service**
Regional Training Agency
Camelon Education Centre
Abercrombie Street
Camelon
FALKIRK FK1 4HA
Tel: 01324 624922

**C14 CRC Community
Education Service**
Adult Learning Base
Carmuirs Primary School
Camelon
FALKIRK
Tel: 01324 637437

**C15 CRC Community
Education Service**
Unit D
131 Church Walk
DENNY FK6 6HS
Tel: 01324 825662

**C16 CRC Community
Education Service**
Grendon House
9 Snowdon Place
STIRLING FK8 2NH
Tel: 01786 442247

**C17 CRC Community
Education Service**
Argyll Community
Education Centre
Princes Street
STIRLING FK8 1HQ
Tel: 01786 461165

**C18 CRC Community
Education Service**
Bannockburn Community
Education Base
Bannockburn High School
Broomridge
STIRLING FK7 OHQ
Tel: 01786 817142

**C19 CRC Community
Education Service**
Bo'ness Recreation Centre
Gauze Road
BO'NESS
Tel: 01506 823308

C20 Denny High School
Anderson Drive
DENNY FK6 5EB
Tel: 01324 823124

C21 Dunblane High School
Highfields
DUNBLANE FK15 9DR
Tel: 01786 823823

**C22 Falkirk College of
Technology**
Grangemouth Road
FALKIRK FK2 9AD
Tel: 01324 624981

**C23 Falkirk College of
Technology**
Grangemouth Road
FALKIRK FK2 9AD
Tel: 01324 632777

**C24 Falkirk Enterprise Action
Trust (FEAT)**
Falkirk & District Business
Park
Newhouse Road
GRANGEMOUTH FK3 8LL
Tel: 01324 665500

C25 Falkirk High School
Blinkbonny Road
FALKIRK FK1 5BZ
Tel: 01324 629511

C26 Graeme High School
Callendar Road
FALKIRK FK1 1SY
Tel: 01324 622576

C27 Grangemouth High School
Tinto Drive
GRANGEMOUTH FK3
OHW
Tel: 01324 485031

C28 Larbert High School
Main Street
Stenhousemuir
LARBERT FK5 4HB
Tel: 01324 554233

C29 Lornshill Academy
Tullibody Road
ALLOA FK10 2ES
Tel: 01259 214331

C30 McLaren High School
Mollands Road
CALLANDER FK17 8JH
Tel: 01877 30156

C31 Prospects Training Centre Ltd
Unit 149
STEP
Kerse Road
STIRLING FK7 7RP
Tel: 01786 450380

C32 Scottish Enterprise Foundation
Women's Enterprise Unit
University of Stirling
STIRLING FK9 4LA
Tel: 01786 467353

C33 St Modan's High School
Barnsdale Road
STIRLING FK7 OPU
Tel: 01786 470962

C34 St Mungo's High School
Merchiston Avenue
FALKIRK FK2 7JT
Tel: 01324 628416

C35 Stirling Enterprise
Stirling Enterprise Park
John Player Building
STIRLING FK7 7RP
Tel: 01786 463416

C36 Stirling High School
Ogilvie Road
STIRLING FK8 2PA
Tel: 01786 472451

C37 University of Stirling
STIRLING FK9 4LA
Tel: 01786 467044

C38 University of Stirling
School of Management
STIRLING FK9 4LA
Tel: 01786 467276

C39 University of Stirling
School of Arts
STIRLING FK9 4LA
Tel: 01786 467490

C40 University of Stirling
School of Human Sciences
STIRLING FK9 4LA
Tel: 01786 467595

C41 University of Stirling
Educational Policy and
Development Continuing
Education
Airthrey Castle
STIRLING FK9 4LA
Tel: 01786 467940

C42 University of Stirling
Educational Policy and
Development Part-Time
Degree Office
Airthrey Castle
STIRLING FK9 4LA
Tel: 01786 467947

C43 University of Stirling
Educational Policy and
Development
Airthrey Castle
STIRLING FK9 4LA
Tel: 01786 467951

C44 University of Stirling
STIRLING FK9 4LA
Tel: 01786 473171

C45 Wallace High School
Dumyat Road
STIRLING FK9 5HW
Tel: 01786 462486

C46 Woodlands High School
Rennie Street
FALKIRK FK1 5AL
Tel: 01324 629615

C47 Training Direct
Management and
Technology Centre
Smith Street
FALKIRK
Stirlingshire FK2 7NA
Tel: 01324 620015

C49 Stirling Business Links Ltd
Stirling Enterprise Park
Kerse Road
STIRLING FK7 7RP
Tel: 01786 450659

C50 Forth Directions
33 High Street
FALKIRK
Stirlingshire FK1 1ES
Tel: 01324 629998

C51 Impact Communications
22 Finistere Avenue
FALKIRK
Stirlingshire FK1 1QP
Tel: 01324 636991

Dumfries & Galloway

D1 Barony College
Parkgate
DUMFRIES DG1 3NE
Tel: 01387 86251

D2 Business Development Centre
Dumfries & Galloway
College
Technology Annexe
George Street
DUMFRIES DG1 1EA
Tel: 01387 67450

D3 Community Education - Kirkcudbright
Community Education
Centre
Kirkcudbright Academy
KIRKCUDBRIGHT DG6 4JN
Tel: 01557 331281

D4 D&G Regional Council
Special Education
Department
30 Edinburgh Road
DUMFRIES DG1 IJQ
Tel: 01671 403530

**D5 Dumfries & Galloway
College**
Heathhall
DUMFRIES DG1 3QZ
Tel: 01387 261261

**D6 Dumfries & Galloway
College**
John Niven Centre
Lewis Street
STRANRAER DG9 7AL
Tel: 01776 706633

D7 LACEN
Lockerbie Continuing
Education Network
Lockerbie Academy
Dryfe Road
LOCKERBIE DG11 2AL
Tel: 015762 202626

D8 Stranraer Academy
McMaster's Road
STRANRAER DG9 8BY
Tel: 01776 706753

D9 Kinharvie House
New Abbey
DUMFRIES
Dumfriesshire DG2 8DZ
Tel: 01387 850433

FIFE

F1 Balwearie Centre
Balwearie High School
Balwearie Gardens
KIRKCALDY KY2 5LY
Tel: 01592 640335

F2 Beath Centre
Beath High School
Foulford Road
COWDENBEATH KY4 9BH
Tel: 01383 512495

F3 Elmwood College
Greenkeeping Section
Carslogie Road
CUPAR KY15 4JB
Tel: 01334 652781

F4 Elmwood College
APL Unit
Elmwood House
Carslogie Road
CUPAR KY15 4JB
Tel: 01334 656726

**F5 Fife College of F & H
Education**
Business Administration
St Brycedale Avenue
KIRKCALDY KY1 1EX
Tel: 01592 262414

**F6 Fife Institute of Phys &
Rec Education**
Viewfield Road
GLENROTHES
Fife KY6 2RA
Tel: 01592 771700

F7 FRC Schools
For location contact
Fife Training Information
Services
9-10 Flemington Road
GLENROTHES KY7 5QF
Tel: 0800 243 260

F8 Glenrothes College
Business Studies Section
Stenton Road
GLENROTHES KY6 2RA
Tel: 01592 775268

F9 Glenwood Centre
Glenwood High School
South Parks Road
GLENROTHES KY6 1JX
Tel: 01592 752244

F10 Inverkeithing Centre
Inverkeithing High
Hillend Road
INVERKEITHING KY11 1PL
Tel: 01383 414688

F11 Kirkcaldy High School
Dunnikier Way
KIRKCALDY
Fife KY1 3LT
Tel: 01592 267111

**F12 Kirkland High School &
Community College**
Methil Brae
METHIL
Fife KY8 3LT
Tel: 01333 424607

F13 Lauder College
Management and Business
Studies Section
Halbeath
DUNFERMLINE KY11 5DY
Tel: 01383 726201

F14 Lochgelly Centre
Bank Street
LOCHGELLY
Fife KY5 9QU
Tel: 01592 780971

**F15 Lochgelly High School
Community Use**
Station Road
LOCHGELLY
Fife KY5 8LZ
Tel: 01592 780353

F17 Tayside Institute Community Centre
High Street
NEWBURGH
Fife KY14 6DD
Tel: 01337 40427

F18 Pitcoudie Primary School
20 Iona Park
Pitcoudie
GLENROTHES KY7 6NU
Tel: 01592 610473

F19 Waid Centre
Waid Academy
St Andrews Road
ANSTRUTHER KY10 3HD
Tel: 01333 310060

F20 Lochmor Meadows Riding Stables
Chapel Farm Road
Crosshill
By LOCHGELLY
Fife KY5 8LY
Tel: 01592 861596

F21 Grosvenor Career Services
Buchan House
Carnegie Campus
Queensferry Road
DUNFERMLINE
Fife KY11 5WN
Tel: 01383 624444

F22 Pine G
67 Nethergate North
CRAIL
Fife KY10 3TX
Tel: 01333 540942

F23 Thornton Primary School
Station Road
THORNTON
Fife KY1 4AY
Tel: 01592 610473

GRAMPIAN

G2 Banff & Buchan College of Further Educ
Henderson Road
FRASERBURGH AB43 5GA
Tel: 01346 515777

G3 Bankhead Academy AE Centre
Bankhead Avenue
Bucksburn
ABERDEEN AB2 9ET
Tel: 01224 713861

G4 Bridge of Don Academy AE Centre
Braehead Way
Bridge of Don
ABERDEEN AB22 8RR
Tel: 01224 703118

G5 Construction Industry Training Board
Scotstown Road
Bridge of Don
ABERDEEN AB23 8MG
Tel: 01224 828181

G7 Ellon Academy AE Centre
Ellon Academy
Schoolhill Road
ELLON AB41 9AH
Tel: 01358 720562

G10 Hayfield Riding School
Hazlehead Park
ABERDEEN AB1 8BB
Tel: 01224 315703

G11 Maritime Rescue International
The Old Pier
STONEHAVEN
Kincardineshire AB3 2JU
Tel: 01569 764065

G12 North of Scotland Consortium
Room FG16
Northern College of Education
Aberdeen Campus
Hilton Place
ABERDEEN AB9 1FA
Tel: 01224 283676

G13 Northfield Community Education Centre
Byron Square
Northfield
ABERDEEN AB2 7LL
Tel: 01224 695416

G14 Open Learning in Scotland
Blackness Avenue
Altens
ABERDEEN AB1 4PG
Tel: 01224 898052

G15 Robert Gordon University
Schoolhill
ABERDEEN AB9 1FR
Tel: 01224 262105

G16 Robert Gordon University
Industrial Unit
Kepplestone
Queens Road
ABERDEEN AB9 2PG
Tel: 01224 263322

G17 Aberdeen College
Gallowgate
ABERDEEN AB9 1DN
Tel: 01224 640366

G18 St Machar Adult Education Initiative
St Machar Academy
31 St Machar Drive
ABERDEEN AB2 3YZ
Tel: 01224 492855

G19 Thames Valley University
Wellington Street
Slough
BERKSHIRE SL1 1YG
Tel: 01753 697695

**G20 Tillydrone Community
Education Centre**
Room 11
Tillydrone Primary School
Formartine Road
ABERDEEN AB2 2TL
Tel: 01224 492528

G21 University of Aberdeen
Centre for Continuing
Education
Regent Walk
ABERDEEN AB9 1FX
Tel: 01224 272449

G22 University of Aberdeen
Vocational Training Unit
Regent Building
Regent Walk
ABERDEEN AB9 1FX
Tel: 01224 272431

G23 University of Aberdeen
Regent Walk
ABERDEEN AB2 1SX
Tel: 01224 272953

**G24 Independent Painters
Workshop**
50 Cotton Street
ABERDEEN
Aberdeenshire
Tel: 01224 211134

G25 RGIT Ltd
338 King Street
ABERDEEN
Aberdeenshire
Tel: 01224 619600

**G26 Slessor Plant &
Commercial Training**
Flobbans
NEW ABERDOUR
Aberdeenshire AB43 4LR
Tel: 01346 561445

G27 Grampian Motor Training
Altens Centre
Hareness Road
Altens
ABERDEEN
Aberdeenshire AB1 4LE
Tel: 01224 874922

**G28 CSV Aberdeen Media
Action**
Leigh House
160 Union Street
ABERDEEN
Aberdeenshire AB1 1QT
Tel: 01224 622777

G29 Huntly Training Ltd.
School Avenue
HUNTLY
Aberdeenshire AB5 4SE
Tel: 01466 794434

G30 Future Training Services
Future Business College
17 Albert Street
ABERDEEN
Aberdeenshire
Tel: 01224 621700

**G31 F.I. Word Processing
Services**
24 Union Wynd
ABERDEEN
Aberdeenshire
Tel: 01224 640891

G32 Grampian Training
Grampian Training
Management Centre
Silverburn Crescent
BRIDGE OF DON
Aberdeenshire AB23 8EW
Tel: 01224 707071

**G33 North East Fishermen's
Joint Group
Training Association**
20 Queen's Road
ABERDEEN
Aberdeenshire
Tel: 01224 633926

G34 Willian Robb Consultants
85 Argyll Place
ABERDEEN
Aberdeenshire AB2 4HO
Tel: 01224 648838

G36 Hospitality Training
76a Countesswells Road
ABERDEEN
Aberdeenshire
Tel: 01224 874922

**G37 National Hairdressers
Federation**
Unit 16
Frederick Street
Business Centre
Frederick Street
ABERDEEN
Aberdeenshire
Tel: 01224 626377

**G38 Tack Training
International**
25 Cairntack Road
Belhelvie Near
ABERDEEN
Aberdeenshire AB23 8YU
Tel: 01358 742470

G39 ITCA Ltd.
49 York Street
ABERDEEN
Aberdeenshire AB2 1DP
Tel: 01224 594808

G40 Ean Jones School of Music
45 Summerfield Terrace
ABERDEEN
Aberdeenshire AB2 1JE
Tel: 01224 641080

G41 University Of Aberdeen
Language Centre
Regent Walk
ABERDEEN
Aberdeenshire AB9 2UB
Tel: 01244 272536

G42 Scota Limited
The Training Centre
Blackness Avenue
Altens
ABERDEEN
Aberdeenshire AB1 4PG
Tel: 01224 899707

Highlands & Islands

H1 Argyll and The Islands Enterprise
The Enterprise Centre
Kilmory Industrial Estate
LOCHGILPHEAD
Argyll PA31 8SH
Tel: 01345 794285

H2 British Red Cross
Forbes House
36 Huntly Street
INVERNESS IV3 5PR
(and local branches)
Tel: 01463 231620

H3 Caithness and Sutherland Enterprise
Scapa House
Castlegreen Road
THURSO KW14 7LS
Tel: 01847 805207

H4 Caithness and Sutherland Enterprise
Scapa House
Castlegreen Road
THURSO KW14 7LS
Tel: 01847 805211

H5 Caithness Jet
Unit 14A
Ormlie Industrial Estate
THURSO KW14 7EB
Tel: 01847 64025

H6 Caithness Jet
Ormlie Industrial Estate
THURSO KW14 7QU
Tel: 01847 66393

H7 Community Education Service (SRC)
2 Tom-a-Mhoid Road
DUNOON
Argyll PA23 7HN
Tel: 01369 6476

H8 Cowal Training Associates
152-156 Argyll Street
DUNOON
Argyll PA23 7NA
Tel: 01369 2001

H9 Cromarty Centre
Burnside Place
CROMARTY
Ross & Cromarty IV11 8XA
Tel: 013817 277

H10 Culloden Academy Swimming Pool
Culloden Academy
Keppoch Road
INVERNESS IV1 2JZ
Tel: 01463 792794

H11 Development Partners Ltd
6 Queensgate
INVERNESS IV1 1DA
Tel: 01463 223993

H12 Easter Ross Jet
Site 8k
Teaninich Industrial Estate
ALNESS IV17 0XS
Tel: 01349 882545

H13 Education Department
Contact local school for details of availability
Tel: LOCAL SCHOOLS

H14 Fish Industry Training Association
7 Ness Way
FORTROSE
Ross-shire IV10 8SR
Tel: 01381 621064

H15 Fish Industry Training Association
GLENELG
By Kyle of Lochalsh
Ross-shire IV40 8JH
Tel: 01599 522240

H16 Goireas
6 Uachdar
BENBECULA PA88 5LY
Tel: 01870 603050

H17 Highland Itec
Unit 6
13a Harbour Road
INVERNESS IV1 1SY
Tel: 01463 226505

H18 Highland Jet
Dochfour Drive
INVERNESS IV3 5EB
Tel: 01463 703001

H19 Highland Printmakers
20 Bank Street
INVERNESS IV1 1QE
Tel: 01463 712240

H20 Highland Scottish Pre-School Play Assoc
Kinmylies Building
Leachkin Road
INVERNESS IV3 6NN
Tel: 01463 703440

H22 Highland Textile Guild
Backacre
Tollie of Brahan
MARYBURGH IV7 8HQ
Tel: 01349 861964

H23 Highlands and Islands Fire Brigade
16 Harbour Road
Longman Industrial Estate
INVERNESS IV1 1TB
Tel: 01463 222722

H24 Inverness and Nairn Enterprise
Castle Wynd
INVERNESS IV1 1QY
Tel: 01463 713504

H26 Inverness College - Lochaber Centre
Lochaber High School
FORT WILLIAM PH33 7ND
Tel: 01397 700421

H27 Inverness College - Seafield Centre
Seafield Centre For Rural Skills
KISHORN
Ross-shire IV54 8XD
Tel: 01520 733300

H28 Isles Telecroft
Unit 1
Baltasound Industrial Estate
Baltasound
UNST
Shetland ZE2 9DS
Tel: 0195 781224

H29 James Watt - Campbeltown Access Centre
Kintyre Community
Education Centre
Stewart Road
CAMPBELTOWN
Argyll PA28 6AT
Tel: 01586 552732

H30 Kirkwall College of Further Education
Kirkwall Grammar School
KIRKWALL
Orkney KW15 1QN
Tel: 01856 872839

H31 Lewis Castle College
STORNOWAY
Isle of Lewis PA86 0XR
Tel: 01851 703311

H32 Linking Education and Disability (LEAD)
Spectrum Centre
Farraline Park
INVERNESS IV1 1LS
Tel: 01463 710023

H33 Lochaber Jet
Lochybridge
North Road
FORT WILLIAM PH33 6TQ
Tel: 01397 704941

H35 Moray Firth Training Group
32 Harbour Road
Longman Industrial Estate
INVERNESS IV1 1UF
Tel: 01463 230036

H36 Stromness Academy
Nautical Department
Victoria Street
STROMNESS
Orkney KW16 3BS
Tel: 01856 851021

H37 North Atlantic Fisheries College
Port Arthur
SCALLOWAY
Shetland ZE1 0UN
Tel: 0159 588328

H38 North West Training Centre
17 Manse Road
KINLOCHBERVIE
Sutherland IV27 4RR
Tel: 01971 521238

H39 Open University
c/o Community Education
Service Office
Ackergill Street
WICK
Caithness KW1 2DT
Tel: 01955 605423

H40 Orkney Opportunities Centre
The Brig
2 Albert Street
KIRKWALL
Orkney KW15 1HP
Tel: 01856 872460

H41 Regional Library Service
Central Services
31A Harbour Road
INVERNESS IV1 1UA
Tel: 01463 235713

H42 Regional Training Unit (HRC)
Dochfour Drive
INVERNESS IV3 5EB
Tel: 01463 702000

H43 Ross and Cromarty Enterprise
62 High Street
INVERGORDON
Ross & Cromarty IV18 9DH
Tel: 01349 853666

H44 Scottish Childminding Association
Rural Tutor
Sliema Essich Road
INVERNESS IV1 2AH
Tel: 01463 715545

H45 Scottish Council on Alcohol
3 Gordon Terrace
INVERNESS IV2 3HD
Tel: 01463 220995

H46 Shetland College of Further Education
Gressy Loan
LERWICK
Shetland ZE1 0BB
Tel: 01595 695514

H47 Skye and Lochalsh Enterprise
King's House
The Green
PORTREE
Isle of Skye IV51 9BS
Tel: 01478 612841

H48 Skye and Lochalsh Jet
Dunvegan Road
PORTREE
Isle of Skye IV51 8HJ
Tel: 01478 612627

H49 Thurso College
Ormlie Road
THURSO
Caithness KW14 7EE
Tel: 01847 896161

H50 University of Aberdeen
Northern Studies Centre
Braal
HALKIRK
Caithness KW12 6XE
Tel: 01847 831420

H51 Western Isles Enterprise
3 Harbour View
Cromwell Street Quay
STORNOWAY
Isle of Lewis PA87 2DF
Tel: 01851 703625

H52 Workers' Educational Association
David Whyte House
57 Church Street
INVERNESS IV1 1DR
Tel: 01463 710577

H53 Inverness College
3 Longman Road South
Longman Industrial Estate
INVERNESS IV1 1SA
Tel: 01463 236681

H54 Craig Dunain Hospital
Training and Guidance Unit
Leachkin Road
INVERNESS
Inverness-shire
Tel: 01463 716853

H55 Bridgehouse Art
ULLAPOOL
Ross-shire IV26 2TG
Tel: 01854 612281

H56 Industrial Rope Access Training
Firthview
Jemimaville
Poyntzfield
DINGWALL
Ross-shire IV7 8LV
Tel: 01463 233119

H58 Highland Regional Council
Adult Basic Education Unit
Spectrum Centre
Margaret Street
INVERNESS
Inverness-shire IV1 1LS
Tel: 01463 710013

H59 Sabhal Mor Ostaig (Canan Ltd.)
SLEAT
Isle of Skye IV44 8RQ
Tel: 01471 4345

H60 Comann An Luchd-Ionnsachaidh
5 Mitchell's Lane
INVERNESS
Inverness-shire IV2 3HQ
Tel: 01463 711792

LOTHIAN

L1 Community Education Service
Department of Education
40 Torphichen Street
EDINBURGH EH3 8JJ
Tel: 0131 229 9166

L2 Craigroyston Community High School
Pennywell Road
EDINBURGH EH4 4QP
Tel: 0131 332 7801

L3 Deans Community High School
Eastwood Park
LIVINGSTON
West Lothian EH54 8PS
Tel: 01506 431972

**L4   Edinburgh University
       Management School**
7 Bristo Square
EDINBURGH EH8 9AL
Tel: 0131 650 8070

**L5   Edinburgh's Telford
       College**
Crewe Toll
EDINBURGH EH4 2NZ
Tel: 0131 332 2491

L6   Heriot-Watt University
Riccarton
EDINBURGH EH14 4AS
Tel: 0131 449 5111

L8   Heriot-Watt University
Research Park
Riccarton
EDINBURGH EH14 4AS
Tel: 0131 449 3393

L10   Heriot-Watt University
Centre for Continuing
Education
Riccarton
EDINBURGH EH14 4AS
Tel: 0131 451 3014

**L11   Heriot-Watt University/
       Stirling Uni.**
School of Planning and
Housing
Edinburgh College of Art
Lauriston Place
EDINBURGH EH3 9DF
Tel: 0131 229 9311

**L12   Institute for Applied
       Language Studies**
University of Edinburgh
21 Hill Place
EDINBURGH EH8 9DP
Tel: 0131 650 6189

**L13   Institute for Applied
       Language Studies**
University of Edinburgh
21 Hill Place
EDINBURGH EH8 9DP
Tel: 0131 650 6200

**L14   Institute for Applied
       Language Studies**
University of Edinburgh
21 Hill Place
EDINBURGH EH8 9DP
Tel: 0131 650 6289

**L15   Inveralmond Community
       High School**
Willowbank
Ladywell
LIVINGSTON EH54 6NH
Tel: 01506 438093

**L16   Jewel & Esk Valley
       College**
Eskbank Centre
Newbattle Road
DALKEITH EH22 3AE
Tel: 0131 654 5236

**L17   Jewel & Esk Valley
       College**
Eskbank Centre
Newbattle Road
DALKEITH EH22 3AE
Tel: 0131 654 5247

**L18   Jewel & Esk Valley
       College**
Eskbank Centre
Newbattle Road
DALKEITH EH22 3AE
Tel: 0131 654 5293

**L19   Jewel & Esk Valley
       College**
Eskbank Centre
Newbattle Road
DALKEITH EH22 3AE
Tel: 0131 654 5296

**L20   Jewel & Esk Valley
       College**
Milton Road Centre
24 Milton Road East
EDINBURGH EH15 2PP
Tel: 0131 657 7238

**L21   Jewel & Esk Valley
       College**
Milton Road Centre
24 Milton Road East
EDINBURGH EH15 2PP
Tel: 0131 657 7240

**L22   Jewel & Esk Valley
       College**
Milton Road Centre
24 Milton Road East
EDINBURGH EH15 2PP
Tel: 0131 657 7241

**L23   Jewel & Esk Valley
       College**
Milton Road Centre
24 Milton Road East
EDINBURGH EH15 2PP
Tel: 0131 657 7242

**L24   Jewel & Esk Valley
       College**
Milton Road Centre
24 Milton Road East
EDINBURGH EH15 2PP
Tel: 0131 657 7248

**L25   Jewel & Esk Valley
       College**
Milton Road Centre
24 Milton Road East
EDINBURGH EH15 2PP
Tel: 0131 657 7284

**L26   Jewel & Esk Valley
       College**
Milton Road Centre
24 Milton Road East
EDINBURGH EH15 2PP
Tel: 0131 657 7285

L27 Jewel & Esk Valley College
Eskbank Centre
Newbattle Road
DALKEITH EH22 3AE
Tel: 0131 660 1010

L28 Jewel & Esk Valley College
Milton Road Centre
24 Milton Road East
EDINBURGH EH15 2PP
Tel: 0131 669 8461

L29 Heriot-Watt University
Centre for Continuing
Education
Riccarton
EDINBURGH EH14 4AS
Tel: 0131 451 3004

L30 Lasswade High School Centre
Eskdale Drive
BONNYRIGG
Midlothian EH19 2LA
Tel: 0131 663 7171

L31 Leith Academy
20 Academy Park
EDINBURGH EH6 8JQ
Tel: 0131 554 0606

L32 MI Technologies Ltd
Motec Campus
Hardie Road
Deans
LIVINGSTON EH54 8AR
Tel: 01506 412695

L33 Moray House Institute of Education
Heriot-Watt University
Holyrood Campus
Holyrood Road
EDINBURGH EH8 8AQ
Tel: 0131 556 8455

L34 Napier University
Language Unit
18 Blantyre Terrace
EDINBURGH EH10 5AE
Tel: 0131 455 2209

L35 Napier University
Merchiston Campus
10 Colinton Road
EDINBURGH EH10 5DT
Tel: 0131 455 2235

L36 Napier University
Merchiston Campus
10 Colinton Road
EDINBURGH EH10 5DT
Tel: 0131 455 2303

L37 Napier University
Merchiston Campus
10 Colinton Road
EDINBURGH EH10 5DT
Tel: 0131 455 2315

L38 Napier University
Merchiston Campus
10 Colinton Road
EDINBURGH EH10 5DT
Tel: 0131 455 2318

L39 Napier University
Merchiston Campus
10 Colinton Road
EDINBURGH EH10 5DT
Tel: 0131 455 2466

L40 Napier University
Merchiston Campus
10 Colinton Road
EDINBURGH EH10 5DT
Tel: 0131 455 2503

L41 Napier University
Merchiston Campus
10 Colinton Road
EDINBURGH EH10 5DT
Tel: 0131 455 2517

L42 Napier University
Merchiston Campus
10 Colinton Road
EDINBURGH EH10 5DT
Tel: 0131 455 2528

L43 Napier University
Merchiston Campus
10 Colinton Road
EDINBURGH EH10 5DT
Tel: 0131 455 2533

L44 Napier University
Merchiston Campus
10 Colinton Road
EDINBURGH EH10 5DT
Tel: 0131 455 2567

L45 Napier University
Merchiston Campus
10 Colinton Road
EDINBURGH EH10 5DT
Tel: 0131 455 2615

L46 Napier University
Merchiston Campus
10 Colinton Road
EDINBURGH EH10 5DT
Tel: 0131 455 2623

L47 Napier University
Merchiston Campus
10 Colinton Road
EDINBURGH EH10 5DT
Tel: 0131 455 2656

L48 Napier University
TAMDU
10 Colinton Road
EDINBURGH EH10 5DT
Tel: 0131 455 2672

L49 Napier University
Sighthill Campus
Sighthill Court
EDINBURGH EH11 4BN
Tel: 0131 455 3324

L50 Napier University
Sighthill Campus
Sighthill Court
EDINBURGH EH11 4BN
Tel: 0131 455 3352

L51 Napier University
Sighthill Campus
Sighthill Court
EDINBURGH EH11 4BN
Tel: 0131 455 3353

L52 Napier University
Sighthill Campus
Sighthill Court
EDINBURGH EH11 4BN
Tel: 0131 455 3358

L53 Napier University
Sighthill Campus
Sighthill Court
EDINBURGH EH11 4BN
Tel: 0131 455 3385

L54 Napier University
Redwood House
66 Spylaw Road
EDINBURGH EH10 5BR
Tel: 0131 455 3409

L55 Napier University
Sighthill Campus
Sighthill Court
EDINBURGH EH11 4BN
Tel: 0131 455 3433

L57 Napier University
Sighthill Campus
Sighthill Court
EDINBURGH EH11 4BN
Tel: 0131 455 3457

L58 Napier University
Sighthill Campus
Sighthill Court
EDINBURGH EH11 4BN
Tel: 0131 455 3474

L59 Napier University
Sighthill Campus
Sighthill Court
EDINBURGH EH11 4BN
Tel: 0131 455 4270

L60 Napier University
Merchiston Campus
10 Colinton Road
EDINBURGH EH10 5DT
Tel: 0131 455 4277

L61 Napier University
Craiglockhart Campus
219 Colinton Road
EDINBURGH EH14 1DJ
Tel: 0131 455 4284

L62 Napier University
Craiglockhart Campus
219 Colinton Road
EDINBURGH EH14 1DJ
Tel: 0131 455 4661

L63 Napier University
Craiglockhart Campus
219 Colinton Road
EDINBURGH EH14 1DJ
Tel: 0131 455 4677

L64 Oatridge Agricultural College
Ecclesmachan
BROXBURN
West Lothian EH52 6NH
Tel: 01506 854387

L65 Queen Margaret College
Admissions Office
Clerwood Terrace
EDINBURGH EH12 8TS
Tel: 0131 317 3247

L66 Scottish Agricultural College-Edinburgh
West Mains Road
EDINBURGH EH9 3JG
Tel: 0131 667 1041

L67 Stevenson College
Bankhead Avenue
Sighthill
EDINBURGH EH11 4DE
Tel: 0131 443 8888

L68 Stevenson College
Bankhead Avenue
Sighthill
EDINBURGH EH11 4DE
Tel: 0131 453 2761

L69 Stevenson College
Bankhead Avenue
Sighthill
EDINBURGH EH11 4DE
Tel: 0131 453 6161

L70 Stevenson College
Leith Adult Education
Resource Centre
4 Duncan Place
EDINBURGH EH6 8HW
Tel: 0131 554 7144

L71 Telford Training & Consultancy Services
Edinburgh's Telford College
Crewe Toll
EDINBURGH EH4 2NZ
Tel: 0131 332 2491

L72 University of Edinburgh
Faculty of Law
Old College
South Bridge
EDINBURGH EH8 9YL
Tel: 0131 650 2010

L73 University of Edinburgh
Faculty of Music
Alison House
Nicolson Square
EDINBURGH EH8 9DF
Tel: 0131 650 2422

L74 University of Edinburgh
Faculty of Science and
Engineering
King's Buildings
West Mains Road
EDINBURGH EH9 3JY
Tel: 0131 650 3094

L75 University of Edinburgh
Faculty of Medicine
Medical School
Teviot Place
EDINBURGH EH8 9AG
Tel: 0131 650 3195

L76 University of Edinburgh
Faculty of Arts Office
David Hume Tower
George Square
EDINBURGH EH8 9JX
Tel: 0131 650 3578

L77 University of Edinburgh
Faculty of Social Sciences
55 George Square
EDINBURGH EH8 9JU
Tel: 0131 650 4085

L78 University of Edinburgh
Faculty of Science and
Engineering
King's Buildings
West Mains Road
EDINBURGH EH9 3JY
Tel: 0131 650 5080

L79 University of Edinburgh
Faculty of Science and
Engineering
King's Buildings
West Mains Road
EDINBURGH EH9 3JY
Tel: 0131 650 5766

L80 University of Edinburgh
Faculty of Divinity
New College
Mound Place EDINBURGH
EH1 2LX
Tel: 0131 650 8900

L81 West Lothian College
Marjoribanks Street
BATHGATE
West Lothian EH48 1QJ
Tel: 01506 634300

L82 West Lothian College
Marjoribanks Street
BATHGATE
West Lothian EH48 1QJ
Tel: 01506 418484

**L83 Wester Hailes Education
Centre**
5 Murrayburn Drive
EDINBURGH EH14 2SU
Tel: 0131 442 2201

L84 Support Training Ltd
Federation House
3 Loaning Road
EDINBURGH EH7 3JE
Tel: 01343 543194

**L85 Centre for Advanced
Maritime Studies**
Albert House
7 John's Place
EDINBURGH
Edinburgh & Lothians EH6
7EL
Tel: 0131 555 0525

**L86 Musselburgh Mathematics
Help Group**
c/o Mr Philip King
45 Kings Road
TRANENT
Edinburgh & Lothians EH33
2HA
Tel: 0131 229 6805

**L87 Creative Learning
Consultants**
Josephine Macleod
15 Saxe Coburg Place
EDINBURGH
Edinburgh & Lothians EH3
5BD
Tel: 0131 332 0893

L88 Royal Mile Tours
16 Jeffery Street
EDINBURGH
Edinburgh & Lothians EH1
Tel: 0131 557 3926

L89 Basil Paterson College
Dugdale-McAdam House
22-23 Abercromby Place
EDINBURGH
Edinburgh & Lothians EH3
6QE
Tel: 0131 556 7695

L90 Yamaha Music School
Keyboard Artistry
33 Sciennes Road
EDINBURGH
Edinburgh & Lothians EH9
1NS
Tel: 0131 667 8477

**L91 East Lothian Riding &
Trekking**
Whiteloch Farm
MACMERRY
East Lothian
Tel: 01875 613662

L92 Leith School of Art
25 North Junction Street
EDINBURGH
Edinburgh & Lothians EH6
6HW
Tel: 0131 554 5761

L93 Institute of Occupational Medicine
Roxburgh Place
EDINBURGH
Edinburgh & Lothians EH8
Tel: 0131 667 5131

L94 Tower Farm Riding Stables
85 Liberton Drive
EDINBURGH
Edinburgh & Lothians EH16 6NS
Tel: 0131 664 3375

L95 Edinburgh Teachers Co-operative
3 Hayfield
Maybury Drive
EDINBURGH
Edinburgh & Lothians EH12 8UJ
Tel: 0131 339 5374

L96 Scottish Wider Access Programme
c/o The University of Edinburgh
57 George Square
EDINBURGH
Edinburgh & Lothians EH8 9JU
Tel: 0131 650 6861

L97 Keil Centre
5 South Lauder Road
EDINBURGH
Edinburgh & Lothians EH9 2LJ
Tel: 0131 667 8059

L98 Edinburgh Dance Centre
10 Westfield Avenue
EDINBURGH
Edinburgh & Lothians
EH11 2QH
Tel: 0131 337 0748

MORAY, BADENOCH & STRATHSPEY

M1 Buckie Further Education Centre
Buckie High School
West Cathcart Street
BUCKIE AB5 1GB
Tel: 01542 832605

M2 Community Education Service (HRC)
Schoolhouse
Milton Park
AVIEMORE PH22 1RR
Tel: 01479 810164

M3 Forres Academy
Burdsyard Road
FORRES IV36 0DG
Tel: 01309 672271

M4 Forres Academy
Burdsyard Road
FORRES IV36 0DG
Tel: 01309 672823

M5 Keith Grammar Adult Education Centre
School Road
KEITH AB5 3ES
Tel: 01542 882028

M6 Lossiemouth FE Centre
Coulardbank Road
LOSSIEMOUTH IV31 6ED
Tel: 01343 542951

M7 Moray College
Moray Street
ELGIN IV30 1NS
Tel: 01343 554321

M8 Moray College Enterprise Ltd
BEST Centre
Marchmont Crescent
BUCKIE AB56 2BY
Tel: 01542 834265

M9 Speyside High - Open Learning Centre
Mary Avenue
ABERLOUR AB38 9QN
Tel: 01340 871522

M10 Balloch Trust Enterprises Ltd.
33 Balloch Road
KEITH
Banffshire AB55 3HW
Tel: 01542 886288

M11 British Association of Ski Instructors
Glenmore
AVIEMORE
Inverness-shire PH22 1QV
Tel: 01479 861717

M12 Glenmore Lodge
AVIEMORE
Inverness-shire PH22 1QU
Tel: 01479 861256

STRATHCLYDE

S1 Anniesland College
Hatfield Drive
GLASGOW G12 0YE
Tel: 0141 332 9427

S2 Anniesland College
Hatfield Drive
GLASGOW G12 0YE
Tel: 0141 357 3969

S3 **Anniesland College**
Hatfield Drive
GLASGOW G12 0YE
Tel: 0141 357 4310

S4 **Anniesland College**
Hatfield Drive
GLASGOW G12 0YE
Tel: 0141 949 4889

S5 **Ayr College**
Dam Park
AYR KA8 0EU
Tel: 01292 260321

S6 **Ayr College**
Dam Park
AYR KA8 0EU
Tel: 01292 265184

S7 **Ayr College**
Dam Park
AYR KA8 0EU
Tel: 01292 286312

S8 **Bell College of Technology**
Almada Street
HAMILTON ML3 0JB
Tel: 01698 283100

S9 **Cambuslang College**
Main Centre
85 Hamilton Road
CAMBUSLANG G72 7NY
Tel: 0141 641 6600

S10 **Cambuslang College**
Allers Centre
Kenilworth
Calderwood
EAST KILBRIDE G74 3PQ
Tel: 013552 24801

S11 **Cambuslang College**
Village Centre
86-88 Main Street
EAST KILBRIDE G74 4JY
Tel: 013552 43018

S12 **Cambuslang College**
Craigneuk Centre
Craigneuk Street
WISHAW ML2 7VY
Tel: 01698 262596

S13 **Cardonald College**
690 Mosspark Drive
GLASGOW G52 3AY
Tel: 0141 883 6151

S14 **Central College of Commerce**
300 Cathedral Street
GLASGOW G1 2TA
Tel: 0141 552 3941

S15 **Clydebank College**
Kilbowie Road
CLYDEBANK G81 2AA
Tel: 0141 952 7771

S16 **Coatbridge College**
Kildonan Street
COATBRIDGE ML5 3LS
Tel: 01236 436000

S18 **Cumbernauld And Kilsyth Itec**
3 Ettrick Way
Town Centre
Cumbernauld
GLASGOW G67 1NQ
Tel: 01236 722111

S19 **Cumbernauld College**
Tryst Road
Town Centre
CUMBERNAULD G67 1HU
Tel: 01236 731811

S20 **Cumbernauld College**
Tryst Road
Town Centre
CUMBERNAULD G67 1HU
Tel: 01236 731822

S23 **Glasgow Caledonian University**
City Campus
70 Cowcaddens Road
GLASGOW G4 0BA
Tel: 0141 331 3000

S24 **Glasgow Caledonian University**
City Campus
70 Cowcaddens Road
GLASGOW G4 0BA
Tel: 0141 331 3155

S25 **Glasgow Caledonian University**
City Campus
70 Cowcaddens Road
GLASGOW G4 0BA
Tel: 0141 331 3157

S26 **Glasgow Caledonian University**
City Campus
70 Cowcaddens Road
GLASGOW G4 0BA
Tel: 0141 331 3213

S27 **Glasgow Caledonian University**
City Campus
70 Cowcaddens Road
GLASGOW G4 0BA
Tel: 0141 331 3256

S28 **Glasgow Caledonian University**
City Campus
70 Cowcaddens Road
GLASGOW G4 0BA
Tel: 0141 331 3277

S29 **Glasgow Caledonian University**
City Campus
70 Cowcaddens Road
GLASGOW G4 0BA
Tel: 0141 331 3358

S30 Glasgow Caledonian University
City Campus
70 Cowcaddens Road
GLASGOW G4 0BA
Tel: 0141 331 3359

S31 Glasgow Caledonian University
City Campus
70 Cowcaddens Road
GLASGOW G4 0BA
Tel: 0141 331 3364

S32 Glasgow Caledonian University
City Campus
70 Cowcaddens Road
GLASGOW G4 0BA
Tel: 0141 331 3381

S33 Glasgow Caledonian University
City Campus
70 Cowcaddens Road
GLASGOW G4 0BA
Tel: 0141 331 3386

S34 Glasgow Caledonian University
City Campus
70 Cowcaddens Road
GLASGOW G4 0BA
Tel: 0141 331 3411

S35 Glasgow Caledonian University
City Campus
70 Cowcaddens Road
GLASGOW G4 0BA
Tel: 0141 331 3417

S36 Glasgow Caledonian University
City Campus
70 Cowcaddens Road
GLASGOW G4 0BA
Tel: 0141 331 3418

S37 Glasgow Caledonian University
City Campus
70 Cowcaddens Road
GLASGOW G4 0BA
Tel: 0141 331 3423

S38 Glasgow Caledonian University
City Campus
70 Cowcaddens Road
GLASGOW G4 0BA
Tel: 0141 331 3434

S39 Glasgow Caledonian University
City Campus
70 Cowcaddens Road
GLASGOW G4 0BA
Tel: 0141 331 3453

S40 Glasgow Caledonian University
City Campus
70 Cowcaddens Road
GLASGOW G4 0BA
Tel: 0141 331 3458

S41 Glasgow Caledonian University
City Campus
70 Cowcaddens Road
GLASGOW G4 0BA
Tel: 0141 331 3464

S42 Glasgow Caledonian University
City Campus
70 Cowcaddens Road
GLASGOW G4 0BA
Tel: 0141 331 3467

S43 Glasgow Caledonian University
City Campus
70 Cowcaddens Road
GLASGOW G4 0BA
Tel: 0141 331 3493

S44 Glasgow Caledonian University
City Campus
70 Cowcaddens Road
GLASGOW G4 0BA
Tel: 0141 331 3507

S45 Glasgow Caledonian University
City Campus
70 Cowcaddens Road
GLASGOW G4 0BA
Tel: 0141 331 3527

S46 Glasgow Caledonian University
City Campus
70 Cowcaddens Road
GLASGOW G4 0BA
Tel: 0141 331 3533

S47 Glasgow Caledonian University
City Campus
70 Cowcaddens Road
GLASGOW G4 0BA
Tel: 0141 331 3604

S48 Glasgow Caledonian University
City Campus
70 Cowcaddens Road
GLASGOW G4 0BA
Tel: 0141 331 3607

S49 Glasgow Caledonian University
City Campus
70 Cowcaddens Road
GLASGOW G4 0BA
Tel: 0141 331 3626

S50 Glasgow Caledonian University
City Campus
70 Cowcaddens Road
GLASGOW G4 0BA
Tel: 0141 331 3630

S51 Glasgow Caledonian University
City Campus
70 Cowcaddens Road
GLASGOW G4 OBA
Tel: 0141 331 3643

S52 Glasgow Caledonian University
City Campus
70 Cowcaddens Road
GLASGOW G4 OBA
Tel: 0141 331 3653

S53 Glasgow Caledonian University
City Campus
70 Cowcaddens Road
GLASGOW G4 OBA
Tel: 0141 331 3657

S55 Glasgow Caledonian University
City Campus
70 Cowcaddens Road
GLASGOW G4 OBA
Tel: 0141 331 3680

S56 Glasgow Caledonian University
City Campus
70 Cowcaddens Road
GLASGOW G4 OBA
Tel: 0141 331 3712

S57 Glasgow Caledonian University
Park Campus
1 Park Drive
GLASGOW G3 6LP
Tel: 0141 331 3724

S58 Glasgow Caledonian University
City Campus
70 Cowcaddens Road
GLASGOW G4 OBA
Tel: 0141 337 4306

S59 Glasgow Caledonian University
Park Campus
1 Park Drive
GLASGOW G3 6LP
Tel: 0141 337 4360

S60 Glasgow Caledonian University
Park Campus
1 Park Drive
GLASGOW G3 6LP
Tel: 0141 337 4361

S61 Glasgow Caledonian University
Park Campus
1 Park Drive
GLASGOW G3 6LP
Tel: 0141 337 4380

S62 Glasgow Caledonian University
Park Campus
1 Park Drive
GLASGOW G3 6LP
Tel: 0141 337 4384

S63 Glasgow Caledonian University
Park Campus
1 Park Drive
GLASGOW G3 6LP
Tel: 0141 337 4385

S64 Glasgow Caledonian University
Southbrae Campus
Southbrae Drive
GLASGOW G13 1PP
Tel: 0141 337 4754

S65 Glasgow Caledonian University
Park Campus
Park Drive
GLASGOW G3 6LP ·
Tel: 0141 337 4776

S66 Glasgow Caledonian University
City Campus
70 Cowcaddens Road
GLASGOW G4 OBA
Tel: 0141 337 4853

S67 Glasgow Caledonian University
City Campus
70 Cowcaddens Road
GLASGOW G4 OBA
Tel: 0141 950 3223

S68 Glasgow College of Building and Printing
60 North Hanover Street
GLASGOW G1 2BP
Tel: 0141 332 9969

S69 Glasgow College of Food Technology
230 Cathedral Street
GLASGOW G1 2TG
Tel: 0141 552 375

S70 Glasgow College of Food Technology
230 Cathedral Street
GLASGOW G1 2TG
Tel: 0141 552 3751

S71 Glasgow College of Nautical Studies
21 Thistle Street
GLASGOW G5 9XB
Tel: 0141 429 3201

S72 Intrain Ltd
19 Bogle Street
GREENOCK PA15 1ER
Tel: 01475 722217

S73 James Watt College
Finnart Street
GREENOCK PA16 8HF
Tel: 01475 721271

S75 James Watt College
Finnart Street
GREENOCK PA16 8HF
Tel: 01475 724433

S76 John Wheatley College
Shettleston Road
Shettleston
GLASGOW G32 9AT
Tel: 0141 771 2283

S77 John Wheatley College
Shettleston Road
Shettleston
GLASGOW G32 9AT
Tel: 0141 771 3382

S78 John Wheatley College
Shettleston Road
Shettleston
GLASGOW G32 9AT
Tel: 0141 778 2426

S79 Kilmarnock College
Holehouse Road
KILMARNOCK KA3 7AT
Tel: 01563 23501

S80 Kilmarnock College
Holehouse Road
KILMARNOCK KA3 7AT
Tel: 01563 44869

S81 Langside College
50 Prospecthill Road
GLASGOW G42 9LB
Tel: 0141 636 6066

S82 Glasgow Business School
University of Glasgow
57 Southpark Avenue
GLASGOW G12 8LF
Tel: 0141 339 8855

S83 Link Training
11 Hume Street
CLYDEBANK
Tel: 0141 951 0534

S84 Link Training
36 Bank Street
IRVINE
Tel: 01294 313212

S85 Link/Pitman Training
Shaftesbury House
5 Waterloo Street
GLASGOW G2 6AY
Tel: 0141 248 7300

S86 Link/Pitman Training
101 Almada Street
HAMILTON ML3 0EX
Tel: 01698 285504

S87 Motherwell College
Dalzell Drive
MOTHERWELL ML1 2BR
Tel: 01698 259641

S88 North Glasgow College
110 Flemington Street
Springburn
GLASGOW G21 4BX
Tel: 0141 558 9001

**S89 Paisley & Renfrew
Enterprise Trust**
27a Blackhall Street
PAISLEY PA1 1TD
Tel: 0141 889 0010

S90 Radix Training (Scotland)
West Sanquhar Road
AYR KA8 9HP
Tel: 01292 261408

S91 Reid Kerr College
Renfrew Road
PAISLEY PA3 4DR
Tel: 0141 889 4225

**S92 Scottish Agricultural
College**
Auchincruive
AYR KA6 5HW
Tel: 0800 269453

S93 Sitms/Metcom
Sandyford Road
PAISLEY PA3 4HW
Tel: 0141 887 2266

S94 Stow College
43 Shamrock Street
GLASGOW G4 9LD
Tel: 0141 332 1786

**S96 Strathclyde Graduate
Business Scho**ol
University of Strathclyde
119 Cathedral Street
GLASGOW G4 0QU
Tel: 0141 553 6000

S98 Cumbernauld College
Tryst Road
Town Centre
CUMBERNAULD G67 1HU
Tel: 0141 777 6043

**S99 Timber Trade Training
Association**
Stocking Lane
Hughenden Valley
HIGH WYCOMBE
HP14 4NB
Tel: 01494 564201

S100 University of Glasgow
Dept of Adult & Continuing
Education
59 Oakfield Avenue
GLASGOW G12 8LW
Tel: 0141 330 4394

S101 University of Paisley
High Street
PAISLEY PA1 2BE
Tel: 0141 848 3000

**S102 University of Paisley
Quality Centre**
High Street
PAISLEY
Renfrewshire PA1 2BG
Tel: 0141 848 3441

S103 University of Paisley
High Street
PAISLEY PA1 2BE
Tel: 0141 889 3225

S105 University of Strathclyde
Curran Building
100 Cathedral Street
GLASGOW G1 1XQ
Tel: 0141 552 4400

S106 University of Strathclyde
Curran Building
100 Cathedral Street
GLASGOW G1 1XQ
Tel: 0141 553 4150

S107 University of Strathclyde
Jordanhill Campus
76 Southbrae Drive
GLASGOW G13 1PP
Tel: 0141 950 3357

S108 University of Strathclyde
Jordanhill Campus
76 Southbrae Drive
GLASGOW G13 1PP
Tel: 0141 950 3462

S109 Continuing Education Centre
University of Strathclyde
McCance Building
16 Richmond Street
GLASGOW G1 1XQ
Tel: 0141 552 4400

S110 Clydesdale Development Co. Ltd
Clydesdale Business Centre
129 Hyndford Road
LANARK
Lanarkshire ML11 9AU
Tel: 01555 665064

S111 In A Word - Options for Change
12 Seyton Avenue
GIFFNOCK
Tel: 0141 638 0903

S112 East Kilbride Itec
30 Hawbank Road
EAST KILBRIDE
Lanarkshire G74 5EX
Tel: 013552 41644

S113 Stewart First Aid Training
20 Rosebank Avenue
BLANTYRE
Lanarkshire G72 9BB
Tel: 01698 824945

S114 Central School of Languages
243 Sauchiehall Street
GLASGOW G2
Tel: 0141 331 1600

S115 Alliance Francaise De Glasgow
7 Bowmont Gardens
GLASGOW G12 9LR
Tel: 0141 339 4281

S117 Nat Systems
37 Adamton Road North
PRESTWICK
Ayrshire KA9 2HY
Tel: 01292 671807

S118 Multiskills 90
95-99 Carron Place
Kelvin Industrial Estate
EAST KILBRIDE
Lanarkshire
Tel: 013552 44442

S119 East Kilbride Arts Centre
Old Coach Road
East Mains
EAST KILBRIDE
Lanarkshire
Tel: 013552 61000

S120 Drauz Language Centre
51 Barassie Street
TROON
Ayrshire
Tel: 01292 318728

S121 Anne B. Wilson L.G.S.M.
Tel: 0141 942 5131

S122 Scottish Agricultural College
(Rob Cockburn
Training Services Officer)
Auchincruive
AYR KA6 5HW
Tel: 01292 520331

S123 Work Wise Ltd
Block 6
Unit E7
Templeton Business Centre
GLASGOW G40 1DA
Tel: 0141 774 5291

S124 Centre for Training & Enterprise
Glasgow College of Building
60 Hanover Street
GLASGOW
Tel: 0141 332 1221

S125 Janet Weir Training Consultants
10 Moorfoot Way
Bearsden
GLASGOW G61 4RL
Tel: 0141 942 8500

S126 North Ayr Training Group
Heathfield Industrial Estate
24/26 Whitfield Drive
AYR
Ayrshire
Tel: 01292 285156

S128 Scottish National Assoc of Youth Theatre
179 Buchanan Street
GLASGOW G1
Tel: 0141 353 1866

S129 British Red Cross
(Jane J. Connelly
Training Administrator)
Alexandra House
204 Bath Street
GLASGOW G2
Tel: 0141 332 9591

S130 Mindstore
Mindstore House
36 Speirs Wharf
Port Dundas
GLASGOW G4 9TB
Tel: 0141 333 9393

S131 Gosta Training
Unit 5F
45 Finnieston Street
GLASGOW G3
Tel: 0141 248 2772

S132 RFM Training
7 Woodside Crescent
GLASGOW G3 7UL
Tel: 0141 332 3224

S133 MacInnes Younger
5 Renfield Street
GLASGOW G2
Tel: 0141 221 8866

S134 Royal Scottish Academy of Music & Drama
100 Renfrew Street
GLASGOW G2 3DB
Tel: 0141 332 4101

S135 Quality College of Scotland
Fleming House
2 Tryst Road
CUMBERNAULD
Tel: 01236 734447

S136 Addapt Ltd
7 Richmond Street
CLYDEBANK G81
Tel: 0141 951 1451

S137 Workers Educational Association
2 Port Dundas Place
(at Killermont Street)
GLASGOW G2 3LB
Tel: 0141 332 0176

S138 BCG Consultancy
Arcadia Business Centre
Miller Lane
CLYDEBANK G81 1UJ
Tel: 0141 248 3063

S139 Chartered Institute of Marketing
29 St. Vincent Place
GLASGOW G1 2DT
Tel: 0141 221 7700

S140 Volunteer Tutors Organisation
Dalreoch Primary School
Kingsway
Castlehill
DUMBARTON
Dunbartonshire
Tel: 01389 742538

S141 North Glasgow College Enterprise Centre
North Glasgow College
186 Rye Road
GLASGOW G21 3JY
Tel: 0141 558 2857

S142 Simpson Tessa Associates
Hillpark House
30 Rostan Road
GLASGOW G43
Tel: 0141 637 2273

S143 College of Piping
20 Otago Street
GLASGOW G12
Tel: 0141 334 3587

S144 Govan Initiative Ltd.
The Training Shop
Unit 10
Govan Cross Shopping
Centre
GLASGOW G51 3JW
Tel: 0141 445 1117

S145 Govan Initiative Ltd.
Industrial Training Unit
Festival Business Centre
Ibrox
GLASGOW G51 1DH
Tel: 0141 314 0015

S146 Construction Industry Training Board
(Mr C. Shearer)
4 Edison Street
Hillington Industrial Estate
GLASGOW G31 2JB
Tel: 0141 810 3044

S147 Strathkelvin Enterprise Trust
Southbank House
Southbank Business Park
KIRKINTILLOCH
Glasgow G66 1QX
Tel: 0141 777 7171

S148 Keil Centre
3 Fitzroy Place
GLASGOW G3 7RH
Tel: 0141 221 2893

S149 Belltec Training Service
3rd Floor
30 Gordon Street
GLASGOW G1 3PU
Tel: 0141 221 9888

S150 Ayr Locality Enterprise Resources Trust (Alert)
Ayr Business Centre
16 Smith Street
AYR
Ayrshire KA7 1TD
Tel: 01292 264181

S151 MEDC
8/14 Storie Street
PAISLEY
Renfrewshire PA1 2BX
Tel: 0141 848 0178

S152 SCDC Ltd.
Templeton Business Centre
GLASGOW G40 1DA
Tel: 0141 554 3797

S153 Reflex
44 Hecla Square
Drumchapel
GLASGOW G15 8LU
Tel: 0141 944 8766

S154 Lillian McNeill School of Dance
29 Marywood Square
GLASGOW
G41 2BW
Tel: 0141 423 0931

S155 CSV Training Options
236 Clyde Street
GLASGOW G1 4JH
Tel: 0141 204 1681

TAYSIDE

T1   Angus College
Keptie Road
ARBROATH DD11 3EA
Tel: 01241 432600

T2   Angus Enterprise Trust
115 High Street
ARBROATH DD11 1DP
Tel: 01356 624779

T3   Carnoustie Further Education Association
51 Dundee Street
CARNOUSTIE DD7 7PG
Tel: 01241 854063

T4   Continuing Education Unit
Mitchell Street
Community Education
Centre
Mitchell Street
DUNDEE DD2 2LJ
Tel: 01382 667297

T5   Fairfield Community Education Centre
Kingspark School
Gillburn Road
DUNDEE DD3 0AB
Tel: 01382 815207

T6   Forfar Assoc for Continuing Education
Forfar Academy
FORFAR DD8 3LB
Tel: 01307 466924

T7   Monifieth Further Education Association
Monifieth High School
Panmurefield Road
MONIFIETH DD5 4QT
Tel: 01382 534638

T8   Perth College
Crieff Road
PERTH PH1 2NX
Tel: 01738 442618

T9   Perth College
Crieff Road
PERTH PH1 2NX
Tel: 01738 621171

T10   SAEA Morgan Academy Evening School
Forfar Road
DUNDEE DD4 7AX
Tel: 01382 450848

T11   St Aidan's Group
Ambleside Terrace
Kirkton
DUNDEE DD3 0DB
Tel: 01382 818877

T12   University of Abertay Dundee
Bell Street
DUNDEE DD1 1HG
Tel: 01382 308080

T13   University of Dundee
Centre for Continuing
Education
Tower Building
Nethergate
DUNDEE DD1 4HN
Tel: 01382 223181

T14   W.S. Training
Pitkerro Training Centre
Pitkerro Road
DUNDEE DD4 8HD
Tel: 01382 500345

T15   British School of Falconry
Gleneagles Hotel
AUCHTERARDER
Perthshire PH3 1NF
Tel: 01764 662231

T16   Apex Trust Scotland Ltd.
Unit G
Hawhill Court
Mid Wynd
DUNDEE
Angus
Tel: 01382 229120

T17 Montrose Fire & Emergency Training Centre
Forties Road
MONTROSE
Angus DD10 9ET
Tel: 01674 672230

T18 Auchterarder Adult Education Assoc.
Mrs Anne Easton
13 Milton Crescent
AUCHTERARDER
Perthshire PH3 1RP
Tel: 01764 664268

T19 Water World Consultants
South Quay
Sea Oil Base
Ferryden
MONTROSE
Angus DD10 9SL
Tel: 01674 671344

T20 Cairnwell Mountain Sports
The Thom
Glenshee
By BLAIRGOWRIE
Perthshire PH10 7QQ
Tel: 01250 885238

T21 University Of Abertay
40 Bell Street
DUNDEE
Angus DD1 1HG
Tel: 01382 308000

T22 Phonetic Skills Project
Additional Skills Company
Douglas Court
West Hendersons Wynd
DUNDEE DD1 5BY
Tel: 01382 200388

T23 Dundee College
Old Glamis Road
DUNDEE DD3 8LE
Tel: 01382 834834

DISTANCE LEARNING

X1 National Extension College
18 Brooklands Avenue
CAMBRIDGE
Cambridgeshire CB2 2HN
Tel: 01223 313586

X2 Highland Libraries Education Services Librarian
Central Services Unit
31a Harbour Road
INVERNESS
Inverness-shire IV1 1UA
Tel: 01463 235713

PUBLISHERS' NOTE

Because of local government re-organisation, details of providers for some courses, in particular for leisure pursuits, cannot be confirmed as we go to print. Libraries and other local sources should be consulted and the Community Education contacts on pages 24 to 26 may also be of assistance.

Other Useful Addresses

Virtually all of Scotland's colleges and universities are included in our Part Two 'Providers' section with appropriate contact details. The following section lists the few who do not appear there as well as other contacts which have direct or indirect links with Part-Time Classes and Courses.

Because of local government organisation, details of providers for some courses, in particular for leisure pursuits, cannot be confirmed as we go to print. Libraries and other local sources should be consulted and the Community Education contacts on pages 24 to 26 may also be of assistance.

COMMUNITY EDUCATION SERVICE
Ayr Division
Wellington Square
AYR KA7 1DR
Tel: 01292 612241

COMMUNITY EDUCATION SERVICE
Lanark Division
Almada Street
HAMILTON
ML30 0AE
Tel: 01698 454466

DUMFRIES & GALLOWAY 'TAP'
The Penninghame Centre
Auchendoon Road
NEWTON STEWART
Wigtownshire
DG8 6HD
Tel: 01671 403530

THE HAMILTON SCHOOL
(The Children's House and Hamilton Training)
80–84 Queen's Road
ABERDEEN
Aberdeenshire
AB1 6YE
Tel: 01224 317155

HUNTLY CONTINUING EDUCATION CENTRE
(Grampian Regional Council Education Dept.)
Castle Street
HUNTLY
Aberdeenshire
AB54 4SE
Tel: 01466 792884

KINDROGAN FIELD CENTRE
Enochdhu
BLAIRGOWRIE
Perthshire
PH10 7PG
Tel: 01250 881286

THE MARY REID SALON & INTERNATIONAL SCHOOL OF BEAUTY
2nd Floor
59 Frederick Street
EDINBURGH
EH2 1LH
Tel: 0131 2253167

NORTH EAST FISHERMENS JOINT GROUP TRAINING ASSOCIATION
12 Commercial Road
BUCKIE

**NORTH EAST FISHERMENS
JOINT GROUP TRAINING
ASSOCIATION**
2 Port Henry Pier
PETERHEAD

THE OPEN UNIVERSITY
10 Drumsheigh Gardens
EDINBURGH
EH3 7QJ

**SCOTTISH COMMUNITY
EDUCATION COUNCIL**
Roseberry House
9 Haymarket Terrace
EDINBURGH EH12 5EZ

**SCOTTISH OFFICE EDUCATION
DEPARTMENT**
Gyleview House,
3 Redheugh Rigg, South Gyle
EDINBURGH EH12 9HH

SCOTVEC
Hanover House
24 Douglas Street
GLASGOW
G2 7NQ

SIGHT & SOUND
Scott House
12–16 South Frederick Street
GLASGOW G1 1HJ

SIGHT & SOUND
181 Pleasance
EDINBURGH
KH8 9RU

THE STUDENT LOANS COMPANY
100 Bothwell Street
GLASGOW
G2 7JD
Freephone: 0800 405010

Abbreviations

AAT	Association of Accounting Technicians
AC	Advanced Certificate
ACC	Advanced Craft Certificate
ACCA	Chartered Association of Certified Accountants
ACIBSE	Associate of the Chartered Institution of Building Services Engineers
ACMA	Associate of Institute of Cost and Management Accountants
ACOP	Approved Code of Practice
ACOPS	Advisory Committee on Pollution of the Sea
AEB	Associated Examining Board
AEC	Architect Engineering Construction
AMSPAR	Association of Medical Secretaries, Practice Administrators & Receptionists
APC	Advanced Proficiency Certificate
APL	Accreditation of Prior Learning
ASME	American Society of Mechanical Engineers
ASNT	American Society of Non-Destructive Testing
ATB	Agricultural Training Board
AVT	Audio Visual Technology
BA	Bachelor of Arts
BASI	British Association of Ski Instructors
BCU	British Canoe Union
BEBOH	British Examining Board in Occupational Hygiene
BEd	Bachelor of Education
BEng	Bachelor of Engineering
BHS	British Horse Society
BPICS	British Production and Inventory Control Society
BS	British Standard
BSc	Bachelor of Science
BTEC	Business & Technology Education Council
C&G	City & Guilds (of London Institute)
CAD	Computer Aided Draughting
CAE	Computer Aided Engineering
CAM	Communication, Advertising and Marketing Foundation
CEC	Continuing Education Certificate
CEELT	Cambridge Examination in English for English Language Teachers
CGLI	City & Guilds of London Institute
CIBS	Chartered Institute of Bankers in Scotland
CIBSE	Chartered Institution of Building Services Engineers
CIBTAC	Confederation of International Beauty Therapy & Cosmetology
CIC	Community Interpreting Certificate
CII	Chartered Insurance Institute
CIM	Chartered Institute of Marketing
CIMA	Chartered Institute of Management Accountants
CIOB	Chartered Institute of Building
CIP	Certificate of Insurance Practice
CIPFA	Chartered Institute of Public Finance & Accountancy
CITB	Construction Industry Training Board
CLAIT	Computer Literacy and Information Technology
CNAA	Council for National Academic Awards
CNC	Computer Numerical Control
CORGI	Council for Registered Gas Installers
COSCA	Confederation of Scottish Counselling Agencies
COSHH	Control of Substances Hazardous to Health
CPC	Certificate of Professional Competence
CPE	Certificate of Proficiency in English
CSYS	Certificate of Sixth Year Studies (SCE)
DALF	Diplome Approfondi De La Langue Francaise
DBA	Doctor of Business Administration
DELF	Diplome D'Etudes De La Langue Francaise
DSA	Dental Surgery Assistants
DTI	Department of Trade & Industry
Dip	Diploma
DipHE	Diploma of Higher Education
DoT	Department of Transport
EARA	Environmental Auditors Registration Association
ECA	Electrical Contractors' Association
ECITB	Engineering Construction Industry Training Board
EEB	English Examination Board
EFL	English as a Foreign Language
ENTRA	Engineering Training Authority
ESOL	English for Speakers of Other Languages
FCE	First Certificate in English
FEPA	Food & Environment Protection Act
FEPIMS	Forum of European Production and Inventory Management Societies
FGA	Fellow of the Gemmological Association
GCE	General Certificate of Education
GCSE	General Certificate of Secondary Education
GRSC	Graduateship of the Royal Society of Chemistry
GSVQ	General Scottish Vocational Qualification
HASW	Health & Safety at Work
HCIMA	Hotel, Catering & Institutional Management Association
HN	Higher National
HNC	Higher National Certificate
HND	Higher National Diploma
HNU	Higher National Unit
HOC	Horse Owners' Certificate (British Horse Society)
HRD	Human Resource Development
HSE	Health and Safety Executive
HTB	Hairdressing Training Board
ICM	Institute of Credit Management
ICSA	Institute of Chartered Secretaries and Administrators
ICW	Institute of Clerks of Works
IEE	Institution of Electrical Engineers
IEEIE	Institution of Electronic and Electrical Incorporated Engineers

ILBS	Institute of Linguistic and Bi-Lingual Skills	PLC	Programmable Logic Controller
IMDG	International Movement of Dangerous Goods	PgC	Post-graduate Certificate
		PgD	Post-graduate Diploma
IMI	Institute of the Motor Industry	REHIS	Royal Environmental Health Institute of Scotland
IPM	Institute of Personnel Management		
IQA	Institute of Quality Assurance	RGN	Registered General Nurse
IRATA	Industrial Rope Access Trade Association	RICS	Royal Institution of Chartered Surveyors
		RIPHH	Royal Institute of Public Health & Hygiene
IRCA	International Register of Certificated Auditors	RLSS	Royal Life Saving Society
		RMN	Registered Mental Nurse
ISM	Institute of Supervisory Management	RSA	Royal Society of Arts
ISO	International Standards Organisation	RSH	Royal Society for the Promotion of Health
IT	Information Technology		
ITD	Institute of Training Development	RTITB	Road Transport Industry Training Board
ITec	Institute of Technology	RYA	Royal Yachting Association
JMB	Joint Matriculation Board	SAC	Scottish Agricultural College
LCCI	London Chamber of Commerce and Industry	SAYFC	Scottish Association of Young Farmers' Clubs
LEAD	Linking Education And Disability	SCA	Scottish Canoe Association
LLM	Master of Laws	SCE	Scottish Certificate of Education
MA	Master of Arts	SCMA	Scottish Child Minders' Association
MAGS	Metal Arc Gas Shielded (Welding)	SCOTCATS	Scottish Credit Accumulation Transfer Scheme
MArch	Master of Architecture		
MBA	Master of Business Administration	SCOTVEC	Scottish Vocational Education Council
MCI	Management Charter Initiative	SEB	Scottish Examination Board
META	Marine Engineering Training Association	SEN	Special Educational Needs
MEd	Master of Education	SJIB	Scottish Joint Industry Training
MIG	Metal Inert Gas (Welding)	SME	Small to Medium Enterprise
MLA	Master of Landscape Architecture	SMLTB	Scottish Mountain Leader Training Board
MLitt	Master of Literature	SNIPEF	Scotland & Northern Ireland Plumbing Employers' Federation
MMA	Manual Metal Arc (Welding)		
MMus	Master of Music	SNNB	Scottish Nursery Nurse Board
MPhil	Master of Philosophy	SNSC	Scottish National Ski Council
MSc	Master of Science	SSTS	Scottish Skills Testing Service
NC	National Certificate	SVQ	Scottish Vocational Qualification
NCC	National Craftsman's Certificate	TAGS	Tungsten Arc Gas Shielded (Welding)
NCM	National Certificate Module	TDLB	Training & Development Lead Body
NDT	Non Destructive Testing	TEFL	Teaching English as a Second Language
NEB	National Examining Board	TEFLA	Teaching English as a Foreign Language to Adults
NEBOSH	National Examination Board for Occupational Safety & Health		
		TESLFACE	Teaching English as a Second Language in Further/Adult/Community Education
NEBSM	National Examining Board in Supervisory Management		
		TESOL	Teaching English to Speakers of Other Languages
NICEIC	National Inspection Council for Electrical Installation Contracting		
		TIG	Tungsten Inert Gas (Welding)
NPTC	National Proficiency Test Council	TQM	Total Quality Management
NSDS	National Skills Development Scheme	TSI	Training Standards Institute
NVQ	National Vocational Qualification	UCAS	Universities and Colleges Admissions Service
NWRAC	North West Region Advisory Council		
OFTEC	Office of Technology	UCLES	University of Cambridge Local Examinations Syndicate
OPITO	Oil and Petroleum Industry Training Organisation		
		UKADT	United Kingdom Association of Dance Teachers
OU	Open University		
PCN	Personal Certification of Non-Destructive Testing	VQ	Vocational Qualification
		WSET	Wines & Spirits Education Trust
PEA	Physical Education Association	YT	Youth Training

When you contact a Provider for further information,
you may wish to make mention of
PART-TIME CLASSES & COURSES in Scotland.

A-Z Subject Heading Index

PUBLISHERS' NOTE

Because of local government re-organisation, details of providers for some courses, in particular for leisure pursuits, cannot be confirmed as we go to print. Libraries and other local sources should be consulted and the Community Education contacts on pages 24 to 26 may also be of assistance.